HOW TO LOVE A CHILD AND OTHER SELECTED WORKS

Dedicated to the legacy of Dr Janusz Korczak, to his children, past, present and future and to all those who are working to keep his legacy alive.

Jerry Nussbaum, President, the Janusz Korczak
Association of Canada

How to Love a Child
and
Other Selected Works

VOLUME 1

Janusz Korczak

Selected by Olga Medvedeva-Nathoo
Edited by Anna Maria Czernow

VALLENTINE MITCHELL
LONDON • CHICAGO, IL

First published in 2018 by Vallentine Mitchell

Catalyst House,
720 Centennial Court,
Centennial Park, Elstree WD6 3SY, UK

814 N Franklin Street
Chicago, Illinois
IL 60610, USA

www.vmbooks.com

Copyright © 2018 by Vallentine Mitchell
Foreword Copyright © 2018 by Olga Medvedeva-Nathoo
English translation © Benjamin Paloff, Danuta Borchardt and Sean Gasper Bye 2018,
and the moral rights of Benjamin Paloff, Danuta Borchardt and Sean Gasper Bye to be
identified as the translators of this work has been asserted in accordance with the
Copyright, Designs and Patents Act 1988.

British Library Cataloguing in Publication Data:
An entry can be found on request

ISBN 978 1 910383 97 1 (Cloth)
ISBN 978 1 910383 98 8 (Paper)
ISBN 978 1 910383 99 5 (Ebook)

Library of Congress Cataloging in Publication Data:
An entry can be found on request

Contents

This publication has been supported by the ©POLAND Translation Program

THE JANUSZ KORCZAK
ASSOCIATION OF CANADA

ADAM
MICKIEWICZ
INSTITUTE

This project has been organized in co-operation with the Adam Mickiewicz Institute. The goal of the Adam Mickiewicz Institute, a state-funded cultural institution operating under its flagship brand Culture.pl, is to promote Poland and Polish culture abroad. Through the presentation of high-quality initiatives and events in the fields of art, music and design, the institute aspires to introduce an international audience to contemporary Polish culture. For more information about Polish culture worldwide: www.culture.pl

Acknowledgements

This two-volume translation of Selected Works of Janusz Korczak, which is of fundamental importance to the dissemination of Dr Korczak's legacy, is now accessible to English-speaking audiences. The translation was a monumental undertaking that would not have been possible without the many people and organizations who have contributed to this effort. We would like to thank them all.

On behalf of the Janusz Korczak Association of Canada we would like to thank the Paul and Edwina Heller Memorial Foundation for the visionary support and generosity towards this project. Without the kindness and understanding of its trustees the translation efforts could not have commenced.

We are grateful to the Polish Book Institute, whose encouragement has inspired us to overcome the many challenges that arose along the way, and whose generosity supported the translation costs.

The Adam Mickiewicz Institute, whose mission is to promote and communicate Polish culture abroad, also generously supported this project.

We would like to acknowledge the long-standing support of Rabbi Dr Yosef Wosk and the generous grant from the Koret Foundation.

The Janusz Korczak Association of Canada also wishes to express its deep gratitude to a large number of people who supported the publication of this translation. We would like to thank Dr Olga Medvedeva-Nathoo, a member of the Janusz Korczak Association of Canada and the author of this selection and Ms Marta Ciesielska, the director of the Korczakianum Center for Documentation and Research at the Museum of Warsaw, who generously shared their expertise and vast knowledge at every stage of the project. We also want to express our deep appreciation to Antonia Lloyd-Jones for her dedication and invaluable help in selecting the translators.

We thank Mr. Toby Harris, of Vallentine Mitchell publishers, for his guidance navigating the requirements of the publishing world. Ms Anna Maria Czernow was invaluable in coordinating the project and collecting and editing the translations. Our thanks go out to all the translators for their dedicated and timely efforts: Sean Bye, Danuta Borchardt, Marta Dziurosz, Alissa Leigh-Valles, Benjamin Paloff, Julia Sherwood and Anna Zaranko.

This was truly a community undertaking and we are profoundly grateful for the many contributions that made this translation a reality.

Jerry Nussbaum, President,
the Janusz Korczak Association of Canada
Anton Grunfeld, Member of the Board,
the Janusz Korczak Association of Canada
Coordinators of the project

Foreword

In the vast legacy left behind by Janusz Korczak, Polish-Jewish doctor, writer, pedagogue and champion of children's rights, there is a short piece, *The Caregiver's Prayer* (1920), concluding with these heartfelt lines:

> Though I be grey and humble before Thee, O Lord, in my request I stand before Thee – in ardent demand. [...]
> Standing upright, I demand, for this is no longer for myself.
> Grant the children good fortune, give aid to their efforts and blessings to their labors.
> Lead them not on the easiest path, but the most beautiful.
> And as a guarantee for my request, take my only jewel: sorrow.
> Sorrow and work.

In this prayer all of Korczak is expressed: humility and, along with it, determination when the time comes to defend the values of life and, no less dear to him, of profession. For the sake of those values he was ready to give his life and he was destined to prove it. Korczak died during the Second World War, in 1942, in the Treblinka extermination camp organized and run by Nazi Germany in occupied Poland. He was murdered in the gas chamber, as were his 200 pupils and staff from the Warsaw Jewish Orphans' Home.

The death of Korczak is enshrined in legend. The only thing that is known for sure is that he had a chance to escape. He was offered the opportunity to leave the Ghetto and hide on the "Aryan" side of the city. For this he had to leave the children. When he had to choose, he reiterated his commitment to the child. This is a story of Korczak's life in facts. On the grapevine, shortly after his death, this account took on legendary, sometimes even "wondrous" guises and continues to be complemented in his semi-fictionalised biographies. Korczak, sharing the tragic fate of his people, became a symbolic figure of the Holocaust, a paragon of self-sacrifice and as such, is an integral part of modern cultural consciousness. The true picture though, of the man and his deeds, often remains overshadowed by Korczak, the legend.

In view of this, it is not surprising that a biography of Korczak often starts with the finale and the most famous of his works – as far as the English-speaking world is concerned – is his *Diary* (known as *Ghetto Diary*). Korczak figures in English also with a number of stories for children, such as *King Matt the First, Little King Matty and the Desert Island, Big Business Billy, When I am Little Again,* and *Kaytek the Wizard*.[1] Most of his work, however, in particular the pedagogical, remained for the English reader unavailable.[2] As the scale of Korczak's oeuvre is truly great, it is sufficient to say that currently in his homeland, Poland, his collected works in 21 volumes are due to be completed.[3] The time therefore has now come for Korczak the educator "to speak" in English. Thus, the objective of the current publication is to acquaint English-speaking readers with Korczak the yet little known in the English world, and afford the opportunity to explore his legacy. No doubt, it may be proposed, a matter of importance for historians of pedagogy, researchers of childhood, educators, teachers, parents, and all those who are not indifferent to the question of the child in all its dimensions.

Olga Medvedeva-Nathoo

Notes

1. These are the original titles of these works: *Król Maciuś Pierwszy* (1923), *Król Maciuś na wyspie bezludnej* (1923), *Bankructwo małego Dżeka* (1924*), Kiedy znów będę mały* (1925), *Kajtuś Czarodziej* (1934).
2. See *Janusz Korczak. A Bibliography. English Sources 1939–2012.* Ed. O. Medvedeva-Nathoo & G. Sanaeva. Vancouver 2012. The bibliography of Korczak's works and those on Korczak in English as of 2012, including books, articles and proceedings of conferences amounts to 318 publications, however, only 43 of them are translations of Korczak's works. Among the books on Korczak a special place is occupied by the oft reprinted biography by Betty Jean Lifton, *The King of Children* (1st edition 1988). It should be noted that in Warsaw, an English anthology of Korczak was published in 1967, though in limited numbers and without the necessary commentaries: *Selected Works of Janusz Korczak.* Trans. J. Bachrach. Ed. M.Wollins.
3. Volume 20 is planned for 2018, 21 for 2019. In Germany, Korczak's collected essays came out in 16 volumes: Janusz Korczak. Sämtliche Werke 16 Bde. 1996–2011. In Israel in Hebrew – collected essays in 9 volumes, 1996-2006. In France, 2009-2017, series of 10 of Korczak's works were published, while in 2018, a selected Korczak, including his most important essays is expected.

How to Love a Child[1]

Translated by Benjamin Paloff

The Child in the Family

Preface to the Second Edition

Fifteen years have passed, many questions, conjectures, and doubts have been raised, distrust toward the stated truths has grown.

An instructor's truths are a subjective assessment of experiences, merely one, the last, movement of considerations and feelings. Its wealth is in the quantity and weight of its unsettling concerns.

Instead of correcting and supplementing, better to note (in the fine print) what has changed around me, and within.

> Yet being born means not the same as resurrection;
> the coffin gives us up, but looks upon us not as mother did.
> Juliusz Słowacki, Anhelli[2]

1. How, when, how many – why?

I sense a great many questions awaiting answers, doubts seeking explanations.

And I respond:

"I don't know."

Whenever you begin to dream the thread of your own thoughts, having set the book aside, the book is achieving its intended aim. If you are quickly flipping through the pages – you will be scanning for formulas and prescriptions, sulking over how few there are – know that if there are suggestions and pointers, they've occurred not just in spite of, but contrary to, the author's will.

I do not know, and cannot, how unfamiliar parents under unfamiliar circumstance can raise a child with whom I am also unfamiliar – *can*, I say, and not *wish to*, nor *should*.

"I don't know": in science it's the haze of becoming, of the hatching of new ideas ever closer to the truth. "I don't know" is, for the mind unschooled in scientific thought, an agonizing void.

I want to teach how to understand and love the wondrous, creative "I don't know," full of life and dazzling surprises, that belongs to contemporary knowledge with regard to the child.

I want it to be understood that no book, no doctor, can replace one's own vigilant mind, one's own attentive observation.

One can often encounter the opinion that motherhood ennobles the woman, that it is only as a mother that one matures spiritually. Yes, in its fervent syllables motherhood brings to mind problems encompassing entire realms of life, external and spiritual; but one might overlook them, put them off to the distant future like a coward or take offense at the fact that one cannot purchase their resolution.

Commanding someone to give out readymade thoughts is to order another woman to give birth to your own child. There are thoughts that, painfully, must give birth to themselves, and these are the most valuable. They decide, mother, whether you will feed from the breast or the udder, whether you'll raise him as a person does or as a female does, whether you will steer him or drag him on the leather strap of coercion, or just play with him, so long as he's little, finding in your caresses with him the complement to the stingy or unkind caresses you receive from your spouse, and later, when he has grown a bit, you'll let him run wild or wish to fight him.

2. You'll say:

"My child."

When do you have the greatest right to this, if not during pregnancy? The beating of a heart as small as a peach pit is an echo of your own pulse. Your breathing gives her oxygen from the air as well. The same blood courses through her and you, and not one red drop of blood yet knows whether it will remain yours or hers or spill out and die as the tribute claimed by the mystery of conception and childbirth. The mouthful of bread you are chewing is, for her, material for building the legs she will run on, the skin that will cover her, the eyes she will see through, the brain in which her thinking will catch fire, the hands that will reach out to you, the smile with which she will call "Mommy."

Both of you have to live through a decisive moment: together you will suffer the same pain. The bell will ring, the voice:

"She's ready."

And at the same time she will say: "I want to live my own life"; you will say, "Now live your own life."

With powerful contractions of your viscera you will cast her out, without a care for her pain; powerfully and decisively, she will break through, not caring about yours.

A brutal act.

No – both you and the child are performing a hundred thousand imperceptible, subtle, wonderfully agile movements so that, claiming her own share of life, she won't claim more than what belongs to her by right – the universal, the eternal.

"My child."

No, even in the months of pregnancy and the hours of labor, the child is not yours.

3. The child you have given birth to weighs ten pounds.

He contains eight pounds of water and a handful of carbon, calcium, nitrogen, sulfur, phosphorus, potassium, iron. You've given birth to eight pounds of water and two of ash. And every drop of this, *your* child, has been the wisp of a cloud, a crystal of ice, mist, dew, a spring, the dregs of an urban storm drain. Each atom of carbon or nitrogen has been bound in millions of combinations.

You've only gathered whatever there was…

The Earth suspended in infinitude.

Its close comrade, the Sun, many millions of miles away.

The diameter of our small Earth is only three thousand miles of fire with a cooled, ten-mile-thin crust.

On that thin, fire-filled crust, amidst oceans – a handful of land is scattered.

On the land, amidst the trees and shrubs, the insects, birds, the animals – it is swarming with people.

Among the millions of people, you have given birth to one more – what? – a mote, a speck – nothing.

So frail it is that it can be killed by a bacterium that, magnified a thousand times, is merely a dot within our field of vision…

But this *nothing* is, in blood and bone, brother to the wave on the sea, to the wind, lightning, the Sun, the Milky Way. This speck is brother to the ear of grain, the grass, the oak, the palm – the chick, the lion cub, the foal, the pup.

Within it is what feels, studies – suffers, desires, rejoices, loves, trusts, despises – believes, doubts, embraces, and rejects.

This speck takes in everything with its mind: stars and oceans, mountains and chasms. And what is the soul's content if not the universe, albeit without dimensions?

This is the contradiction in the human creature, arisen from the dust that God inhabited.

4. "My child," you say.

No, this child is shared, by mother and father, grandparents and great-grandparents.

Someone's distant "I," which has slept in the line of ancestors, the voice of a decayed, long-forgotten coffin, suddenly speaks out in this child.

Three hundred years ago, in war or peace, someone seized someone, in the kaleidoscope of intersecting races, nations, classes – with consent or in violence, in a moment of terror or erotic elation – betrayed or seduced, no one knows who, when, but God had written it into the book of destiny, the anthropologist wishes to piece it together from the shape of a skull and the color of hair.

Sometimes the sensitive child fantasizes that she is a foundling in her parents' house. It happens: her parent died before her time.

The child is a parchment crammed with tiny hieroglyphs, only a part of which you will succeed in making out, and some you will succeed in wiping away or merely scratching out, and you will fill in your own content.

A terrible truth. – No, a beautiful one. In each of your children, it provides the first link in the generational chain. Look for the particle of yourself dormant in your alien child. You might make it out, you might even develop it.

The child and infinitude.

The child and eternity.

The child – a speck in space.

The child – a moment in time.

5. You say:

"It should… I want it to…"

And you're seeking a pattern for what it should be like, you are seeking the life you wish it to have.

No matter that all around is mediocrity and averageness. No matter that you are surrounded by greyness.

People bumble around, keep busy, bustle – minute worries, faint aspirations, run-of-the-mill goals…

Unfulfilled hopes, gnawing regret, eternal longing…

Injustice reigns.

Cold indifference pierces with ice, hypocrisy stifles the breath.

What has fangs and claws goes on the attack, what is quiet folds into itself.

And not only do they suffer, but they are tarnished.

Who is he supposed to be?

A fighter, or merely a worker? A commander, or a private? Or merely happy?

Where is happiness – *what* is happiness? Do you know the way? Are there people who might?

Will you make it?...

How do you foresee, how do you protect?

A butterfly over the bubbling stream of life. How do you make it hardy and not burden its flight, fortify it without wearing out its wings?

With one's own example, then, with help, advice, a word?

And if he rejects it?

In fifteen years, he staring into the future, you – into the past. In you, memories and habits, in him – changeability and impudent hope. You doubt, he anticipates and hopes; you fret, he hasn't a care.

Youth, if it does not mock, does not curse, does not spurn, always desires to change the flawed past.

As it should be. And yet...

May he seek that he not wander, may he climb that he not fall, may he clear the wood that he not bloody his hands, let him struggle, if carefully – carefully.

He will say:

"I see it another way. Enough looking after me."

So you do not trust me?

So you don't need me?

My love is holding you down?

Impulsive child, who knows nothing of life, poor child, ungrateful child.

6. Ungrateful.

Is the earth grateful to the sun for shining? Is a tree grateful to the seed it grew from? Does the nightingale sing to the mother who warmed it with her breast?

Do you return to the child what you had taken from your parents, or do you only lend in order to take back, meticulously recording and calculating the interest?

Is love a service for which you demand payment?

"The mother-crow thrashes around like mad, perches almost on the boy's shoulders, clings to his stick with her beak, hangs down right over him and bangs her head like a hammer into the stem, gnaws off little twigs – and caws in a croaking, strained, dry voice of despair. When the boy tosses the chick aside, she throws herself to the ground, dragging her wings, she opens her beak, wants to caw – her voice is gone, so she beats her wings and hops crazily, comically, to the boy's feet. When they have killed all her children, she flies off to the tree, visits her empty nest, and, spinning in circles upon it, ponders something." Żeromski.[3]

Maternal love is elemental. People have altered it in their own way. The entire civilized world, excluding those masses untouched by culture, commits infanticide. A marriage that produces two children when it could have had twelve is the murderer of the ten who were not born, of whom there was one, the one, "their child." Among the unborn they may have killed the most dear.

What, then, to do?

One must raise not those children who were not born, but those who were and are going to live.

> *An immature skulk.*
>
> *For long I did not want to understand that there must be an accounting and concern for the children who are born. In the unfreedom of Partition[4], subjugated, not a citizen, I indifferently neglected the fact that, alongside the children, one must give birth to schools, apprenticeships, hospitals, the cultural conditions of being. Today I regard imprudent fertility as harm and simpleminded excess. – We may be on the eve of new laws dictated by eugenics and population politics.*

7. Is the baby healthy?

It is still strange that it is no longer she. Not long ago, in their double life, worrying about the child was a part of worrying about herself.

So great was her desire for it all to be over, so much did she want this moment to be done with. She thought that she would be freed from concern and care.

And now?

A strange thing: before, the child had been closer to her, more her own, she was more certain of her safety, she understood her better. She thought she knew that she would know what to do. Since someone else's hands – experienced, paid for, confident – took the child into their care, she, shunted to the background, has felt unease.

The world is already taking her away.

And in the long hours of compulsory inactivity, a raft of questions arise: What have I given her, how have I equipped her, how have I protected her?

She is healthy, so why is she crying?

Why is she thin, why doesn't she latch, doesn't sleep, sleeps so much, why is her head so big, why are her legs shriveled, fists clenched, skin red, why are there white pimples on her nose, why does she squint, hiccup, sneeze, choke, get hoarse?

Is she supposed to do that? And what if they're lying?

She looks at this helpless little thing, unlike any of the equally toothless little things she has spotted on the street, in the park. Could it really be that this is what she will be in three, four months?

And maybe they're mistaken?

Maybe they're not taking her seriously?

The mother listens distrustfully to the doctor's voice, follows him with her gaze: she wishes to read into his eyes, the shrug of his shoulders, the lift of his brow, the wrinkles on his forehead: is he telling the truth, isn't he hesitating, is he sufficiently focused?

8. Beautiful? I don't care. This is what mothers say, dishonestly, when they want to emphasize their serious regard for the task of childrearing.

Beauty, grace, posture, a pleasant-sounding voice: these are the capital that you have given your child; like health, like reason, they ease life's course. It does not do to overestimate the value of beauty unsupported by other values, it can come to ill. All the more does it demand a sensitive mind.

One must raise a beautiful child one way, an ugly one another. And there is no childrearing without the child's own participation, so one must not embarrassedly hide the issue of beauty from the child when doing so is the very thing that spoils him.

This ostensible disdain for looks is a relic of the Middle Ages. Ought a person sensitive to the beauty of a flower, a butterfly, a landscape, be indifferent to the beauty of a person?

Do you wish to hide from the child the fact that he is lovely? If one of the numerous individuals surrounding him in the home doesn't say so, strangers will, on the street, at the store, in the park, everywhere – with a shout, a laugh, a glance, adults or peers. The way ugly and unsightly children are held back will tell him. He will understand that beauty offers privileges, as he understands that a hand is his hand, for him to use as he pleases.

Just as a weak child can develop successfully, and a healthy one fall victim to catastrophe, so too can a pretty one be unhappy, and one armored in ugliness – the undistinguished, the unnoticed – can live happily. Because you have to, absolutely have to remember that life, having discerned every positive value, will desire to buy, swindle, or steel what is precious. On this balance, with its innumerable shifts, there arise surprises that amaze the caregiver in a frequently painful "why?"

"I don't care about beauty!"

You're starting off from error and falsehood.

9. Is she smart?

If at first a mother inquires apprehensively, before long she's going to be demanding.

Eat, though you are sated, even with revulsion; go to sleep, perhaps with tears, though you will wait an hour for sleep to come. Because you have to, because I demand that you be healthy.

Do not play in the sand, wear well-fitting trousers, don't tousle your hair, because I demand that you be pretty.

"She's not talking yet... She's older than...and still, she hasn't... She doesn't learn well..."

Instead of watching so as to recognize and know, you take up the first example of a "successful child" you come across – and place a demand on your own child: here is the pattern to which you should conform.

It cannot be that the child of well-to-do parents should become an artisan. Better that she be an unhappy and demoralized person. Not the love of the child, but the egotism of the parents; not the good of the individual, but the ambition of the flock; not the seeking of paths, but the constraints of the template.

Intellects come active and passive, lively and apathetic, steadfast and moody, submissive and contrary, creative and imitative, brilliant and diligent, concrete and abstract, realistic and literary; memory, outstanding and mediocre; cleverness in the use of what information one has attained and honesty in hesitation, an innate despotism, thoughtfulness, and criticalness; development is premature or delayed, interests one- or many-sided.

But who cares?

"Let her at least finish the fourth grade," the parent's resignation says.

Sensing a great renaissance of physical labor, I see candidates for it from every social class. Meanwhile, the struggle of the parents and the school with every exceptional, atypical, weak, or imbalanced intelligence.

It's not *whether* she's smart, but *how* is she smart.

> *A naive appeal to the family to assume a heavy sacrifice. Intelligence tests and psychotechnical examinations will truly suppress selfish ambitions. That is to say, the song of the distant future.*

10. The good child.

One must be careful not to confuse good with – convenient.

He doesn't cry, he doesn't wake us up at night, he's trusting, cheerful – good.

Bad, moody, whiny, for no apparent reason he gives his mother more unpleasant emotions than pleasant ones.

Regardless of how they feel, newborns are innately patient, more or less. For some a dose of complaint suffices to bring about the reaction of ten doses of wailing, while over there another child reacts to ten doses of ailment with a single dose of crying.

One is sluggish – lazy movements, slow nursing, the wail without real tension or clear affect.

A second is excitable: lively movements, sensitive sleep, frenzied nursing, wailing to the point of cyanosis.

He sobs, loses his breath, has to be revived, sometimes has a hard time coming back to life. I know: an illness, we treat it with fish oil, phosphorus, a non-dairy diet. But this illness allows the baby to grow into an adult with a formidable will, an impetuous drive, and an ingenious mind. Napoleon sobbed as a baby.

All of contemporary childrearing wishes for the child to be convenient, step-by-step it consistently strives to anaesthetize, to suppress, to destroy everything that is the will and freedom of the child, the fortitude of his spirit, the force of his demands and intentions.

Polite, obedient, good, convenient, and without a thought, he'll be internally passive and practically ineffectual.

11. The painful surprise that the young mother encounters is her child's wail.

She had known that children cry, but she had overlooked this when thinking of her own; she'd expected only charming smiles.

She'll see to his needs, raise him in a judicious, modern fashion, under the direction of an experienced doctor. Her child shouldn't cry.

But there comes a night when she's baffled with the living echo of the hard hours she's endured, which have lasted ages. She has barely felt the sweetness of fatigue without worry, of indolence without reproach, of rest following work completed, desperate effort, the first in an overdelicate life. She has barely yielded to the illusion that it's over, because he – this other – is now breathing. Plunged into quiet emotions, capable of posing to nature only questions that are filled with mysterious whispers, not even demanding an answer.

When suddenly...

The despotic wail of the child, who demands something, is complaining about something, needs help, and she does not understand.

Keep watch!

"When I cannot, I don't want to, I don't know."

This first wail by the light of the night lamp heralds a bifurcated life: one life mature, compelled to make concessions, renunciations, sacrifices, defends itself; the second one new, young, which wrests its rights – its own – for itself.

You don't accuse him today; he does not understand, he's suffering. But the hand of time points to the hour when, in the future, you will say, "I, too, feel, and I, too, am suffering."

12. There are newborns and infants that cry little, all the better. But there are also those who wail so that the veins stand out on their brow, their fontanelle puffs out, a scarlet hue washes over face and head, the lips go blue, the toothless jaw trembles, the belly swells, the fists are tightly clenched, the legs beat the air. Suddenly, helplessly, she goes silent, with an expression of complete surrender, she looks "reproachfully" at her mother, squints, begging to sleep, and after a couple of quick breaths there's a similar, and perhaps stronger, fit of wailing.

How can the tiny lungs, small heart, and young brain stand this?

Help! Doctor!

It's ages before he arrives, listens with an indulgent smile to all her anxieties, this stranger, an unapproachable professional, for whom this child is one of a thousand. He's come only to depart a moment later for other maladies, to hear other complaints, he's come now, in daylight, when everything seems cheerier: because there's sun, because people are walking outside, he's come when the child happens to be sleeping, no doubt exhausted from her sleepless hours, when the ghastly night's faint traces are barely discernible.

The mother listens, sometimes she listens inattentively. Her dream of the doctor as friend, as supervisor, as guide on an arduous journey, dissolves forever.

She hands over the fee and is again left alone with the bitter conviction that the doctor is an indifferent stranger who doesn't understand. And, anyway, he hesitates, too, he hadn't had anything solid to say.

13. If only the young mother knew how decisive these first days and weeks are, not so much for the health of her child today as for both their futures.

And how easy it is to squander them!

Having established this, instead of getting used to the idea that, as far as the doctor is concerned, her child is an object of interest only insofar as he brings an income or satisfies ambitions, just as he is nothing to the world, she alone thinks him precious…

Instead of getting used to the contemporary state of knowledge, which thinks things out, strives to know, investigates and takes a step forward – it knows, but nothing is certain, it brings help, but it doesn't make guarantees…

Instead of stating it valiantly: raising a child is not a pleasant pastime, but a challenge that requires one to pay with the effort of sleepless nights, the capital of difficult experiences, and much consideration…

Instead of re-forging it, in the fire of feeling, as a firm awareness without illusions, without childish sulking and selfish bitterness, she can move the child and his nanny to a far-off room, because she "cannot bear to see" the little thing's suffering, she "cannot bear to hear" the pained cries, maybe she'll summon the doctor and doctors over and over again, not having gained anything from her experiences, only she's ill-served, stupefied, stunned.

How naive a mother's joy is when she understands her child's first, indistinct speech, pieces together the mispronounced and incomplete expressions.

Only now...? That's it...? Nothing else...?

And the speech of crying and laughter, the speech of glancing and grimacing, the speech of movements and sucking...?

Do not renounce these nights. They provide what no book, what no advice can. For the value here is not only in knowledge, but in the deep spiritual revolution that does not allow one to return to futile meditations on what could have been, what should be, what would be nice if..., but learns to work under conditions as they are.

A wondrous ally may be born during these nights, the child's guardian angel: the intuition of a maternal heart, the clairvoyance of which an inquisitive will, sensitive mind, and undimmed feeling consist.

14. It has sometimes happened: a mother calls me over.

"In fact, my child is healthy, she's fine. I just wanted you to have a look at her."

I look her over, offer a few tips, answer her questions. How healthy, sweet, happy she is!

"Goodbye."

And that evening or the following morning:

"Doctor, my child has a fever."

The mother had discerned what I, a doctor, didn't know how to see in a superficial examination during a short visit.

In her hours hunched over the little one, without methods of observation, she does not know what she has discerned; not trusting herself, she doesn't dare admit to the subtle observations she has made.

Yet she has noticed that the child, who does not have a sore throat, has a somewhat rough voice. She is babbling somewhat less or more quietly. Once, in her sleep, she shuddered more violently than usual. Upon waking she burst into laughter, but more weakly. She sucked somewhat more slowly, maybe with longer pauses, as if she were distracted. Did she grimace while she was laughing, or did it just seem like she had? She threw her favorite toy away angrily – why?

By the hundred symptoms the mother's eye, her ear, her nipple had perceived, by her child's hundred micro-complaints, she had said:

"I am indisposed. I'm feeling rotten today."

The mother did not believe that she was seeing what she was seeing, since she had not read about any comparable symptoms in a book.

15. A mother who gets by doing odd jobs brings her few-week-old infant to the free clinic:

"He doesn't want to nurse. He's barely grasped the nipple, he lets it go with a cry. He feeds greedily from a spoon. Sometimes in his sleep, or else when he's awake, he'll suddenly cry out."

I examine the mouth, the throat – I see nothing.

"Please give him your breast."

The child brushes the nipple with his lips, he doesn't want to nurse.

"He's become so untrusting."

Finally he grabs the breast, quickly, he pulls it several times, as if desperately, and lets it go with a cry.

"Look: he has something on his gum."

I take a second look, there's a reddening, but odd: it's only on one gum.

"Oh, here, there's something black. A tooth perhaps?"

I see it: hard, yellow, ovular, with a black line around its perimeter. I pry it loose, it moves, I pick it out, beneath it a small red depression with bloody edges.

I finally have the "something" in my hand: it's the husk of a seed.

A canary cage hangs over the child's cradle. The canary had tossed out a husk, it had fallen onto the lip, been licked into the mouth, dug into the gum.

The course of my thoughts: stomatitis catarrhalis, thrush, stomatitis aphtosa, gingivitis, tonsillitis, etc.

She: pain, something in his mouth.

I performed an examination, twice… What did she do?

16. If the precision and meticulousness of her observations sometimes amaze the doctor, it is on the other hand equally amazing to him how the mother oftentimes cannot even discern the simplest symptom, let alone understand it.

The child has been crying since she was born, that's all she's seen. She keeps crying!

Does the crying erupt suddenly and immediately reach a peak, or does her plaintive wail gradually build into a scream? Does she calm down quickly, right after producing a stool or urine, or after vomiting (or spitting up her food), or does she scream suddenly and violently while being bathed, dressed, or picked up? Does she protest, crying at length, without sudden eruptions? How does she move when she's doing it? Does she rub her head against her pillow or make a sucking motion with her mouth? Does she calm down when she's being carried, when she's unswaddled, placed on her belly, when her position is changed often? After crying does she fall into a long, deep sleep, or does she wake up at the slightest rustle? Does she cry before or after nursing, more in the morning, evening, or at night?

Does she calm down while she's nursing? For how long? Does she refuse to nurse? How so? Does she let go of the nipple, has she barely taken it into her mouth, or is it as she is swallowing, suddenly, or after a certain point? Is she firm in not wanting it, or can she be persuaded to nurse? How is her sucking? Why doesn't she?

If she has a cold, how is she going to nurse? Eagerly and strongly, because she's thirsty, then quickly and superficially, unevenly, with pauses, because she's out of breath. Then it hurts when she swallows – now what?

Crying occurs not only because of hunger or "tummy ache," but from pain on the lips, gums, tongue, throat, nose, finger, ear, bone, the pain of a scratch that an enema left on the anus, painful urination, nausea, thirst, overheating, itching on skin that does not yet have a rash, though there will be one in a couple months, crying because of a chafing ribbon, a crease in the diaper, a tuft of cotton that got stuck in the throat, the seed husk from the canary's cage.

Call the doctor for ten minutes, but keep watch yourself for twenty hours.

17. The book, with its readymade formulas, has dulled their vision and slowed their mind. Living on someone else's experience, research, viewpoint, their faith in themselves is so far gone that they don't want to look for themselves. As if what some printed rag contains were a revelation, and not the product of research – only someone else's, not mine, somewhere, into someone, and not today, into my own child.

And school has enhanced the cowardice, the anxiety not to betray that I don't know.

How many times has the mother, having jotted down the questions she wants to pose to the doctor, not mustered the courage to articulate them? And how exceptionally rare is it that she hands him the paper – because "what she wrote is stupid."

Hiding that she herself does not know, how many times has she forced the doctor to conceal his doubts, his hesitations – to say decisively. How reluctantly people at large accept conditional answers, how they dislike it when the doctor thinks aloud over the cradle, how often the doctor, forced to be a prophet, becomes a charlatan.

Sometimes the parents don't want to know what they know – or see what they see.

Childbirth in a sphere ruled by the fanaticism of comfort is something so singular and maliciously exceptional that the mother categorically demands a generous prize of nature. If she has consented to the renunciations, the trials, the afflictions of pregnancy and the suffering of childbirth, the child should be just as she had wished.

What's worse: having grown accustomed to being able to purchase anything with money, she doesn't want to resign herself to the fact that something exists that a pauper can receive and that a magnate couldn't scrounge together.

How many times, in searching for what is summarily labeled "health" on the open market, have parents bought counterfeits that either do not help, or else bring harm.

18. For the baby, it is her mother's breast, regardless of whether she was born because God had blessed the marriage or that a girl had lost her shame; of whether the mother whispers, "My dearest," or else sighs, "Woe is me, what am I to do?"; of whether they humbly congratulate Her Ladyship or cast "Ew, the slut" at the country lass.

Prostitution, which serves men's purposes, finds its societal compliment in the wet nurse, for a woman's purpose.

One must have a complete consciousness of the hallowed, bloody crime against the poor child – even against the good of the rich child. For the wet nurse can feed two children: her own and someone else's. The mammary gland gives as much milk as they demand of it. And the wet nurse loses her milk only when the child drinks less than the breast provides.

The formula: an ample breast, a tiny child – a waste of milk.

A strange thing: in less important cases, we're inclined to ask the advice of many doctors, in so important a matter as whether a mother can nurse we make do with one opinion, sometimes dishonest, whispered by whomever happens to be around.

Every mother can nurse, they all have an adequate amount of milk; only unfamiliarity with the technique of nursing deprives them of their natural capacity.

Pain in the breasts, blistering of the nipples – these are a certain impediment; but here the suffering occupies the awareness that the mother has gone through her entire pregnancy without casting any of its burdens onto the shoulders of a wage slave. For nursing is a continuation of pregnancy, "only the child has moved from within to without, cut from the placenta, it has seized the breast, it drinks not red blood, but white."[5]

The child drinks blood? Yes, the mother's, for this is nature's law, and not the starved co-nursing child, which is the law of man.

> *An echo of the living struggle for the child's right to the breast. The question of housing has come to the fore among today's challenges. What will it be tomorrow? – Thus the author apportions his interests according to the moment we are living through.*

19. Maybe I should write an Egyptian dream book of hygiene for mothers' use.

"Weighing three and a half kilos at birth means: health, auspiciousness."

"Green stools with mucus: anxiety, bad news."

Perhaps I, too, could put together a romantic treasury with advice and pointers.

But I have become convinced that there is no prescription that uncritical extremism won't bring to the level of the absurd.

The old system:

Breast thirty times a day, alternating with castor oil. The infant passes from one set of hands to another, rocked and bounced by every cold-addled aunt. They carry him to the window, to the mirror, they clap, they rattle, they sing – it's a fair.

The new system:

Breast every three hours. The child, seeing the preparations for the feast, grows impatient, angry, cries. The mother looks at the clock: four minutes to go. The child sleeps, the mother wakes him up, because the hour has struck; she tears the hungry child from the breast, because the minutes have passed. He's lying down – not allowed to move. Don't let him get used to being held! Bathed, dry, sated, he should sleep. He doesn't. One must walk on tiptoe, cover the windows. A hospital room, a morgue.

No: thinking labors, but a prescription gives orders.

20. Not "how often to feed," but "how many times a day."

When the question is put this way, it gives the mother her freedom: let her set the timetable that's best for her and her child.

How many times should the child nurse in a day?

From four to fifteen.

How long should she lie on the breast?

From four minutes to forty-five and more.

We encounter: breasts that work more or less easily, that feed poorly or copiously, with nipples that are good or bad, hearty or fragile. We encounter children whose suck is powerful, fussy, or lazy. So there is no general prescription.

A poorly developed nipple, but resilient; an eager baby. Let her nurse often and long to "break in" the breast.

A rich breast, a weak baby. It may be better to squeeze out some milk before feeding to compel the child to feed. Can't manage it? Then give her the breast, and squeeze out the rest.

A somewhat difficult breast, a sleepy child. She only starts drinking after ten minutes.

One swallowing motion can coincide with one, two, five sucking motions. The amount of milk in a gulp can be smaller or greater.

She licks the breast, tugs at it, but does not swallow, does so rarely, does so often.

"It dribbles down her chin." Perhaps because there's a lot of milk, perhaps because there's too little, because, ravenous, she pulls hard and chokes, but only on the first couple gulps.

How can one provide a prescription without the mother and child?

"Five rations a day, ten minutes each" – that's a formula.

21. Without a scale, there is no technique for breastfeeding. Everything we do will be a game of blind man's buff.

Besides the scale, there is no way of finding out whether the child sucked out three spoonsful of milk or ten.

And this determines how often, how long he should suck, whether from both breasts or one.

The scale can be an unerring advisor when it says what is, it can become a tyrant when we want to hold to a formula for the child's "normal" growth. Let us not fall from the superstition about "green stools" into superstitions about "ideal growth charts."

How do we weigh?

It is worth emphasizing: there are mothers who have spent many hours on scales and etudes and yet find it too burdensome to acquaint themselves with a scale for weighing. Weigh him before and after nursing? What a pain! There are others who surround their beloved family doctor's scale not with attentiveness, but affection.

Cheap scales for infants, their popularization, such that they'd be strewn far and wide – this is a social challenge. Who will take it up?

22. How does it happen that one generation of children has grown up under the banner of milk, eggs, and meat, while another receives oatmeal, vegetables, and fruit?

I could answer: advances in chemistry, in research on the transformations of matter.

No, the change's essence goes deeper.

The new diet is an expression of science's confidence in the living organism, its tolerance for its will.

When proteins and fats were available, one wanted to compel the system to develop through a specially selected diet; today we give everything: let the living organism choose for itself what it needs, what brings a benefit, let it control the forces it possesses, the agents of the health it has received, the potential energy for its development.

Not what we give the child, but what she assimilates. Because every violence and excess is ballast, every one-sidedness a potential mistake.

Even those close to the truth can commit a minute error, and repeating it consistently over the course of months we hurt or hinder the organism's work.

When do we supplement the child's feeding, how, with what?

When it is not enough for the child to suck a liter of milk, gradually, always waiting to see how the organism reacts, we can supplement anything, depending on the child, on her response.

23. And powdered supplements?

One must distinguish between health science and the health trade.

Hair tonic, tooth elixir, skin-youthening compound, teething powders – these are most often the shame of science, and never its pride, its breakthroughs and achievements.

With his powder, the manufacturer guarantees normal stools, and impressive weight, it pleases the mother and tastes good to the child. But it doesn't help the tissues assimilate properly, maybe it weakens them, it doesn't give vitality, maybe in adding weight it even reduces vitality; it doesn't make the child resistant to infection.

And it always discredits the breast, albeit cautiously, raising doubts, incidentally, slowly digging away, tempting and indulging the weaknesses of the crowd.

Someone will say: world-renowned names are voicing their approval. But scholars are people: among them there are those who are more or less incisive, the cautious and the rash, the honest and the mendacious. How many are generals of science not by genius, but by cunning or the privilege of wealth and birth! Science requires expensive training, which one comes by not only through essential value, but also slickness, subservience, and scheming.

I was present at a meeting where unabashed insolence plundered the work of twelve years' diligent research. I know a discovery that was fabricated for a well-known international conference. The nutritious preparation whose contents had been confirmed by a dozen or more "stars" turned out to be counterfeit; there was a trial: the scandal was quickly covered up.

No: who has approved the powder, but who hasn't wanted to, despite its agents' efforts. And they really know how to insist. Enterprises that make millions have influence; it's a force that not everyone will resist.

Many instances in these chapters echo the proceedings of my divorce from medicine.[6] *I saw a lack of care and an ineptitude of aid. (Besides Kamieński, who has not received the recognition he deserves, Brudziński was the first to speak up for and win equal rights for pediatrics.)*[7] *The international remedy industry had started to prey insistently upon poverty and neglect. – Today we have walk-in clinics, factory daycare, summer camps, health spas, a school nurse, a sick fund. There is still disorder and insufficiency, but we've lived to see the beginning. – Today one can believe in powders and medicines; their purpose is to support, not to replace, good hygiene and social care for the child.*

24. The child has a fever. A stuffy nose.

Isn't she in some danger? When will she be healthy?

Our answer comes out of a line of thinking based on what we know and what we have managed to discern.

And thus: a strong child will fight off a weak infection in a day or two. If the infection is stronger or the child weaker, the ailment will last a week. We'll see.

Or: minor discomfort, but the child is young. A runny nose in infants often moves from the mucous membranes in the nose to the throat, the windpipe, the bronchi. We'll know soon enough.

Finally: for every hundred similar cases, ninety end in a quick return to health, in seven the ailment drags out, in three the disease develops, perhaps leading to death.

A caveat: and what if mild congestion masks some other illness?

But the mother wants certainty, not supposition.

One can complement the diagnosis by examining the nasal secretion, urine, blood, cerebrospinal fluid, one can take an X-ray, call in the specialists. The likelihood of the diagnosis and prognosis, even of the treatment, will increase. But isn't this addition offset by the harm of multiple examinations, the presence of many doctors, of whom any might carry a more serious infection in his hair, in the folds of his clothes, on his breath.

Where could she have caught cold?

It could have been avoided.

And doesn't this minor infection make the child more resistant to the stronger one she will encounter in a week, a month, doesn't it improve the defense mechanism, in the brain's thermal center, in the glands, in the components of the blood? Can we isolate the child from the air she breathes, and which contains thousands of bacteria in one cubic centimeter...

Will the new clash between what we would wish and what we must yield to be yet another attempt at arming the mother, not with education, but reason, without which one cannot raise a child well?

25. So long as death reaped women in childbirth, little thought was given to the newborn. He was noticed when asepsis and the technique for providing aid safeguarded the life of the mother. So long as death reaped infants, all the attention of science had to be directed toward the bottle and the diaper. Now it won't be long before, apart from the vegetal, we will clearly discern the child's character, his life and mental development through the first year. What we have done to this point is not yet the beginning of our work.

An infinite line of psychological puzzles and those that stand on the border between the infant's soma and psyche.

Napoleon had tetany. Bismarck had rickets, and now it's beyond question that each and every prophet and murderer, hero and traitor, great and small, athlete and wretch, was an infant before becoming an adult person. If we want to study the amoebas of thoughts, feelings, and aspirations, before they have developed, been differentiated and defined, then it is to the infant that we must return.

Only limitless ignorance and superficial treatment can overlook the fact that the infant embodies a certain, precisely defined individuality composed of his innate temperament, the strength of his intellect, his general state, and his life experiences.

26. A hundred babies. I lean over each of their beds. There are those who count their lives in weeks and months, those of different weights and their own past growth chart, those who are sick, convalescent, healthy, and barely holding on while just on the surface of life.

I encounter different gazes, from the dim, misted-over, expressionless, through the stubborn and painfully focused, to the lively, warm, aggressive. And the sudden, welcoming, friendly smile, or a smile following a moment of sharp observation, only in answer to a smile and an affectionate word – wakey-wakey.

What at first seems accidental to me is repeated over the course of many days. I note it, mark the trusting and the mistrusting, the consistent and the fussy, the cheerful and the sullen, the uncertain, anxious, and hostile.

Consistently cheerful: she smiles before and after nursing, woken from sleep and with sleep overcome: she'll lift her eyelids, smile, and fall asleep. Consistently sullen: she greets you uneasily, almost in tears, in three weeks she has smiled but once, in passing...

I inspect the throats. A vigorous, tempestuous, passionate protest. Or else just a halfhearted wince, an impatient movement of the head, and already a kind smile. Or suspicious vigilance over a foreign hand's every move, an explosion of anger before it has even touched her...

Mass pox vaccination[8], fifty in an hour. That's an experiment. Again, in some, an immediate and firm reaction, in others a gradual and uncertain one, in a third group – indifference. One is content with surprise, another becomes uneasy, a third sounds the alarm; one will quickly regain her balance, the second remembers for a long time, doesn't forgive...

Someone will say: that's infancy. Yes, but only to a certain extent. The speed of orienting oneself, of recalling what they have lived through. Oh, we know children who have acquired painful experience from knowing a surgeon, we know there are those who do not want to drink milk because they have been given a white camphor emulsion.

But what else does a mature person's mental expression consist of?

27. One baby.

He is born and is already accustomed to the chill of the air, the coarse diaper, the disturbance of noises, the work of nursing. Diligent nursing, calculated and confident. Now he's smiling, now he's babbling, now he's using his hands. He grows, investigates, develops, crawls, walks, prattles, speaks. How and when did this take place?

Clear, unclouded development...

Another baby.

A week has passed before he has learned to nurse. A couple of restless nights. A week without trouble, a one-day storm. Somewhat sluggish development, arduous teething. Ups and downs in general, but now everything is alright: calm, sweet, amusing.

Perhaps born phlegmatic, the care not sound enough, the breast not working well enough – a happy development...

A third baby.

Violent. Jolly, he gets easily worked up, provoked by an unpleasant impression, external or internal, he struggles desperately, he doesn't save his energy. Vigorous movements, sudden changes, today something different from yesterday. He learns one moment, forgets the next. A discontinuous development, with powerful rises and dips. Surprises, from the most pleasant to the seemingly ominous. Hard not to say: "At last."

Erethic, touchy, a fussy strength, perhaps a significant value…

A fourth baby.

If you are to count the sunny days and the drizzly ones, there won't be many of the former. Dissatisfaction as the fundamental background. There's no pain, there are unpleasant sensations; no screaming, but unrest. It would be good if… Never without reservation.

The child is flawed, raised unwisely…

The room temperature, a hundred grams too much milk, a hundred grams too little drinking water: these influences have to do not only with hygiene, but upbringing. A baby, which has so much to examine, think through, get to know, get used to, to love and hate, to guard wisely against and demand, must enjoy wellbeing regardless of its innate temperament, its innately sprightly or sluggish intelligence.

> *Instead of the neologism foisted upon us,* osesek *[Polish, "suckling" or "nursling" – Tr.], I use the older "infant." The Greeks said* népios, *the Romans* infans. *If that's what the Polish language had wanted, then why translate the ugly German word* Säugling? *– One cannot mine a dictionary of old and important expressions without discussion.*

28. Vision. Light and darkness, night and day. Sleep: something very weak is happening; wakefulness – it's happening more powerfully; something good (breast) or bad (pain). The newborn is looking at the lamp. No, she is not: the eyeballs turn apart and together. Later, following a slowly moving object, at each moment she fixes it and loses it.

The contours of a shadow, the trace of the first lines, and all of it without perspective. One meter away, the mother is already a different shadow from when she is leaning in close. The profile of a face is like the crescent moon; only the chin and mouth, when she is looking from below, propped on the knees; that very same face with eyes looks still different, with hair, when she is more tilted. And the senses of hearing and smell say that it's the same.

The breast, a bright cloud, the taste, smell, warmth, goodness. The infant releases the breast and looks, uses her vision to examine that strange something that is constantly appearing over the breast and from which flow sounds and a wafting, warm stream of breath. The infant doesn't know that the breasts, the face, the hands form a single whole – the mother.

Someone new stretches hands toward her. Deceived by a familiar movement, an image, she gladly passes into them. Only now is the error apparent. This time the hands remove the infant from the familiar shadow and bring it closer to something foreign, arousing distress. With a sudden motion she returns to her mother and, safe once more, looks and is surprised, or else hides behind her mother's shoulder to avoid the danger.

Finally, the mother's face stops being a shadow explored with the hands. Many times has the infant snatched at the nose, touched the strange eye that is by turns sparkling and again matted beneath the covering of the eyelid, explored the hair. And who hasn't seen her pull back the lips, watch the teeth, peer into the mouth, in concentration, seriously, with furrowed brow. Only she's hindered by nonsense talk, kisses, jokes – what we call "child's play." We're the ones who are playing; she's studying. She already has certainties, speculations, and problems born of her research.

29. Hearing. From the din of the street beyond the windowpanes, from distant sounds, the ticking of a clock, of conversations and knocking, to the whispers and words addressed to the child directly, all of it creates a chaos of irritations that she must categorize and comprehend.

Here we must add the sounds that the infant herself produces, and so her cry, babbling, rumbles. Before she realizes that it is she herself, and not an invisible someone who is babbling and crying – a lot of time passes. When she is lying there saying "abb, aba, ada," she is listening and studying the feelings that she experiences in moving her lips, her tongue, her voice box. Unaware of herself, she confirms only her freedom to create these sounds.

When I speak to a baby in her own language – "aba, abb, adda" – she stares in amazement at me, a mysterious creature producing sounds she knows well.

Were we to dig deeper into the essence of the infant's consciousness, we would find far more there than we think, only not the what or how that we think. "Poor baby, poor little thing, she wants yum-yum, she wants milky-milky." The infant understands perfectly, she waits for her feeder to unbutton her brassiere, place a napkin under the chin, she grows impatient when they delay the final expected sensation. And yet the mother has delivered this whole long tirade to herself, not to her child. The latter would more quickly retain those sounds that a housekeeper uses to summon domestic fowl: "cheep-cheep, quack-quack."

A baby thinks through the anticipation of welcome sensations and the fear of unpleasant ones; that she thinks not only in images, but also in sounds, can be judged at the least from wailing's infectiousness: wailing heralds misfortune, or: wailing automatically sets in motion the mechanism that expresses dissatisfaction. Pay close attention to a baby when it hears crying.

30. A baby strives arduously to seize control over the outside world: he wishes to overthrow the evil, enemy forces surrounding him, to press good, protective spirits into serving his cause. A baby has two spells at his disposal before he scores a third, wonderful tool of his will: his own hands. These two spells are: wailing and sucking.

If at first the baby wails because something is bothering him, he quickly learns to wail so that something won't. Left alone, he cries, but he settles down upon hearing his mother's footsteps; he wants to nurse, he cries, but he stops crying when he sees preparations for feeding.

He operates within the scope of the information he possesses (not much) and the means at his disposal (which are weak). He makes mistakes, generalizing particular phenomena and binding together two successive facts as cause and effect (*post hoc, propter hoc* [after this, therefore because of this]). Doesn't the interest and affection he has for his bootees have their root in the fact that it is to the bootees that he ascribes his ability to walk? So too is his little coat the magic carpet from the fairytale that carries him into a world of wonders – on a walk.

I have the right to make similar conjectures. If a historian has a right to guess at what Shakespeare intended in creating *Hamlet*, the pedagogue has a right to make even erroneous conjectures that, absent others, nevertheless provide practical outcomes.

And so:

The room is stuffy. The infant has dry lips, too little saliva, which is thick and stringy, he's sulky. Milk is food, but he's thirsty, so give him water. But he "doesn't want to drink": he turns his head, he knocks the spoon from the hand. He wants to drink, only he does not yet know how. Sensing the desired liquid on his lips, he throws back his head, he looks for the nipple. I immobilize his head with my left hand, I place the spoon against his upper lip. He doesn't drink, but sucks the water, sucks greedily, he's drunken five spoonsful and falls quietly to sleep. If I'll give him liquid from a spoon clumsily once or twice, he'll choke and have an unpleasant experience, and then he really won't want to drink from a spoon.

A second example:

The infant is constantly fussy, dissatisfied; he settles down at the breast, during changing or bathing, with frequent shifts in position. This infant has an itchy rash. They respond that there is no rash. Surely there will be. And after two months the rash appears.

A third example:

The infant sucks at his hands; when something is bothering him, any unpleasant sensations, thus also the disquiet of impatient expectation, he wishes to soothe it with beneficial, quite familiar sucking. He sucks at his fists when he's hungry, thirsty, when overfeeding leaves a bad taste in his mouth, when he's in pain, when he's too hot, when his skin or gums itch. Where does the doctor get the idea that it's the teeth, that the infant is clearly experiencing unpleasant sensations in his jaw or gums, though no teeth appear over several weeks? Don't teeth irritate the tiny nerve branches in the bone itself as they are breaking through? Here I will add that a calf suffers similarly before its horns grow.

And here the path is as follows: the sucking instinct, sucking so not to suffer, sucking as pleasure or habit.

31. Again: the fundamental tone, the content of the infant's mental life, is the striving to master the unknown elements, the mystery of the world around him, from which good and evil flow. Wanting to master it, he wishes to know.

Again: a sense of wellbeing fosters an objective examination; any unpleasant sensations flowing from within his organism, and thus pain first and foremost, cloud a shaky awareness. To confirm this, one must examine him in health, suffering, and illness.

When feeling pain, the infant not only wails, but he also hears the wail, he feels this wail in his throat, sees it in blurry images through his squinting eyes. All of this is powerful, menacing, incomprehensible. He must remember these moments well, he must fear them and, not yet knowing himself, tie them to incidental images. And here we most certainly have the source of many of the infant's inexplicable sympathies, antipathies, fears, and oddities.

Researching an infant's intellectual development is exceedingly difficult, since he learns and forgets over and over again: this is development in a series of advances, retreat, and reversals. Perhaps the shaky sense of wellbeing plays an important role in this, perhaps the most important role?

The infant examines his hands. He stretches them out, moves them right and left, farther away, closer, he splays his fingers, squeezes them into a fist, speaks to them and waits for an answer, grabs his left hand with his right and pulls, takes his rattle and looks at the oddly altered image of his hand, shifts the rattle from one hand to the other, he examines it with his mouth, suddenly withdraws it and is again looking slowly, attentively. He tosses the rattle, pulls at a button on his quilt, investigates the reason for the resistance he's experiencing. He is not playing around: use your eyes, blast it, and note the willful effort to comprehend. This is a scientist in his laboratory, immersed in a problem of the greatest gravity that slips away from his understanding.

The infant imposes his will by wailing. Later, by miming with his face and hands, and then finally – through speech.

32. Early morning – five o'clock, let's say.

She's woken up, she smiles, babbles, moves her hands, sits, stands. The mother wants to keep sleeping.

The clash of two wants, two needs, two conflicting egoisms; the third instance in a single process: the mother suffers, and the child is born into life; the mother wants to rest after giving birth, the child demands to be fed; the mother wants to sleep, the child wishes to stay up; there will be a long series of these. This is not a trifle, but a challenge; have the courage of your feelings and, handing the child over to a paid nanny, say clearly: "I don't want her," even if the doctor were to tell you that you may not do so, because that's what he'll always say on the first floor, but never in the attic.

Or perhaps it's like this: the mother surrenders her own sleep to her child, but she demands payment in return, and so she kisses her, caresses her, she hugs the warm, pink, silken creature. Beware: this is a dubious act of overblown sensuality tucked away and hidden in the love not of the maternal heart, but of the body. Know that if the child will willingly hug, blushing from a hundred kisses, with radiant joy in the eyes, this means that your eroticism finds an echo therein.

So you should renounce kissing? I cannot demand this, recognizing kissing, when wisely administered, as a precious component of caregiving; a kiss soothes pain, mitigates harsh words of rebuke, arouses remorse, rewards effort, is a symbol of love, just as the cross is a symbol of faith and functions as such; I say that it is, not that it should be. And anyway, if this odd desire to hug, caress, nuzzle, to absorb the child into oneself raises no doubts, do as you please. I don't prohibit or prescribe anything.

33. When I watch a baby open and close a box, put a pebble inside and take it out, shake it and listen; a one-year-old on unsure legs pull a small table and buckle under the weight; a two-year-old, when told that a cow says "moo," add, "ada – moo," and "ada" is the name of the dog; he's committing super-logical linguistic errors that should be noted and published.

When, among a little kid's junk, I see nails, string, rags, pieces of glass, because they "come in handy" in executing a hundred schemes; when she tests who will "hop" farther, works, bustles, organizes a group game; inquires, "When I am thinking of a tree, do I have an itty-bitty tree in my head?"; gives a beggar not a couple groszy[9], so as to win approval, but twenty-six groszy, all she possesses, because he's so old and poor and is going to die soon.

When an adolescent applies saliva to smooth his mop of hair because his sister's girlfriend is supposed to come over; when a girl writes me a letter that says the world is foul, and people are animals, though she doesn't say why; when a youth tosses out a proudly rebellious thought or provocation that's already worn-out, rancid...

Oh, I kiss these children, with my eyes, with my mind, with a question: what are you, wondrous mystery, what do you bear? I kiss them with an effort of will: how can I help you? I kiss them the way an astronomer kisses a star that has been, is, will be. This kiss ought to occupy the same place between the ecstasy of the scientist and a humble prayer; but he who, in seeking freedom, has lost God in the crowd, will not know its magic.

34. The child doesn't speak yet. When will she start to speak?

Speech is indeed an indicator of a child's development, but it is neither the only one, nor the most important. Impatiently awaiting the first expression is a mistake, proof of the parents' immaturity in childrearing.

If a newborn shudders and throws her arms in the bath, having lost her balance, she's saying, "I'm afraid," and this anxiety reflex in a being so far from understanding danger is exceedingly interesting. You give her your breast, she doesn't take it, she's saying, "I don't want it." She stretches her hands toward a desired object: "Give." With her mouth screwed into a cry, with a defensive movement, she is telling a stranger, "I don't trust you," sometimes asking her mother, "Can I trust him?"

What is the inquisitive look of a child, if not the question: "What's this?" She reaches for something, with much effort she gets it, she sighs deeply, and with this sigh of relief she's saying: "Finally." Try taking it away, in a dozen ways she'll tell you: "I'm not giving it back." She raises her head, sits, stands: "I'm taking action." What is a smile of mouth and eyes if not "Oh, how good I have it."

She speaks with facial speech, she thinks in the speech of images and emotional memories.

Her mother puts her little coat on her, she's happy, she turns her torso toward the door, grows impatient, wants her mother to hurry. She's thinking in images of a stroll and with the recollection of what she has felt on one before. A baby is friendly toward the doctor, but seeing a spoon in his hand she immediately recognizes an enemy.

She understands speech, not in words, but that of countenance and voice modulation.

"Where's your nose?"

Not comprehending any of these three words, she knows from the voice, the movement of the lips, that they demand a given response from her.

Not knowing how to speak, the baby carries on a very complex conversation.

"Don't move," her mother tells her.

Regardless, she reaches for the forbidden object, tilts her head gratefully, smiles, tests whether her mother will renew her prohibition more firmly or, disarmed by her refined coquetry, yield, allow her.

Not having yet uttered a single word, she lies, she lies shamelessly. Wanting to free herself from the unkind individual, she gives the agreed-upon sign, an ominous signal, and sitting on you-know-which vessel she looks upon her surroundings with triumph and derision.

Try to make fun of her, offering and taking back the object she demands, she won't always get angry, sometimes she'll just be offended.

An infant knows how to be a despot without words, to keep pushing persistently, to tyrannize.

35. Very often, when a doctor asks the question of when a child started to speak and walk, the embarrassed mother timidly provides an approximate answer:

"Early, late, normal."

She thinks that the date of so important a fact should be precise, that any doubt casts her in a poor light in the doctor's eyes; by way of proof, I recall how unpopular it is among the general public to remain cognizant that it is only with difficulty that even precise scientific observation manages to sketch an approximate line of the child's development, how common is the schoolboyish urge to conceal one's ignorance.

How are you to distinguish between "am, an, ama" and the infant saying "mama" for the first time, between "gaga" and "grandma"? How can we describe when the expression "mama" is now tied precisely in his mind to the image of his mother and with no other?

The baby bounces on his knees, stands, held up or leaning on his own against the edge of the bed, he stands for a moment without help, he's taken a couple of steps along the floor and several in the air, he shuffles, creeps, crawls, shoves a chair before him, not losing his balance, quarter-, half-, three-quarter-walking, before he finally walks. And here, yesterday, all week he's been walking, and again he doesn't know how. Slightly weary, he's lost his inspiration. He's tipped over and gotten scared, he's afraid, a two-week break.

The little head dropping helplessly on the mother's shoulder is not proof of grave illness, but of every ailment.

In every new movement, a child is similar to a pianist who needs a sense of wellbeing, complete balance, in order to perform a difficult composition;

even the exceptions to this rule are similar to each other. Sometimes the child "was weak already, but wouldn't give up and maybe walked, played, talked all the more"; here we have the self-accusation: "So I thought that it only seemed to me that he was weak, and I took him for a walk"; the justification: "It was such lovely weather"; and the question: "Could that have done him harm?"

36. By when is the child supposed to be walking and talking? When she walks and talks. When are her teeth supposed to come in? At precisely the time they come in. And the fontanelle is supposed to close at just the time it closes. And a baby should sleep as many hours as she needs to in order to be well-rested.

But we know when these things generally happen. In every popular pamphlet, transcribed from textbooks, one finds these little truths about children in general and lies about your child in particular.

For there are babies that require more or less sleep; there are early teeth that are already rotten during teething and the later, healthy teeth of healthy children; the fontanelle closes in the ninth and the fourteenth month of life in healthy children; dimwitted kids start prattling early, smart ones sometimes do not speak for a long time.

The numbers on cabs, the rows of seats in the theater, the deadline for paying the rent, everything that people have come up with for order can be respected; but whoever is willing to reach, with a mind raised on police regulations, for nature's living tome is going to be smacked on the head with the whole enormous weight of unrest, disappointments, and surprises.

I credit myself for having answered the aforementioned questions not by rattling off figures that I called little truths. For it is unimportant whether the upper or lower teeth come in first, the incisors or the canines, anyone who has a calendar and eyes can tell that much; but what is the living organism, and what does it need, this is a great truth, and one only now being investigated.

Even conscientious doctors must have two measures of conduct: with prudent parents they are naturalists, they have doubts, conjectures, difficult challenges, and interesting questions; with the imprudent ones, they are cold tutors: from here to there, and a nail mark in the primer.

A spoonful every two hours.

An egg, half a glass of milk, and two ladyfingers.

37. Attention. Either we come to an understanding now, or we part ways forever. Every thought that wishes to slip away and hide, every feeling running wild should be brought to order and placed in a disciplinary line through an effort of will.

I am calling for a Magna Carta[10], for the rights of a child. There may be more; I have dug out three basics:

1. A child's right to die.
2. A child's right to the present day.
3. A child's right to be what a child is.

One must recognize them in order to commit the fewest possible errors in furnishing these rights. For errors there must be. Let us not fear them: he will correct them himself with amazing vigilance provided that we not dull his precious capacity, his mighty defensive power.

We gave him too much food or the wrong kind, too much milk, an unfresh egg – he threw it up. We delivered indigestible information, he didn't understand, worthless advise, he didn't digest it, didn't listen. It is not an empty cliché when I say: it is humanity's good fortune that we cannot force children to submit to their caregivers' influences or to didactic attacks on their sound mind and healthy, human will.

> *Not yet crystallized within me, not yet affirmed, was the understanding that the first, indisputable right of a child is to articulate his own thoughts and take an active role in our discussions and verdicts about him. When we grow toward respect and trust, when he himself will trust and say what is his right – there will be fewer riddles and mistakes.*

38. A mother's intense, understanding, even-tempered love for her child must give him the right to an early death, to conclude the cycle of life not in sixty revolutions of the Earth around the sun, but in only one spring or three. A cruel demand on those who do not want to bear the difficulties and costs of the postpartum period more than once, twice.

"The Lord gave, and the Lord hath taken away" – so says the folk-naturalist who knows that not every seed yields a stalk, not every chick is born capable of life, not every shrub fills out into a tree.

There is a notion going around that the higher the child mortality among the proletariat, the stronger the generation that survives and grows up. But no: the poor conditions that kill the weak weaken the healthy and strong. Whereas it strikes me as true that the more a mother from affluent circles is terrified by the thought of her child's possible death, the less the child will encounter conditions for becoming an at least adequately developed person physically and a passably autonomous one spiritually. Whenever I see, in a room whitewashed with oil paint, among furnishings varnished white, in a white dress, with white toys, a white child, I get a bad feeling: this room, not a child's, but an operating room, is where a bloodless soul must grow up in an anemic body.

"The white drawing-room, with electric bulbs in all the corners, made me feel that, any moment, I might have an epileptic fit," Claudine says.[11] Perhaps further research will conclude that overfeeding the nerves and tissues with light is just as injurious as the lack of light in a gloomy basement.

We have two expressions: freedom and liberty. Freedom, it seems to me, signifies possession: I am in charge of my own person. In liberty we have an element of will, and thus of the act born of aspiration. Our child's room with its symmetrically arranged furniture, our licked-clean urban parks, are no terrain where freedom can manifest itself, nor a workshop where the child's active will would find its tools.

The small child's room arose from the midwife's clinic, whose regulations are dictated by bacteriology. On our guard against diphtheria bacteria, let's be careful not to bring the child into an atmosphere permeated by the mustiness of boredom and acquiescence. Today there isn't the stuffiness of dried diapers, but there is the stuff of iodoform.

Very many changes. Now not just the white varnish of the furniture, but beaches, excursions, sports, scouting. And that's just the beginning. A bit more freedom, yet the life of the child remains muted, stifled.

39. A boo-boo: poor baby, where does it hurt?

The child makes an effort to track down the minute traces of scrapes from the day before yesterday, she points to the place where the bruise would be if she had been hit harder, she achieves an expertise in discovering blemishes, specks, and marks.

If every "pain" is accompanied by a tone, gesture, and facial expression of helpless humility, of hopeless resignation, then "ew, ugh, foul" merges with manifestations of revulsion and hatred. One must see how the baby holds her chocolate-soiled hands, all her disgust and helplessness, before mommy wipes her with a batiste napkin, to ask the question:

"Wasn't it better when the kid, having knocked her skull against a chair, slapped it back, and when she was bathing, her eyes full of soap, spat and kicked her nanny?..."

A door – she'll pinch her finger, a window – she'll lean out and fall, a pebble – she'll choke, a chair – she'll topple it onto herself, a knife – she'll cut herself, a stick – she'll poke her eye out, she's picked a box up off the ground – she'll catch an infection, a match – fire, she'll burn up.

"You'll break your arm, you'll get run over, the dog will bite you. Don't eat plums, don't drink water, don't walk around barefoot, don't run in the sun, button your coat, wrap your scarf. You see: you weren't listening. Look: a cripple, look: a blind man. Help, blood, who gave you scissors?"

A bump is not a bruise, but fear of brain swelling; vomiting is not dyspepsia, but fear of scarlet fever. There are traps and dangers everywhere, everything is threatening and ominous.

And if the child believes it, she won't eat a pound of unripe plums on the sly, and having dropped our vigilance she won't light matches in some corner with pounding heart, if she obediently, passively, trustingly surrenders to the demand to evade all experience, to renounce trying anything, to abandon all effort, every impulse of the will – what will she do when, in herself, within her spiritual essence, she senses something that hurts, that burns, that stings?

Do you have a plan for raising the child from infancy through childhood and into puberty, when, like lightning, the surprise of blood befalls a girl, and an erection and nocturnal emissions befall a boy?

Yes, she's still nursing at the breast, and already I'm asking about her giving birth. Because that's the problem one cannot ponder too much over two decades.

40. In the fear of having one's child snatched away by death, we snatch the child away from life; not wanting him to die, we do not allow him to live. Ourselves raised in the corrupting, helpless anticipation of what will be, we are constantly rushing into a magic-filled future. Lazy, we do not want to seek beauty in the present day, in order to prepare ourselves to receive tomorrow morning with dignity: tomorrow has to bring inspiration on its own. What is that "If only he already walked, talked" – what, if not the hysteria of anticipation?

He will walk, he'll knock into the hard corners of an oak chair. He will speak, he'll grind the chaff of daily dullness with his tongue. How is the child's today worse or more priceless than his tomorrow? If it's a matter of hardship, it will get much harder.

When tomorrow arrives at last, we await another. For the basic view – the child is not, but will be, doesn't know, but will, cannot now, but then will be able to – compels us toward constant anticipation.

Half of humanity does not exist; their life – it's a joke, their striving naive, their emotions fleeting, their views silly. Children are different from adults, something is missing from their lives, and there is more of something than in ours; but this life, so disparate from our own, is a reality, not a delusion. What have we done to know the child and create conditions in which he might exist and mature?

Worry over the child's life overtakes worry about disability, the worry over disability latches onto the cleanliness necessary for good health, here a belt of prohibitions shifted onto a new wheel: the cleanliness and safety of the dress, stocking, tie, glove, bootee; no longer a hole in the brow, but on a trouser knee. Not the health and good of the child, but our own ambition and pocket. A new belt of proscriptions and prescriptions turns the wheel of our own comfort.

"Don't run, because you'll get run over by a carriage. Don't run, because you'll get muddy. Don't run, because I have a headache."

(And yet running is something we allow children to do as a matter of principle: it's the one act by which we allow them to live.)

And the whole monstrous machine operates over long years to crush the will, grind down the energy, to reduce a child's power to ashes.

For tomorrow, one disregards what amuses the child today, what saddens, surprises, angers, occupies him. For tomorrow, which he neither understands, nor has any need to understand, one steals years, many years of life.

"Children should be seen and not heard."

"You have time. Wait until you're older."

"Oh my, you're in your long pants! Whoa, you have your own watch. Show me: your moustache is growing."

And the child thinks:

"I'm nothing. The thing is to be a grownup. Right now I'm just an older nothing. How many more years must I wait? Just wait till I'm grown up…"

He waits and lives lazily, he waits and suffocates, he waits and bides his time, waits while his mouth waters. A lovely childhood? No, a boring one; and if it contains lovely moments, they're fought-for, more often than not stolen.

> *Not a word on free public education, rural schools, garden cities, scouting. Such things were unimportant and hopelessly distant. – A book depends on the kinds of experiences and encounters the author has dealt with, the kind of terrain and methodology, the kind of soil that has nourished his mind. This is why we come across the naive views of authorities, foreign ones all the more.*

41. So then is everything permissible? Never: of a bored slave we'll make a bored tyrant. With our prohibitions, after all, we harden the will, albeit only toward restraint and renunciation, we cultivate inventiveness on restricted terrain, skill in slipping out of others' control, we arouse the critical faculty. And this is precious as a one-sided preparation for life. In allowing that

"everything goes," in indulging whims, let's be all the more cautious not to stifle desires. One way, we weaken the will, another, we poison it.

It's not "do as you please," but "I will do, I will buy, I will give you everything you want, but demand only that which I can give, buy, or do for you." I pay for you not to do anything, I pay for you to be obedient.

"Eat your meat, and mommy will buy you a little book. Don't go out for a walk, I'll give you chocolate."

The childish "gimme," even just wordlessly reaching out the hand, has to be met with our "no"; a whole enormous segment of childrearing depends on our "you can't have it, you're not allowed, you may not."

A mother doesn't want to see challenges: she prefers to defer, lazily, in a cowardly manner, to put it off to later, to afterwards. She doesn't want to know that childrearing cannot dispense with the tragic collision of an unreasonable, unfeasible, inexperienced wish with an experienced prohibition, that one cannot exclude the still more tragic clash of two wishes, of two rights on the same terrain. She wants to put a lit candle in her mouth, I cannot allow her to; she demands a knife, I'm afraid; she reaches her hands toward a vase, which would be a pity; she wants to toss a ball, I want to read a book. We have to establish the boundaries of her right and mine.

The baby reaches for a glass, her mother kisses the hand, it doesn't help, she gives her a rattle, it doesn't help, she tells someone to take the temptation out of her sight. If the baby tears her hand away, throws the rattle to the floor, seeks the hidden object with her eyes, looks angrily at her mother, I ask who's in the right: the mother-deceiver, or the baby who despises her?

Whoever doesn't think the problem of proscriptions and prescriptions all the way through when there are few of them will not grasp it, will get lost, when there are many.

42. Little Jędrek from the countryside. He's already walking. He holds himself up by the doorframe and saunters over the threshold from the main room to the entrance. From the entrance, over two stone steps, he crawls on all fours. He met a cat in front of the cottage: they looked at each other and went their separate ways. He stumbled on a lump, stopped, looked. He's found a stick, sits down, digs in the sand. There's a potato peel, he puts it in his mouth, sand in his mouth, he's grimaced, he spits, throws it away. Back on his feet, he'll run opposite a dog; the brute has knocked him over. With a grimace, he's about to cry, but doesn't; he's remembered something, he's dragging a broom. His mother is going to get water; he's gotten hold of her dress and is now running more certainly. A group of older children, they have a wagon, he watches: they've driven him away, he's standing off to the side, he watches. Two roosters are fighting, he watches. They've sat him in the wagon, they're

giving him a ride, they've tipped it over. The mother calls. This is the first half-hour of sixteen hours in the day.

No one tells him that he's a child, he feels for himself what is beyond his power. No one tells him that the cat scratches, that he doesn't know how to descend stairs. No one sets parameters for dealing with older children. "As little Jędrek grew up, so too did the course of his raids take him farther and farther from his cottage" (Witkiewicz).[12]

He makes mistakes, errs often; thus the bump, thus the big bump, thus the scar.

But no: I do not wish to exchange an excess of care for a lack thereof. I am merely indicating that the country yearling is already living when for us the mature youth has not yet begun to. Merciful God – when will he?

43. Bronek wants to open the door. He pushes a chair. He stops and rests, but he doesn't ask for help. The chair's heavy, he's gotten tired. Now he's dragging one leg, then the other, in turn. The labor is slower-going but easier. Now the chair is near the door, it seems to him that he's going to make it, he clambers up, stands. He's wavered, gotten scared, he climbs down. He pulls the chair right up to the door, but off to the side of the handle. Another failed attempt. Not a trace of impatience. He's at it again, just with longer breaks. He climbs up for the third time; leg up, grasp of the hand and propping on a bent knee, he hangs, catches his balance, a new effort, the hand hooks the edge – he's lying on his belly; pause, a forward thrust of the body, he kneels, gets his legs tangled in his smock, stands up. What poor Lilliputians these are in the land of giants. Head always looking up to see something. The window somewhere high up, like in prison. You have to be an acrobat just to sit on a chair. Strain every muscle and the whole intellect just to finally reach a door handle.

The door open – he has sighed deeply. We see this deep sigh of relief already in infants after every willful effort, every lasting expenditure of attention. When you finish an interesting fairytale, the child sighs the same way. I should like this to be understood.

Such a deep, individual sigh demonstrates that the breathing beforehand had been slowed, shallow, inadequate; with bated breath the child is looking, waiting, following, until his oxygen is depleted, until his tissues are poisoned. The organism immediately alerts the breathing center; there follows a deep gasp, which restores balance.

If you know how to diagnose a child's joy and the intensity thereof, you have to note that the greatest joy is in a hardship overcome, a goal attained, a mystery revealed. The joy of triumph and the happiness of self-sufficiency, mastery, dominium.

"Where's mommy? Mommy's gone. Look for her." He's found her. Why is he laughing so hard?

"Run, mommy's going to get you!" Oh, she can't catch him. My, what a happy child.

Why does he want to crawl, walk, tear himself from your hands? Such a common scene: he's toddling around, farther from his nanny, he sees his nanny running after him, so he bolts, he loses his sense of danger, he speeds blindly ahead in an ecstasy of freedom – and either he stretches out on the ground or, caught, he wrenches himself free, kicks his legs, screams.

You'll say: an excess of energy; that's the physiological side, I'm seeking out the psychophysiological one.

The question I'm asking is why he wants to hold the glass himself while he's drinking, and for his mother not to touch it at all with her hand; why he doesn't want to eat anymore but is eating because he's allowed to feed himself with a spoon. Why is he so joyful in extinguishing a match, pulling on his father's slippers, bringing a footrest for his grandma? Is it imitation? No, it's something much greater and more precious.

"I do!" he cries a thousand times with a gesture, with a look, with a laugh, with begging, anger, tears.

44. "And do you know how to open the door yourself?" I asked a patient whose mother had warned me that he was afraid of doctors.

"Even to the bathroom," he hastened to reply.

I burst out laughing. The boy was embarrassed, but I was even more so. I had extracted a confession of hidden triumph and had laughed it off.

It is not difficult to imagine that there had once been a time when all doors had stood open before him, but the one to the bathroom had resisted his efforts, it was the focus of his ambition; it had been similar for the young surgeon dreaming of performing a difficult operation.

He hadn't confided in anyone, because he knows that among those around him he will find no echo of what composes his inner world.

Perhaps at times he'd been menaced or spurned with a suspicious question.

"What are you hanging around there for, why are you always puttering around there? Don't move, you'll break it. Go straight to your room."

Thus he had been working in secret, on the sly, and finally opened it.

Have you paid attention to how frequently, when the bell rings in the foyer, you hear this request:

"I'll get it!"

First of all, the latch on the front door is difficult, and second: the sense that behind the door there stands a grownup who cannot manage it on his own and is waiting for him, a little kid, to help.

Such minute triumphs are celebrated by a child who is already dreaming of long journeys, who in his sleep is Robinson Crusoe on a deserted island and in reality is happy when he's allowed to look out a window.

"Can you get onto a chair by yourself?"

"Can you hop on one leg?"

"Can you catch a ball with your left hand?"

And the child forgets that he doesn't know me, that I'm going to look down his throat, that I'm going to prescribe him medicine. I bring up what surpasses feelings of embarrassment, fear, aversion, and so he joyfully responds:

"Yes I can."

Have you seen how a baby, with an impassive face, parted lips, and concentration in his eyes slowly, patiently puts on and takes off a stocking or slipper? It's neither a game, nor imitation, nor thoughtless fooling around, but work.

What sustenance will you provide his will when he's three years old, or five, or ten?

45. Me!

When a newborn scratches herself with her own nail; when a baby is sitting down and pulls her foot into her mouth, topples over onto her back, and angrily looks around her for the culprit; when she pulls her own hair, grimaces in pain, but then tries it again, when she hits herself in the head with a spoon, she looks up for something that she does not see, though she senses – she does not know herself.

When she is examining the movements of her hands; when, sucking on her fists, she looks at them carefully; when, at the breast, she suddenly stops nursing and compares her foot to her mother's breast; when, toddling around, she stops and looks down, and she is seeking that something that is holding her up quite differently from how maternal hands do; when she compares her right, stockinged foot to her left one, she wishes to recognize and to know.

When she investigates the water in the bath, discovering herself, a conscious droplet in the many unconscious drops, then she has an inkling of the great truth contained in the brief expression: I.

Only a Futurist painting can give us what a child is to herself: fingers, a little fist, feet less distinct, maybe the belly, maybe even the head, but only in faint outlines, like a map of the polar regions.

Work still unfinished, she is still turning and bending back to see what's hidden behind her, she studies herself before a mirror and stares at a photograph, she discovers the depression of the belly button, the rise of her own nipples, and already there's a new job: to pick yourself out from your surroundings. Mommy, father, mister, missus, some appear often, others rarely, lots of mysterious figures whose purpose is obscure and deeds doubtful.

She's only just established that mommy serves to fulfil or oppose her demands, daddy brings home money, and her aunts – chocolates – when, in her own thoughts, somewhere within herself, she discovers a new, even stranger, invisible world.

Moving forward, she'll have to pick herself out in society, in humanity, in the universe.

So then – grey hair, unfinished work.

46. Mine.

Where is the protozoan of thought and feeling hidden? Perhaps it is conjoined with the concept of the *I*? Perhaps just as the baby protests against her hands being restrained, she struggles for them as "mine," and not as "I." If you take away the spoon she's banging against the table, you deprive her not of *her* property but of *the* property by which her hand expends energy; she is expressing herself by a different means, through sound.

This hand, not quite her own, rather Aladdin's obedient spirit, clutches a ladyfinger, attaining yet another precious property, and the child defends it.

To what extent is the concept of property bound to the concept of increased power? For the savage[13], a bow was not only one's property but an improved arm that strikes from a distance.

The child does not want to give back the torn newspaper because she's examining it, because she's practicing, because it's a material like the hand, it's a tool that makes no sound, has no flavor, but alongside the bell it speaks, alongside a roll it supplements nursing with additional, pleasant impressions.

Imitation, emulation, the desire to get up – these only come later. Because property brings respect, raises value, gives power. Without the ball he'd stand in shadow, unnoticed, but having the ball he can assume an eminent place in the game regardless of what he can do; with a small sword, he becomes an officer, having reins makes him a coachman; and whoever doesn't have these things is a private, a horse.

"Gimme, lemme, come on" – the request that tickles one's ambition.

I'll give it or I won't – depends on my whim – because it – is mine.

47. I want to have it, I have it, I want to know, I know, I want to be able to, I can; three branches of the shared trunk of the will, whose roots are two emotions: satisfaction and dissatisfaction.

The baby does everything he can to know himself, the world around him, living and dead, because his success is bound to this. Inquiring, "What's that?" – in speech or a look – demands not a name, but an assessment.

"What's that?"

"Ew, let go, that's foul, don't pick it up."

"What's that?"

"It's a flower," and a smile, and a gentle expression on the face, and permission.

When a child inquires about an indifferent object and receives a name without the emotional qualification of a facial expression, it happens that, looking at his mother in surprise, almost in disappointment, he repeats the name, drawing out the expression, unsure of what he's supposed to do with the response. He has to gather experience in order to understand that, beside the desirable and the undesirable, there also exists an indifferent world.

"What's that?"

"Cotton"

"Coooooootton?" and looking into his mother's face he waits for an indication of what he is supposed to think about it.

If I were to journey with a native through a subtropical forest, I would ask a similar question – "What's that?" – upon noticing a plant with unfamiliar fruit, and he, figuring the question out, would answer with a shout, a grimace, or a smile that it's poison, tasty food, or useless junk, not worth putting in one's travel sack.

The childish "What's that?" means: What's it like? What's it for? What benefit does it hold for me?

48. A common and curious scene.

Two children, still unsteady on their shuffling feet, encounter one another; one has a ball or some gingerbread; the other wants to take it away from her.

The mother is sorry when her child grabs something away from another, doesn't want to give, share, "lend." It's embarrassing that the child exceeds an accepted norm, an established convention.

The scene we're describing can follow a threefold course:

One child grabs, the other watches, surprised, then turns her gaze toward her mother, expecting an appraisal of an incomprehensible situation.

Or: one tries to grab, but her net's come up empty: the one under attack keeps the desired object away, she repels her attacker, she knocks her over. The mothers run over to help.

Or: the children look, approach each other apprehensively, one reaches with an uncertain movement, the other defends herself anemically. The conflict arises only after long preparation.

The age of both children, the store of their experience, plays a role here. When a child has older siblings, she has already come out in defense of her rights or property many times, sometimes she herself was the attacker. But after we toss aside what is accidental, we discern two opposed organizations, two deeply human types: the proactive and the reactive, the active and the passive.

"Good kid, gives everything away."

Or:

"Silly thing: lets them take everything she has."

This isn't goodness, and it isn't silliness.

49. Gentleness, a weaker vital drive, a lower surge of will, reluctance to act. Avoiding sudden movements, intense experiences, difficult undertakings.

Doing less, he wins fewer factual truths, so he is forced to trust more, to surrender for longer.

Is the intellect less precious? No, just different. Passive, he has fewer bruises and unpleasant missteps, so he lacks a painful experience of them; but perhaps he has a better memory of the experiences he has attained. Active, he has more bumps and let-downs, maybe he forgets them faster. The former maybe experiences fewer things and more slowly, but more thoroughly.

The passive child is more comfortable. Left alone, he won't fall out of his carriage, does not call the house to alarm for any old reason, when in tears he's easily assuaged, his demands are not overly insistent, he's less likely to smash something, bawl, destroy.

"Give it" – he does not protest. "Put it on, take this, take it off, eat this" – he yields.

Two scenes:

Not hungry, but a spoon of oatmeal is lying on the saucer, so he has to eat, because the portion has been fixed by the doctor. He reluctantly opens his mouth, chews long and lazily, swallows slowly and with effort. The second one, not hungry, so he clenches his teeth, energetically throws his head around, pushes it away, spits it out, defends himself.

And their upbringing?

To judge children from two diametrically opposed child types is to speak of water on the basis of the properties of full boil and ice. The scale has a hundred degrees, where does our child belong? But a mother can know what's innate, what's hard-fought – and she should remember that everything attained through drilling, pressure, and force is short-lived, uncertain, unreliable. And when a submissive, "good" child suddenly becomes stubborn and unruly, it doesn't do to get angry that the child is what he is.

50. A peasant staring at the sky or the earth, a product and creature of the earth, knows the scope of human authority. A horse is clever, lazy, timid, skittish; a hen egg-laying, the cow a milk-cow, the soil fertile and barren, the summer drizzly, the winter snowless – everywhere he encounters something that can be slightly altered or greatly improved with oversight, toil, the whip, but it can happen that nothing does the trick.

City folk have too great a notion of human power. Potatoes had a bad year, but they're there, you just have to pay a little more for them. Winter, you put on a fur; rain – boots; drought – they spray the street to keep the dust down. Everything can be bought, everything can be remedied. The child's feeble – the doctor; she doesn't learn well – a tutor. And a book, in telling you what you ought to do, offers the illusion that everything is attainable.

How are you to believe that the child must be what she is, that, as the French say, eczema can be bleached, not cured.

I wish to nourish a scrawny child, I do it slowly, carefully, and it's worked: I got a kilogram. But all it takes is a minor ailment, a runny nose, a pear given at the wrong time, and the patient will lose the lousy, hard-fought two pounds.

Summer camp for poor children.[14] Sun, forest, river, they soak in the merriment, the refinement, the goodness. Yesterday a little savage, today a kind partaker of the fun. Bullied, timid, and vacant, a week later she's brave, lively, full of initiative and song. Here change happens from hour to hour, there from week to week, elsewhere no change at all. It's not a miracle and the lack thereof, just that there is what was there and waiting, and there isn't what there wasn't.

I teach an underdeveloped child: two fingers, two buttons, two matches, two coins – two. She's already counting to five. But change the question's order, intonation, gesture – she doesn't know again, she doesn't know how.

A child with a heart defect. Gentle, slow in her movements, speech, smile. She's out of breath, every vigorous movement is a cough, suffering, pain. She has to be this way.

A woman is ennobled by motherhood when she sacrifices, renounces, resigns; she is corrupted when, shielding herself with the alleged good of the child, she makes her prey to her own ambitions, predilections, habits.

My child is my property, my slave, my lapdog. I tickle her between the ears, I pet her on the back, I take her for a walk adorned in ribbons, I train her so that she'll be clever and polite; and when she annoys me:

"Go play. Go study. Time for bed!"

This is supposedly the basis for treating hysterics:

"You claim, sir, that you are a rooster. So be a rooster, just don't crow."

"You're impetuous," I tell a boy. "Fine. Punch, just not too hard. Get angry, but only once a day."

If you please, in this one sentence I have summarized my entire method of childrearing.

51. You see that little kid running, shouting, rolling around in the sand? He'll be an excellent chemist someday, he'll make discoveries that will bring him high regard, an outstanding position, an estate. Yes, between the revelry and the ball – the bore will suddenly lose himself in thought, lock himself in his study, and emerge a scientist. Who would have suspected?

You see that other one, his sleepy eyes indifferently observing his peers at play? He's yawned, stood up – maybe he'll approach the playful group? Now he's sat back down. And he will be an excellent chemist, he'll make discoveries. Odd: who could have thought?

No, neither the little rattlebrain nor the dullard will be a scientist. One will be a gymnastics teacher, the other a postal clerk.

It is a passing fashion, an error, nonsense that everything that's not outstanding strikes us as pointless, worthless. We're sick with immortality. Whoever hasn't grown into a monument on the town square wants to have at least a little street named after him, an everlasting testament. If not four newspaper columns after his death, then at least a mention in the text: "He played an active role, he left a great many in mourning."

Streets, hospitals, shelters have carried the names of patron saints, and this made sense, then – of those in power, this was a mark of the time, and today of scientists and artists, and this doesn't make sense. Now they'll erect monuments to ideas, to nameless heroes, to those who have no monument.

A child is not a lottery ticket that's supposed to win you a portrait in a board room at city hall or a bust in the theater vestibule. Each has his own spark that can kindle a fire of happiness and truth, perhaps ten generations hence it will blow up into a blaze of genius and consume the child's own kin, giving humanity the light of a new sun.

A child is not soil that heredity plows to sow life; we can only help foster the growth of that which begins to grow in great rushes well before it's taken its first breath.

New kinds of tobacco and fresh brands of wine need publicity, but people do not.

52. Thus the doom of heredity, ruthless predestination, the bankruptcy of medicine, of pedagogy? Cliché hurls lightning.

I have called the child parchment crammed with writing, earth already seeded; let's dispense with comparisons that lead us astray.

There are cases in the face of which, given the state of our knowledge today, we are helpless. These are fewer today than yesterday, but they're there.

There are cases in the face of which, given the conditions of life today, we are helpless. And there are a bit fewer of those.

Here's a child for whom the highest will and greatest effort will bring little. Here's another who would gain much by them, but the conditions are stacked against her. For one the countryside, the mountains will not bring much, while they would help the other, only we cannot provide them.

When we meet a child languishing for want of care, air, clothing, we do not blame the parents. When we see a child harmed by excessive attention, overfed, overheated, protected from imaginary danger, we're inclined to accuse the mother, it seems easy to us to remedy the wrong so long as there is a desire to understand. No, one must have a great deal of fortitude to resist the regulations incumbent on a given class or stratum, not with empty criticism, but action. If in one place the mother cannot wash her child or wipe her nose, in another the child cannot be allowed to run around in worn-out bootees with a filthy face. If in one place the mother tearfully takes the child out of school and apprentices her for work, in another, with just as much pain, the mother must send her to school.

"I'll squander the kid without school," says one, taking away the books.

"I'll squander the child in school," says the other, purchasing a stone's weight in new textbooks.

53. For people on the whole, heredity is a fact that blocks out any exception one encounters; for science, it is a riddle currently being researched. There is a vast literature that aspires to untangle one question alone: Is a child of consumptive parents born sick, or just predisposed, or is he infected after birth? Or, in thinking about heredity, have you taken into account such simple facts that, besides the inheritance of disease, there exists the inheritance of health, that siblings are not siblings in the pluses and minuses, the resources and flaws they have received – one should and must. Healthy parents bear their first child, the second will be the child of syphilitics if the parents have contracted that illness; the third will be the child of syphilitic consumptives if the parents have then become infected with tuberculosis. These three children are strangers: without baggage, with baggage, and double-burdened. Turned around, the ill father has recovered, of the two siblings the first is a sick man's child, the second the child of a healthy parent.

Is a nervous child that way because he was born of nervous parents, or because he was raised by them? Where is the line between nervousness and a subtlety of nervous structure, a spiritual progeneration?

Does a ne'er-do-well father bear a wastrel son, or does he infect him with his example?

Tell me who bore you, and I'll tell you who you are. But not always.

Say who raised you, and I'll say who you are – and not that, either.

Why do healthy parents have weak offspring? Why does a scoundrel grow out of a virtuous family? Why does an ordinary family produce an exceptional descendent?

Beside the province of heredity it is necessary to conduct concurrent research in the province of childrearing; then quite a few riddles may find their solution.

The province of childrearing is what I call the family's dominant soul; individual members cannot assume any stance they please in the face of it. This driving soul commands, it will not tolerate resistance.

54. The province of dogmatism.

Tradition, authority, ritual, the dictate as absolute law, compulsion as life imperative. Discipline, order, and consistency. Seriousness, spiritual balance, wellbeing flowing from fortitude, a sense of stability, resolve, self-confidence, the righteousness of one's tasks. Self-restraint, self-overcoming, work as law, morality as habit. Deliberation to the point of passivity, the one-sided failure to recognize rights and truths not handed down by tradition, not sanctified by an authority, not preserved by a mechanized course of action.

If self-confidence doesn't pass into willfulness, simplicity into crudeness, then the fertile province of childrearing will break the child, who is spiritually alien to it, or it will indeed carve out a beautiful person who will respect strict managers because they didn't fool around with her and took an arduous path to a clearly defined goal.

Unfavorable conditions, the pressure of physical needs – these do not change the province's spiritual essence. Meticulous labor passes into drudgery, calm into resignation, there is abnegation to the point of digging in with the will to survive, sometimes there's shyness and humility, always a sense of righteousness, trust. Apathy and energy are not a child's weakness, but her strength, which someone else's ill will bats at in vain.

Dogma can be land, church, fatherland, virtue and sin; it can be science, volunteer and political activity, estate, struggle, God, as well as hero, idol, effigy. It's not what you believe in, but how.

55. The province of ideology.

His courage is not in the fortitude of his spiritual endurance, but in his momentum, drive, push. Here one doesn't work, one joyfully performs. Creates, not awaits. There is no compulsion, there's eagerness. There are no dogmas, there are challenges. There is no deliberation, there's zeal, enthusiasm. Its brake is a revulsion for filth, moral aestheticism. He might dislike for a time, he never spurns. His tolerance is not the imperfection of his own convictions, but respect for human thought, joy at its soaring free at different heights in different directions, weaving, descending, and rising, that it is filling the vastness with itself. Courageous in his own action, he greedily catches the echoes of other people's hammers, with interest awaits a tomorrow of new admirations and amazements, recognitions, wanderings, struggles, doubts, assertions, and contradictions.

If the province of dogmatism fosters the rearing of a passive child, the province of ideology tends to cultivate active children. I believe that many painful surprises find their source here: to one they give ten commandments etched in stone when he wants to burn them up with his own fire in his own breast, another they press into seeking truths that he has to accept readymade. You cannot see this when you approach the child with "I'm going to make a human being out of you" instead of inquiring: "What might you be, human being?"

56. The province of happy use.

I have as much as I need, thus not much as an artisan or clerk, thus a lot as the owner of a spacious manor. I want to be what I am, thus a master craftsman, stationmaster, lawyer, novelist. Work is not a duty, a job, a goal, but a means to attain comforts, desirable conditions.

Happiness, serenity, a mild thrill, friendliness, goodness, as much sobriety as is required, as much self-knowledge as one can attain without too much trouble.

There is no *stubbornness* in preserving and enduring, nor *stubbornness* in seeking and striving.

A child breathes inner promise, the lazy custom that preserves the past, forbearance toward the day's currents, the charm of the simplicity that surrounds her. Here she can be everything: on her own, from books, conversations, encounters, life experiences, she spins the fabric of her own worldview, she chooses her own path.

I will add the love of one's parents for one another: rarely does the child sense its lack when it's missing, but she soaks it in when it's there.

"Daddy is angry at mommy, mommy isn't talking to daddy, mommy was crying, daddy slammed the door" – this is a cloud that obscures the blue sky and cuts down the eager din of the child's room with frosty silence.

In the Preface I said:

"Commanding someone to give out readymade thoughts is to order another woman to give birth to your own child."

It might have occurred to a few:

"What about a man? Doesn't someone else bear his child?"

No: not someone else, but the beloved.

57. The province of appearance and career.

Again we see stubbornness, but it stems not from inner need but cool calculation. There is no room here for content and fullness, there is only a crafty form, the nimble exploitation of someone else's values, the artificial assumption of an essential void. The catchphrases one can make money on, the convention one must humble oneself before. Not a value, but clever advertising. Life not as work or rest, but sniffing around and soliciting. Insatiable vanity, rapacity, ferment, haughtiness and humility, envy, anger, and spite.

Here children are neither loved, nor cared for, here they are only appraised, lost and earned, bought and sold. Obeisance, a smile, a squeeze of the hand, all of it calculated, to be sure, marriage and fertility. One earns in money, promotion, honors, relations in "spheres."

If positive value grows in a comparable province, it happens that it's just an appearance, that it's just a more skillful game, a more tightly fitting mask. It does happen, however, that in the province of disintegration and decay, in torment and spiritual rift there will grow the proverbial "rose from the muck." Such instances indicate that besides the recognized law of suggestion in childrearing there is yet another, the law of antithesis. We see it in instances when the miser raises a spendthrift, the heathen a God-fearing man, the coward a hero, which one cannot explain by "heredity" alone.

58. The law of antithesis depends on the power that defies the suggestions that flow from various sources and employ various means. This is the defense mechanism of resistance, of self-defense, the spiritual system's vigilant, automatically functioning instinct for self-preservation.

If moralizing has already been sufficiently discredited, then it is the suggestion of example, the environments that enjoy absolute confidence in childrearing. So why is it that suggestion so often falls short?

I am inquiring as to why the child, after hearing a curse word, wishes to repeat it, despite prohibitions, and after yielding to the threat retains it in her memory?

Where is the source of this apparently ill will, when the child resists where she could easily give in?

"Put on your coat."

No, she wants to go without her coat.

"Put on your pink dress."

She actually wants her blue one.

If you don't insist, she'll obey, if you're going to insist, by request or threat, she'll dig in and will yield only when compelled.

Why is it that, most often during puberty, our banal "yes" is met with her "no"? Isn't this one of the symptoms of that deep resistance toward temptations that come from inside, and that can come from outside?

"A pitiful irony which gives virtue nostalgia for vice and vice nostalgia for virtue." Mirbeau.[15]

Persecuted faith attains all the more fervent adherence. The wish to temper national self-knowledge arouses it all the more effectively. It may be that here I have mixed the facts of two different fields; it's just that for me personally the hypothesis of the law of antithesis explains many paradoxical reactions to instructive stimuli and turns me away from too numerous, frequent, and powerful suggestions in even the most desirable direction.

The soul of the family? Sure. "But where is the spirit of the age? It halted at the borders of trampled freedom; we hid the cowardly child from it." Brzozowski's Legend of Young Poland[16] *has not protected me from a parochial view on life.*

59. What is a child? What is he, even just physically? He's a growing organism. Surely. But putting on weight and size is just one occurrence beside many. Science is already familiar with a couple episodes in this growth: it is uneven, there are periods of vigorous and subdued tempo; we know that the child does not just grow, but changes proportion.

The vast majority doesn't even know this much. How many times has a mother summoned the doctor, complaining that her child has gone sickly, lost weight, his body has become limp, his little face and head have shrunken. She doesn't know that a baby entering the first phase of childhood loses folds of fat, that as the ribcage develops the head sinks into the broadening shoulders, that the limbs as well as the organs have disparate development, that the brain, heart, stomach, skull, eye, and long bones all grow differently, that if it were otherwise an adult person would be a monster with an enormous head on a short, bulky trunk, that he wouldn't be able to move on the two fat shafts of his legs, that growth is accompanied by a change in proportion.

We have tens of thousands of measurements, some not entirely consistent charts of average growth, we know nothing about what purpose the observed accelerations, delays, and deviations in growth serve. For knowing just the tip of the iceberg of an anatomy of growth, we do not know its physiology, for we have diligently researched the sick child and have only just begun to examine the healthy one from afar. Because for nearly a hundred years the hospital has been our clinic, and the childcare institution has not yet begun to be.

60. The child has changed. Something has happened to her. While the mother doesn't always know how to indicate what the change is based on, she has a ready answer to the question of what to ascribe it to.

"The child changed after her teeth came in, after being vaccinated for smallpox, after she was weened, after she fell out of bed."

She had already been walking, suddenly she stopped walking; she would mumble to be pottied, now she wets herself again; she eats "nothing," sleeps poorly, too little, or too much, has become fussy, overactive, or listless – she's lost weight.

Another phase:

After starting school, after coming back from the countryside, after the measles, after her prescribed baths, after she was terrified by a fire. A change in sleep or appetite, a change in character: she used to be obedient, now she's willful, used to be diligent, now she's absentminded and lazy. Pale, she's hunched over, has some nasty habits. Maybe it's friends who've been brought up poorly, maybe it's school, maybe she's sick?

A two-year stay at the Orphans' Home, observing rather than studying the child, has allowed me to establish that the child goes through everything that is known as the instability of puberty several times in a less extreme form, as little crises, equally "critical" years, just less eye-catching, and thus unnoticed.

Striving for unity in their view of the child, some people wish to examine her as a weary organism. Thus we see a greater need for sleep, a weak resistance to disease, the vulnerability of the organs, a weak mental resilience. It's an accurate view, but not for every stage of development. The child is by turns strong, lively, cheerful, then weak, exhausted, and gloomy. If in the critical period she gets sick, we are inclined to believe that the illness had already been bothering her; I think that the illness developed in passing, on weakened terrain, that either it was lying in wait for the most auspicious conditions for attack, or it just happened to be carried in from outside and, having found no resistance, made itself at home.

If, in the future, we no longer divide the cycle of life into the artificial – baby, child, youth, adult, elder – the guideline for dividing it will not be external growth and development but the as yet unknown, deep transformation of the system as a whole, which Charcot[17] elaborated in his lecture on the evolution of arthritis, from cradle to grave, across two generations.

61. Between the first and second year of the child's life one often changes family doctors. During this time I have gained the patients of mothers embittered toward my predecessor, who had apparently comported himself incompetently in the child's care, and the opposite, the mothers' firing me, complaining that this or that undesirable symptom arose from my neglect. Both groups are right enough, that the doctor has taken a baby for healthy when, suddenly, an unexpectedly unforeseen, previously undiscernible flaw surfaces. It suffices, however, to wait out the critical period patiently, and the child with slight hereditary baggage quickly reaches a momentarily shaky balance and, in a more heavily burdened state, an improvement follows, and the young life's further development again proceeds nicely.

If in this first period of disrupted function – like the second, during the school years – one applies certain treatments, it is to them that the improvement is attributed. And if today we now know that an improvement in pneumonia or typhus follows the completion of the disease's course, here the confusion has to remain up until we establish the order of the child's developmental stages, until we sketch out distinct developmental profiles for different kinds of children.

The child's developmental curve has its own springs and autumns, periods of intensive labor and of rest so as to complete, to hasten to conclude the work that's been performed and gather supplies preparatory to further construction. A seven-month-old fetus is already capable of life, and yet for two long months more (almost a quarter of the pregnancy) it matures in its mother's womb.

A baby that initially triples his weight in a year has a right to take a break. The lightning-fast path his mental development is taking also gives him a right – to forget a bit of what he knew how to do, and what we had counted prematurely as a permanent acquisition.

62. The child doesn't want to eat.

A small arithmetic problem.

The child had weighed a little over eight pounds at birth, he tripled his eight after a year, now he weighs twenty-five. If he had to keep growing at this same rate, at the end of the second year he would weigh 25 lbs. x 3 = 75 lbs.

At the end of the third year: 75 lbs. x 3 = 225 lbs.

At the end of the fourth year: 225 lbs. x 3 = 675 lbs.

At the end of the fifth year: 675 lbs. x 3 = 2025 lbs.

This five-year-old monster, weighing 2000 pounds, consuming from a seventh to a sixth of his weight daily, as babies do, would require 300 pounds of groceries every day.

A child eats little, very little, much, very much, depending on his growth mechanism. The weight curve provides slow or sudden rises; sometimes it doesn't change over months. It is inexorable in its consistency: when unwell, the child loses weight over a couple days, and over the following days he gains as much, in accord with his inner imperative, which announces: "this much and no more." When a healthy child is underfed, impoverished, and switches to a normal diet, he makes up the deficit and reaches his level within a week. When a child is weighed every week, after a certain time he starts to guess whether he's lost or gained weight:

"Last week I lost three hundred grams, today I'm sure I'll weigh five hundred more. Today I'll weigh less, because I haven't had supper. I've gained again, thanks..."

The child wants to indulge his parents, because it's not nice to make your mother worry, because satisfying your parents brings incalculable benefits. Therefore, if he doesn't eat his cutlet, if he doesn't finish his milk, it's because he cannot. If they're going to force him, the regularly recurring digestive trouble and diet will regulate the normal increase in weight.

The principle is: the child should eat as much as he wants, neither more, nor less. Even when a sick child is pressed to eat, one can modify his diet only with his participation and administer treatment under his control.

63. Forcing children to sleep when they don't feel like it is a crime. The chart that declares how many hours of sleep a child needs is absurd. Establishing the number of hours for a given child is easy when someone has a clock: as many hours as she sleeps without interruption, to wake up well-rested. I say "well-rested," not "refreshed"; there are periods when the child requires more sleep, there are those when she wants to lie in bed without sleeping, because she's tired, not sleepy.

The period of weariness: she goes to bed in the evening reluctantly because she doesn't feel like *sleeping*; in the morning she's reluctant to get out of bed, because she doesn't feel like getting up. In the evening she pretends she's not sleepy because they won't let her lie there cutting out little pictures, playing with blocks or a doll, they'll turn off the light and forbid her from talking. In the morning she pretends she's sleeping because they'll immediately order her to get out of bed and wash up with cold water. How joyfully they greet some cough, a fever, because it allows them to stay in bed without sleeping.

The period of happy balance: she falls asleep quickly, but she wakes up before dawn full of energy, the need to move, and playful initiative. Neither an overcast sky, nor the chill of the room will discourage her: barefoot, in a shirt, she'll warm up jumping across the table and chairs. What should you do? Put her to bed late, even, the horror!, at eleven. Allow her to play in bed. I ask why it is that talking before bedtime is supposed to "disturb one's sleep," while vexation at how she has to be naughty in spite of herself does not.

Parents have forged the principle of early to bed, early to rise, regardless of whether it's appropriate, into another: more sleep means better health. To the day's indolent boredom they add the irritating boredom of an evening's anticipation of sleep. It's difficult to imagine a more despotic imperative, bordering on torture, than:

"Go to sleep!"

People who go to sleep late happen to be ill because they spend their nights drinking and carousing and, forced by their professional work to get up early, sleep too little.

A neurasthenic who has risen once at dawn feels perfectly suggestible.

That a child who goes to bed early spends less time in artificial light is after all not so great a positive in a city where she cannot run out into the fields in the morning light, and she lies next to lowered blinds, now indolent, now sulky, now fussy, a poor forecast for a day only just beginning…

As with all the issues raised in this book, I cannot elaborate on the subject in a few dozen lines. My task is to spark vigilance…

64. What is the child as a spiritual arrangement, as distinct from our own? What are the child's qualities, what unnoticed potential does she conceal? What is this half of humanity, which lives with and alongside us, tragically cut off? We load them down with the burden of future man's obligations without providing any of present man's rights.

If we divide humanity into adults and children, and life into childhood and maturity, then there is a whole lot of this child in the world and in life. It's just that, intent on our own struggle, our own worry, we can't perceive her, as before we didn't perceive woman, peasant, subjugated classes and peoples. We've set ourselves up so that children cause us the least disturbance, work out little for themselves about what we are and, indeed, what we do.

In a Parisian orphanage I saw two banisters on the stairs: a high one for the grownups, a low one for the kids. Besides that, a genius inventor had outdone himself on one school bench. That's little, very little. Have a look at the beggarly playgrounds, with a chipped cup on a rusty chain beside the well, in the aristocratic gardens of Europe's capitals.

Where are the houses and gardens, the workshops and practice fields, the instruments of work and learning for children, the people of tomorrow? One more window, one more small passage dividing the classroom from the loo, that's as much as architecture has provided, plus an oilcloth horse and a little tin sabre, that's as much as industry has given; drawings on the walls, and sloyd, not much; a fairytale, we're not the ones who came up with it.

Before our eyes the human woman has emerged from the concubine. For centuries, through violence, she had submitted to the role imposed on her, she had created a type molded by the willfulness and egoism of man, who did not wish to see a woman-worker among the people, just as he still does not see the child-worker.

The child did not speak, she still keeps listening.

The child, a hundred masks, the hundred roles of a capable actor. One way toward her mother, another toward her father, grandmother, grandfather, another toward the strict teacher and the gentle one, another in the kitchen, among her peers, another toward the rich and the poor, another in her daily clothes and her Sunday best. Naive and sly, meek and haughty, gentle and vindictive, well-behaved and willful, she knows how to hide until the time is right, to wall herself in, so that she deceives and exploits us.

On the plane of instincts she lacks only one, or rather it's there, but diffuse, like the mist of erotic inklings.

On the plane of emotions her power exceeds ours because of their unformed restraints.

On the plane of the intellect she is at least our equal, she just lacks experience.

This is why mature people are so frequently children, whereas she is a mature person.

All the difference that remains is that she doesn't earn a wage, that, being supported, she must submit.

> *Children's homes are now less akin to barracks and convents; they're almost hospitals. There's hygiene, but there's no smile, joy, surprise, fooling around; they're just differently serious, if not severe. Architecture has not yet noticed; there is no "child style." An adult facade, adult proportion, the coolness to the details is all that's needed. A Frenchman says that in monastic education Napoleon replaced the bell with a drum – correct; I would add that what hangs over the spirit of modern childrearing is the factory whistle.*

65. Inexperienced.

An example and attempt at an explanation.

"I'll whisper it in mommy's ear."

And wrapping his arms around his mother's neck, the child says secretively:

"Mommy, ask the doctor if I can have a roll (or chocolate, or compote)."

Meanwhile, he frequently looks at the doctor, wooing him with a smile in order to purchase, to extort his consent.

Older children whisper into the ear, younger ones speak in their normal voice...

There was a time when the people around him regarded the child as sufficiently mature for moralizing:

"Some wishes are not to be uttered. There are two kinds: those that one should not have at all, and if you do, you should be ashamed, and those that are acceptable, but only among your family."

It's nasty to be pushy, nasty to ask for a second candy after eating the first. Sometimes it's nasty to ask for candy at all; you have to wait until it's given.

It's nasty to go in your underpants, but it's nasty to say "I have to pee," they'll laugh at you. So that they don't laugh, you have to whisper it in the ear.

Sometimes it's nasty to ask aloud.

"Why doesn't that man have any hair?"

The man laughed, everyone laughed. You can ask, but whisper it into the ear.

The child doesn't understand right away that whispering into the ear is intended for just one trusted person to hear; thus he speaks into the ear, but aloud:

"I have to pee. I want cake."

If he speaks quietly, he still doesn't understand why. For what's the point of hiding what those present will learn from his mommy anyway?

He's not supposed to ask strangers for anything, so why is he allowed to ask the doctor out loud?

"Why does that little dog have such long ears?" the child asks in his quietest whisper.

More laughter. You can ask that out loud, because the little dog isn't going to be offended. And yet it's nasty to ask why that girl has a nasty dress on. Yet the dress isn't going to be offended.

How can you explain to a child how much outrageous grownup insincerity there is in all of this?

How can you clarify later on why whispering into the ear is nasty in general?

66. Inexperienced.

She looks with curiosity, she eagerly listens and is trusting.

Apple, aunt, flower, cow.

She is trusting.

Pretty, tasty, good – she is trusting.

Nasty, don't touch it, you're not allowed, no – she trusts.

Give a kiss, bow, say thank you – she is trusting.

The child gets bumped; show me, mommy will kiss it; it doesn't hurt anymore.

She smiles through her tears; mommy gave her kisses; it doesn't hurt anymore. She got bumped, so she runs for medicine, a kiss.

She trusts.

"Do you love me?"

"I do..."

"Mommy's sleeping, mommy has a headache, you can't wake mommy up."

So she approaches very quietly on tiptoe, carefully tugs at the sleeve, and whispers her question. She's not waking mommy, she's only asking, and then: "Sleep, mommy, you have a headache."

"God's up there. God gets angry at rude children, and to polite ones he gives rolls and cakes. Where's God?"

"Up there, high up."

And a strange man, all white, is coming down the street. "Who's that?"

"A baker. He bakes rolls and cakes."

"Really? So that man is God?"

Grandpa has died, and they've buried him in the ground.

"They buried him in the ground?" I ask, surprised. "How do they feed him?"

"They dig him up," the child answers. "They dig him up with an ax."

A moocow gives milk.

"A cow?" I ask in disbelief. "And where does the cow get the milk from?"

"From the well," the child replies.

The child trusts, because whenever she wants to think up something herself she's wrong; she has to believe.

67. Inexperienced.

The child dropped a drinking glass on the ground. Something very strange happened. The drinking glass disappeared, although entirely different objects showed up. He leans over, picks up the glass, cuts himself, pain, blood flows from his finger. Everything is full of mysteries and surprises.

He's pushing a chair in front of him. Something has suddenly flashed before his eyes, jerked, banged. The chair has been altered, and the child is sitting on the floor. Again, pain and fright. A world full of marvels and dangers.

He tugs at a blanket to extricate himself from it. Losing his balance, he grabs at a nightgown. Climbing up, he takes hold of the bed's edge. Now rich in experience, he pulls the tablecloth down from the table. Again, catastrophe.

He looks for help, because he can't manage it himself. He only knows defeat when he tries on his own. Dependent, he loses patience.

Even if he doesn't trust them or trusts them part way, for they've tricked him many times, he has to follow adults' directions, just as an inexperienced employer is forced to tolerate a dishonest, indispensable employee, just as a paralytic has to accept a brusque nurse's help and put up with his fickleness.

I repeat, every helplessness, every ignorant amazement, error in the application of experience, unfortunate attempt at imitation, every dependency – these recall a child, regardless of age. It is not difficult for us to find childish qualities in the sick, the old, the soldier, the prisoner. The country person in the city, the city person in the countryside, have a child's astonishment. The layman asks childish questions, the parvenu makes childish faux pas.

68. The child imitates adults.

Only by imitating does the child learn to speak, to fill out the greater part of worldly forms, she creates the appearance of acquainting herself with the milieu of adults, whom she cannot understand, who are spiritually foreign to her and incomprehensible.

We make our most fundamental mistakes in our judgements about a child precisely because her essential thoughts and feelings are lost in the expressions they have assumed, in the forms they use, investing them with their own, quite different content.

The future, love, fatherland, God, respect, duty – concepts fossilized in expressions, they live, are born, grow, change, strengthen, weaken, they're something else in every period of life. One must expend a great deal of effort not to confuse the pile of sand the child calls a mountain with a snowy peak in the Alps. For the person who thinks deeply about the spirit of the expressions people use, the difference between a child, youth, grownup, boor, and sage is erased, there emerges an intellectual being beyond age, social class, level of education, acculturation, as a reasoning being within a range of greater or lesser experience. People of disparate beliefs (I am speaking not of political slogans, which are sometimes dishonest, violently enforced) are people with disparate experiential frames.

The child does not understand the future, does not love her parents, has no sense of fatherland, does not comprehend God, respects no one, knows no duty. She says, "When I grow up," but she doesn't believe in it, she calls her mother "dearest," but she doesn't feel it, her fatherland is the garden or the courtyard, God is a kindly uncle or an annoying grouch, she feigns respect, surrenders to duties embodied in whomever has given an order and is in charge; one need only remember that you can give an order not only with a whip, but a request, a gentle look. The child sometimes has a sense, but those are just moments of wondrous clairvoyance.

The child is imitating? And what does the traveler do when a Mandarin asks him to take part in a local ritual or ceremony? He watches, tries not to stand out, not to cause confusion, he grasps the essence and how the episodes tie together, proud that he's played his role well. What does an uncouth boor do when admitted to a feast among gentlemen? He adapts. And the steward, the office clerk, the officer – in speech, movements, smile, dress, facial hair, doesn't he imitate his patron?

There's one more form of imitation: if a girl lifts her short dress when walking across mud, it means she's a grownup. If a boy imitates his teacher's signature, he's testing his qualifications for high office. We will find this form easily among adults as well.

69. The egocentrism of the childish worldview is also a lack of experience.

From individual egocentrism, where his consciousness is the center of all things and all phenomena, the child passes into familial egocentrism, which lasts more or less time, depending on the conditions in which he is being raised; we ourselves maintain it by exaggerating the value of the family home, portraying the dangers, real and imagined, that menace beyond the reach of our help and care.

"Stay with me," auntie says.

The child presses against his mother, tears in his eyes, he won't stay at her place for anything.

"He's so attached to me."

The child stares with amazement and dread at other mothers, who aren't even his aunts.

But a time comes when he calmly starts to compare what he sees in other houses with what he himself possesses. At first he wishes merely to have the same kind of doll, garden, canary as well, but at his house. Later he perceives that there are other mommies and daddies out there, also good, perhaps even better?

"If she were my mom…"

A child of the yard and the rural cottage is earlier to gain pertinent experience, to know sorrows that no one shares, joys that please only those closest to him, he understands that his name day is a holiday for him alone.

"My dad, at our house, my mommy" – the exaltation of one's own parents, which we find so often in arguments among children, is rather a polemical formula, sometimes the tragic defense of an illusion he wants to believe in, is starting to doubt.

"You wait, I'm going to tell my father…"

"Like I'm really afraid of your father."

That's right: only I find my father threatening…

I would ascribe the child's egocentric view of the current moment to the fact that, lacking experience, he lives only in the now. A game deferred until next week ceases to be a reality. In summer, winter becomes legend. Saving a cake "for tomorrow," he renounces it, yielding to obligation. It's difficult to understand that the deterioration of objects makes them not immediately unusable, just less lasting, more prone to breaking down. The stories of when mommy was a girl are a curious fairytale. With amazement bordering on fear he looks upon the strange arrival who speaks to his father by his given name, his childhood friend.

"I wasn't alive yet…"

And youthful egocentrism: doesn't the world begin with us?

And the egocentrism of party, class, nation – how many people grow into a consciousness of a person's position in humanity and the universe? How much effort did it take for us to reconcile ourselves to the notion that the Earth revolves, that it is merely a planet? And what of the deep conviction of the masses, in the face of reality, that the horrors of war are impossible in the twentieth century?

Isn't our attitude toward children an expression of the egocentrism of adults?

> *I didn't know that the child remembers so much, waits so patiently. Many errors come from the fact that the child we encounter is one of obligation, bondage, drudgery, disfigured, miserable, rebellious; one must think hard about what the child is in essence, how he could be.*

70. The child's perceptiveness.

On the screen of the cinematograph, a shocking drama.

Suddenly, a child's sonorous shout resounds.

"Oooo, a doggie…"

No one noticed, but she spotted it.

One sometimes hears similar shouts at the theater, in church, during many ceremonies; they disconcert loved ones, provoke a smile in the public.

Not comprehending the whole, mind unoccupied by the incomprehensible content, the child, happy, welcomes the familiar, the familiar detail. But in the same way we, too, gladly welcome a familiar face encountered by chance in abundant, indifferent, restrictive company...

Incapable of living idly, a child visits every nook and cranny, peers into every gap, seeks, inquires, she finds interest in the moving speck of an ant, a shiny bead, an expression or statement overheard. How like children we are in a foreign city, in an exceptional environment...

A child knows her surroundings, its moods, habits, foibles, knows them and, one might add, skillfully exploits them. She senses kindliness, guesses at hypocrisy, has an instant grasp of ridiculousness. She reads a face the way a country person can predict the weather by reading the sky. Because she, too, spends entire years gazing and studying; in schools and orphanages, this labor of penetrating us is conducted as a group effort. Only we don't want to know; so long as she doesn't disturb our peace, we prefer to delude ourselves that she is naive, doesn't know, doesn't understand, is easily deceived by appearances. Another viewpoint would confront us with a dilemma: either to openly renounce the privilege of our ostensible perfection, or else to rid ourselves of that which, in their eyes, debases, humiliates, and impoverishes us.

71. In seeking increasingly new enjoyments and impressions, the child seems unable to occupy himself with anything for long, even play quickly becomes boring, and who was a friend an hour ago is already an enemy, only to be a dear companion again a while later.

A true observation in general: a child in a train car is fussy; he grows impatient when set down upon a garden bench, nagging during a visit; his favorite game is already tossed into a corner; he fidgets in class; even at the theater he won't sit still.

Let us consider, however, that while traveling he is excited and exhausted, that he has been planted on the bench, that on a visit he is self-conscious, that his game and partner were chosen for him, he's forced to go to class, and he was roused for the theater because he had believed it would be a pleasant time.

How frequently we resemble a child who has dressed his cat up in a ribbon, treats him to a pear, gives him a drawing to look at, and is surprised that the good-for-nothing wishes to get away tactfully or, desperate, scratches.

On a visit, the child would like to see how the box on the console table opens, what it is shining over there in the corner, whether there are pictures in the big book; he would like to catch the little fish in the aquarium and gobble down a lot of chocolate. But he won't betray his desires, because it's rude.

"Let's go home," says the poorly behaved child...

A game is announced to him: there will be flags, artificial fires, a performance; he waited and was disappointed.

"Well, are you having fun?"

"It's perfect," he answers, yawning, or else stifling his yawn so as not to cause offence...

Summer camp. I'm telling a fairytale in the forest. While I'm telling it, one of the boys leaves, then another, then a third. I'm surprised, so I ask about it the following day: the first had placed a rod under a bush, remembered it during the story, and was afraid someone would take it; the second had a cut on his finger that was hurting, and the third doesn't like made-up stories. Won't an adult leave a performance that's not interesting him, when pain is bothering him, when he's forgotten his billfold in his coat pocket?

I have abundant evidence that a child can occupy himself with the same thing for many weeks and months and won't want a change. One of his toys, his favorite, will never lose its charm. He listens to the same fairytale many times with equal curiosity. And, on the other side, I have evidence that a mother grows impatient with the monotony of her child's interests. How often have mothers turned to the doctor so he will "vary the diet, because the child has already grown tired of porridge and compote."

"It is you, and not the child, who has grown tired of them," I have been forced to explain.

72. Boredom, a subject for thorough study.

Boredom, loneliness, lack of impressions; boredom, too many impressions, the racket, the commotion. Boredom: don't, wait, careful, it's not proper. The boredom of a new dress, of self-consciousness, embarrassment, prescriptions, proscriptions, duties.

The half-boredom of the balcony and looking out the window, of a stroll, a visit, of playing with accidental, ill-suited companions.

Boredom as acute as a high fever, and chronic, festering, with restrictions.

Boredom, the child's lack of well-being; thus too much heat, cold, hunger, thirst, too much feeding, sleepiness and too much sleep, pain and fatigue.

Boredom-apathy, indifference toward stimuli, poor mobility, reticence, a weakening of life's rhythm. The child gets up lazily, walks with a slouch, dragging her feet, stretches, answers by making a face, in monosyllables, in a quiet voice, with a grimace of distaste. She doesn't make demands, but she meets every demand directed at her with hostility. Discrete, sudden explosions, incomprehensible, poorly justified.

Boredom, increased mobility. She doesn't sit still for a moment, won't busy herself for long with anything, is fussy, combative, malicious, she provokes, she pesters, takes offense, cries, gets angry. At times she'll deliberately start a fight in order to receive, in the anticipated punishment, the strong impression she desires.

We often see the obstinacy of conscious ill will where there is actually the bankruptcy of will, an excess of energy where there is the despair of fatigue.

Boredom does at times assume the quality of collective psychosis. Unable to organize games, or embarrassed, or poorly matched in age and temperament, or in unusual circumstances, they fall into a frenzy of pointless noise.

They shout, bump into each other, pull each other's legs, knock each other down, spin around until they lose consciousness, and they fall to the ground, they get each other worked up, they laugh a forced laugh. Most often a catastrophe interrupts the "game" before the response has ripened: a scuffle, torn clothes, a broken chair, a participant gets knocked too hard, thus commotion and mutual accusation. Sometimes the noise's mood burns out, somebody's "Stop acting nuts" or "Shame on you, what are you up to," the initiative passes into energetic hands – and there's a fairytale, singing in chorus, conversation.

I'm afraid that some caregivers are inclined to regard these infrequent pathological states of collective, oversensitive boredom as a normal game of children "running wild."

73. Even child's play, understood journalistically, has not received thorough clinical study.

One must remember that it's not just children who play, but adults as well, that children don't always play readily, that not everything that we call play is indeed play, that many child's games are an imitation of serious adult acts, that play is different on open ground, different within the walls of a city or of a room, that we are allowed to examine a child's games solely in light of the position he occupies in contemporary society.

A ball.

Watch the efforts of the youngest child to pick it up from the ground, to roll it along the floor in an intended direction.

Watch an older child's arduous practice at catching it with the right hand and the left, bounce it several times on the ground, against a wall, pop it up with a stick-bat, hit his target. Who gets it farthest, who highest, who most accurately, who the most times? Emulation, learning one's value through comparison, triumphs and defeats, getting better.

Surprises, very often of a comical nature. He had it, and it slipped away; it bounced off one and landed right in the other's hand; catching it, they bonked heads; it landed under the wardrobe and came out meekly on its own.

Getting worked up. The ball fell on someone's lawn, risky to pick it up. It was lost, then searching for it. A window was nearly broken. It flew onto the wardrobe, how to get it down, a group discussion. Did it hit you or not? Who's at fault: the one who threw it off target, or the one who didn't catch it? A heated argument.

Individual variations. He feints: he pretends he's throwing; he aims at one and beams into the other; he's hidden it nimbly, like it's not there. He blows at the tossed ball so it will fly faster; does a sort of flip while snatching it; tries to catch it in his mouth; pretends to be afraid when they throw it to him; pretends they beamed it at him too hard. He beats the ball: "I'll show you, ball." "Something's rattling in the ball," they shake it, they listen.

There are children who themselves don't play but like to watch, as adults do with those playing billiards or chess. Here, too, there are moves that are interesting, wrong, and ingenious.

A move's usefulness is just one of many qualities that make the sport pleasurable.

74. Play is not so much an element of the child as it is one area where we allow her initiative of narrower or broader scope. The child at play feels to a certain extent independent. Everything else is a fleeting grace, a momentary concession, but a child has a right to play.

Playing horse, army, cops and robbers, fire brigade, she expends her energy in apparently purposeful movements, momentarily surrenders to the illusion or consciously escapes from the junk of her actual life. This is why children so prize the participation of peers with lively imaginations, multifaceted initiative, a supply of themes culled from books, they submit so humbly to their often despotic authority that, thanks to them, the hazy delusion more readily assumes the appearances of reality. Children are self-conscious in the presence of adults and strangers, they're ashamed of their games, realizing their vacuity.

How much one finds in children's games the bitter awareness of the absence of real life and the painful longing for it.

To a child, a stick is not a horse, in the absence of the real thing she has to make do with a wooden one. If they sail around the room on an overturned chair, it's not them taking a small boat over a pond.

When the child has a day plan of unlimited swimming, woods and berries, the fishing pole, bird's nests in high trees, a dovecote, chickens, rabbits, plums in someone else's orchard, the flower bed in front of the house, play becomes superfluous or completely changes its character.

What child would exchange a real live dog for a stuffed one on wheels? What child would give up a pony for a hobby horse?

She turns to her game when compelled, escapes to it from serious boredom, huddles away from the threatening emptiness, hides from cold obligation. Yes, a child prefers even play over cramming her memory with grammatical structures or the multiplication table.

A child grows attached to a doll, a goldfinch, a little potted flower, because she doesn't yet have anything else; a prisoner or old person becomes likewise attached, because they no longer have anything. A child will play with anything to kill time, because she doesn't know what to do, because that's all there is.

We hear a girl lecture her doll on the rules of good behavior, instruct and chasten her; but we do not hear her complaining to her in bed about her surroundings, confiding in her about her worries, failures, and dreams.

"I'll tell you, dolly, only don't repeat it to anybody."

"Oh, you're a good doggy, I'm not angry at you, you didn't do anything bad to me."

The child's solitude gives the doll a soul.

This is not the child's paradise, but a drama.

75. A cowherd prefers a game of cards to a ball: he runs around enough chasing after the cows. A little papergirl or errand-boy just at the start of a career runs hard; they soon learn to apportion their effort, spreading it out over the entire day. A child who has to take care of a baby doesn't play with a doll; on the contrary, he flees from the unpleasant duty.

So does the child dislike work? An impoverished child's work is utilitarian, not instructive, it doesn't take account of his strengths, nor of his individual qualities. It would be ridiculous to offer them as an example – the lives of poor children; there's boredom here as well, the winter boredom of a cramped room and the summer boredom of the yard and the roadside ditch; it just has a different form. Neither they, nor we, are able to fill a child's days so that their sequence, logically consequent, would unfurl life's colorful contents, from yesterday through today to tomorrow.

Countless children's games are work.

If four of them build a fort, dig with a scrap of tin, with glass, hammer in the pegs, tie the stays, cover it with a roof of branches, lining it with moss, working now strenuously and silently, now sluggishly, but designing improvements, developing their further plans, sharing the results of the observations they have made – this is not play, but unskilled labor with imperfect tools, inadequate material, thus not very productive, but organized so that everyone, regardless of age, strength, competence, puts in as much effort as he has to give.

If the children's room, despite our prohibitions, is so often a workshop and a warehouse for junk, and therefore for material used in executing planned projects, then shouldn't that be the course toward which we direct our search? Maybe it is not linoleum that's needed in a small child's room, but a wagonload of healthy yellow sand, a large bundle of sticks and a wheelbarrow of stones? Maybe a plank, some cardboard, a pound of nails, a saw, a hammer, a lathe – maybe these would be a better gift than a "toy," and a teacher of handicrafts of greater benefit than a master gymnast or pianist. But one would have to drive the hospital-like silence from the children's room, the hospital cleanliness and the fear of scraping a finger.

It is with a sense of distress that judicious parents give the command to "Go play," and it is with pain that they hear the answer: "It's always just 'go play, go play.'" What will they come up with when they have nothing else?

Much has changed. Games and play are no longer condescendingly tolerated, they've now entered the school program, there is an increasingly vocal demand for playgrounds. The changes are happening by the hour, the mentality of the average paterfamilias and the caregiver cannot keep up.

76. Despite what was said above, there are children who are neither overly tormented by solitude, nor feel the need of an active life. In the home one "does not hear" these quiet ones, whom others' mothers raise as examples. They do not get bored, they find games for themselves that they initiate on demand, and on demand they obediently cut them off. These are passive children, they want little and weakly, thus they submit easily, delusion replaces their reality, all the more because this is how adults would have it.

They get lost in the pack, injure themselves painfully against its rough indifference, they don't follow its rapid current. Instead of recognizing this, here, too, mothers wish to rework it, to impose by force what can only be slowly and carefully acquired through tiresome effort, by a road strewn with the experience of many failures, unsuccessful attempts, and painful humiliations. Every immoderate order worsens the state of things. "Go play with the children" harms them the same as "Enough of this game" harms others.

How easy it is to recognize them in a crowd.

Example: playing in the park, in a circle. A couple dozen are singing, holding hands, and two in the middle are playing the main role.

"Well, go play with them."

She doesn't want to, because she doesn't know this game, doesn't know these children, because once when she tried they told her, "We don't need you, we have enough already," or, "You're a klutz." Maybe tomorrow, in a week, she'll try again. But the mother doesn't want to wait, she makes room, she pushes forcefully. Timid, the girl reluctantly takes her neighbors' hands, wishes to go unnoticed, she'll stand there, maybe she'll slowly become interested, maybe she'll take the first step in coming to terms with the new, collective life. But her mother makes another faux pas: she wishes to encourage her with the lure of livelier participation.

"Girls, why is it always the same ones in the circle? Oh, this one hasn't been in yet: choose her."

One of the ringleaders refuses, two others assent, but reluctantly.

The poor understudy in an unwelcoming troupe.

This scene ended in the child's tears, the mother's anger, confusion among those taking part in the circle.

77. A circle observed in the park as a practical exercise for caregivers: a number of noteworthy events. General observation (difficult – all the children taking part in the game), individual observation (of one randomly selected child).

Initiative, the circle's germination, blossoming, and collapse. Who gives the signal, organizes, leads, and whose withdrawal dissolves the gathering? Which children choose their neighbors, and which take two random hands? Which ones part willingly to make room for a new participant, and which ones protest? Which ones change places frequently, which ones occupy the same place the whole time? Which ones wait patiently during the breaks, and which ones grow impatient: "Come on, hurry up, let's start." Which ones stand motionless, which ones shift on their legs, swing their arms, laugh out loud? Which ones yawn but don't leave, which ones quit the game, whether because it doesn't interest them, or because they're offended; which ones push persistently until they get one of the main roles? A mother wants to tack on a small child; one says, "No, he's too little," another, "What's it to you, let him stand there."

If a grownup were to manage the game, he or she would introduce turns, a superficially fair distribution of roles, and, believing that it helps, make it obligatory. Two children, nearly always the same ones, run (duck, duck, goose), play (tops), choose (round dancing); surely the others get bored? One looks on, another listens, a third sings in a whisper, under his breath, out loud, a fourth has an obscure desire but is wavering, his heart beating fast. And the ten-year-old ringleader-psychologist quickly evaluates, takes it in, takes control.

In every group activity, and thus in every game, doing the same thing, they differ in at least one tiny detail.

And we recognize what the child is in life, among people, in action, what he's worth, not latently, but on the market, what he absorbs, what he is able to contribute, how the crowd values it, how autonomous he is, how resistant to group suggestion. From intimate conversation we know what he desires, from observing him in the pack what he's able to carry out: here, how he relates to people, there, the hidden motives behind those relations. If we only ever see a child by himself, we will know him one-sidedly.

If he enjoys respect, how did he get it, how does he use it; if not, does he crave it, does he suffer, does he get angry, does he sulk, does he envy passively, insist, or yield? Does he protest often or seldom, is he right or not, is he driven by ambition or fickleness, does he impose his will tactfully or brutally? Does he flee from those who lead, or does he cling to them?

"Listen, let's do it like this. Wait, this would be better. This is no fun. Okay, so tell me how you want it."

78. What are the peaceful games of children if not a conversation, an exchange of ideas, the spinning of fantasies on a given theme, a dramatized dream of power? At play, they voice their views, like an author does in the plot of a novel, rolling out its principal idea. This is why you will frequently spot an unconscious satire of adults here, as they're playing school, paying a visit, welcoming guests, entertaining their dolls, buying and selling, hiring and dismissing the help. Passive children take playing school seriously, they wish to win praise; active children choose the role of pranksters, whose larks often provoke collective protests; do they not unknowingly betray that this is what their actual attitude toward school is like?

Unable even to enter the garden, a child all the more eagerly takes a journey over oceans and desert islands; without even a dog to listen to her, she is a tough commander to her regiment; being nothing, she wants to be everything. But is it true only of children? Don't political parties, as they gain influence on the course of public affairs, exchange castles on clouds for the whole grain of actual conquests?

There are certain games, inquiries, and attempts that we would rather not see. The child walks on all fours and barks to see how the animals get along, she pretends to be lame, to be a hunched old person, she squints, stutters, staggers like she's drunk, imitates the nutcase she saw on the street, walks with eyes closed (blind), shuts her ears (deaf), lies still and holds her breath (dead), looks through glasses, drags on a cigarette, winds a watch on the sly; she plucks out a fly's wings (how is it going to fly?); she catches a pen nib with a magnet; she looks into your ears (what are those little drums?), your throat (what are those almond shapes?); she suggests a game of doctor with the opposite sex in the hope of seeing what's down there; she runs into the sun with a magnifying glass, listens to the sound inside a shell, bangs stone against stone.

Everything there is for her to see about she wants to see, test, experience, and still there remains so much that she has to take on faith.

They tell her there's one moon, and you can see it from anywhere.

"Listen, I'll stand behind the fence, and you stand in the garden."

They close the gate.

"Well, is the moon in the garden?"

"Yes."

"It's here, too."

They change places and check again: now they're certain that there are two moons.

79. Games whose purpose is to test strength, to know one's worth, have their own place; and this can only be achieved through comparison with others.

So, who takes bigger steps, how many steps does he take with his eyes closed; who can go longer standing on one leg, without blinking an eye, without laughing when looking straight into someone else's eyes, who can go longer without breathing? Who will scream the loudest, spit the farthest, release a stream of urine or throw a stone the highest? Who will jump from the greatest number of stairs, the highest, the farthest; who will hold out longest against the pain of a squeezed finger? Who will run to the finish line fastest, who will lift, drag, knock over whom?

"I can. I do. I know. I have."

"I can better. I know more. Mine are better."

And then:

"My mommy and daddy can, they have."

In this way one garners respect, assumes the appropriate position in one's milieu. And we must remember that a child's good fortune does not depend exclusively on how adults rate him, but to the same degree, or perhaps more so, on the opinion of his peers, who have different, and nevertheless durable bases for rating the value of, and apportioning rights to, members of their own society.

A five-year-old can be admitted into the company of eight-year-olds, and they may be tolerated by ten-year-olds, who already roam the streets and have a locked pencil case and notebook. Someone who's two classes older will explain away many doubts, for half a cake or for free; he'll initiate, he'll educate.

A magnet attracts iron because it's magnetized. The best horses are Arabians, because they have thin legs. Kings don't have red blood, but blue. A lion and an eagle surely have blue blood, too (he'll have to ask someone about that later). If a corpse grabs someone by the arm, you cannot pull it away. In the forest there are women who have serpents instead of hair; he saw it once in a picture, he even saw it in the forest, but from far away, because if she looks when she's up close a person turns to stone (he must be lying?). He saw a drowning victim, knows how children are born, and knows how to make a coin purse out of paper.

And not only does he say that he knows, but he did make a coin purse out of paper: mommy doesn't know how to do that.

80. Were we not to disregard the child, her feelings, aspirations, wishes, and thus her games as well, we would understand how it's appropriate that she eagerly remains with one, flees from another, meets her under duress and plays reluctantly. She might get into a fight with her best friend, but they soon reconcile, but she doesn't want to associate with someone unpleasant without a clear argument.

She cannot play, because she cries at the drop of a hat, is immediately offended, complains, screams and goes crazy, brags, punches, wants to lead, gossips, cheats – insincere, clumsy; small, stupid, dirty, ugly.

One such small, squeaky and irritating child spoils the whole game. Observe the children's efforts to render her harmless! The older ones willingly let the little one join the fun, too, since she, too, might contribute; but let her make do with a secondary role, don't let her get in the way.

"Give it to her, go ahead, let her: she's little."

Not true: adults don't give in to children, either…

Why doesn't she like going there to visit? There are children there, and she's eager to play with them.

Eager, but at her home or in the park. And there's a man there who yells, they're always pressing kisses on you, the maid has offended her, the older sister will tease her, they have a dog she's afraid of. Pride does not allow her to give her real motives, and her mother believes it's fickleness.

She doesn't want to go to the park. Why not? Because an older boy has threatened to beat her up, because one little girl's nursemaid had warned that she would complain, because the park-keeper had threatened with a stick when she sat on the lawn after playing ball, because she had promised to bring a boy a postage stamp and misplaced it somewhere.

There are fickle children, I've seen a couple dozen of them in my hours of seeing patients. These children know what they want, but that's not what they get: they're breathless, they're stifled under the weight of loving care. If children generally have a cool attitude toward adults, these pathologically fickle children spurn and despise those around them. It is possible to torture children with mindless love; the law should take them in its care.

81. We've dressed children up in the uniform of childhood and believe that they love us, respect us, trust us, that they're innocent, credulous, grateful. We play the role of disinterested guardians flawlessly, we are moved by the thought of the sacrifices we have borne and, one could say, we're fine with them for a time. They believe us at first, then doubt us, endeavor to expel insidiously sneaking suspicions, sometimes try to struggle against them, and seeing the struggle's fruitlessness they start to deceive us, buy us out, exploit us.

They swindle with a request, a grateful smile, a kiss, a joke, obedience, they buy with the concessions they've made, rarely and tactfully they let it be known that they have certain rights, at times they extort spitefully, at times they ask openly, "And what do I get in return?"

The hundred varieties of submissive and rebellious slave.

"Not nice, not healthy, a sin. Teacher said so. Oh, if only mommy knew."

"If you don't want it, you can go. You and your teacher both think you're so smart. Let mommy know too: what will it do to me?"

We don't like when a chastened child "mumbles something under his breath," because in his anger honest words are writhing in his mouth that we're not interested in.

A child has a conscience, but his voice is silent in minute, everyday squabbles, while out flows a hidden aversion toward the despotic, and therefore unfair, authority of the strong, and therefore the irresponsible.

If a child loves a cheerful uncle, it's because it's thanks to him that he has a moment of freedom, because he brings in life, because he's given him a gift. And a gift that is all the more precious for having fulfilled a long-harbored dream. The child values presents far less than we believe, he accepts them reluctantly from unkind people: "She thinks she's doing me some favor," he seethes, humiliated.

82. Adults are not smart; they don't know how to use the freedom they have. They're so happy, they can buy anything, they're allowed to do anything, yet they're always fuming over something, screaming about whatever comes up.

Adults do not know everything: their answers are often to brush you off, or are a joke, or else are impossible to understand; one says this, another that, and you don't know who's telling the truth. How many stars are there? What's the African word for "daybook"? How does a person fall asleep? Is water alive, and how do we know that there's a zero degrees, that it's supposed to make ice. Where is Hell? How did that man make scrambled eggs out of watches in his hat, and the watches are undamaged, and the hat didn't tear: is that a miracle?

They're not good. Parents give their children food, but they have to so that we don't die. They don't let their children do anything, they laugh when you're saying something, and instead of explaining they tease on purpose, they make jokes. They're unfair, and when someone else is deceiving them they believe him. They love it when you suck up to them. When they're in a good humor, they'll let you do anything, but when they're angry everything bothers them.

Adults lie. It's a lie that you get worms from eating candy, and that when you don't eat your food you dream of Gypsies, and that if you play with fire you'll wet yourself, and when you swing your legs you're rocking the devil. They don't keep their word: they promise, then forget, or else they weasel out of it, or it's like they don't let you do something as punishment – and they wouldn't have let you do it anyway.

They order you to tell the truth, and when you do they get offended. They're insincere: they say one thing to your face, another behind your back. When they don't like someone, they pretend that they do. It's constantly just "please, thank you, excuse me, a very good evening to you," one would think they mean it.

I insistently ask people to turn their attention to the expression on a child's face when she runs cheerfully, says something enthusiastically, or does something wrong and is severely reprimanded.

Father is writing; the child runs in with news and grabs at his sleeve. She hasn't any sense that there's now an ink blot on an important document. Chastised, she looks with eyes full of wonder: what's just happened?

The experience of a couple of inappropriate questions, unsuccessful jokes, of secrets betrayed, of imprudent confidences teaches a child to treat adults like tame, but wild animals, of which one can never be too certain.

83. Besides condescension and aversion, one may also discern a certain disgust in children's attitude toward adults.

A prickly beard, a rough face, the smell of a cigar – these irritate a child. So long as it's not forbidden, he wipes his face conscientiously after every kiss. The majority of children cannot stand being taken onto someone's knee; when you take them by the hand, they gently, slowly come away. Tolstoy[18] noticed this trait in country children, but it's typical of all those who have not been corrupted, cowed into submission.

Of body odor, the strong smell of perfume, the child says with revulsion, "It stinks" – until he's taught that this is a nasty expression, that perfumes smell, he just doesn't know yet…

Those various ladies and gentlemen who have indigestion, body aches, incontinence, a bitter taste in the mouth, who are bothered by drafts, damp, are afraid of eating before bedtime, are stifled by a cough, are missing teeth, have trouble walking up stairs, are red, obese, who pant – this is all somehow foul.

Those cutesy expressions of theirs, the stroking, cuddling, patting, the overfamiliarity, nonsensical questions, laughing at who-knows-what.

"Who's he take after? My, my, so big. Look at him grow."

The embarrassed child is waiting for this to be over…

It's nothing for them to say in front of everyone, "Hey, your underpants are coming down," or "You're going to wet the bed." They're indecent…

A child feels cleaner, better-raised, worthier of respect.

He's afraid to eat, she's afraid of damp. Cowards: I'm not afraid at all. If they're afraid, let them sit by the stove, why do they forbid us from going out?

Rain: he'll run out in secret, stand in the downpour, run away laughing, pat his hair down. Frost: he'll fold his arms, hunch over, raise his shoulders, he holds his breath, tenses his muscles, his fingers go numb, lips blue, he watches a funeral, a street brawl, runs off to warm up; brrr, I'm frozen, what fun.

Those poor old people who are bothered by everything.

And the one good feeling the child constantly feels for us may well be – pity.

"You can see something's bothering them when they're not happy."

Poor daddy works, mommy's feeble, they don't have much time left, the poor things, I shouldn't worry them.

84. A caveat.

Besides the aforementioned feelings that a child undoubtedly experiences, besides his own reflexes, a child understands obligation; he does not break entirely free from imposed views and emotional suggestions. They are living through the conflicts of a bifurcated ego, the active child more distinctly and swiftly, the passive one later and more vaguely. The active child arrives on his own, the passive child has his "eyes opened" by a companion in misery, in slavery; neither of them systematizes it the way that I have. A child's soul is just as intricate as our own, filled with similar contradictions, tragically struggling within the eternal: I want to, but I can't, I know I have to, but I'm not up to it.

The caregiver who frees rather than forces, lifts rather than drags, shapes rather than pinches, teaches rather than dictates, asks rather than demands, will experience many inspired moments with a child, will not infrequently watch teary-eyed as the angel fights with the devil, with the white angel carrying the day.

He lied. He took jam from the cake on the sly. He lifted a girl's dress. He threw stones at frogs. He laughed at a hunchback. He broke a figurine and set it up so no one would know. He smoked a cigarette. He was angry and cursed his father in his mind.

He has behaved badly and feels that it's not the last time, that something will tempt him again, that they'll talk him into it again.

It does happen that the child suddenly becomes quiet, meek, affectionate. Adults know this: "She clearly has something on her conscience." Often this strange change is preceded by an explosion of feelings, tears stifled into a pillow, resolutions, a solemn vow. It happens that we're prepared to forgive if only we receive an assurance, oh, not a guarantee, but the illusion that the mischief will not be repeated.

"I won't be any different. I can't promise."

It's not obstinacy that dictates these words, but honesty.

"I understand what you're saying, sir," a twelve-year-old boy said, "but I don't feel it."

We encounter this respectable honesty even in children with bad inclinations:

"I know that one shouldn't steal, that it's shameful and a sin. I don't want to steal. I don't know that I won't steal again. It's not my fault!"

A caregiver lives through some painful moments, seeing his own powerlessness in the helplessness of a child.

85. We are susceptible to the illusion that a child can be satisfied for long with an angelic worldview, where everything is simple and accommodatingly reasonable, that we'll manage to shield him from our ignorance, weakness, contradictions, our failures and shortcomings – and our lack of a formula for happiness. The prescription of pedagogical manuals that we raise children consistently, that a father not criticize the mother's actions, that adults not discuss things around children, that the housemaid not lie that "Mr. and Mrs. So-and-So are not at home" when an unwanted guest calls – this is naive.

And why isn't one allowed to torment animals when flies die in torment on sticky paper by the hundreds? Why does mommy buy a pretty dress, but it's rude to say that a dress is pretty? Does a cat have to be insincere? Lightning; the nanny crossed herself and said, "My God," but teacher says it's electricity? What do you have to respect grownups for, and do you respect a thief, too? Uncle said, "I busted a gut," but that's rude to say. Why is "dammit" a curse? The cook believes in dreams, but mommy doesn't. Why do people say "healthy as a horse" when horses get sick, too? Do monkeys have fun in barrels? Why is it rude to ask how much a present costs?

How to conceal, how to explain, without deepening the misunderstanding?

Oh, those answers of ours...

It happens to be the case that I have twice witnessed people explaining what a globe is to a child in front of a bookstore display.

"What kind of ball is that?" the child asks.

"A ball is all," her nanny responds.

Another time:

"Mommy, what's that sphere?"

"It's not a sphere, it's the Earth. There are houses, little horses, mommy."

"Mommmy?" The child looked at her mother with compassion and fear and did not press the question.

86. We see children in stormy manifestations of joy and sadness, when they differ from us; we do not notice the cheerful moods, quiet reveries, profound emotions, painful shocks, the festering suspicions and humiliating doubts in which they are most similar to us. A "true" child is not only one hopping on one leg, but also one pondering the mysteries of the bizarre fairytale that is life. One needs only exclude the truly "artificial" children, those that make a show of repeating the clichés they've learned or snatched from adults. A child cannot think "like a grownup," but she can wonder in a childish way over the serious conundrums of adults; lack of knowledge and experience forces them to think differently.

I tell a fairytale: wizards, dragons, fairy godmothers, enchanted princesses; an apparently naive question suddenly arises:

"Is this true?"

And I hear one of them explain in a superior tone:

"But he told us it's a fairytale."

Neither the characters, nor the plot, is improbable; this could be, but it is not because we have warned them that fairytales are not true.

Speech, which was to have defused the terrors and oddities of the surrounding world, has on the contrary deepened and widened ignorance. Formerly, the small ongoing life of personal needs had demanded a certain number of firm responses; the new, great life of the word has been flooded with all the riddles at once, yesterday's and tomorrow's, distant and farthest away. There is no time, not to weigh them all, nor even to consider them. Theoretical knowledge is breaking away from everyday life and soaring beyond verifiability.

Here, the active and passive temperaments transform into intellectual types: the realist, and the reflective.

The realist believes and does not, depending on the will of an authority: what is more convenient, advantageous to believe; the reflective inquires, concludes, counters, rebels in thoughts and deeds. The unconscious falsity of the former we oppose to the latter's will to knowledge; it's a mistake that hinders diagnosis and renders instructional therapy ineffectual.

In psychiatric clinics, a stenographer transcribes the patients' monologues and conversations; it will be the same in future pedological clinics.[19] Today we have only the material of a child's questions.

87. Life's a fairytale. A fable of the animal world.

In the sea there are fish that swallow people up. Are these fish larger than a ship? When one swallows a person, does he suffocate? What if it swallows a saint? What do they eat if no ship crashes apart? Can you catch such a fish? How can regular fish live in the sea? Why don't they catch all of those fish? Are there lots of them, a million? Can you make a little boat out of a fish like that? Are they antediluvian fish?

Bees have a queen, so why not a king? Did he die? If birds know how to fly to Africa, they're smarter than people because no one ever taught them. Why is it called a centipede if it doesn't have a hundred legs, and how many does it really have? Are all foxes sly, can't they help it, why are they that way? If someone tortures and beats a dog, is it still loyal? And why aren't you allowed to watch when a dog mounts a dog? If stuffed animals were once alive, can you stuff a person? Is it very uncomfortable in there for a snail; will it die if you pull it out; why is it so wet, is it a fish; does it understand when you say, "Hey snail, stick out your antennae"? Why are fish cold-blooded? Why doesn't it hurt snakes to shed their skin? What do ants talk about with each other? Why do people pass away, when animals just die? Does a spider die if its web breaks, and where does it get the thread to make another one? How can a hen be born from an egg, and do you have to bury the egg in the ground? An ostrich eats stones and iron; how does it go potty? How does a camel know how many days of water it has in reserve? Does a parrot understand at least a little bit of what it says, is it smarter than a dog, why can't you trim a dog's tongue so it would talk, was Robinson Crusoe the first to teach a parrot to talk, is it hard to teach, how do you do it?

A colorful fairytale about plants.

A tree lives, breathes, dies. An oak grows out of a small acorn. A small flower turns into a pear – can you see it? Do shirts grow on trees? Teacher said at school (he swore to God she did), is it true? Father answered, "Don't talk nonsense," mommy, that they don't grow on trees, just that linen grows in a field, and in school your teacher said you can't talk about it during arithmetic, that she'll explain another time. So it's not a lie: if only to see but one such tree.

What is a dragon beside such marvels? There's no such thing, but there could be. How could King Krakus[20] kill the dragon if there's no such thing? If there aren't any mermaids, why do they draw them?

88. A fairytale – the nations.

A Negro is black no matter how much he washes.[21] His tongue is not black, nor his teeth. He's not a demon: he has neither horns, nor a tail. Their children are black, too. They're horribly savage: they eat people. They don't believe in God, only in frogs. They all used to believe in a tree, they were stupid; the Greeks also believed in stupid things, but they were smart, so why did they believe? Negroes walk around their streets without any clothes on and are not at all embarrassed. They stick shells through their noses and think it's pretty; why don't they tell them not to do that? They're happy: they eat figs, dates, and bananas, they keep monkeys, the don't go to school at all, a little boy joins the hunt right away.

The Chinese have braids; they're very funny. The French are the smartest, but they eat frogs and say "bone-jore." Supposedly smart, yet they talk so funny: "bo-po-fo-bzdo." Then there's the Germans, der-di-doubt, sauer and kraut. Jews are afraid of everything, they call out, "Oy vey," and they cheat. A Jew has to cheat no matter what; because they murdered Lord Jesus. They have Poles in America, too – what do they do there, why did they leave, is it nice there? Gypsies will steal children, break their legs, and order them to beg or give them away to the circus. It must be nice performing in the circus, though they rough you up. If they rough you up once, can you do tricks forever? Is there such a thing as dwarves, why not, and if not, how do we know what they look like? And a little man was walking down the street, everybody stared, do Lilliputians never grow up, are they small as a punishment? Were the Phoenicians wizards? How did they make glass out of sand? Is it hard? Are sailors a nation, can they live in water, is it harder being a diver or a sailor: which is more important?

At times a question will cause a disturbance:

"If I were to smear myself all over with ink, would Negroes recognize me?"

A child has a hard time assimilating information that has no practical application. She would like to do it, too, to try it out, and would most like to see up close.

89. A fairytale – a person.

Are there people whose eyes are made of glass, can they take their eyes out, can one see through those eyes? What are wigs for, and why do people laugh when someone's bald? Are there people who speak through their tummy, are there any who speak through their bellybutton, what's a bellybutton for? Are there real drums in the ears? Why are tears salty, and why is the see salty? Why does a girl have long hair, and why is she different down there, too? Do mushrooms grow in the heart – why are there drawings with mushrooms on a heart for April Fool's Day? Must one die? Where was I before I was in the world? The maid said you can get sick from someone giving you the eye, and if you spit three times you won't get sick. What happens inside your nose when you sneeze? Is a crazy person sick, is a drunk sick, what's worse: drunk, or crazy? Why do I have to wait to learn how children are born? Does wind come from when someone has hanged himself? Is it better to be blind or deaf? Why do children die, but old people live? Should you cry more when your grandmother dies, or when your little brother does? Why can't a canary go to heaven? Does a stepmother have to beat the children? Is breastmilk from cows, too? When you dream of something is it real, or does it only seem so? What makes hair red? Why can't you have a child without a husband? Is it better to eat a poisonous mushroom or get bitten by a viper? Is it true that standing in the rain makes you grow faster? What's an echo, and why is it in the forest? Why is it that when you make a tunnel with your hand and look through it, you can see your whole house: how does it fit in there? What is a shadow, why can't you get away from it? Is it true that if someone with a moustache kisses a girl, she'll grow a moustache? Is it true that there are bugs on your teeth, only you cannot see them?

90. A fairytale – authorities.

A child has numerous gods, demigods, and heroes.

Authorities are divided into: the visible and the invisible, the living and the dead. Their hierarchy is exceedingly complicated. Mommy, father, grandmother, grandpa, aunts, uncles, hired help, police officer, soldier, king, doctor, older people in general, priest, teacher, more experienced friends.

Dead, visible authorities: the cross, the Torah scroll, the prayer book, holy images, portraits of ancestors, monuments to great people, photographs of strangers.

Invisible authorities: God, health, the soul, the conscience, the dead, wizards, devils, angels, spirits, wolves, distant relatives who are frequently mentioned.

Authorities demand obedience; a child understands this, understands it painfully well. They demand love, which is much harder to deal with.

"I love daddy and mommy more."

Little ones are venturing an incomprehensible answer to a misunderstood question. An older child can't stand the question: it humiliates and embarrasses her. She loves now more, now less, now so-so, as much as is absolutely necessary, sometimes she hates, yes, it's awful, but what can you do when she hates.

Respect is such a complex feeling that the child renounces her own decision, she relies on the experience of older people.

Mommy gives the housekeeper orders, the housekeeper is afraid of mommy. Mommy got angry at the nursemaid. Mommy has to inquire with the doctor whether it's allowed. The policeman can punish mommy. A friend doesn't need to listen to mommy. Daddy's superior at work got angry with him, that's why daddy is sad.

A soldier is afraid of an officer, an officer a general, a general a king. Everything here is understandable, maybe that's why boys are so interested in military ranks, and maybe that's why children are so precise in how they apportion respect according to grade level, so that this, too, is easy to understand.

Quite worthy of respect are the mediators between visible and invisible authorities. The priest was in conversation with God, the doctor is in some kind of cahoots with health, a soldier has dealings with the king, and a maid knows a lot about spells, terrors, and spirits.

There are moments, however, when the person most deserving of respect is the shepherd who whittles a figurine with a pen knife: that's something neither mommy, nor a general, nor a doctor can manage.

91. Why do unripe fruit make your belly ache? Is health in the belly, or in the head? Is health the same as the soul? Why can a dog live without a soul, but a person dies? Does a doctor get sick, does he die, and why? Why have all the great people died? Is it true that there are those who write books and are alive? Kings die: they don't get buried. Does a queen have wings? Was Mickiewicz[22] a saint? Has the priest seen God? Can an eagle soar up to heaven? Does God pray? What do angels do, do they sleep, do they eat, do they play ball, who sews their dresses? Do devils hurt a lot? Is it devils who put the poison in poisonous mushrooms? If God gets angry at bandits, why are we told to pray for them? When Moses saw God, did he get really scared? Why doesn't daddy pray, did God give him permission? Is thunder a miracle? Is the air God? Why can't you see air? Does air enter an empty bottle right away, or after a little bit, how does it know there's no water in there? Why do poor people curse? If it's not a miracle, why can't anyone make it rain? What are clouds made of? My aunt who lives far away, does she live in a casket?

How childish parents' hope is (only don't call them progressive) that, having told their children "There is no God," they will facilitate their understanding of the world around them. If there is no God, what is there, who made it all, what will happen when I die, where did the first person come from? Is it true that if you don't pray, you live like a beast? Daddy says there are no angels, but I saw one with my own eyes. If it's not a sin, why aren't you allowed to kill? After all, doesn't a chicken feel pain, too?

Nothing but doubts and disturbing questions.

92. A grim fairytale, mysterious poverty.

Why is he hungry, why is he poor, why is he cold, why doesn't he buy, why doesn't he have money, why don't they give him a "yes"?

You say:

"Poor children are dirty, they say nasty things, they have bugs in their hair. Poor children are sick, you can catch something from them. They fight, throw rocks, they poke their eyes out. You're not allowed to go into the yard, into the kitchen: there's nothing interesting there."

And life states:

"They're not sick at all, they run around happily all day, they drink water from the well, they buy delicious dyed candies. The boy sweeps with a broom, tidies the yard, shovels the snow, it's very nice. They don't have bugs, that's not true, they don't throw stones, they have both their eyes, they're not fighting, they're wrestling. The nasty things they say are funny, and it's a hundred times more pleasant in the kitchen than in this room."

You tell the child:

"One should love and respect the poor, they're good, they work hard. You must be grateful to the cook, because she prepares lunch, and to the custodian, because he keeps order. Play with the custodian's children."

And life states:

"The cook has killed a chicken, tomorrow we're going to eat it, mommy's going to eat it, too, because the chicken's cooked, it doesn't feel pain; and the cook killed it fresh, mommy can't even look. The custodian drowned some puppies, how cute they were. The cook has rough hands, she pokes around in dirty water. A peasant stinks, a Jew stinks. You don't say 'that lady,' but 'the seller,' not 'that gentleman,' but 'the custodian.' Poor children are dirty; as soon as they're shown something, right away they say, 'Gimme that,' and if you don't, they toss off your hat, they laugh, and one spat, spat right in my face…"

The child hasn't yet heard of evil sorcerers, and despite this approaches an old beggar fearfully to give him a penny.

The child knows that they don't tell her everything here, either, that in this, too, something nasty is hidden that they do not, or cannot, explain.

93. The oddities of social life and good position.

It's improper to stick your finger in your mouth, to pick your nose, to sniffle. It's improper to ask, to say, "I don't want it," to pull back when someone is kissing you, to say, "That's not true." It's improper to yawn audibly, to say, "I'm bored." It's improper to prop yourself up on your arm, to extend your hand first to an adult. Swinging your legs is naughty, as is keeping your hands in your pockets, looking around when you're on the street. It's improper to make loud remarks and point your finger.

Why?

These prescriptions and proscriptions flow from various sources; children cannot grasp their essence and interconnection.

It's improper to run in one's shirt and improper to spit on the floor.

Why is it improper to answer grownups' questions while sitting? Are you supposed to bow to your father on the street as well? What do you do if someone says something that's untrue, for example, when your uncle says, "You're a girl," but you're a boy, or else, "You're my fiancée," or "I've bought you from your mommy," even though that's a lie?

"Why do you have to be polite for the girls?" a pupil asked me.

"It has a historical significance," I responded.

"Why did you write 'returnd' without the second 'e'?" I asked a few moments later.

"It has a historical significance," he responded with a mischievous smile.

To the same question, one of the mothers responded:

"See: a girl is going to bear children, is going to get sick, etc."

It wasn't long before an argument again arose between the brother and sister.

"Mommy, what does it have to do with me if she's going to have children? What matters to me is that she's not a crybaby."

The explanation that seems least felicitous to me is the one most frequently encountered:

"They're going to laugh at you."

It's convenient and effective: children are afraid of being ridiculous.

But they'll laugh at him for listening to his mommy, for confiding in her, for not wanting to play cards, drink vodka, go to the public house in the future.

Fearing ridiculousness, parents commit preposterous mistakes as well. The most harmful mistake being covering up the child's faults and the oversights in his upbringing; for a time the child pretends toward guests to be well raised, for a generous price; and later it backfires.

94. Native speech; it's not regulations and morals selected for and suited to the child, but air that his soul breathes in tandem with the collective soul of the entire nation. Truth and doubt, faith and custom, love, aversion, willfulness and seriousness, utter dignity and baseness, wealth and poverty, everything that a prophet created in his inspiration and a thug threw up in a drunken rant, centuries of noble work and gloomy years of slavery.

Who has thought this over, who's written about it, who's studied how to exterminate the bacteria and saturate this element with ozone? Maybe it would turn out that, no, it's not the healthy demotic "take a shit," but the genteel "worth the sin," that contains the germs of decay?

Praise be. God is punishing him. The devil made him do it. Just like heaven. On cloud nine. All hell broke loose. Good riddance. Snug as a bug in a rug. The Lord shall provide. To rattle off prayers. Goody two-shoes. Arty-farty. Without two pennies to rub together. Heart in your mouth. He'd sell his soul to the devil. He has peccadillos. He still has some gas left. I'm making a day of it.

To health. Your health. Friday's an unlucky day. Ears burning, someone's talking about you. She's smitten, she's over-salted the soup. He's dropped his knife, a stranger will come a-knocking. He ate the priest's cracklings. One foot in the grave.

Chinese ceremony. Gypsy wedding. Jewish word. A gentleman's agreement. A numbskull. An orphan's lot.

An old bore, old idiot, toothless crone. Brat, dummy, pup, greenhorn, wet behind the ears.

Blind? No, visually impaired. Old? No, advanced in age. Crippled? No, disabled.

This weather's for the dogs. He's gone to the dogs. Sumbitch, ain't that a bitch. Go nuts with anger. Like a headless chicken. Hungry like a wolf. Beat to a pulp.

Doesn't have a good head on shoulders, it's in the clouds. Pulls the wool over your eyes. Has a screw loose. Bursts with laughter. Gets out of a pickle. Knows it like the back of the hand. Now that'll be the day. It's sucking the life out of me.

What is this? Where did it come from? What's all this for?

"Table, noun, table, subject."

"But why 'dumb as a table leg'? Was the guy who came up with grammar smart?"

95. Children do not like incomprehensible expressions; sometimes they try to use them to dazzle those around them. They have a choice in assimilating adult speech, clearly resisting some of our frequent turns of phrase.

"Look, give it. Listen, let me have it. Look, show me."

"Look," "listen," these correspond to our "please." Asking is begging (a beggar asks). A child does not like a humiliating expression.

"You think I'm going to keep asking? Don't ask him. Like I'd ask. Wait, you ask me."

I know only one exceptionally ceremonial turn of phrase.

"You see how you are: please, I'm asking you."

Even when addressing adults, a child prefers the form "Mommy, do this," "Sir, do that," and only asks when required to.

A child uses the expression "look" to replace the no less disagreeable "I'm sorry."

"Look, I didn't mean to. Look, I didn't want to. Look, I didn't know."

And there's a wealth of expressions of persuasion and admonition to escape violent scenes.

"Stop, leave it, don't start, go away, leave. Drop it. I told you to stop. I'm begging you, stop (here the request is a very firm command). Won't you go away? Listen: won't you stop already?"

A threat:

"Do you want me to let you have it? Do you want to get it? You'll see, you'll be sorry. I'll give you something to cry about."

The dismissive doubling of an expression:

"Fine, fine… I know, I know… Hold on, hold on."

We force the child to be afraid.

"Like I'm really afraid. You think I'm afraid. Like I'd be afraid of him."

All of a child's property is disputable: he may not give it away without asking, may not destroy it, he has a right to use it (and so values an unshared possession all the more).

"Your bench, your table?"

"Mine! (Or else: maybe it's yours?)."

"I was here first."

The "first" took the place, started playing, started digging. Grownups, seeing to their own peace and quiet, judge children's disputes quite superficially.

"He started it. He did it first. I was standing here, then he…"

The "or else" formulation is curious:

"Or else I'm going to bump into him. Or else I'll start running away. Or else we'll start laughing."

The story's content – willfulness; maybe the "or else" is an echo of prohibitions.

"You promised, remember. You gave your word. You broke your word."

Whoever doesn't keep his promise is swine. Grownups should remember that.

A wealth of material for study.

96. A child is not utterly unamenable to the poor: she likes the kitchen, and she likes it not because there are prunes and raisins down there, but because something is going on in the kitchen while nothing is going on in the rooms, she likes it because a fairytale is more interesting down there, because besides a fairytale she'll get to hear a true-life story, because she'll tell something herself, and they listen to her with interest, because in the kitchen she's a person and not a miniature pinscher on a satin pillow.

"So you want a story? Alright then. So what was it I was saying? Aha, so that's how it was. One moment, let me remember."

Before the fairytale begins, the child has time to choose a comfortable spot, fix her clothes, clear her throat, ready herself for a long listen.

"So she was walking, walking through the forest. And it's dark, can't see anything, not a tree, not a beast, not a stone. Dark and dark. So she's so afraid, so afraid. Right, she crossed herself once, her terror left her a little, she crossed herself again and walked on."

I've tried to tell a story like this; it's not easy. We don't have the patience, we rush it, we respect neither the fairytale, nor the listener. A child doesn't keep up with our story's tempo.

Maybe if we knew how to talk like this about a length of linen, then the child wouldn't think that shirts grow on trees, or that earth is sewn with ash...

An actual occurrence:

"I get up in the morning, and I see everything double, I look at one thing and see two. I look at a chimney, two chimneys, I look at a table, two tables. I know there's one, but I see two. I wipe my eyes, it doesn't help. And there's a pounding, a pounding in my head."

The child waits for the riddle's solution, and when a foreign name finally arrives – typhus – is prepared to accept the foreign term.

"Doctor says, 'typhus'..."

A pause. The narrator rests, and the listener rests, too.

"So, when I came down with this typhus..."

And on flows the story.

A simple story about how there was a farmer in a village who feared no dog, how he bet he could take a dog as mean as a wolf and carry it on his arm like a calf, it turns into an epic. And how at a wedding one guy dressed up like an old woman, and no one recognized him. And how a farmer looked for his stolen horse.

Keep an eye out, maybe a russet-coated storyteller would appear on the stage, would teach us how to speak to children in a way that will be heard.

One must be alert; we prefer to forbid.

97. Is it true?

One has to understand the essence of this question, which we merely dislike, thinking it pointless.

If mommy, if a schoolteacher has said something, that means it's true.

Nay, the child has become convinced that every person possesses merely partial knowledge, that, for example, a coachman knows even more about horses than his father does. Furthermore, not everyone who knows says so. Sometimes they don't feel like it, sometimes they bend the truth to the child's level, often they conceal or consciously falsify.

Besides truth, there's also belief; one person believes, another doesn't: grandma believes in dreams, mommy doesn't. Who's correct?

Finally, there's lying as a joke and lying to puff oneself up.

"Is it true that the Earth is a sphere?"

Everyone says it's true. If one person says it's not, it will leave a shadow of doubt.

"You were in Italy; is it true that Italy is like a boot?"

The child wants to know whether you saw it for yourself or know it from others, where you know it from; he wants answers to be short and firm, comprehensible, identical, serious, honest.

"How does a thermometer measure a fever?"

One person says "mercury," another says "quicksilver" (why is it quick?), a third that bodies expand (is a thermometer a body?), a fourth that you'll find out when you're older.

The fairytale about the stork offends and angers children, as does any playful answer to a serious question, whether it's "Where do children come from?" or "Why does a dog bark at a cat?"

"Don't make my job easier if you don't want to, but why do you make it harder, why do you mock me for wanting to know?"

A child taking revenge on his playmate pronounces:

"I know something, but now I'm not going to tell you."

Yes, he won't tell as a punishment, but what are adults punishing him for?

I note a couple more childish questions:

"Doesn't anyone in the world know? Isn't it something you can know? Who said that? Everyone, or just one? Is it always like that? Does it have to be that way?"

98. Can I?

They don't allow it, because it's a sin, because it's unhealthy, because it's improper, because she's too little, because they said so, and that's that.

And here we find dubious and intricate problems. Now and then something is unhealthy when mommy's angry, now and then they even let a little kid do it when father is in a good mood or guests are over.

"Why do they forbid what would bother them?"

It's a lucky thing that the consistency prescribed by theory is, in practice, unfeasible. Because what, you want to draw the child into life with confidence that everything is correct, fair, reasonably motivated and invariable? In the theory of childrearing we forget that we're supposed to teach the child not only to value the truth, but also to recognize a lie, not only to love, but to hate as well, not only to respect, but also to despise, not only to agree, but also to be outraged, not only to submit, but also to rebel.

We often encounter mature people who feel outraged when it would suffice to disregard, who despise where they should sympathize. For when it comes to negative emotions we are autodidacts, because in teaching the ABCs of life they teach us just a couple letters and hide the rest. Is it any wonder we don't know how to read right?

A child feels unfreedom, suffers in fetters, longs for freedom but will not find it because, changing the form, they retain the content of prohibition and obligation. We cannot change our adult life because we are raised in unfreedom; we cannot offer the child liberty so long as we ourselves are in chains.

If I were to cast away everything in childrearing that burdens my child prematurely, it would meet the harsh judgement of his or her peers as well as from adults. Would the compulsion to blaze new trails, the hardship of pushing against the current – wouldn't this be an even heavier yoke? For free birds from country manors, how painful is their penance in school dormitories, after a couple years of relative freedom in the field, the stable, the servants' quarters…

I wrote this book in a field hospital, under artillery fire, during the war; the very program of understanding was insufficient.

99. Why does a girl at a neutral age already differ so much from a boy?

Because, besides the impairment of youth, she is subject to additional limitations as a woman. A boy is deprived of rights because he's a child, he's seized the privilege of his sex with both hands and does not let it go, does not feel like sharing it with a girl the same age.

"I'm allowed, I can, I'm a boy."

A girl is an interloper in their circle. One in ten of them will always ask: "What's she doing with us?"

Let an argument arise, and boys resolve it on their own, without injury to ambition, without threatening banishment, but for a girl they have a rough:

"You won't like it, go do your own thing."

Preferring to remain among the boys, the girl becomes someone who is suspicious within her own circle:

"You don't want to, go hang out with the boys."

Disadvantage answers contempt with contempt; it's a self-defense reflex of pride under attack.

An exceptional girl will not be discouraged, she disregards their opinion, she's superior to the crowd.

And how is the hostility of children in general toward girls who continue to play with boys expressed? Perhaps I am not mistaken in asserting that this hostility has created an absolute, cruel rule:

A girl is disgraced if a boy sees her underpants.

This rule, in the form in which it has been adopted among children, was not thought up by adults.

A girl cannot run free, for if she falls over, before she straightens out her dress, she'll hear a malevolent shout:

"Ooo, her underpants!"

"Not true," she says, blushing, confused, humiliated, or, defiantly, "Yeah, so what?"

Just let her try fighting, and immediately the shout will stop her, incapacitate her.

This is why girls are less nimble, and therefore less deserving of respect, they don't fight, so they get offended, argue, complain, and cry. And then it's older people who demand respect for them. With what joy children say of an adult:

"I don't need to listen to him."

And you're supposed to step aside for a girl – why?

Until we free girls from "it's inappropriate," which has its source in their organism, efforts to make them playmates to boys are pointless. We have solved the problem in another way: we have decked boys out in long hair and entangled them in an equal number of recipes for decency, and they play together; instead of manly daughters, we have doubled the number of effeminate sons.

> *Short dresses; bathing suits and sports clothes; new dances – a bold attempt to solve the problematic on new bases. How many deliberations are concealed within fashion decisions? Not frivolously, I trust.*
>
> *One cannot sulk and criticize; in discussing ostensibly sensitive topics, we maintain the prejudice of circumspection.*

*

I will not renew the attempt to discuss every stage of the development of every child in a brief brochure.

100. The child who at first sails joyfully along life's surface, unaware of its murky depths, treacherous currents, hidden monsters, the hostile forces lying in wait, trusting, enchanted, smiling at colorful surprises, awakes suddenly from her sky-blue half-sleep and, with an unmoving gaze, baited breath, and quivering lips tremulously whispers:

"What's this, why, what for?"

A drunk staggers, a blind man feels the way with his cane, an epileptic falls on the sidewalk, a thief is led away, a horse dies, a rooster gets slaughtered.

"Why? What's all this for?"

Father speaks in an angry voice, and mommy cries and cries. Uncle kissed the maid, she threatened him, they're laughing, they look into each other's eyes. They speak in outrage about someone having been born under a bad sign, so he will have to have his bones broken.

"What's this, why?"

She doesn't dare ask. She feels tiny, alone, and helpless in the face of mysterious powers in conflict with one another.

She, who had once been in charge, whose wish had been a command, armed with tears and a smile, rich with her bounty of mommy, daddy, and nurse, perceives that it is they who have her for their entertainment, that she is for them, not the other way around. Alert like an intelligent dog, like a slave-prince, she looks all around and looks at herself.

They know something, they're hiding something. They are not what they call themselves, and they demand that she not be what she actually is. They praise the truth, they themselves lie, they order you to lie. They speak one way to children, a completely different way among themselves. They make fun of children. They have their own lives and get angry when a child wants to penetrate it; they want the child to be gullible, they're happy when her naive question betrays that she does not understand.

Death, animal, money, truth, God, woman, reason, it's as though there's falsehood in everything, as though there's a nasty riddle, an evil secret. Why don't they want to say how things really are?

And the child recalls her childhood years with regret.

101. The second period of instability, on which I can say nothing more categorically, only that it exists, I have called the school period. It is an excuse name, an ignorance name, an avoidance name, one of many labels that science puts into circulation, creating the appearance, and luring laymen to believe, that it knows, whereas we're just barely starting to think it through.

School-age instability is not a crisis at the boundary between babyhood and early childhood, and it is not adolescence.

Physically: a change for the worse in appearance, sleep, appetite, a diminished resistance to disease, the appearance of latent hereditary flaws, a poor sense of well-being.

Mentally: self-isolation, spiritual unrest, hostility toward those around oneself, easy submission to moral blight, the rebellion of innate inclinations against the imposed influences of caregivers.

"What happened to him? I don't recognize him – it's a trait he gets from his mother."

Sometimes:

"I thought that it was sulkiness, I got angry, I reprimanded him, but he's obviously been ill for a long time."

For the mother, the close link between the physical and psychological changes she has observed comes as a surprise.

"I ascribed it to the poor influence of his friends."

Yes, but why, out of those numerous influences, did he choose the poor ones, why were those heeded so easily, why did they prevail?

The child, tearing himself painfully away from his loved ones, still weakly integrated with the society of children, feels all the more grief at their not wanting to help him, at having no one to turn to for advice, no one to hold.

When we encounter these small changes in the orphanage with a significant number of children, when today there's one out of a hundred, tomorrow a second "goes bad," suddenly becomes lazy, clumsy, sleepy, petulant, touchy, incorrigible, deceitful, only to regain his balance after a year, "get back on track," it is difficult to doubt that these changes are dependent on the growing process, of whose laws objective, impartial tools provide us a certain understanding: weight and height.

I foresee a time when weight, height, perhaps other tools acquired by human genius, will be the seismograph of the organism's hidden powers, will allow us not only to recognize, but to predict.

102. It is untrue that a child wants the panes from the windows and the stars from the sky, that she can be bribed with understanding and acquiescence, that she is a born anarchist. No, the child has a sense of obligation unimposed by violence, she likes a plan and order, she does not renounce rules and obligations. She only demands that the burden not be too heavy, that it not injure her back, that she find understanding when she hesitates, slips, when, weary, she stops to catch her breath.

Let's test it out: just see whether you can handle it, how many steps you'll take under the load, whether you can carry as much every day – this is the chief principle of orthophreny.[23]

The child wants to be taken seriously, she demands confidence, a hint, and advice. We treat her jokingly, we suspect her constantly, we reject her with misunderstanding, we refuse help.

The mother who has come to the doctor for advice does not want to cite a fact, she prefers the general:

"She's nervous, sulky, disobedient."

"Facts, dear lady, symptoms."

"She bit her friend. I'm ashamed to say. She likes her, they're always playing together."

Five minutes of conversation with the child: she hates her "friend," who makes fun of her, of her dresses, and called her mommy a trash-picker.

Another example: a boy is afraid to sleep alone in his room; he despairs at the thought of the approaching night.

"Why didn't you tell me?"

"But I have been telling you."

The mother had disregarded it; it's shameful for such a big boy to be afraid.

A third example: he spat on his nursemaid, latched onto her hair, it was hard to get him off.

The nursemaid would take him to bed at night and order him to press against her; she threatened that she would put him in a trunk and throw it into the river.

A child can be dreadfully lonely in his suffering.

103. Prepubescence – good cheer, quietude. Even "nervous" children become calm again. Vibrancy returns, childish robustness, the harmony of vital functions. There's even respect for one's elders, and obedience, and good posture; there are no disturbing questions, sulkiness, or acts of mischief. The parents are once again satisfied. Externally, the child assimilates the worldview of his family and environment, taking advantage of his relative freedom, he doesn't demand any more than they give him, he's careful not to disclose his views, knowing in advance which of them will find a hostile reception.

School, with its powerful tradition, its buzzing and colorful life, timetable, demandingness, worry, defeat, and triumph, a companionable book – these make up life's content. Facts provide no time for futile inquiry.

Now the child gets it. He knows that everything is not alright in the world, that there is good and evil, knowledge and ignorance, justice and injustice, liberty and dependence. Sure, he doesn't understand, but then what does that matter to him? He's resigned, he goes with the flow.

God? You have to pray, in moments of doubt you supplement the prayer with some charity, the same as everyone else. A sin? You feel remorse, and God forgives.

Death? Yes, one has to cry, wear mourning, remember with a sigh, like everyone does.

They demand that he be exemplary, cheerful, naive, grateful toward his parents – by all means, at your service.

Please, thank you, excuse me, mommy sends her regards, I wish it with all my heart (not just half). It's so simple, easy, and it wins praise, it's the price of peace.

He knows when, to whom, and how, and which request will hit the mark, how to extricate himself nimbly from an unpleasant situation, how to indulge whom and with what, and merely calculates "whether it's worth it."

A sense of spiritual wellbeing, physical favor – these make him amenable, inclined to compromise: when it comes down to it, his parents are good, the world on the whole is fine, life, when you skip over the trifles, is beautiful.

This stage, which parents can exploit to prepare themselves and their child for the new tasks awaiting them, is a period of naive calm and unworried rest.

This has been aided by arsenic or iron, a good teacher, an ice rink, a stay in a summer apartment, a confession, a mother's sermon.

Parents and their child delude themselves that they have already come to understand each other, that they have overcome the difficulties, when the reproductive function, no less important than growth, and controlled the least by modern mankind, before long starts tragically entangling the ever-ongoing function of personal development, unsettling the spirit and attacking the body.

104. Again, an effort to evade the truth, a slight relief in understanding it, the danger of the error that it has already been grasped when we have merely a shadow, a couple strokes of the general outline.

Neither a period of disruption, nor of equilibrium, is an explanation of the phenomenon, just its popular headline. We depict mysteries mastered as objective mathematical formulas, while others, against which we stand helpless, disconcert and anger us. Fire, flood, hail are a catastrophe, but only in the value of the harms they bring; thus we organize a fire brigade, we build dams, we insure, we stand guard. We have adapted to spring and autumn. We struggle unsuccessfully with a person because, not knowing her, we do not know how to bring her into harmony with life.

It's a hundred days until spring. There is not yet a single blade of grass, not one bud, but in the ground and in the roots there is already the imperative of spring, which goes on in secret, vibrates, is lurking, lying in wait, swelling – beneath the snow, in the naked boughs, on the frosty gale, in order to burst suddenly into bloom. Only superficial study sees disorder in the volatile weather of a March day: what is deep within is ripening logically, hour by hour, it's gathering and falling into line, we just don't distinguish the iron law of the astronomical year from its accidental, fleeting intersections with a law that is less familiar or not familiar at all.

There are no border posts between the periods of life; we have placed them the way we have painted the map of the world in various colors, having arranged the countries' artificial borders, changing them every few years.

"She'll grow out of it, it's a transitional age, it will change" – and with a forgiving smile the caregiver waits for the help of a happy accident.

Every researcher loves his work for the ordeal of experimentation and the delight of the struggle, but the conscientious one hates it – the fear of the errors it introduces, the false appearances it creates.

Every child lives through periods of senile weariness and the drunken fullness of vital processes, but this does not mean that one should yield and guard, it doesn't mean that one should struggle and harden. The heart does not keep up with growth, so give it some rest, and perhaps rouse it to livelier action, that it grow stronger, bigger? This problem can be resolved only in a given instance and at a given moment, but we would have to gain the child's trust, and she would have to deserve our faith.

And above all knowledge would have to know.

105. We must thoroughly revise everything we ascribe today to adolescence, which we take into serious account, and rightly so, but don't we also do so excessively, one-sidedly, and in particular without separating the factors it consists of? Hasn't our identification of the earlier developmental stages allowed us a more objective examination of this new period of instability (though one of many), similar in its features to those that came before, depriving it of its unhealthy, mysterious exceptionality? Haven't we, somewhat artificially, dressed the maturing youth in the very same uniform of instability and unrest as children – of cheerfulness and serenity; doesn't this suggestion infect him? Doesn't our helplessness influence the course's turbulence? Isn't there too much about awakening life, matins, spring, and spurts, and too little factual data?

The main thing: does the phenomenon belong to fecund growth in general, or merely to the development of particular organs? What is dependent on changes in the circulatory system, of the heart and blood vessels, on an impaired or qualitatively altered oxidation of the brain tissues and how they get nutrients, and what on the development of the glands?

If certain phenomena trigger panic among youth, hurting painfully, taking a rich toll of victims, breaking ranks and bringing destruction, it's not that this is how it must be, but that this is how it is under today's social conditions, that everything fosters such a course for this fragment of life's orbit.

A weary soldier submits easily to panic; it's easier when he looks distrustfully upon those leading him, suspecting treachery or seeing the indecision of those in charge; it's easier still when he's wracked with anxiety, ignorance of where he is, what's ahead of him, what's on his flanks or behind him; it's easiest when the attack comes without warning. Solitude fosters panic; a tight column, shoulder to shoulder, heightens serene courage.

The youth, wearied by growing and alone, without a judicious leader, lost in the labyrinth of life problems, suddenly encounters an enemy and, having an exaggerated sense of this enemy's brittle power, doesn't know where he came from, how to hide, or how to defend himself.

One more question.

Don't we confuse the pathologies of adolescence with physiology, and hasn't our view been constructed by doctors, who see only *maturitas difficilis,* difficult, abnormal maturation? Aren't we repeating the hundred-year-old error that ascribed all the undesirable symptoms of a child under three years old to teething? What has remained of the myth of "teething" might remain a hundred years from now of the myth of "sexual maturation."

106. Freud's research on the sexual life of children has tarnished childhood, but by the same token hasn't it cleansed youth? Dispelling the beloved illusion of the child's pristine whiteness has dispelled another agonizing illusion: that suddenly "the beast within will wake up, and she'll fall into the gutter." I've printed this common cliché in order to emphasize all the more how fatalistic is our view of the evolution of a drive as bound to life as growth is.

It is no stain, the haze of scattered emotions to which only conscious or unknowing depravity lends shape prematurely; it is no stain, even the initially faint "something" that slowly, over the course of several years, colors the feelings of the two sexes all the more clearly until such a time when, at the moment of the drive's maturation and the organs' complete maturity, a new living thing is conceived, the heir in the generational line.

Sexual maturity: the organism is ready to give healthy issue without harm to its own prospects.

Maturity of the sexual *drive*: the clearly crystallized desire for normal coupling with an individual of the opposite sex.

In a male youth, sexual life is sometimes initiated before the drive matures; in girls, it becomes tangled, depending on whether it is a case of marriage or rape.

A difficult issue, but all the more unreasonable is serenity when a child knows nothing, or moodiness, when she figures something out.

Isn't this why we brutally reject her whenever the question crosses into forbidden territory, to make her shy – so that she won't dare to address it in the future when she begins not only to sense, but to feel?

107. Love. Art leased it, attached wings, and put it in a straightjacket, by turns kneeling before it and smacking its gob, sitting it on a throne and ordering it to nod at passersby on the street corner, committing a hundred absurdities of adoration and disgrace. And bald science, having set its glasses on its nose, then recognized it as worthy of attention when it could have studied its abscesses. The physiology of love knows only the one-sided "It serves to preserve the species." That's a bit too little, too shabby. Astronomy knows more than that the sun shines and gives warmth.

And so it was that life is generally dirty and zany, and always suspect and ridiculous. The only thing worthy of respect is attachment, which always arrives after the shared birth of a legitimate child.

Thus we laugh when a six-year-old gives a girl his half of a cake; we laugh when a girl goes beet red when a schoolboy bows at her. We laugh, having caught the lad staring at her photograph; we laugh at her jumping to open the door for her brother's tutor.

But we furrow our brow when he and she are playing too quietly somehow or have fallen breathlessly to the ground while wrestling. But we fly into a rage when the love of a daughter or son runs against our intentions.

We laugh because it's far away, we grow glum because it's getting closer, we're outraged when it messes up our calculation. We injure our children with mockery and suspicion, we desecrate emotions that bring no profit.

And so they cover it up, but they're in love.

He loves her because she's not a silly thing like all the others, because she's cheerful, because she doesn't quarrel, because she wears her hair down, because she doesn't have a father, because she's somehow so nice.

She loves him because he's not like the other boys, because he's not a rat, because he's funny, because his eyes shine, because he has a lovely name, because he's somehow so nice.

They cover it up, and they're in love.

He loves her because she's like the angel in the picture on the side altar, because she's pure, whereas he'd been on a certain street deliberately to see "that kind of girl" standing by her door.

She loves him because he'd agree to marry her under one condition: that they'd never, ever get undressed in the same room. He'd kiss her twice a year on the hand, and once for real.

They'll experience all the emotions of love but one, the brutal suspicion of which rings in the brusque:

"Instead of romancing, you'd better… Instead of filling your head with lovey-dovey, it would be better if…"

Why did they hound, and why do they antagonize?

Is it wrong that she's in love? She's not even in love, she just really likes him. More than her parents? Maybe that's the sin.

What if one of them had to die? Oh God, but I want everybody to be healthy.

Adolescent love is nothing new. Some love even while they're children, others sneer at love as children.

"She's your girlfriend; has she shown it to you?"

And the boy, wanting to prove that he doesn't have a girlfriend, sticks his foot out in front of her on purpose or pulls hard at her braid.

In beating premature love out of their heads, aren't we beating premature debauchery in?

108. The period of maturation, as if all the preceding periods were not also gradual maturation, now slower, now more vigorous. Let us examine the weight curve, and we'll understand the fatigue, the awkwardness, laziness, half-sleepy reveries, the airy halftones, paleness, sluggishness, lack of will, sulkiness, the indecision characteristic of this age of, let's say, great "instability," to differentiate it from the periods before.

Growing is work, hard work for the organism, and the conditions of life do not sacrifice a single hour of school to it, nor a single day at the factory. And how often it flashes by as a state akin to illness, because it's premature, because it's too sudden, because it deviates from the norm.

For a girl the first menstruation is a tragedy because she has been taught to be horrified by the sight of blood. The development of her breasts saddens her because she has been taught to be ashamed of her sex, and breasts unmask her, everyone is going to see that she's a girl.

A boy, who lives through the same thing physiologically, has a different mental response. He awaits the first fuzz of a moustache with yearning because it's an announcement to him, a promise, and if he's embarrassed by his cracking voice and his windmill arms it's because he's not ready yet, that he has to keep waiting.

Haven't you ever noticed the envy and aversion of disadvantaged girls toward privileged boys? Yes, before, when she was punished, there was always at least a shade of guilt, but here, how is it her fault that she's not a boy?

Girls begin their transformation earlier and gladly display this, their one privilege.

"I'm almost grown up, but you're still a brat. In three years I can already get married, when you'll still be sitting over a book."

The nice childhood playmate receives the contemptuous smile.

"Go get married, then, but is someone going to have you? I gain my rights without getting married."

She grows into love earlier, he into romance, she into marriage, he into the pub, she into motherhood, he into coupling with a female, as Kuprin says, "Something on the nature of these flies [...]. They're stuck together on the window sill, and then in some sort of fool wonder scratch their backs with their little hind legs and fly apart forever."[24]

The former aversion of the two sexes now assumes a new hue, only to change its face again before too long, when she hides, he hunts after her, only to settle into his hostile attitude toward his spouse, who is a burden to him, assume his privileges, benefit from them herself.

109. The long-hidden aversion to the surrounding adults takes on an awful hue.

Such a common phenomenon: the child's to blame, he's broken a window. He should feel guilty. When we offer the appropriate reproaches, we're less likely to get remorse than rebellion, anger on his furrowed brow, in glances cast from a lowered head. The child wants his caregiver to show him kindness precisely when he is guilty, when he's bad, when he's met misfortune. The broken pane, the spilled ink, the torn clothes – these are an unsuccessful undertaking, albeit committed against all warning. And adults, having lost in the poorly conceived to-do – how will they take the sulkiness, anger, and reproach?

This aversion toward strict and absolute masters occurs just as the child is regarding adults as creatures superior to himself. He suddenly catches them red-handed.

Aha, so that's how it is, so that's your secret, so you were hiding something; there was something to be ashamed of.

He had heard it before but hadn't believed it, he had had doubts, but it was nothing to do with him. Now he wants to know, he has to find out from someone, he needs this information for his struggle against them, at last he feels himself embroiled in this matter. Before it had been "I don't know it, but I'm certain of it," and now everything is clear.

So one can want children and not have them, so that's why an unmarried girl can have a child, so she can not give birth if she doesn't feel like it, so they do it for money, so there are diseases, so everyone?

And they just go on living, and among themselves they're not ashamed.

Their smiles, glances, prohibitions, fears, embarrassments, monosyllables, everything that had been unclear before now becomes comprehensible and is shockingly real.

That's just fine; we'll get even.

The teacher of Polish shoots a look at the mathematician.

"Come here: I'll whisper something in your ear."

And the laugh of evil triumph, and the peeping through the keyhole, and the drawing of a burning heart on blotting paper or a chalkboard.

His old woman has dressed up. His old man is preening himself. His uncle pulls him by the chin and says, "You brat."

No, a brat no longer: "I know."

They're still pretending, they're still trying to lie, and thus he must track down and unmask the deceivers, avenge himself for the years of enslavement, for his stolen trust, the extorted cuddles, for the confidence they wangled from him, the respect they demanded.

Respect them? No – disdain them, mock them, spit on them. Fight against the loathsome dependency.

"I'm not a child. What I think is my business. I wish I'd never been born. What, mommy, are you jealous? Grownups aren't so holy either."

Or else pretend that he doesn't know, take advantage of their not daring to speak openly, and to say only with a mocking glance and half-smile, "I know," while the mouth says:

"I don't know what's wrong in that, I don't know what you want."

110. One must remember that a child is incorrigible and malicious not because she "knows," but because she suffers. Happy good cheer is forgiving where treacherous weariness is truculent and trifling.

It would be a mistake to think that understanding means evading difficulty. How many times does the sympathetic caregiver have to temper his or her good feelings, have to reign in horseplay in order to maintain discipline in the child's actions, even though there is none in the caregiver's own thoughts. Here a great deal of scientific training, a great deal of experience and balance, is exposed to a hard trial.

"I understand and forgive, but people, the world – they don't forgive."

On the street you have to behave decently, restrain yourself from too-rowdy manifestations of glee, give no outlet to fits of anger, refrain from remarks and judgments, show respect to your elders.

It can be hard, difficult with good will and mental effort; and does the child find the conditions for impartial deliberation in the family home?

When she's sixteen, her parents are past forty, an age of painful reflection, sometimes the final protest of one's own life, a moment when the balance sheet of the past displays a clear deficit.

"What do I get out of life?" the child asks.

"And what did I get?"

The intuition says that the child, too, will not win life's lottery, but we have already lost, whereas the child has hope and, because of this illusory hope, is hungry for the future, not perceiving and indifferent to the fact that she's putting us in our graves.

Do you remember the time you were awakened from your sleep by prattle early in the morning? Back then we paid ourselves for the trouble with a kiss. Yes, for a gingerbread we would receive the jewel of a grateful smile. Slip-on shoes, a hood, a bib, it's all so cheap, nice, new, amusing. And now everything's expensive, gets destroyed easily, and you get nothing in return, not even a good word. How many soles one will wear through in chasing her ideal; how quickly she grows without wanting to wear clothes with room to grow.

"Here's some pocket money."

She has to enjoy herself, has her own minor needs. She takes it out of cool obligation, like alms from an enemy.

A child's pain painfully offends the pain of the parents, the parents' suffering incautiously slams into the child's pain. If the clash is so strong, how much stronger would it be if the child, against our will, in her own lonely effort, were not to prepare herself slowly for the fact that we're not omnipotent, omniscient, and perfect.

111. If we closely examine not the collective soul of children of that age, but its component parts, not the lot of them, but individuals, we again see two diametrically opposed organizations.

We find the child who whined quietly in the cradle, slowly rose under his own steam, gave back the sponge cake without protest, observed those playing in a circle from a distance, and now muffles his rebellion and pain in tears that go unnoticed in the night.

We find the one who screamed till he was blue, couldn't be left alone for a moment without terror, wrenched the ball from his peer, led in "Everybody, stop and stand, take your partner by the hand," and now imposes his program of rebellion and his active anxiety on his coevals, on all of society.

I have searched arduously for an explanation to the painful dilemma that in collective life, of youths as well as of adults, an honest thought must so often be concealed or quietly instilled when outright arrogance crashes garishly around, that kindness is synonymous with stupidity or incompetence. How often a prudent social activist and conscientious politician, himself not knowing what he's yielding to, would find an explanation in Jellenta's words:

"I have not the audacious maw to respond to their witticisms and barbs, and I know not how to speak and reason with those who have a ready, mouthy, pimpish reply to everything."[25]

What can we do so that the active and the passive might assume equal places in the organism's circulating juices, so that the elements of all fertile terrain might circulate freely within it?

"I'm not giving it away," active rebellion says. "I already know what I'm doing. I've had enough."

"Let it rest. What's it to you? Maybe that's just how you see it."

These simple sentences, expressions of honest hesitation or sincere resignation, are a salve, they have greater power than the artful phraseology of tyranny that we, the grownups, unfurl, wanting to subjugate children. There's no shame in hearing a peer out, but letting an adult convince you, let alone move you, is to allow yourself to be taken in, to be deceived, to admit to one's own poverty; unfortunately, they're right not to believe.

But how, I repeat, to shield reflection from insatiable ambition, quiet deliberation from the shouting match, how to teach to differentiate an idea from "appearances and career," how to shield dogma from derision and a youthful idea from experienced, treacherous demagoguery.

The child takes a step forward into life, not into sexual life; he matures, he doesn't sexually mature.

If you understand that you will not succeed in untangling any of these riddles without their participation, if you say everything that's been said here, and after your meeting is over you hear:

"Well, passive kids, let's go home."

"Don't be so active, or you'll get hit in the head."

"Hey there, province of the dogmatic, you took my hat…"

Don't think they're mocking you; don't say, "Not worth it…"

112. Dreams.

The game of Robinson Crusoe has turned into dreaming of travel, playing cops and robbers into dreaming of adventures.

Again, life is not enough, so dreaming is an escape from it. Without material for thought, its poetic form appears. Feelings that find no outlet flow into dreams. Dreaming is a program for living. If we knew how to decipher it, we'd see that dreams come true.

If a country boy dreams of becoming a doctor but becomes an orderly, he has realized his life program. If he dreams of riches and dies on a daybed, it only seems that his dreams have been shattered: he hadn't dreamt of the work of acquiring, but of the delights of wasting; he'd dreamt of getting drunk on champagne, but he guzzled rotgut, dreamt of salons, but lived it up in a dive, he'd wanted to throw gold around, but he threw around coppers. He dreamt of becoming a priest, but he's a teacher, no, just a doorman; but he became a priest of a teacher, a priest of a doorman.

She dreamt that she was a terrifying queen; and doesn't she tyrannize her husband and children, having married a minor clerk? She dreamt she was a beloved queen; and doesn't she reign in her peasant school? She dreamt she was a famous queen; didn't she find renown as an extraordinary, exceptional seamstress or bookkeeper?

What pushes youth toward a bohemian life? Some, the dissipation, others, the exoticism, still others, drive, ambition, career; and only this one loves art, this one, out of the whole bunch of them, is truly an artist, this one does not sell his art; he died in poverty and oblivion, but he had dreamt of victory, and not of honors and gold. Read Zola's *The Masterpiece*; life is more logical than we think.

She dreamt of the convent, she found herself in a house of ill repute, but she remained a sister of mercy who, outside of business hours, looks after her sick coworkers, soothes their sorrows and sufferings. Another wished to have fun and has tons of it in the cancer ward until the dying man smiles listening to her prattle, following her pleasant figure with his fading eyes...

Poverty.

A scholar *thinks* about it, researching, sketching, creating theories and hypotheses; a youth *dreams* that he'll build hospitals, distribute alms...

There is Eros in children's dreams; for the time being there is no Venus. The one-sided formula that love is the egoism of the species is harmful. Children love individuals of the same sex, old people, people they've never seen, even those who don't exist. Even as they experience feelings of desire, they have much longer to love an ideal, not the body.

The need for struggle, quiet, chit-chat, work, sacrifice; the urge to possess, use, seek; ambition, passive imitation – all this finds expression in dreaming, independent of its form.

Life realizes one's dreams; out of a hundred dreams of youth, it molds a single statue of reality.

113. The first stage of adolescence: I know, but I still don't feel, I feel, but I still don't believe, I'm a harsh judge of what nature does to others; I suffer, because it threatens me, I'm not at all sure I'll get away. But I am blameless in disdaining them, I'm just afraid for myself.

The second stage: in sleep, in half-sleep, in dream, in the excitation of play, despite the resistance, despite the revulsion, despite the prohibition, a feeling arises more and more often that, to the painful conflict with the external world, piles on the burden of a conflict with one's very self. A violently rejected thought imposes itself like a harbinger of disease, like the first shudder of fever. There is an incubation period to sexual feelings, which are surprising and disconcerting, then arouse trepidation and desperation.

The epidemic of secrets whispered with a giggle dies away, the ticklish bits of bawdiness lose their appeal, the child enters the period of confidences; friendship deepens, the beautiful friendship of orphans astray in the thicket of life, who swear that they will support each other, won't abandon each other, won't let go in a time of need.

The child, himself unhappy, addresses every impoverishment, suffering, impairment, now no longer with the formula he's been taught and the gloomy anxiety of being surprised, but with a fervent compassion. Too occupied with and worried about himself, he cannot be moved for too long by others, but he'll find a moment and a tear for a girl led astray, a child knocked around, a dimwitted convict.

Every new slogan, idea, and powerful cliché finds a sensitive listener and a fervent backer in him. He doesn't read books, he laps them up like an addict, and he prays for a miracle! The childhood God is a fairytale; later, God is a wrongdoer, the ur-source of all misfortune and offense, the one who can, yet does not want to, return as God, a mighty mystery, God, forgiveness, God, reason over weak human thought. God, a calm harbor in the hour of the hurricane.

Before: "If grownups are forcing me to pray, clearly even prayer is a lie; if they drive my friend away, then apparently he's the one to show me the way," because how can I trust them? Today it's different: hostile aversion gives way to compassion. The epithet "filthy talk" does not suffice; something is hidden here that is infinitely more complex. But what? A book dispels the doubts only apparently and for the moment; a peer is himself weak and helpless. There is a moment when one can again recover the child: he's waiting, he wants to listen.

What is there to tell him? Just so long as it's not about how flowers are fertilized and hippopotamuses multiply, and not that onanism is harmful. A child senses that this is about something significantly more important than cleanliness of the fingers and sheets, that what hangs in the balance is his spiritual thesis, the sum total of his worldly responsibility.

Oh, to again be an innocent child, believing, trusting, not thinking.

Oh, to be an adult at last, to flee from the "transitional" age, to be like them, like everyone.

The monastery, quiet, reverent contemplations.

No – fame, heroic deeds.

Travels, a change of scenery and emotions. Dances, games, the sea, the mountains.

Death is best, because what's there to live for, why suffer?

Depending on what he has prepared for this moment over many long years of closely observing the child, the caregiver can provide him a program for knowing himself, for overcoming himself, for what kind of effort to use, how to seek one's own way in life.

114. Abundant willfulness, empty laughter, the merriment of youth.

Yes, joy at being part of the crowd, the triumph of a dreamed-for victory, an inexperienced burst of faith that, contrary to reality, we will shake the earth to its foundations.

So many of us, so many young faces, clenched fists, so many healthy, sharp teeth – we won't give up.

A glass of wine or pint of beer dispels what doubt remains.

Death to the old world, long live the new!

They don't notice the one who, with eyes slightly squinting, sneers, "Dumb," they don't see the other one who, with a sad look, says, "Poor things," they don't see the third who wishes to take advantage of the moment and get something started, take some oath that his noble excitation will not drown in an orgy, not break apart in hollow exclamations...

We often take collective merriment for an excess of energy when it is only a manifestation of the oversensitive weariness that, feeling momentarily unfettered, is aroused in delusion. Recall the merriment of the child in the railway car who, not knowing where she's going or how long it will take, as if satisfied with impressions, fussy about their excess and the anticipation of what will be, ends the cheerful laughter in bitter tears.

Explain why the presence of adults "ruins the fun," discomfits, introduces a constraint...

Ceremony, pomp, a serious mood – adults are stirred up so skillfully, suited so well to the moment. And these two, they're looking into each other's eyes and suffocating, dying from laughter, straining to the point of tears not to crack up, and unable to restrain themselves from the perverse urge to nudge each other with their elbows while whispering a malicious remark, increasing the danger of scandal.

"Just remember not to laugh. Just don't look at me. Just don't make me."

And after the ceremony:

"Her nose was so red. His tie was askew. They almost broke down. Show me: you do that so well."

And an endless story about how funny it was…

One more thing:

"They think I'm happy. Let them. One more proof that they don't understand us…"

The eager work of youth. Some kind of preparations, a forceful effort, an act with a clear goal, when necessary, speed of hand and ingenuity of mind. Here the youth is in her own element, here you will behold healthy merriment and cheerful excitation.

Planning, pondering, wearing oneself out, seeing it through, laughing at unsuccessful attempts and difficulties overcome.

115. Youth is noble.

If you will call it courage that a child leans out a fourth-floor window without being scared; if you will call it kindness that he gave a crippled old man the gold watch his mommy had left on the table; if you will call it a crime that he threw a knife at his brother and poked out his eye, then sure, youth is noble, having no experience of the enormous, half-of-life-sized territory of gainful employment, social hierarchy, and the laws of social life.

The inexperienced believe that one can display friendliness or aversion, respect or disdain, depending on the feelings they've nurtured.

The inexperienced believe that one can voluntarily establish and break off relations, submit to or dismiss accepted forms, agree to or break from customary laws.

"I don't give a hoot, I spit on that, I don't care what they say, I don't want to and that's it, what's it to me?"

Barely have they drawn breath, having wrenched themselves partially free of their parents' authority, and whoa, here are new shackles!

Because someone rich or some Right Honorable so-and-so, because someone somewhere can think or say something?

Who teaches the youth which compromises are a practical necessity and which can be evaded and at what cost, which cause pain but leave no mark, which corrupt? Who indicates the boundaries where hypocrisy is the decency of not spitting on the floor, not wiping your nose on the tablecloth, and not a misdeed?

We would tell the child:

"They're going to laugh at you."

Now one would have to add: "and starve you."

You say, "the idealism of youth." The illusion that you can always persuade someone and set everything right.

And what do you do with this nobility? You grind it to the hilt in your own children and rub lasciviously against idealism, the joy of the anonymous "youth," as once you did against innocence, gratitude, and the love of your own children. And the illusion takes shape that the ideal is as much a sickness as the mumps or chickenpox, that it's just an innocent obligation, like visiting a gallery of paintings on your honeymoon.

I, too, have been a *faris*. I've seen Rubens.

Nobility cannot be the morning mist, but a shaft of light. If we can't afford it yet, for now let's merely raise honest people.

116. Fortunate is the author who, in finishing his work, is aware that he has said what he knows, what he has read, assessed according to stated models. Committing it to print, he has a serene sense of satisfaction that he has called forth a mature child capable of an independent life. It can be otherwise: he does not see the reader who demands mediocre science with a readymade recipe and an indication for its use. Here the creative process means becoming engrossed in one's own unestablished, unlearned, suddenly arising thoughts. Here is the work's conclusion – a cool balance sheet, the painful jolt from sleep. Every chapter looks with reproach at having been abandoned before it came to be. The book's final thought is not the conclusion of the whole, and isn't it strange that that's all there is, that there's nothing more?

So should I add something? That would mean starting over again, casting aside what I know, encountering new problems that I will hardly think through, writing a new book, equally unfinished.

- - -

A child brings a wondrous song of silence into her mother's life. The song's content, its program, strength, creativity, consists of the number of hours the mother spends near her when the child requires nothing, but lives, of the thoughts she diligently enfolds the child in. Through the child the mother matures, in quiet contemplation, into the inspirations that the work of caregiving demands.

Not from a book, but from herself. Then any book will have meagre value; and mine has fulfilled its task if it is convincing in that.

In wise solitude, keep watch…

The Orphanage. Summer Camp.
The Orphans' Home.

Foreword to the second edition

1. Fifteen years ago I wrote the following in this book:

"May no opinion be an absolute conviction, nor a conviction for all time. May this day forever be merely a passage from the sum of yesterday's experiences to the greater one of tomorrow's… Only under these conditions will this work be neither monotonous, nor hopeless."

So it was, and so it has remained. I don't know how to say where I have matured, where I have merely gotten older, what is confidence *gained* in my attitude toward the child and life, and what is an illusion *lost,* that a caregiver can, through persuasion or suggestion, invest the child with his own sense of life and its obligations.

2. The wheel of history turns slowly. A person is a product of her place and time – plus the store of her own health, powers, emotions, imagination, intelligence, talents, beauty, of her ability to commune, to reconcile the divergent wants of herself and others.

First and foremost, perhaps, people divide themselves into species: *homo rapax* [rapacious man], *vulgaris* [common], and, only a certain portion of them, *sapiens* [wise]. The task of eugenics will be selecting positive traits, limiting the increase of socially undesirable types. Has Mendel's law already found its echo in pedology?[26]

We treat one form of mental impairment with a course of organotherapy (myxedema – thyroid hormone); won't the study of the glands' internal secretions do away with pedagogical therapies?

3. Every living thing wants to be well; it avoids pain, or else it *finds satisfaction* in it.

I have long wracked my brains over the question of what the self-preservation instinct actually is. I have explained the creative role of suffering for daily use.

So too is the ratio of good and evil, the strength and number of what injures and agitates, or else soothes and creates, the topic of targeted experiments in the observation of collective life.

Mental lunges through a small cluster of orphanage children into the adult world, its phenomena and rules – increasingly clear: from children's self-governance to the parliaments of the world.

4. The codex of the collegial court seems to me an incomplete, but promising attempt to evade the generally applied system of punishments and repressions. The number of summary (and therefore accidental) punishments has diminished considerably.

Torture's time is over. It is pointless today. Confinement, imprisonment – perhaps these are unnecessary in many instances? Anyway, the law has grown more vigilant. There are no longer enough jails for every harmful individual and every immoral act.

Perhaps one should begin with juvenile courts and forgive the young delinquent (see articles numbered 1-99)[27] or say, "You have acted inappropriately, badly, very badly," and not always call the parents.

I don't know; I'm aiming high.

5. I explain my present attitude toward the child and the society of children in my pamphlet *A Child's Right to Respect*.[28]

Maria Falska's[29] small book *Our Home* can give a sense of how student government looks in broad outline.

A decade of student government, its history – this is serious study. Unfortunately, I don't have the time – there is still so much work: the preschool age, youth – and current matters besides: what few years we have would be wasted looking back.

The documents are in the orphanage newspapers, the reports from student government meetings, dispute testimonies, statistics. An additional facet of the system is the fact that it allows us to archive moments of life.

J.K.

The Orphanage

1. I wish to write a book about the urban orphanage, where a hundred child-orphans, boys and girls of school age, are raised in the care of a modest number of professionals, in their own building with a modest staff.

The orphanage cannot boast a rich literature. We find either works of an exclusively hygienic nature, or else a passionate critique of the very basis for raising children collectively.

I learned the colorless and gloomy mysteries of the orphanage while serving as a caregiver in the dormitory, lavatory, recreation hall, cafeteria, yard, and the toilet. I do not know children in their formal classroom attire; I know them in the dishabille of their everyday lives.

This book may be of interest to the caregiver not only in the barrack-like prison that is the orphanage, but also in the cell-like prison that, for the modern child, is the family.

In both the orphanage and the family, children are tormented; the more energetic try to deceive those watching over them, to break free of vigilant control; they fight stubbornly and hopelessly for their rights.

I fear that the reader will be willing to trust me – and then this book might bring him harm. A warning, then: the road I have elected to take toward my goal is neither the shortest, nor the most convenient, but it is the best for me, because it is mine, because it is my own. I have discovered it not without toil, not without pain – and only once I had understood that all the books I had read, alien experiences and strangers' opinions, were lying.

Publishers sometimes print the golden thoughts of great people; how much more useful it would be if they were to assemble a compendium of the falsehoods uttered by classics of truth and knowledge. Rousseau opens *Émile* with a statement that all our modern knowledge of heredity contradicts.

2. This book has to be quite brief because I intended it first and foremost for a young colleague who had suddenly fallen into a whirlpool of the most difficult childrearing challenges, the most tangled practical conditions, and, stunned, embittered, he's calling for help.

The poor fellow has no time for studies. He'd been awakened twice at night: a child had a toothache, she'd started crying; he had to comfort and treat her. Barely had he fallen asleep when another woke him; she'd had a bad dream: the dead, robbers had wanted to kill her, to throw her into the river, so again he offered reassurance, lulled her to sleep.

A drowsy person cannot read thick pedagogical works in the evening because his eyes are heavy, because if he doesn't get enough sleep he'll be irritable, impatient, incapable of putting the learned work's salutary principles into action. I will remain brief so as not to disturb his night's rest.

3. The caregiver has no time in his day for study. Hardly has he sat down to read, the first child arrives to complain that as he was writing his neighbor jostled him, leaving an ink blot, and now he doesn't know whether to start all over again or to leave it as it is or to tear the page out. A second child is limping: he has a nail in his shoe, he cannot walk. A third is asking whether

he can have the dominoes. A fourth is asking for the key to the cupboard. A fifth hands over a handkerchief he has found: "I found it, I don't know whose it is." A sixth gives him the four groszy he received from his aunt for safekeeping. A seventh runs in for the handkerchief: "It's mine, I set it on the window for a moment, and he took it right away."

There, in the corner, a little oaf is playing with scissors: he'll make a mess, cut himself; who gave him scissors? A lively dispute in the middle of the room, it will soon come to blows: must put a stop to it. The one whose tooth hurt in the night is now running around like mad: again, she'll jostle one of the kids who's writing, or she'll knock an inkpot to the floor; and perhaps her tooth will start aching again in the night.

The caregiver must really want to if he's to be able to manage to read even a short book.

4. But he doesn't really want to, because he doesn't believe.

Through his many citations, the author demonstrates that he is learned. He'll again repeat what is widely known. The same wishful thinking, warmhearted lies, unexecutable suggestions. The caregiver should... should... should... And, ultimately, in all matters, minor and major, he must decide for himself how and what he knows and, most importantly, what he can do.

"That's fine in theory," he consoles himself pitifully.

And the caregiver feels an aversion toward the author because the latter sits quietly behind a comfortable desk and dictates prescriptions with no need for immediate contact with the moving, whining, vexing, and unruly lot to whom anyone who doesn't want to be their tyrant is their slave, and among whom there are those who so thoroughly poison his life on a daily basis that all the rest have a hard time cheering him up.

Why do they tease him with the mirage of great knowledge, momentous tasks, lofty ideals, when he is, and must remain, a workhorse-like Cinderella?

5. He senses that he is losing the enthusiasm that had brought him to the work of its own accord, independently of anyone's sermon. He used to be delighted by the thought of arranging a game, preparing a surprise for the children. He wanted to bring a joyful breath of fresh air into the grey and monotonous life of the orphanage. Now he's delighted when he logs a hopeless "nothing happened." If none of the children has thrown up, if they haven't smashed a window, if he hasn't heard a harsh reproach – that means the day has been well spent.

He's losing his energy: today he looks at minor infractions through his fingers, he tries to see less, to know less, no more than what is most necessary.

He's losing his initiative: it used to be that if he would receive sweets, a toy – he already had a plan to make the most of them. Now he's swift to hand treats out: let them eat them as swiftly as possible, for again there will be disputes, complaints, grievances. A new device or object, so he'll again have to take care, because they'll break it, bust it. Some plant on the window, a painting on the wall – there's so much to do, but he doesn't know, he doesn't want to or cannot. And he doesn't notice it anyway.

He's losing faith in himself. It used to be that not a day went by that he didn't spot something new in the children or in himself. The children would cling to him, now they keep their distance. Does he still love them? He's rough, at times brutal.

Maybe it won't be long before he becomes like those to whom he'd wanted to be an example, for whom he'd felt an aversion because of their coldness, passivity, and negligence?

6. He resents himself, his surroundings, the children.

A week ago he'd received a letter about a sister who was ill. The children found out, they respected his sorrow: they went to bed quietly. He was grateful to them.

And at some point a new ward arrived. They wheedled out of him all the sweets he'd been given by his family, and a pencil case, and pictures – they threatened to beat him up if he complained – and even those he'd taken for honest took part in the nasty affair.

A child will throw her arms around his neck and say "I love you" – and will ask for a new outfit.

That's a child for you; just when he is moved, marveling at how she comes by so much subtle tact and deep feeling, he is again repulsed by her rapacious perversity.

Now it's "I want to, I have to, I should," then it's a hopeless "Is it worth it?"

Theoretical assumptions have become so tangled with personal daily experience that he has lost the thread: the longer he thinks, the less he understands.

7. He doesn't understand what's going on around him.

He tries to limit the prescriptions and proscriptions to the smallest number necessary. He gives the children their freedom; unsatisfied, they demand more.

He wants to probe their concerns. He approaches a boy who has withdrawn uncharacteristically into a corner, quiet and indifferent. "What's wrong? Why are you sad?" "Nothing's wrong, I'm not sad at all," he answers reluctantly. He wants to stroke his head – the boy pulls away roughly.

Over there a group of children is having a lively discussion. He approaches them; they go silent. "What were you talking about?" "Nothing."

It seems like they like him. But he knows they make fun of him. They have confidence in him – and are always hiding something. They appear to take him at his word, but they listen to evil whispers with a willing ear.

He doesn't understand, doesn't know, and it's strange to him, and hostile, and hard on him.

Cheer up, caregiver. You're already casting off your prejudiced, sentimental view of the child. You already know that you don't know. It's not like you believed, so things are different. Not getting by, you're already looking for a way. Are you getting lost? Remember that it's no shame to wander in the enormous forest of life. Even as you wander, look about you with curiosity, and you'll behold a mosaic of beautiful images. Are you suffering? The truth is born in pain.

8. Be yourself; seek your own path. Know yourself before wanting to know children. Come to terms with what you're capable of before you begin plotting the extent of the children's rights and responsibilities. Of them all, you yourself are the child you must first get to know, raise, and educate.

One of the nastiest errors is to believe that pedagogy is the science of the child, and not of the human being.

Stirred up, a violent child would hit, where the violent adult would kill. A kindhearted child is swindled out of a toy, where the adult is swindled out of a signature on a promissory note. A frivolous child would buy sweets with the ten zlotys given her for a notebook, where an adult would lose his entire estate at cards. There are no children – they're people, only with a different range of concepts, with a different store of experiences, different drives, a different play of emotions. Remember that we do not know them.

Immature!

Ask an old man, he'll take you, at forty years old, for still immature. Hey, whole social classes are immature, since they're weak. Entire peoples require someone else's care – they're immature, too, because they don't have cannons.

Be yourself, and make careful observation of children just when they can be themselves. Observe them, and don't make demands. For you will not force a lively, aggressive child to be quiet and focused; a distrustful and surly one will not become sincere and outgoing; a proud and willful one is not going to be gentle and submissive.

And what about you?

If you don't have an imposing bearing and a powerful chest, you will struggle in vain to quiet the crowd's roar with a sonorous voice. You have a nice smile and patient eyes: don't say anything – maybe they'll settle down on their own? Seek your own path.

Don't demand of yourself that you be a serious, mature caregiver already, with a psychological ledger in your heart and pedagogical code in your head. You have a wonderful wizardly ally – youth – yet you're appealing to a grouchy slouch – experience.

9. Not "what should be," but "what can be."

You want to be loved by the children, but you have to press them into the tight, stifling forms of modern life, modern hypocrisy, modern violence – in conscientious, obligatory, required labor. They don't want it, they defend themselves, they have to resent you.

You want them to be honest and well-raised when the worldly forms are deceptive, and honesty is audacity. The boy whom you asked why he was sad yesterday – do you know what he was thinking? He was thinking, "Leave me alone." He's already being dishonest; he didn't say what he was thinking; he merely withdrew hostilely, and even that hurt you.

One shouldn't complain, backbiting is nasty – yet how will you acquaint yourself with their affairs, pains, sins?

Not punishing, and not rewarding. But there have to be both a rule and a signal that must be obeyed. The bell has to gather all of them for lunch – but if they're late, if they don't arrive, if they're unwilling?

You have to be a model. But how do you defend against your own flaws, vices, quirks? Do you try to conceal them? You'll no doubt succeed: the more carefully you conceal them, the more carefully the children will pretend they don't see them, don't know about them. And they will make fun of you only in the quietest whisper.

Difficult, even very difficult – sure. But everyone has difficulties, and still, there are different ways of resolving them. The answer will be only relatively precise. For life is not a collection of arithmetic problems, where there is always just one answer, and at most two means of arriving at it.

10. Securing the freedom of children to develop all their spiritual powers harmoniously, extracting the fullness of their latent strengths, raising them to venerate the good, beauty, and liberty... You're naive – just try it. Society has given you a little savage so that you'll hew him, shape him, make him easily digestible – and it's waiting. The state, the church, the future employer – they're all waiting. They demand, wait, keep watch. The state demands stately patriotism, the church churchly faith, the job-giver honesty, and everyone mediocrity and humility. It will break whoever's too strong, it

will mistreat the quiet, it will sometimes bribe the perverse, it will always bar the way of the poor: "it" who? No one: life.

You think that the child is of little value. An orphan – a fledgling fallen from its nest: she'll die, no one will notice, her grave will grow over with weeds. Try – you'll see, it'll make you cry. Read the history of Prévost's refuge for children in the free French Republic.[30]

The child has a right to want, to speak up, to demand – she has a right to grow and mature and, having matured, to bear fruit. And the aim of childrearing: don't make noise, don't wear out your shoes, listen to and carry out orders, don't criticize, but believe that all things aim exclusively toward your best interest.

Harmony, an easy tempo, freedom – this is a commandment: love thy neighbor. Have a look at the world – smile.

11. The new ward.

You've clipped and trimmed his nails, washed him up, changed his clothes, and now he's like everyone else.

Now he even knows how to bow, he doesn't say "I want," but "please"; when a stranger enters, he knows that he is supposed to greet him. Now he will declaim a little poem at the recitation, he'll wipe his muddy shoes; he doesn't spit on the floor, he uses a tissue.

Don't deceive yourself that you've erased the dark recollections from his memory, the poor influences and painful experiences. The clean and cleanly dressed will long remain crumpled, aching, weathered – there are unclean wounds that one must patiently dress for months, and then scars still remain, always ready to fester anew.

The orphan's facility is a clinic where you encounter all manner of illness of body and soul in a weakly resistant organism, where a sickly inheritance delays and hinders one's recovery. And if the orphanage will not be a moral rehabilitation center, it is in danger of being a hotbed of infection.

You've bolted the orphanage's doors, but you won't be able to keep the evil whisper of the street from seeping in, the unfiltered and brutal voices that no moralizing prayer will drown out. The caregiver can lower his eyes and pretend not to know, but the children will know all the more wickedly.

12. You say: I consent to compromises, I accept the child material as life brings it to me, I humble myself before the necessary work conditions, though they are very difficult. But I demand freedom in the little things, help and assistance in the actual technique of the work.

Naive: you cannot demand anything.

Your superior will fault you for the scraps of paper scattered on the floor, the little scatterbrain who's bumped her head, for the smocks not being clean enough, and the beds not made up neatly enough.

You want to remove a child, have regarded it as necessary for the good of the others. They ask you not to expel her: maybe she'll improve?

It's cold in the rooms, and the majority of your anemic children have frostbitten fingers. Coal, heat – these are expensive, but chill withers them physically and spiritually. No, the children have to toughen up.

You're surprised two eggs have yielded less than a full spoonful of omelet. You hear the curt reply that it's not your forte.

Your colleague certainly knew where the key to the cupboard was, maybe he'd hidden it himself, he'd deliberately let you look for it. When he goes out in the evening, he leaves the dormitory unattended; he doesn't let you peak in on his room, his children.

The despotic whim and ignorance of authority, the dishonesty of the administration, the ill will and negligence of a coworker. Add: the crudeness of the staff, the fight with the laundress over a thrown sheet, as if you'd done it, with the cook over the scalded milk, with the custodian over the sullied stairs.

If a caregiver will find favorable work conditions, all the better. If just these, may he not be surprised or indignant, but apportion his powers and energy judiciously – for a longer haul than the first few months.

13. A bird's-eye view of the orphanage.

Prattle, movement, youth, merriment.

Such a pleasant little country of naive little people.

So many children, and so clean.

The harmony of the uniform they wear, the rhythm of the choral singing.

At the signal, they all fall silent. Prayer, they sit at their tables. Neither scuffles, nor arguments.

A cheery face will flit by, smiling eyes will flicker. One of them is so gaunt – poor thing.

The caregiver is gentle, calm. Some kid had run up with a question; he's responded. From a distance, he threatened someone jokingly with his finger – "Yes, sir!" A small flock of the most loyal surround you in a tight circle.

"How do you like it here?"

"Good."

"Do you love the person in charge of you?"

They laugh, they lower their heads coyly.

"It's rude not to answer when you're asked. Do you love him?"

"We do."

Pleasant work, a thankful task. Minor worries, minor needs – the small world of children.

"Here's some gingerbread, go on."

They've given polite thanks. No one was first with outstretched hands.

14. Casual guest, look rather upon those children who keep their distance.

Somewhere in the shadow there's a gloomy one, her finger wrapped in a rag. Two older ones, whispering something with an ironic smile, follow you closely with their gaze. Several busy children don't even notice your arrival. Others are deliberately pretending to read so as not to have a pro forma question directed at them. Another takes advantage of the caregiver's being occupied to slip quietly away, to get up to no good without retribution.

There's the one who waits impatiently for you to leave because she wants to ask the caregiver for something. Another approaches on her own because she wants to be seen. Another is lying in wait in order to be the last to go up to you, only to be alone beside you, because she knows that the caregiver will say, "This is our singer, this is out little helper, this is the victim of a tragic story."

Under similar clothes beat a hundred different hearts, and each of them is another difficulty, another labor, another worry and fear.

A hundred children – a hundred people who, not at some point, not soon, not tomorrow, but already, now, today, are people. Not their little world, but the world, of values, merits, vices, aspirations, desires that are not minor, but significant, not innocent, but human.

Instead of asking whether they love an authority figure, ask how it is that they listen, that there's order, a program, and reason.

"There are no punishments…"

"Lie."

15. What are your duties? "To keep watch." If you want to be a caretaker, you can do nothing. If you're a caregiver, you have a sixteen-hour workday, without breaks, without holidays, a day consisting of work, lending itself to neither definition, nor notice, nor control, consisting of words, thoughts, feelings, whose name is – a thousand. External order, and things apparently well-arranged, making a show of training – these require only an iron fist and numerous prohibitions. And children are always the martyrs of worry about their alleged success; the most frequent harms find their source in this worry.

The caregiver knows as well as the caretaker that a child hit in the eye can go blind, that he's always in danger of breaking an arm or dislocating a leg, but he remembers that there are numerous accidents when the child nearly loses an eye, almost falls out a window, gets seriously banged up and could break a leg, whereas actual misfortunes are relatively rare, and what's most important is that it is impossible to shield children from them.

The more miserable your spiritual level, drab your moral character, great your concern for your own peace and comfort, the more prescriptions and proscriptions there will be, dictated by an ostensible concern for the children's wellbeing.

The caregiver who does not want to have unpleasant surprises, does not want to carry the responsibility for what can happen, is the children's tyrant.

16. The caregiver who tends to the children's morality becomes a tyrant.

Pathological suspicion can reach the point where it is no longer children of the opposite sex whom we will take for our enemy, nor every pair of children who move off to the side, but the child's own hands.

Some anonymous someone, somewhere, at some time, dictated a ban on keeping one's hands under the blanket.

"When I'm cold, when I'm afraid, I can't fall asleep."

If it's warm in the room, she'll uncover not just her hands, but all of her. If she's sleepy, she'll fall asleep in five minutes. How many similarly thoughtless suspicions are based on unfamiliarity with the child…

I once noticed a couple of older boys whispering something secretively as they led little ones to the water closet; after a certain time the latter came back to the room embarrassed. It took a lot of effort for me to keep sitting there and writing calmly. But the game was innocent. One of the boys (he works for a photographer) was covering a cigar box with his apron; he was placing those who wished to be photographed under the faucet installed in the wall of the water closet, and when those who were waiting motionless for the picture to be taken, a pleasant expression on their faces, at the count of three he would release a stream of cold water on their heads.

A perfect lesson for the little ones in reasonable caution; doused in water, they won't go to the water closet again at the first secretive whisper.

Caregiver, you who watch too one-sidedly over the children's morality, I worry that you yourself are not alright.

17. The theoretician divides children into categories according to temperament, intellectual type, likes; the practitioner knows that children are first of all easy and not-easy – average, the ones you need not concern yourself with, and exceptional, the ones who take up a lot of time.

Not-easy: the youngest, less than the average age, the oldest: they're critical and willful; the awkward, the languid and frail, the violent and impudent.

The child who is already growing weary, who has outgrown the rigors of the orphanage, who is humiliated by the general rules of the dormitory, the cafeteria, of prayer, play, a stroll.

The child who has stuff coming out of his ear, who's gotten a sore, whose fingernail is peeling off, whose eyes water, whose head hurts, who's running a fever, who has a cough.

The child who dresses slowly, washes slowly, combs his hair slowly, eats slowly. His is the last bed to be made, his towel the last to be hung up, you have to wait for his plate or mug; he delays cleaning the dormitory, clearing the table, sending the dishes to the kitchen.

The child who turns to you every moment with a question, a complaint, a grievance, a lament, doesn't enjoy the other children's company, clings to you importunately, always has something he doesn't know, asks for something, needs something, has something important to say.

The child who has answered roughly, has insulted a member of the staff, has gotten into an argument, into a fight, thrown a stone, deliberately broken or torn something, says that he doesn't want to.

The sensitive and finicky one who finds pain in a minor remark, a surly look, the punishment of cool indifference.

The kind prankster who will clog your sink with pebbles, who will swing on your door, twist off the faucet handle, shut the flue, unscrew the bell, doodle on the wall in blue pencil, scratch the windowsills with a nail, carve letters into the table. He's murderously inventive and unpredictable.

These are the plunderers of your time, the tyrants of your patience, the ferment of your conscience. You struggle with them, and you know it's not their fault.

18. The children rise at six o'clock. All you have to say to them is: "Get up, children." That's all.

In actual fact, if you tell a hundred children to get up, the eighty easy ones get up, get dressed, get washed, are ready for the next announcement, that of the morning's breakfast. But for eight children you have to repeat it twice; for five of them, three times: get up. You have to yell at three. Two you have to wake up yourself. One has a headache: is she sick, or maybe pretending?

Ninety children get dressed, but you have to help out two, because they won't manage. One has misplaced his sock garter, one has a cold-stiffened finger and can't put on his shoe. One has gotten a knot in his shoelace. Someone keeps someone else from making his bed. Someone doesn't want to hand over the soap, another jostles or splashes while washing, has switched towels, pours water on the floor. He's put his right shoe on his left foot, can't button up his smock because a button's popped off; someone has taken his top, it was there a minute ago. Someone is crying: that's his basin, that's the one he always uses to wash up – but today that other kid got there first.

Eighty children devoured five minutes' time, ten swallowed up a minute, and you were busy with two for almost half an hour.

It will be the same tomorrow, only another one will lose something, another will feel unwell, another will do a poor job making his bed.

It will be the same in a month, in a year, in five years.

19. All you had to say was: "Get up, children" – nothing more. And yet you wouldn't have managed.

You wouldn't have managed if one of the easy children hadn't found a misplaced sock garter or top, a second hadn't brought spare slipper for a chilly foot, a third hadn't untied a knot.

Because the sock garter was so hidden that one had to crawl under the bed for it, the slipper had to be brought in from a distant room, and your assistant was working on the knot for a long time, first with a fingernail, then a tooth, then a small nail he'd found yesterday, and finally with a crochet hook borrowed for this purpose.

You cannot help but notice that one of the children more often loses, another more often finds; one makes knots, the other unties them. One is often sick, the other always well. One requires your help, the other provides it. Let's assume you don't wish ill upon the first, you don't feel gratitude toward the second.

But today the one who'd talked long into the evening in the dormitory is having a hard time getting up. But the younger one has done a better job making his bed than the older one. But the one who's throat hurts had drunken water from the tap, though you'd warned him that the water is cold, and he's sweaty. Work out for yourself what you'll say, though you know, understand, are resigned, forgive.

For the more of these difficult children there are, the more of your sixteen hours of daily work will be swallowed up by shuffling around, bustling, grumbling, and the less will remain for the sublime, the lofty – read: "The caregiver should."

Less time and less strength…

20. The help that the children render to the caregiver may be completely selfless. She helps because she wants to, she helps because she wants to today, it says nothing about tomorrow.

But this little helper, finicky, ambitious, and honest, will not take every activity upon herself. She will be easily disheartened when she encounters unexpected difficulties, she will get offended when the caregiver shows dissatisfaction; she has doubts, so she asks, she demands inspections and instructions. She won't force her pesky help on you; you have to seek her out, bolster her, encourage her; when you ask her, she'll do it eagerly, when you order her, she won't want to. You cannot depend on her, because she can disappoint just when she's most needed.

The caretaker will have no difficulty finding another little helper among the children. Clever, energetic, impudent, insincere, and self-interested, he will impose his help on you, spurned he will return, when needed he'll pop up out of nowhere, he'll guess your wish from a look, he'll carry out every order, he'll take on everything.

If he does a bad job, he'll weasel out of it, lie; berated, he'll feign humility. He'll always report back: "Everything's fine."

If he doesn't grasp the "minor" affairs and concerns of children, the unconscientious, incompetent, or exhausted caregiver will surrender his authority to such a child hall monitor, the hall monitor will take over, replace him without a problem. From the child who will seek, summon, bring, tidy up, babysit, remind – he knows, has heard, will say – a genuine substitute will soon be made.

This is not the innocent bootlicker of school, but the dangerous staff sergeant of the dormitory/barracks.

21. The hall monitor has an easier time getting on with the pack than the adult does. For the adult in charge, if he strikes someone, it's not with full force, if he threatens, it's with a certain restraint, if he punishes, it's for an offence. But the child hall monitor strikes not the back, but the head or stomach, because then it will hurt more; he threatens not with a punishment, but with something that is ostensibly naive: "You wait, when you're asleep at night I'm going to butcher you with a switchblade"; in the coldest of blood he'll accuse the innocent and force him to confess to a crime he never committed: "Tell them it was you who ate it, took it, broke it" – and the little kid, trembling, says, "I broke it, I stole it."

The great majority of children fear him more than they do the caregiver, because the hall monitor knows everything, because he's with them constantly. The recalcitrant ones hate him, rarely avenge themselves, more often they pay him off.

Now the little tyrant already has his own helpers and substitutes. He no longer does anything himself, he just gives orders, informs on the recalcitrants, and answers for everything to the authorities.

One must draw a clear distinction: this is not a favorite, not the caregiver's pet, he's a genuine helper, factotum, right-hand man. He sees to his master's comfort, his master tolerates him – because he knows that he lies, deceives, exploits, but he cannot get by without him, and anyway, he's holding out for a better job.

22. Insidious and mysterious threats replace prohibited fights, which are overt and noisy:

"You wait, I'm going to tell on you. You wait, I'll get you back tonight."

These are the magical spells by which the clever yet perverse one forces the younger, weaker, dumber, the more honest into silence, submission, humility.

The lavatory and dormitory – these are the two open grounds where secrets are exchanged, where the institution's conspiratorial life is concentrated. And caregivers err in thinking that the dormitory and lavatory require only one kind of vigilance.

I know of a case where a boy crept into his enemy's bed at night and pinched him, pulled at his ears, his hair, warning him:

"Be quiet. If you scream and wake him up, you'll get kicked out."

I know of a case where a boy had water poured deliberately on his bed at night so that the caretaker would cover it in a shameful oilcloth.

I know of a case where the hall monitor would trim her unpopular peers' fingernails until they bled. Another monitor deliberately poured a cold bath for a boy he was on bad terms with.

The terrorism of evil powers can take root in the orphanage, poisoning the atmosphere, spreading moral epidemics, causing havoc and harm. And it is just in an atmosphere of lying, coercion, suppression, pressure, violence, of quiet battles, false denunciations, of fear and silence, in an atmosphere saturated with the miasma of moral decay that epidemics of self-abuse and criminal acts arise.

And the caregiver, having fallen into a similar cesspool, flees, and if he cannot flee, he withholds any mention.

23. Children quickly discern that the caretaker hides things from his superiors, that those who have won praise gain his affections, while those on whose account the caretaker has heard a sardonic remark fall into disfavor.

There is a quiet compact between the caretaker and the children: we will mutually pretend that things are as good as they can be, we will conceal it when "one of those things" happens.

And now little reaches the ears of the director-in-chief in his cloistered office, and nothing leaks out beyond the facility walls. The children commit a string of illicit and reprehensible acts, and he tolerates them through his bumbling or malicious neglect.

Perhaps this is why the children in the orphanage are so timid and quiet, why they are eager to respond only to banal questions – "How are you? Do you listen?" – and they maintain their discreet silence when they could "give it away." Might this be why the orphanage has a whiff of dark secrets about it, and a conversation with a child who exchanges momentary glances with his caregiver is awkward and unpleasant?...

In the third part of this book I will say how, in organizing the Orphans' Home[31], we secured the children's help without fear of poor outcomes, how we introduced openness into the life of the orphanage.

24. A day of ordinary worry and draining bustle has its easy children and its difficult ones, and the day of a visitation or festive fair has them as well.

For the caregiver who leads them in song, the easy child is the one with the most resounding voice; for the caregiver-gymnast, it's the most nimble. The first is thinking of an exemplary choir, the second of a public tournament.

Children who are capable, polite, brave – they do the house's honors during formal visits, they represent the institution well, they reflect well on the caregiver; and the pretty child will give the bouquet to the honored guest.

Can the caregiver not be grateful to them? What if she sang, played the violin, performed her role imaginatively in the little sketch? He can't take credit for that. And the conscientious, scrupulous caregiver, committing a violation against himself, conceals his warm feelings.

Is this appropriate? Can feigned indifference deceive, and if it does, doesn't that cause harm? For the child this is an important day, ceremonious, memorable; a bit bewildered, more alarmed, among strangers, numerous honored guests, she runs to the one who is closest to her because she values his praise above anyone else's, she demands it, she has a right...

Do not let it go to their heads, but you have to give them some recognition...

But then what happens to the rule about the absolute equality of all the children? That rule is a lie, after all.

25. The caregiver-practitioner has children toward whom he has warm feelings, they reward him for the hardships he endures, they are the children dearest to his own heart – beloved quite independently of their worth or the benefit they bring.

Nice, because he's cute; nice, because he's cheerful, because he' happy, because he's charming, because he smiles; nice, because he's quiet, serious, focused, and sulky; nice, because he's small, clumsy, absent-minded; nice, because he's critical, bold, and rebellious.

Depending on the spiritual character and ideals of the caregiver, different children are close or dear to different people.

One impresses with his energy, another moves with his kindness, a third arouses memories of one's own childhood, a fourth a wistful concern for his future, in a fifth it's the high flight that arouses anxiety, in a sixth it's the meek apprehensiveness. And among these many nice children there's one you love most dearly, whom you wish the best, whose tears sting you the most, whose good will you most strive for, who you want never to forget you.

How did this happen? When? You don't know. It came suddenly, unbidden, unexpectedly – like love.

Don't hide it: your smile, tone of voice, your gaze will give you away.

And the remaining children? Do not worry, they won't hold it against you; they have their favorites, too.

26. Young and tender caregivers are inclined to love the quietest ones, apprehensive in a crowd, with sad eyes and a soul filled with longing. They turn toward these forgotten ones, in shadow, with fervent affection, they desire to win their trust, they wait to be taken into their confidence. What does she feel, what is she thinking about, this tired-winged angel?

The children in general are surprised. What's there to love when she's so stupid? The favorite, long since passed over as a nothing, at most shoved aside when she stood in the way – now they follow her consciously and deliberately. They envy her, because the choice was ill-conceived.

The caregiver is initiating an asymmetrical battle for his favorite – and is losing. Recognizing his error, he tries to push her ever so slightly away. She's understood, moved away, she looks sadly, as if reproachfully, with her moist eyes. The caregiver suffers: he gets angry at himself and at the children.

O Poet, if only you knew that this poetic child has but one secret in those great big eyes with the long lashes – the secret of being burdened with tuberculosis – instead of waiting to be taken into a confidence you might rather wait for a cough, instead of kisses you might provide guaiacol oil. And you would spare her, yourself, and the children many unpleasant moments.

27. It happens that your love for a child is not reciprocated. He wants to play ball, or race, or war, and you wish to caress him, cuddle him, pet him. This angers him, he grows impatient, humiliated – and either he withdraws from these unnecessary affections or casts his arms around your neck and asks for new clothes. It's your fault, not his.

It happens that a couple members of staff vie for the favor of a single child; the little darling then cunningly maneuvers so as not to offend anyone.

For you'll let him go to bed later, the housekeeper will replace the torn stockings, and the cook will treat him to an apple or raisins.

It happens that a sensuous or depraved child finds satisfaction in caresses. He likes to stroke an arm because it's so very cuddly, he'll say he likes how your hair smells, he'll kiss you on the ear or neck or on each of your beloved little fingers in turn. Keep your eyes wide open: these are lecherous caresses.

Erotic feelings are alive in the child. Nature has prescribed that life grow and multiply; this law encompasses mankind, animal, plant. Sexual feeling does not grow suddenly and out of nowhere; it still lies dormant, but you already hear its quiet breathing. And there are movements, and embraces, and kisses, and children's games that are secretly or openly sensual.

But the caregiver need not raise his eyes to heaven or drop his hands dumbstruck, nor distance himself in outrage.

Give the life of the child momentum so that he not grow bored, allow him to run and make noise, sleep only as much as he feels like, and his sexual feeling will calmly sprout, neither sullying, nor causing harm.

28. The probing eye of science has discerned the root of sexuality in the affection of the parents. The mother who nurses her baby submits to this as much as the father does when he brings his dead child's cold hands to his lips.

Innocently stroking the child's face or hair, tucking her in under her blanky, even praying for her happiness beside her cradle's headboard as she is quietly sleeping, these are a normal manifestation of healthy erotic feeling, and leaving the child in the servants' care, finding a higher satisfaction in the airy chatter of the café – these are its atrophy.

For atrophied, blunted senses, these affections, are too gentle and already imperceptible. Here the mother must shower the child's little feet, back, and belly with kisses in order to experience the affection that a light touch would give a healthy mother. The decently sensuous does not suffice – she requires the lascivious.

You're surprised? You don't want to believe it? Maybe I have said what you have sensed, suspected, but angrily rejected?

Because you do not know that the reproductive instinct, in its manifold stirrings, oscillates between the most sublime creative stimulus and the most shameful crime.

You must appreciate the affection you harbor for children and keep watch over it, because the children can also deprave you, who are not only raising the children but are yourself raised by them.

The four walls of a house, school, orphanage – they conceal dark secrets. At times a criminal scandal casts a flash of lightning on them for a moment. And, again, darkness.

In the sanctioned violations that modern childrearing permits itself to perform against the souls of children – in bondage, in secret, in unappealable authority – there must lurk both lawlessness and crime.

29. The caregiver-apostle. The future of the nation. The happiness of future generations.

But where is my own life in this? My own past, my own happiness, my own heart?

I hand out my ideas, advice, admonitions, feelings, I hand them out lavishly. When another child approaches every other minute, always with a new demand, request, or question, taking up your time, mind, emotion, you feel at times bad that, being the sun to this flock, you yourself grow cold – that, in shining, you yourself lose one ray after another.

It's all for the children, and what's for me?

They grow strong on knowledge, experience, moral instruction, they're filling their stock – and I'm expending. How do you keep managing the store of your own spiritual powers so as not to go bust?

Let's assume that the caregiver no longer has his youth, which calls for its rights; a family, which shackles him; material worries, which cause concern; physical ailments, which trouble. Completely devoted to the sacred matter of caregiving, he has to have affection. How is he to keep it from being shattered?

And when he returns to the home, which is supposed to be his home, unable to greet everyone sincerely, doesn't he have the right to smile at one? When he leaves the dormitory in the evening, unable to say affectionate goodbyes to them all, doesn't he at least sometimes have a right to single out one or two with a targeted "Sleep, my son, sleep, you little rascal"? In reprimanding someone for a minor infraction, doesn't he have a right to forgive more clearly with his eyes while making bitter accusations?

Even if he's mistaken, having chosen one who is not the most precious— so what? The pleasant emotion that that child provides will cover over a raft of negative ones; the caregiver will treat many to the smile received from a beloved child.

There may be caregivers to whom all children are uniformly unimportant or repugnant, but here are none to whom they would all be uniformly pleasant and dear.

30. Let's assume absolute equality. There are no easy or difficult children, no pleasant or unpleasant ones. They all receive uniform pieces of bread and portions of soup, a uniform number of sleeping and waking hours, uniform strictness and forbearance – an absolute uniformity of dress, portion, rules,

affection. Despite its clear preposterousness, let's assume this is how it should be. No privileges, no exceptions, no singling out – because that ruins everything.

And even then the caregiver has a right to make a wrong move, to take the consequences of the mistakes he's made.

Pestalozzi's[32] letters about his time in Stanz are the most beautiful work of a caregiver-practitioner.

"…one of my very favorite wards abused my love and permitted himself to make an unjustified threat against another; this infuriated me; I was quite harsh in expressing my dissatisfaction to him."[33]

Odd: the great Pestalozzi had favorites, lost his temper…

He erred, whether with excessive confidence or a surfeit of praise; and he himself was punished above all: he was disappointed.

It is sometimes amazing how quickly, how severely, the caregiver has to atone for the mistakes he's made. May he be vigilant in correcting them.

Unfortunately, sometimes with the most important problems he cannot be.

31. Stop making noise!

Children expend only part of the energy they have in their throats, their lungs, their souls, only part of the shout they have in their muscles. When they listen, they restrain it insofar as it is possible.

"Quiet" – is the noise of the classroom.

"No noise during lunch."

"No noise in the dormitory."

Children make noise so quietly it's moving, run so carefully it brings tears to the eye, so as not to shift the table they let each other slide in, they yield rather than let an argument break out or let something happen, for again they will hear the despised "No noise!"

Even in the yard you're not allowed to shout, since it bothers the neighbors. And their only crime is that every meter of land in the city costs a lot of money.

"You're not in the woods" – a cynical remark, a brutal way of bullying a child for not being able to be where he should.

Allow them to run around a meadow and there won't be any screaming, just the pleasant twitter of human birds.

A significant majority of children, if not all, like movement and commotion; their physical and moral health depends on freedom to move and shout. And you, aware of this, have to admonish them:

"Sit calmly – and quietly."

32. You are forever and always committing the same error of combating the proper resistance of the child.

"I don't want to!"

I don't want to sleep, for while the clock has struck the hour, the evening is redolent, it is smiling with a scrap of star-strewn sky. I don't want to go to school, because the first snow fell in the night, and the world has become merry. I don't want to get up, because it's cold, I'm sad. I prefer not to eat lunch, just let me finish this game of rounders. I won't beg the teacher's pardon, because she punished me unfairly. I don't want to do the assignment because I'm reading *Robinson Crusoe*. I won't put on short pants because they'll laugh at me.

You have to.

There are commands you give because you were commanded, angrily and without conviction, but you weren't allowed not to fulfil them.

Now don't listen just to me, who weighs every order before it is declared, but also to the many anonymous persons whose laws are cruel and unjust.

"Learn! Respect! Believe!"

"I don't want to" is the cry of the child's soul, and you have to suppress it because modern man lives not in the woods, but in society.

You must – otherwise, it will be chaos.

The more gently you stifle stubbornness, the better; the more swiftly and thoroughly, the less painfully you will ensure the necessary discipline of the flock: you'll achieve the minimal necessary order. And woe unto you if, being gentle, you don't manage to do this.

Without organization, let loose, only a few exceptional children can develop successfully; dozens will be wasted.

33. There are mistakes that you are always going to make because you're a person and not a machine.

Sad, exhausted, ill, embittered, you perceive in the child the quality that makes adults evil and harmful: insincerity, cool calculation, ugly haughtiness, miserable deceit, rapacious greed – will you not act too rashly?

It doesn't add up for me. Every moment another child comes in, though the children are absolutely forbidden from entering the office. The last to come in is a little lad carrying a bouquet for me as a gift: I throw the bouquet out the open window, lead him out the door by his ear.

Why add to the examples of unreasonable and brutal deeds…

But the child will forgive. He'll be offended, get angry…think it over… and very often will ascribe the fault confidently to himself. A few sensitive ones will steer clear of you when you're angry or busy. They'll forgive when they experience your kindliness.

It isn't some supernatural intuition on the part of the child that he knows who loves him, but the vigilance of a dependent creature who must know things thoroughly because his success rests in your hands. Similarly, an office-slave spends so much time observing and pondering his boss, until he knows his every habit, liking, mood, tremble of the lip, movement of the hand, glint in the eye. And he knows when to ask for a raise or a vacation, and at times he patiently waits long weeks for the right moment. Give them independence, they'll lose this perspicacity.

A child will forgive a faux pas or injustice, but will not get attached to a caregiver-pedant or cold despot. And he will spurn every insincerity with distaste, or mock it.

34. One will not avoid mistakes that flow from commonplace words, widely accepted acts, from the common attitude that children are lower creatures, insane, amusing in their naive inexperience.

You will treat their worries, wishes, questions disdainfully, jokingly, patronizingly; you will always cause some of them pain.

She has a right to demand respect for her misfortune, even if it was losing a pebble, a wish, even if it was taking a walk without a coat when there was frost outside, a seemingly preposterous question. You don't share in the loss; you cast the request aside with a terse "No"; with one "You fool" you nip doubts in the bud.

Do you know why the boy wanted to wear a cape on a hot day? Because he has an ugly patch on the knee of his pants, and the girl he loves will be in the park…

You don't have time, you can't always watch over them, meditate on it, seek out the hidden motives of a blatantly nonsensical wish, initiate yourself into the unfathomable depths of a child's logic, fantasy, search for truth – you can't always bend to the child's aspirations and tastes.

You will make these mistakes, because the only one who doesn't is the one who does nothing at all.

35. I am impulsive. Neither Olympian calm, nor philosophical equilibrium, is my lot. Too bad. What can I do about it?

When Mr. Life takes me down a peg as a steward, I get angry that the child-slave doesn't understand what I endure to get him shackles that are one link longer, one gram lighter. I see resistance where I am not allowed to yield, and as a bureaucrat I say, "You must," and as a naturalist I say, "You cannot." The farmhand in me is annoyed that the herd is running wild, the person in me is happy that the children – live. I am by turns the warden of a jail seeing to the order dictated by regulations, an equal among equals, a slave among comrades rebelling against despotic law.

When I am banging my head against some riddle that leaves me powerless, when I hear a harbinger of menacing phenomena I cannot prevent, being myself anxiety and anticipation already, seeing their carefreeness and confidence I feel raging pain or a genuine kindliness.

When I perceive in a child the immortal spark of the fire stolen from the gods, the flash of undisciplined thought, the dignity of rage, a rush of enthusiasm, the sadness of autumn, the sweetness of sacrifice, an apprehensive dignity, the courageous, joyful, confident, aggressive searching after reasons and goals, arduous attempts, a menacing reflex of the conscience – I humbly take a knee, for I am worse, weak, and a coward.

What am I to you, children, if not ballast to your free flight, the spider web to your colorful wings, the shears that have the bloody duty of mowing down lush sprouts?

I stand barring your way or bumble around helplessly, I grumble, I nag, I keep silent, I persuade falsely, uninspiring and laughable.

36. The good caregivers differ from a bad one only in the number of mistakes they make, of injuries they cause.

There are mistakes that the good caregiver makes only once and, having assessed them critically, does not repeat; he remembers the mistake he's made for a long time. If he acts unfairly, tactlessly, in exhaustion, he directs all his efforts toward automating minor, if bothersome, activities, because he knows that things go wrong for lack of time. The bad caregiver assigns blame for his own errors to the children.

The good caregiver knows it's worth thinking about a minor episode because it contains a hidden problem; he doesn't disregard it.

The good one knows what he does at the demand of a prevailing authority, a dominating church, a forceful tradition, an accepted custom, under the iron dictate of circumstance. He knows that the order has the children's best interest in mind only insofar as it teaches them to give in, submit, settle accounts, train themselves for the compromises of the future, when they will grow up.

The bad caregiver thinks that the children in fact shouldn't make noise, soil their clothes, that they should conscientiously learn little grammatical formulas by heart.

The judicious caregiver doesn't sulk over not understanding the child, but ponders, seeks, questions the children. They will teach him not to cause them too much harm – if only he wants to learn.

37. "I don't mete out punishments," the caregiver says, and sometimes he himself does not suspect not only that he does, but that they're quite severe.

There is no dark torture chamber, but there are isolation and loss of freedom. Only he'll stand you in the corner, seat you at a separate table, not allow you to visit your family. He'll take away your ball, magnet, picture, bottle of perfume – so there is forfeiture of property. He'll forbid you to go to sleep with the older children, won't let you put new clothes on for the holiday – so there's deprivation of specific rights and privileges. In the end, isn't it a punishment when I show him coolness, aversion, dissatisfaction?

You impose punishments, you've just tempered them or changed their form. The children worry about whether the punishment will be big, small, or merely symbolic. Understand: the children are afraid, so there is discipline.

One can whip the child's ego, his affection, as his body used to be whipped.

38. No punishments, I just explain that she did a bad thing.

How will you explain?

You'll say that if she doesn't straighten out, you'll be forced to expel her. Naive, you hold the death penalty over her. You're not going to expel her: the one you expelled a year ago was sick, abnormal, and this one is a healthy, nice little rascal who will grow into a courageous person; you just want to frighten her. My, even a nanny won't give a child away to a beggar, won't lead her into the woods for the wolves to eat her – for her it's just a threat, too.

You summon the tutors for a conference: that's an even more refined threat.

You threaten that she's going to sleep in the corridor, eat on the stairs, that you'll make her wear a bib; you always threaten her with a punishment one degree higher than those in use.

Sometimes the threats are incorporeal, vague:

"This is the last time I'll tell you." "You'll see, this will end badly." "You're finally going to get it." "I'm through with repeating it: you can do as you please." "Now I really am on to you." The multitude of expressions itself shows how widely they circulate and, I would add, are abused.

The child sometimes believes, always half-believes:

"What will happen to me now?"

He hasn't punished me, and if he will, then when – and how? The fear of the unknown, the unexpected.

If you have punished her, the next day she's already distanced herself from the painful experience, gotten closer to reconciliation, forgetting. Waking up the day after a verbal threat, she may have gotten closer to the moment of hard reckoning.

One can use threats to maintain the child in great discipline; with mild criticism, one can think that it is a gentle mode of operating – when a threat unfulfilled is a big punishment.

39. There is an erroneous conviction, based on superficial observation, that a child quickly forgets his sorrows, traumas, resolutions. He was just crying, and already he's laughing. They were only just fighting, already they're playing together. An hour ago he'd promised he'd do better, and he's misbehaving again.

That's not how it is: children remember a trauma for a long time; he'll remind you about an injury sustained a year ago. He doesn't keep the promise you forced out of him because he cannot.

He runs and plays because he's allowed himself to be seized by the general merriment, but he will return again to worry-filled thoughts – when it's quiet, with a book, in the evening before falling asleep.

At times you perceive that some child is avoiding you. He doesn't approach with a question, doesn't smile as he's passing by, doesn't come into your room.

"I thought you were still angry," he'll respond when asked.

With difficulty, you recall that the week before, because of a minor infraction, you'd said something relatively unpleasant to him in a relatively raised voice. And the child, ambitious or sensitive, has spent many unpleasant moments in silence, unseen.

The child remembers.

A widow in deep mourning will forget herself in a humorous conversation and burst into loud laughter; suddenly she will sigh, "Oh, I'm laughing, but my poor late husband." Because she knows she has to. You will soon teach the children this art; give one a strict scolding for being cheerful when he should be sad and broken – he'll obey. It happens that I've often seen one who was taking an active part in a game suddenly assume a distressed look after meeting my surly gaze. "Oh, right, you shouldn't have fun when they're angry with you."

Remember that there are children who feign indifference: do not think that he is afraid, worried, that he remembers. If the punishment was calculated to humiliate them, honor dictates precisely not to make a fuss over it. It is children who feel perhaps most acutely and remember for a long time.

40. There are no punishments, only berating, admonition, words. But if this word conceals a readiness to shame…

"Just look at the state of your notebook. Do you know what you're like? You've done a fine job. Everyone look what he's done."

And the audience, one's comrades, they have a duty to smile ironically, to express amazement, contempt. Not all of them do it; the fairer they are, the more restrained they are in expressing an unflattering judgment.

There are other kinds of punishment – constant disdain and demeaning resignation:

"You still haven't finished eating? You're the last one again? You've forgotten again?"

A reproachful look, throwing up one's hands, a sigh of despair.

Feeling guilty, the delinquent hangs his head, sometimes full of rebellion and disgust he glares from under his brow at the pack antagonizing him, only to settle the score with whomever he needs to in a free moment.

"Give me that," one of the boys would say more often than the others.

I rebuked him for the nasty habit in a rather severe way. A year later, when I was noting the nicknames that had been given to the children, I heard an echo of my own tactless speech: among the others, the boy had the most painful nickname: "Gimme That the Beggar."

Ridicule is a serious, painful punishment.

41. You appeal to their emotions.

"This is how you show your love for me? You make a promise, and this is how you keep it?"

A gentle request, a sincere reproach, a kiss as a deposit on an improvement you've demanded, finally the forcing out of a new promise.

And you leave the child with an affection that is heavy on his soul: obligated by kindness, by magnanimous forgiveness, feeling his own helplessness, oftentimes not believing in the possibility of improvement, he renews his pledge, he resolves once again to fight a decisive battle against his impetuousness, laziness, absentmindedness – against himself.

"And what if I forget again, am late, hit someone, give an impertinent answer, lose something?"

At times a kiss places heavier shackles than a switch does.

Have you not noticed: if a child does something once after promising to be better, pay attention, for the first infraction will be followed by a second, and a third.

It is the pain of the defeat he has suffered and an aversion toward the caregiver that has forced him, with a promise extracted deceitfully, into unequal battle. You will renew the exasperating appeal to his conscience, his affection – he'll spurn you violently.

You respond to his anger with stormy anger – shouting. The child doesn't listen, he only feels that you are casting him out of your heart, you're withdrawing your kindness. Alien, alone – he's deserted. And you, elated, impose all the punishments: threatening, and reproach, and mockery, and actual repressions.

See how compassionately his comrades look at him, how gently they try to cheer him up:

"He was only talking. Don't be afraid, it's nothing. Don't worry, he'll forget."

And all of it cautiously so as not to fall into the caregiver's bad graces, not to get it from the rebellious victim.

Whenever I have made a "big scene," besides disgust I have experienced clear affection; I have wronged one, but I have taught many a great virtue: solidarity in misfortune. The little slaves know how it hurts.

42. Sometimes, while reprimanding a child, you read a hundred rebellious thoughts in her eyes.

"Maybe you think I've forgotten. I remember everything just fine."

The child, poorly faking remorse, tells you with a hostile look, *It's not my fault you have such a good memory.*

I: "I've been patient. I was waiting for you perhaps to straighten out."

She: *That's a real shame. There was no need to wait.*

I: "I thought you would finally come to your senses. I was wrong."

She: *If you're so smart, you shouldn't be wrong.*

I: "You think that because I forgive you you can do whatever you want?"

She: *That's not what I think at all. When is this finally going to be over?*

I: "I can't keep putting up with you any longer."

She: *Blah, blah, you're bristling with rage today, so you're picking on me...*

Sometimes in the tumult the child maintains an amazing stoicism.

"How many times have I told you not to jump on the beds?" I fume. "The beds are not for playtime. That's what we have balls and puzzles for..."

"And what are puzzles?" he inquires curiously.

For that he got a slap on the wrist...

Another time, after a tumultuous conversation, I was asked:

"Sir, why is it that a person turns red when he gets mad?"

While I was straining my voice and mind to set him on the path of virtue, he was closely following the play of colors on my face in my fit of passion. I gave him a kiss: he was charming.

43. Children rightly despise being accused as a group.

"One cannot be kind to the lot of you... Again, you've... If you all don't straighten out..."

Why do they all have to answer for the guilt of one or a few?

If a little cynic has given cause for fury, he'll be satisfied: instead of receiving the whole portion of rage, he has received just a fraction. A decent one will be wounded too harshly, seeing so many innocent victims of his crime.

Sometimes reprimands fall upon a certain group of children: the boys are worthless, or the opposite – the girls are exceptionally immoral, most often "the older kids, instead of giving an example… Look how well-behaved the little ones are."

Here, besides the justifiable anger of the innocent, we cause the embarrassment of those we praise, who know their own numerous sins, remember how they themselves have been pilloried. Ultimately we achieve the evil triumph of the little scoffers: "Ha, now you've done it!"

I once wanted to react exceptionally solemnly to an unexplained theft. I went into the boys' dormitory, where they were already falling asleep, and, rhythmically beating the bedrail, said in a sonorous voice:

"Another theft. This has to end. Raising thieves is a waste of work…"

I repeated this same, rather long speech in the girls' dormitory.

The following day the boys had a conversation with the girls:

"And he yelled at you, too?"

"He sure did."

"He said he'd have everybody expelled?"

"He did."

"And he banged his fist on the bed?"

"With all his might."

"And whose bed was it? Because with us it was Maniusia's."

Whenever I have accused them as a group, I have saddened the most good-natured and annoyed them all, I have made a fool of myself in the eyes of the critical ones: "It's nothing, let him get a little angry – it's healthy."

44. Doesn't the caregiver understand that a significant percentage of the punishments are unjust?

A scuffle.

"He hit me first." "Because he was annoying me… He took it and didn't want to give it back." "I was only joking… He butted in, he messed it up." "No I didn't, he pushed me."

And so you punished either both of them (why?), or the older one, who is supposed to yield to the younger one (why?), or the one who, by simple accident, caused the greater hurt or harm. You punished, because fighting's not allowed. Is tattling?

He spilled it, knocked it over, broke it.

"It was unintentional."

He repeats your own statements: you tell them to forgive if they cause harm unintentionally.

"I didn't know... I thought you could."

He was late because... She knows how, but...

You cast aside the right reasons as excuses. That's a double injustice: you have both disbelieved him, though he's telling the truth, and you have punished him unjustly.

Sometimes the case makes a relative prohibition absolute. Sometimes it stops being a prohibition.

One is not allowed to make noise in the dormitory, but one is allowed to converse in a lowered voice. If you're cheerful, you will yourself burst out laughing at an innocent prank; when you're tired, you'll rebuke them for the usual dormitory chatter, albeit only with a harsh remark:

"That'll be enough talk already... Not one more word ... Whoever speaks again..."

One is not allowed to enter the office, but children do. It happens that today is monthly bookkeeping – you need peace. He didn't know, so he walked in and got a licking. Even if he hadn't been led out by the ear, if he were only told, "What are you doing in here? Get out of my sight this instant" – your anger would still be an undeserved punishment.

45. While playing ball he shattered a windowpane; you forgave him, because windows rarely get broken, because you don't know who was actually to blame, because you don't like to punish.

But when the fourth window is broken, when the guilty party is the chronic prankster, who furthermore has the sin of a poor grade in school, you punish him with yelling, threatening, exasperation.

"It was by accident," he responds boldly, and as far as you're concerned – proudly.

A fourth window... prankster... bad student... loafer... and he answers proudly besides... Caregiver, I assure you that you will rap his knuckles. After all, the child cannot understand – and has no need to reconcile himself with the fact – that you have punished him as an example, that he, being less sensitive, is a suitable medium for applying a more effective punishment, that you have not meted out this punishment for this one fact, but for the totality of what he has done.

He knows that you forgave child A, B, C, but you have punished him unfairly...

You go another way: you've taken a ball away.

"No more ball."

Unfair: the punishment affects dozens of innocent children.

Gentler still: you announce that if a window is broken again, then you'll take the ball away: you're using the punishment unfairly, threatening everyone when there were four guilty.

And of these four not all of them are guilty, because one shattered the window, which was already a little cracked; a second didn't shatter the whole thing, just a little corner; the third really did break it, but he had been pushed; and the truly guilty one was the fourth, who will always do the sort of thing that makes his caregiver angry.

46. You have forgiven unconditionally. You believe that you have done the right thing. You're wrong.

"If I had done that," one thinks.

"He can do whatever he likes," thinks another, "because he likes him so much."

Unfair again.

There are children for whom furrowing your brow, a harsh remark, or a gentle "You've upset me" is sufficient punishment. If you want to forgive him, the children must understand why you're doing it, and let the child understand that he's not allowed to do more than the others. Otherwise he runs rampant, you'll spoil him, leave him prey to a pack that's gotten a taste of their rights. You'll be mistaken: both he, and the children, are meting punishment out to you.

Forget for a moment about the four broken windows (and really just two, because one was already cracked, and a second only lost a little corner). Forget it, have a look around at how many groups are pondering and remarking on the mishap. In each group, someone else is shaping opinion, to your advantage or not.

The right wing states that windowpanes are expensive, that you're going to have trouble from the board, because they're going to say that you're too good, and the children don't listen to you, and there's no order: the punishment should have been more severe.

The left wing (supporters of playing ball):

"You're not allowed to play anything – they prohibit everything. As soon as somebody does something, right away there's shouting, threatening, fighting. But it's not like we can sit all day like painted dolls."

Only the center accepts everything with confidence and resignation.

Don't smile indulgently: it's not a joke, not a trifle – it's the actual life of children in barracks.

So renounce punishments once and for all, fundamentally and in all cases, and give the children total freedom?

And if a willful individual child limits the rights of the community? The willful one does not learn himself and hinders the others, he won't make his own bed and will dishevel others', he'll misplace his own coat and put on someone else's – what then?

47. "Complaining is nasty. I don't permit complaining."

But what should a child do if someone steals from him, disrespects his father or mother, badmouths him to his friends, threatens him, talks him into something bad?

It's nasty to complain. Who sanctified this principle? Did children receive it from bad caregivers, or did caregivers get it from bad children? Because it's a convenient principle – for bad people, for the worst.

The quiet and helpless will be wronged, exploited, robbed – and they won't be allowed to call for help or demand justice. The wrongdoers triumph, the wronged suffer.

For the unconscientious, clumsy caregiver, it's convenient not to know what's happening among the children, because he disdains their arguments, because he doesn't know how to weigh them judiciously.

"It would be best for them to settle it themselves." And here, where it is a matter of his own convenience, his confidence in the children extends so far that he believes in their reason, experiences, and fairness, that in so important an area he leaves them with the freedom to act.

Freedom? Well, no: they're not allowed to fight, not allowed to argue, you don't even allow them to exclude each other from games, you won't let them withdraw from one. He got angry and just doesn't want to sleep next to him, doesn't want to sit at his table or walk beside him. So appropriate, so natural a demand – is not allowed.

The children are quarrelsome? Untrue. They are both amicable and understanding. Just take a serious look at the conditions of their work and cohabitation. Try planting forty office clerks in the same room, keep them five hours on uncomfortable benches, doing responsible work under a supervisor's constant, watchful eye: they'll scratch each other's eyes out.

Listen closely to the children's complaints, examine them, and you'll find ways to assuage and find compensation for more than one problem. My neighbor bumped the exposed corner of my notebook, making an ugly line across the middle of the page, or the nib tore into the paper, spraying ink. – The class's most frequent complaint.

48. The complaints of school recess have a special character.

"He doesn't let me play, he butts in…"

Recess brings certain children to a state of wild half-consciousness. They run, jump, jostle: mindless screaming, pointless movements, irresponsible deeds. A child runs aimlessly, pushes those who are walking, swings her arms, lets out shouts, finally knocks into whoever's there. Pay attention to how often the one who has been pushed or knocked into turns away angrily, doesn't say anything, steps aside.

There are children who won't leave the kid who gets picked on for no reason in peace. "Go away, leave me alone" – for them, this is the signal not to go away. The children don't like them, and they despise their lack of ambition and tact – and they're the ones who bring the complaint.

"We're having fun, but then he... Please, he's always... When we start playing, right away he..."

The complainant is in a fit of rage ("seething"), her tone of voice evidences her despair. Recess is brief, every precious minute is wasting, and he's souring it, stealing their moments of liberty.

Remember that the child, all out of patience, helpless, not wanting to fight, only turns to you as a last resort. She loses time uselessly, exposes herself to a careless or harsh response. You must have a reflexive, habitual opinion – it will save you the work of thinking.

"He's butting in?" I ask. "Tell him to come here."

Often that's the end of it. It was a matter of driving the nuisance away: seeing that his friend is going to complain, he's hidden, so the goal has been achieved.

If the complainant comes back – "He doesn't want to come over" – then I say threateningly, "Tell him to get over here this instant."

On the whole the children complain rarely and quite reluctantly. If a certain number of them complain quite often, one ought to investigate and think over why. You will never know the children while having contempt for their complaints.

49. "Sir, can I, may I, will you let me?"

It seems to me that the caregiver who doesn't like complaints is equally intolerant of requests. Wanting, however, to find the appropriate motive here, too, he leans on the principle that states:

"All children have the same rights. No exceptions, no privileges."

Is that appropriate? Perhaps it's merely convenient?

The necessity of the oft-repeated "You may not, I don't allow it, you can't" is unpleasant for a caregiver. When it seems that we've reduced the proscriptions and prescriptions to the minimum, it angers us when they demand further concessions. And at times, recognizing the appropriateness of a request, we refuse, because one request granted calls forth an entire series of requests from many children. We wish to achieve the ideal that the children recognize the need for a fixed limit and not demand more.

If, however, you will surrender to the hard duty of refusing, though hearing out their appeals, if you will note them down and file them away, you'll learn that there are very frequent, everyday requests – and those that are utterly exceptional.

Requests to switch their places at the tables were constant and exasperating. We have allowed the children to change place once a month. One could write an expansive monograph about this minor reform, given how many positive angles there were to it, and we have only the irritating requests to thank.

Woe to the children, and to the caregiver who manages to stifle every wish that is not addressed in the regulations. For it is thanks to their wishes, as it is also thanks to their complaints, that you will learn the greater part of the child-soul's secrets.

50. Besides the children who turn to the caregiver on their own business, we also have requests from their envoys.

"He's asking whether it's allowed, whether you'll let him."

These kinds of supplicants made me angry for a long time, and for many reasons:

The envoys are often those children who have enough problems of their own, whose frequent demands have already caused annoyance; they typically arrive at a bad time, when you're in a hurry, you're busy, in a bad mood, their requests are often such that the answer is clearly negative; this creates what looks like a patronage system – won't the envoy take the credit for a favorable decision?; finally, there is something like contempt in all this: come to me yourself, deign to take the trouble, and don't ask through your lawyer.

The fruitlessness of battling these kinds of requests forced us to look into the deeper causes within the phenomenon. And I discovered one.

I discovered a panhuman, and not exclusively childish, subtlety of spirit.

A brusque response does not offend the petitioner on someone else's behalf. The petitioner, and not the interested party, does not see the reluctant expression, the unpleasant grimace, the impatient movement of the hand. She just receives the refusal.

I have happened to see the actual applicant watching from a distance to see what effect her request triggers, ready to appear herself at the first summons to set out further explanations.

When we introduced a system of written agreements with the children at the Orphans' Home, the number of requests from envoys fell significantly. And we came up with a standard response:

"Have him write down what he wants and why."

51. The imperative to respond to children's questions is repeated *ex cathedra* [with complete authority] to the point of nullity. And the poor caregiver, believing it uncritically, enters into conflict with his conscience, because he cannot, he doesn't know how, he doesn't have the patience to be constantly asked, always answering. And he doesn't even suspect that the more often a brief "Don't pester me" is forced out of him, brushing the little pest off, the better a caregiver he is.

"Did I do a good job, writing, polishing my shoes, cleaning my ears?"

If the first inquires because there are doubts, those who follow desire only to draw attention to themselves, to interrupt labor once initiated, to receive superfluous praise.

There are difficult questions that are better left unanswered than brushed off with a superficial, incomprehensible explanation. He'll understand when he has studied physics, cosmography, chemistry. He'll understand when he has studied physiology. And no one knows that one, not even adults, not even your teacher – no one knows.

One ought to pay attention to the child himself, focused or superficial, the intention of the question: idle curiosity or the desire to solve a vexing puzzle, a mystery of nature, an ethical dilemma, and – finally – the possibility of answering. And my "Look it up" or "You won't understand" or "I don't know" or "Ask me in a week" or "Don't waste my time with this" will be the result of much consideration.

It is with a suspicious eye that I look at a caregiver who claims that he answers children's questions patiently. If he is not lying, then perhaps he is so alien to the children that it is only rarely and exceptionally that they come to him with their questions.

52. If complaints, requests, and questions are the key to understanding the child's soul, then the whispered confession is the wide road that leads us to it.

This is a confidence freely given several months after the fact:

"We were really mad at you, sir, he and I. So we agreed that at night one of us would go into your room through the little window, take your pince-nez, and throw it into the toilet. Then we thought it would be a waste to throw it away, that we would just hide it. We didn't sleep, we just waited till midnight. When I was already getting up to go, one of the boys woke up and went to do his business. But then later I got up again. I went in through the little window – my heart was beating hard – and the pince-nez was sitting on the table. You were asleep. So I snatched it up and hid it under my pillow. Then we got scared. Now we didn't know what to do. Then he said to put it back. So I told him to do it. But he didn't want to. So I got up again, but this time I didn't go in through the window, I just slid it through and pushed it a bit."

Knowing both of them, I know where the initiative came from, how the plan of action slowly came about, why the revenge was not brought to its conclusion.

One could devote an entire lecture to this one occurrence, it's that rich in food for thought.

53. If you smile at a child, the expected response should be a smile. If you're saying something interesting, you expect interest. You're angry, one ought to show remorse.

This means that you receive a normal reaction to a stimulus. But it can be otherwise: the child responds paradoxically. You have a right to be surprised, you ought to wonder about it, but do not get angry, do not be cross.

You approach a child in a friendly manner, he withdraws reluctantly, sometimes he is clearly avoiding you: perhaps you've wronged him, perhaps he's done wrong, done something bad – and honesty does not allow him to receive an undeserved cuddle. Note it down, inquire after a week, a month: maybe he'll forget, maybe he'll say, maybe he will reveal with a smile or embarrassment that he remembers but doesn't want to say. Respect the secret.

I once severely reprimanded the children:

"What's with this whispering around corners, cowering in class, secrets? You know I don't like it."

In response: stoic resignation, spiteful contrariness, mischievous good cheer. The clear lack of remorse was supposed to catch my attention. I didn't understand, I suspected the indecent scheming of our recalcitrants. And they were secretly rehearsing a little sketch that they'd decided to regale us with. I still blush today at the thought of how very funny I must have been in my foul temper.

54. "My child keeps no secrets from me – she entrusts all her thoughts to me," a mother says.

I don't believe it would be so, but I do believe that she demands it – and is wrong.

Example:

The child sees a funeral outside. A solemn procession, lanterns, gravity. A child in mourning is walking behind the casket: in a crepe-trimmed dress, she is a participant in a ritual filled with mysterious poetry. And a fleeting thought occurs to her: that must be pleasant; if only mommy would die... She looks terror-stricken at her mother: oh, she doesn't want her mother to die, wherever did such a thought come from?

May one – can one – confide such a thought? Do we have the right to bully the child in the very instant of her menacing conflict of conscience?

If a child entrusts a secret to you, be glad, because her confidence is the greatest prize, the highest stamp of approval. But do not force it, because she has a right to her secret; don't force it, not by asking, nor by trickery, nor by threat – all means will be equally contemptible; they won't bring you closer – rather, they'll distance you from your ward.

One must convince the children that we respect their secrets, that the question "Can you tell me?" does not mean "You have to." To my "Why?" let them answer not with an excuse, but with an honest "I can't tell you. I'll tell you sometime. I'll never tell."

55. I once noticed an eleven-year-old boy approach the girl he loved and whisper something. She blushed in response, lowered her head shyly, shrugged her shoulders in refusal.

A couple days later I inquired as to what he'd approached her about. No embarrassment – an honest desire to recount it.

"Oh, I asked her if she knew how much is sixteen times sixteen."

I was so grateful to him: he had sparked so many good, heartfelt thoughts in me.

Another time the news reached me that one of the girls had had some mysterious adventure when she was passing through a park in the evening. Our children go into town themselves, and by themselves; it's in our educational program, and it would be very painful to renounce this principle. Vigilance was advised. The adventure in the park unsettled me. So I insisted that she tell me; I threatened that if she didn't she wouldn't be allowed to go by herself.

She said that when she was walking through the park, a bird flying by sullied her hat: "It pooped on my head."

It seems to me that, of us two, I was the more embarrassed.

If we were not so unsubtle in our attitude toward children, how often we would be forced to be shame-faced at the sloppiness of the life they have discovered, and from which we are helpless to defend them.

56. The quiet whisper of a confidence is at times the whisper of denunciation.

Do not be falsely outraged: you will hear the informant out, for you are obliged to do so.

"He curses you, sir, he used bad words about you."

"How do you know he curses me?"

"A lot of the boys have heard."

So it's something heard by accident, not deliberate eavesdropping.

"Alright, then, but why are you telling me?"

Discomfiture: he was just saying.

"And what is it you'd like me to do to him?"

Discomfiture: he doesn't know what he wants me to do.

"And do you know why he cursed me?"

"He was angry that you..."

Trivial content, vague intention. Surely he had been counting on the caregiver's interest; he might have been impressed by the idea that, having come into an important secret, he'd share it with an elder.

"And do you not curse when you're angry?"

"Sometimes I do."

"Don't. It's a nasty habit."

Don't preach morals to him; perhaps he was directed by genuine good will. And if not, a couple of discomfiting questions and a lack of interest in the news one has received are sufficient punishment.

57. Immoral intent: the desire for revenge.

"The older boys are telling dirty jokes, they have some obscene pictures and little rhymes."

"What pictures and rhymes?"

He doesn't know. He had been hiding so that they wouldn't see him, he'd been intentionally eavesdropping. He's telling because such pictures are not allowed. He wants them to be punished.

"And you didn't ask them to show you the pictures?"

He did, but they didn't want to; they said he's still too little.

"And can I tell them who told me?"

No, he won't allow that: they'd beat him up.

"If you don't let me say who told me, I can't do anything to them. Because they'll suspect somebody else, and he's the one they'll beat up."

Fine, then, he's not afraid: go ahead, sir, do as you please.

"Thank you for telling me. I'll speak to them when I have a chance; I'll ask them not to do it again."

I thank him: he has seen what it had been my duty to see. If I want to point out the ugliness of revenge, I'm setting the moral aside for later. Enough for today: he's failed, he'd been expecting a different effect; his shot missed its mark.

58. The matter may be important, the intention pure:

She was in a house where there's scarlet fever. The little ones gather in the cloakroom, they smoke cigarettes, they might set the house on fire. X talks Y into stealing. Z takes food out to the watchman, gets an apple in return. Yesterday some man on the street asked a girl if she wanted to go with him to a pastry shop, take a ride in his automobile.

She knows why she's telling. Having spotted danger or a punishable act, she hesitated, didn't know what to do. She comes for advice on how to proceed, because she trusts you. They'll get angry, they'll avoid her – tough, nothing to be done about it. The child has met her obligation: she's alerted you.

I have to treat her as an adviser in solving a difficult puzzle. She's rendered me a great service. And now we are thinking together about what to do next.

Remember that whenever a child comes to you with someone else's secret, she's always making an accusation:

"You haven't done your duty: you don't know." And you don't know, because you enjoy their trust, but only relatively – the trust of children, but not of them all.

59. From the moment you know, don't rush.

Don't let the dishonest informant crow, "I've gotten his attention, I've carried out an important mission." You have a duty to protect the honest child from the revenge of being ostracized; deferring a discussion of the matter to a later time, you have the possibility of seeing for yourself through heightened vigilance.

Furthermore: if, having observed the offense, you immediately raise the alarm, you assure the children that whenever you're quiet about it, you don't know.

"How did you know? When did you find out? Why, sir, didn't you say something right away?" These are the most common questions when you recall a sin committed long before.

Furthermore: if, in no hurry, you wait for the right moment to discuss the matter, when the child is pleasantly disposed, when the matter has grown trivial over time, lost its immediacy. Oh, that was a long time ago, a month. He'll tell you honestly what inclined him toward the evil deed, how he did it, what he felt before, during, and after.

Furthermore: you won't lose your temper – you have time to weigh it, think it over, prepare. Your future attitude toward the child or the group sometimes depends on a judicious resolution of some matter...

Taking advantage of your good humor, a boy asks for a small locking drawer.

"By all means. It will be easier for you to hide your obscene pictures so the small children don't find them."

Embarrassed, bewildered, amazed.

Now he's going to want to speak with you. Don't hurry! When he cools off, he'll gladly give you the picture (it's lost the charm of its novelty), tell you from whom he got it, whom he allowed to see it. The more calmly you speak, the more you trivialize the matter – the more judicious you are, the closer you will become.

60. A principle.

Let the child sin.

Let us not strive to forestall every action, to immediately show the way whenever there's hesitation, to run to help whenever things go awry. Let's remember that we may be absent at a moment of great need.

Let her sin.

When the still-weak will battles passion, let the child be defeated in battle. Let's remember that her moral resistance trains itself and grows in skirmishes with her conscience.

Let her sin.

For if she does not err in childhood, but is sheltered and protected, she won't learn to get a grip on temptation, she'll grow up to be moral passively, for never having had the chance, and not actively, through the power of restraint.

Don't say:

"Your sin disgusts me."

But rather:

"It doesn't surprise me that you sinned."

Remember:

The child has the right to have lied, swindled, extorted, stolen. She doesn't have the right to lie, swindle, extort, steal.

If not once in her childhood has she had the opportunity to pick the raisins from the tart and gobble them up in secret, then she is not and will not be honest when she matures.

"I'm outraged."

Liar.

"You disgust me."

Liar.

"I would never have expected this from you... So even you I cannot trust?"

It's bad that you never expected it. Bad that you trusted unreservedly. You're a hopeless caregiver: you don't even know that the child is a person.

You're outraged not because you perceive danger for the child, but because she jeopardizes the opinion of your institution, your approach to childrearing, your person: you're concerned for no one but yourself.

61. Allow the children to make mistakes and to strive joyfully toward correction.

Children want to laugh, run, frolic. Caregiver, if life for you is a cemetery, allow them to see the meadow therein. You yourself, in a hair shirt, a failure in worldly happiness or a devout penitent, wear the wise smile of forbearance.

What must – must – reign here is an atmosphere of broad tolerance for a joke, prank, malicious remark, trick, falsehood – for a naive sin. There's no room here for ironclad duty, stony seriousness, hard compulsion, and absolute conviction.

Whenever I have fallen into the tone of a monastery bell, I have erred.

Believe me when I say that the reason the life of the orphanage is so opaque is that we set too high an idealistic bar for it. A hundred times, in the barrack life of the orphanage, you are not cultivating a wondrously uniform integrity, nor fretful cleanliness, nor the pristine innocence of affections that know not that there is evil.

And besides, isn't this why you so love your righteous ones, self-sacrificing, gentle, because you know how bad they'll have it?

And besides, can there be the adoration of truth without a familiarity with the roads tread by falsehood? Do you want the sobering reality to arrive suddenly, when the world will smash into ideals with a brutal fist? Isn't that when, having perceived your first lie, the child will immediately cease to believe all your truths?

Besides that, when life demands claws, have we the right to arm them solely with a shameful blush and a quiet sigh?

Your duty is to raise people, not little sheep – workers, not preachers – healthy physically and morally. And health is neither tender, nor self-sacrificing. I wish hypocrisy would accuse me of immorality.

62. Children lie.

They lie when they're afraid and know that the truth will not be revealed.

They lie when they're ashamed.

They lie when they're forced to tell a truth they cannot or do not want to say.

They lie when it seems necessary.

"Who spilled this?"

"I did," a child will admit, and she will try to justify herself if she knows that you'll only say, "Get a washcloth and clean it up" – and add, at most, "oaf."

And she'll admit to a serious offense when she knows that the caregiver will investigate strenuously, has resolved to expose the truth regardless.

Example: water has been poured onto an unpopular boy's bed. No one admits to it. I have announced that I won't let anyone out of the dormitory until the guilty party comes forward. The time for the older boys to go to their jobs has passed, and breakfast time is approaching for everyone. They'll eat their breakfast in the dormitory. Some won't go to school – some are already late for work as it is. In the dormitory, a murmur of close councils. There is a group of the absolutely innocent, others that are less so, the more and most suspect. Now they're certainly figuring it out, maybe they already know – maybe they'll talk him into admitting it.

"Excuse me, sir..."

"It was you?"

"Yes."

A punishment would be superfluous: this type of offense will no longer be repeated…

Allow the children to keep their secrets; give the child the right to say, "I know, but I won't tell." He won't be lying that he doesn't know.

Allow the children to confide openly those of their secrets that do not fit the hallowed commandments.

63. "How the children love you," a sentimental person says.

There are allegedly prisoners who love their sympathetic jailors. But is there a child who wouldn't bear a grudge against his caregiver, for some unwelcome command, some sharp word spoken at some point, a latent desire that he won't reveal because "nothing will come of it"? If they believe they love you, it's because that's how it's supposed to be, because that's what their elders tell them; others, because they don't want to be left behind; a certain number doesn't know for themselves – now it seems to them that they love you, and then they hate you again; and everyone, seeing my faults, would wish to rework me a bit, make me better. Poor things, they don't know that my deepest guilt is over my having stopped being a child.

"How the children love you."

How they ran up to me, hugged me, crowded me when I came back from the war. But wouldn't they have been happier if white mice or guinea pigs suddenly showed up in the room unexpectedly?

Mother, father, caregiver – if your child has showered deep, always consistent, selfless love upon you, prescribe him mild hydrotherapy, even a bit of bromide.

64. There are instances when a child loves you limitlessly, when you're as necessary to her as God in a disaster: the child in illness and the child terrified by a bad dream in the night.

I remember a night spent in the hospital by the bed of a sick little girl. From time to time I would administer oxygen. Dozing, she held my hand tightly. Every movement of my hand was accompanied by her half-conscious words, which she whispered without opening her eyes: "Mommy, don't go."

I remember how, trembling, in the throes of hopeless despair, a boy came to my room terrified by a dream of the dead. I took him into my bed. He narrated the dream about his dead parents, about staying with an uncle after they'd died. He spoke in a sincere, tear-filled whisper, perhaps wanting to compensate me for my interrupted rest, perhaps fearing that I'd fall asleep before his bad visions finally withdrew.

I have a letter from a boy filled with complaints against me and the Orphans' Home. He had written it in farewell. He complains that I didn't understand him, that I was mean and unfair to him. As proof that he knows how to judge goodness, an example: he'll never forget that once, when he had a toothache at night, I didn't get angry that he'd woken me up, I wasn't too disgusted to apply medicated cotton to his tooth. Of his two-year residence, he regarded this one fact as worthy of more heartfelt mention. Yet the caregiver must remove sick children from the orphanage, and at night he must sleep after a long day's work.

65. Let us not demand sacrifices from the children, whether individual or collective.

A father who works hard, a mommy who's head hurts, an exhausted caregiver – this will manage to move them once or twice, but in the long term it will wear down, bore, anger. We can cow children into responding to our first grimace of pain or dissatisfaction with whispered speech and walking on eggshells, but they will do so reluctantly, fearfully, not out of attachment.

They will be polite and solemn because their caregiver has troubles. But let that happen seldom and exceptionally.

And we, the adults, are we always prepared to submit to the whims of the old, their venerable views and senile fancies?

I believe that many children grow up with a revulsion toward virtue because they are constantly being drilled, overfed, on good words. Let the child slowly discover for himself the need, beauty, and sweetness of altruism.

Whenever I point out to children their obligation toward their family, a younger sibling, I'm always afraid that I am making a mistake.

They themselves bring pictures or raffled sweets into the home because they find satisfaction in a younger brother's joy, or maybe it's just the ambition to be like adults, that they have something to give, too.

A child withdraws a saved ruble from his account, gives it to his sister for shoes. A beautiful deed. But is he aware of the value of money? Maybe it's just recklessness?

It's not the deed, but the motive that marks the child, his moral fiber, his potential future development.

66. We have depressed children with the duty that they be grateful, respectful – with our authority. They feel everything, but differently, each in his or her own way.

They respect you because you have a watch, because you received a letter with a foreign stamp, because you have the right to carry matches and go to bed late, because you sign your name in red ink, because you have a locked drawer, because you have all the privileges of adults. They respect you much less for your education, in which they are always discerning gaps. And do you know how to speak Chinese, sir? Can you count to a billion?

A caregiver tells nice fairytales, but you can get nicer ones from the janitor, the cook. The caregiver plays the violin, but a classmate hits the ball higher at rounders.

Good-natured children are impressed by everyone; the critical ones don't bow their heads before intellect, nor before our morality. Grownups lie, cheat, are insincere, make cheap excuses. If they don't smoke cigarettes in secret, it's only because they can smoke them openly, that they do as they please.

The more stridently you tend to the maintenance of your authority, the more it eludes you; the more carefully you comport yourself, the more easily it will slip from your fingers. Unless you're extremely funny, utterly clumsy, you don't try stupidly to wheedle into children's good graces, fishing for complements and turning a blind eye: they'll respect you in their own way.

In their own way how? I don't know.

They'll laugh at you for being tall and thin, fat, bald, for having a wart on your forehead, for how your nose moves when you're angry, for how your head shrinks into your shoulders when you laugh. And they will imitate you and wish to be thin or fat and for their nose to move when they get angry.

Allow them, in a heartfelt, exceptional moment, in a rare friendly conversation, to say what they think of you.

"You're so weird, sir. Sometimes I like you, but sometimes I could kill you I'm so angry."

"Sir, when you say something, I feel like it's all true. But when I think it over I see that the only reason you say it is because we're children."

"We can't ever tell what you really think of us."

"And you're not that much fun, sir, because you're only funny sometimes."

67. No one objected when in my short story for children entitled *Fame*[34] I allowed one of the protagonists to steal. I hesitated for a long time, but I could have it no other way: this boy, with his great want and lively imagination, had to steal just once.

For a child steals when he desires to have something so badly that he cannot resist.

A child steals when there's a lot of something, so he can take one. He steals when he doesn't know the owner. He steals when he has been stolen from. He steals because he needs it. He steals because he's been talked into it.

The object of his theft can be a pebble, a nut, a caramel wrapper, a small nail, a matchbox, a shard of red glass.

It happens that all the children are stealing, that stealing is tolerated. These minor, worthless objects make up property that is part personal, part collective.

"Here are some rags you can play with."

And if they start arguing – what then?

"Stop fighting: you have plenty, give a few to him as well."

He's found a pen nib; he gives it to you.

"Go ahead and throw it out."

He's found a torn picture, a string, a bead. If you're allowed to throw it out, you're also allowed to keep it.

And it slowly becomes such that the nib, the needle, the piece of eraser or the pencil, the thimble, ultimately any object lying on the windowsill, the table, the floor, is sort of collective property. If a hundred arguments arise in a family because of this, in the orphanage there will be thousands of them daily.

There are two ways: one – the base one – is not to allow the children to hold onto "knickknacks"; the second – the proper way – is that every object has an owner, everything that is found should be returned, regardless of its minimal or zero value. Every mislaid object should be looked for immediately.

In this way the child has clear directives; there remains only the one, first kind of theft, and sometimes it is not the worst children who give in to temptation.

68. Deception is merely a variant of theft – theft in disguise.

Pleading for presents, overtly preposterous wagers, gambling and "spinning the wheel," "fleecing," finally trading valuable objects (a pocket knife, a pencil case, the box from some chocolates) for worthless ones. Finally, borrowing something indefinitely.

Most often the caregiver, concerned for his own comfort, forbids trades, making gifts, playing with the intention of gain. This prohibition bars once and for all the injured party's path toward what remains an accursed complaint.

Hundreds of the most vital, interesting, peculiar affairs don't reach the caregiver's attention, but one, glaring, unmasked, gives him an opening to make a rhetorical display, a sermon filled with practical untruth. An even more categorical prohibition – silence, again, until the next incident. Because a prohibition has force for a brief window of time, for life casts it aside.

How many nasty, corrupting, injurious affairs there are – resulting from manufactured debts, presents received under false pretenses, transactions intended to swindle.

The child who has lost a borrowed pocket knife or ball can become a slave.

69. The caregiver who drops in with the sweet illusion that he is entering a little world of pure, affectionate, and sincere little souls whose favors are so easily won, their trust so easily gained, is soon disappointed. And instead of bearing a grudge against those who have led him astray, and himself for believing them, he will be cross at the children for squandering his trust. And are they to blame for your having been shown the work's allure while its thorns were hidden?

There are as many bad people among children as there are among adults, only they have neither the need nor the opportunity to show it. Everything that happens in the filthy world of adults happens in the world of children. You will find representatives of all kinds of people and instances of all their despicable deeds. For children imitate the life, the conversations, the aspirations of the environment in which they were raised, for they have all their passions in embryonic form.

And if I meet a group of children tomorrow, today I should already know who they are. There will be the gentle, passive, good-natured, trusting ones – up through those who are the most malicious, those who are openly hostile and filled with perverse initiative, or the duplicitously docile, the conspiratorially malicious – the schemers and child criminals.

I fully expect to struggle over the regulation and security of the callous and the decent. I will call the positive values of the flock into service, I will stand them up against the forces of evil. And only then will I commence my planned work as a caregiver, clearly coming to terms with the limits of a caregiver's influences in a given area.

I can foster a tradition of truth, order, diligence, honesty, sincerity, but I will not remake any of the children into something different from what he or she is. A birch will remain a birch, an oak an oak, a burdock a burdock. I can awaken what slumbers in the soul; I can create nothing. I'll be ridiculous if I get cross at myself or the child.

70. Among honest caregivers I have noticed an aversion toward dishonest children. I would wish to turn their attention to how the bondage we hold children in brings out falseness, as well as deviousness in exploiting your preferences, and a two-faced desire to please, and the self-interested farce of attaching themselves to you. Everyone has a touch of this disease to some degree.

Peek into the souls of the insincere. They're poor children. Sometimes ambitious, but without real value, maybe unacknowledged, sometimes physically weak and ugly, kicked around, sometimes with side training in duplicity, spoiled and injured by both you, who don't like them, and by those who have not perceived the falseness of their attachment, gratitude, and exemplarity – and give them privileges.

If the cool and malicious child gets close to you, cuddles up to you, though you know that this is a calculated act, you have no right to turn her away. Perhaps she just doesn't know how, perhaps others deceive you more skillfully, more gracefully, perhaps they're more deceitful because they give in to the suggestion of their own game?

Among those who encircle you more than you'd like, perhaps there are those who are weak and disliked, and they want you to give them more care, to protect them from harm?

Perhaps someone has whispered to them to "be sincere, give him a posy and a kiss – and then ask." Perhaps the child is carrying out the recommendation without conviction, against her own sincere, if cold, nature, and thus on command, awkwardly, incompetently.

I was surprised when one of the boys, reserved, cold, without affect, introverted, a misanthrope, suddenly began to show me sincerity, the first to laugh at my joke, let me pass, anticipate my wishes. He would do so awkwardly, with a clear desire to draw attention to what he was doing. It went on like this for quite a while; I hid the distress I was experiencing… When he finally asked that his younger brother be taken into the Orphans' Home, I could feel the tears welling in my eyes: the poor thing, how much effort it had cost him to spend so much time being what he in fact is not.

71. Children disliked by children and their favorites, the ringleaders. An important topic, the research perhaps would give us a key to solving more than one riddle of success in life, not on a scale of worth and power, but of something elusive, unknown.

Children who are pleasant, healthy, cheerful, who have initiative, are bold, talented, always have friends, allies, admirers; the overly ambitious have enemies as well. Thus, camps. There are the momentary darlings of childhood communities, which bring them to the top in order to take pleasure in their fall.

Don't be surprised that a child who knows how to organize a game, knows stories, likes to play and knows how, is well-regarded by his friends: he provides merriment, imagination, the way others share fruit. And at the end of the day what do they love if not the abundance of treats or of spirit they draw from.

Children do not like the sluggish and irritating ones, and what are they if not poor in body and weak in spirit? They turn to the caregiver because, unable to offer anything to the other children, they get nothing in return.

It has to be that the children who absorb you most and surround you most closely are those who are not the most worthy. Do not demand full rights for them; they themselves don't demand much.

But do not spurn them.

72. The child tries and, I would add, has a right to make use of all the plusses she possesses, all the positive values at her disposal, to draw attention to herself: thus, a nice appearance, nimbleness, memory, articulateness, a sonorous voice, background. If we constrain her without having gotten her to go along with it, we'll arouse dislike: she'll discern a malicious barb, maybe envy.

"This is our singer, this is our gymnast."

Maybe that's inappropriate? Maybe it spoils her? And maybe it only encourages her to express honestly what she thinks: yes, she's proud that she sings the best, that she's the most nimble.

Isn't it a greater faux pas to tell the child brusquely:

"You think because you sing so beautifully, because your daddy's an alderman, you can do whatever you want?"

Or:

"You think you'll lead me astray with a smile? You give me a kiss because you want something?"

Sure she does, but you do the same thing, too.

Don't you fill in the lack of your own thoughts with memory, or your lack of memory with intelligence? Don't you try to win their obedience with a smile because you don't know how to make threats, or don't like to? Don't you want to gain improvement with a kiss?

Don't you conceal your own faults and vices?

Why do you take from the child a right that you yourself enjoy, having the enormous privilege of age and authority?

A substantial majority of children does not yet have wisdom. They avail themselves of their cunning. Locke calls cunning the ape of wisdom. The better the conditions for growing up you provide your wards, the faster your amusing little apes will become people.

73. The last and delayed children – these are the test of the caregiver's patience.

The bell – the uninitiated do not know how much effort is required of the caregiver, how much persistent good will from the children, for the hundred of them to fall in line on command.

Just one more line of unfinished dictation, one number of the raffle being announced, one word of unfinished conversation, not to the end of the chapter, but to the period of the story he's reading.

Leaving the room, you wait for the door to close. Noisily, jostling each other, they all run too hurriedly, except for one or two for whom you must wait before they put something in or take something out at the last moment.

You're handing out shoes, coats – it's the same thing again.

And you're waiting by the open cabinet, by the lamp (to turn it off), by the bath (to drain it), by the table (to clear it) – for this one or two you wait to begin or conclude an activity. And their hats are always misplaced when they were supposed to have left already, the nib is broken as you're beginning the dictation.

"Hurry up... Get moving... Is this going to take long?... Would you be so kind?"

Don't be mad: they have to be like this.

74. A prohibition, ostensibly not an onerous one. You struggle fruitlessly, and the children don't listen. Don't be mad.

We forbade evening conversation in the dormitory.

"You've had all day to chat. Now go to sleep."

Apparently something isn't allowing the children to yield to the sensible command, because the children are talking under their voices, in a whisper, a quiet whisper. There's a murmur.

You've yelled; quiet, but not for long.

Today, yesterday, tomorrow – the same thing. So what's left is the cane, violence – or research.

"What were you talking about yesterday in the dormitory?"

"I was telling him how we lived at home when daddy was still alive." "I was asking him why Poles don't like Jews." "I was telling him to straighten out and you won't always be angry with him." "I was saying that when I'm big I'm going to go to the Eskimos and teach them to read and build houses."

With a brutal "Quiet in there!" I would have cut these four conversations short.

Instead of an infraction, you are observing one of the deep, sincere worries of these children's souls. In the noise and riotous bustle there's no room for a quiet confidence, wistful remembrance, sincere advice, private questioning. The all-day noise tires you, you wish to find a moment's peace before sleep – that's what they want, too…

You forbid them from conversing in the morning, before the appointed hour? And what is the one who has woken up early to do, the one who wakes up earlier every morning?

The pointlessness of fighting for morning peace has again awarded victory to the children, and to me it has given the discovery of balance, if not a decisive one, then at any rate no small thing.

75. Another example.

I've often posed these kinds of questions to children:

"What are you up to, what's new with you, why are you sad, how are your people back home?"

I have often received the reply:

"Nothing, everything's fine, I'm not sad."

This would satisfy me. To show the child my interest, my good will, I lost the lesser part of a minute. Often I was petting whomever was in the passage.

After a certain time it came to my attention that the children like neither these questions, nor the caresses. Some would answer reluctantly, as though with a certain embarrassment; they'd answer with cool reserve, sometimes with an ironic smile. Once a boy turned to me a moment later on a rather important matter, after he had given a stock answer to the question. Some of the children, affectionate and emotional otherwise, clearly dodged being petted.

I admit that this irritated me; I got angry; finally, I understood. In these habitual, casually tossed-off questions, the child sees neither sincere interest, nor the possibility of making a request. He's right. When offering an entire box of sweets, you're counting on your guest to take one, and not the largest. You treat the child to a fraction of a minute, and he gives you the required answer – "Everything's fine" – but paying off his debt for being raised well, he bears a grudge against you for the insincerity of your feigned interest in him as an individual; he doesn't want to be treated as someone to brush off, in passing.

"Well, now – feeling better?" the doctor inquires while making his hospital rounds.

From his tone of voice, his movements, the patient sees that the doctor is in a hurry, so he reluctantly answers:

"Yes, better, thank you."

76. Children have no experience in the insincerity of social forms, or, I would add, in the ordinary lies of common speech:

"I'm throwing up my hands; it should be as quiet as church; everything he has goes up in smoke; whatever he gets his hands on he breaks; I've said it a hundred times; I'm done repeating it."

To the child, these are lies.

How is it not shameful to say you're throwing up your hands when you move them around freely? Church isn't the least bit quiet. His pants were torn when he was going through a fence, and they can be mended; they didn't burn at all. He gets his hands on lots of things and doesn't break them, and the fact that one thing did get broken, well, that happens. You didn't say it a hundred times, but five at most, and you'll repeat it plenty more.

"Have you gone deaf, or what?"

No, she has not gone deaf. The question is also a lie.

"Don't let me set eyes on you again."

And this order is a lie, because at lunch they'll order him to sit at the table.

How many times does a child behave rebelliously because she'd rather get a couple of thumps, if only the awful speech would end. Maybe the child, convinced of the necessity of respecting caregivers, suffers for seeing this respect collapsing into ruin? For how much easier it would be for her to yield if she were convinced of their essential moral superiority.

77. We introduced a reform at the Orphans' Home: during breakfast, lunch, and dinner, the children have the option of receiving as much dry bread as they'd like. But they are not allowed to throw it around or leave it. Let them take as much as they can eat. Not right away, the children acquire the relevant experience, for fresh bread is a delicacy for many of them.

Evening, dinner is over, the little ones have been called to the dormitory.

At the same moment, one of the older girls, having bitten off a modest mouthful of bread, ostentatiously tosses the remaining portion onto the table where I'm sitting and walks on, dragging her feet. I was so dumbfounded that I didn't say anything more than "You're a deplorable, insolent brat." In response, a disdainful shrug of the shoulders, tears, and, offended, she set off for the dormitory.

I was surprised when I found her already asleep in bed a short time later.

A few days after that I understood the cause of her obviously nonsensical act when this same girl declared that she wants to go to bed early, at the same time as the little ones.

A proud girl, she couldn't decide right away to go to sleep with the little kids, which would be humiliating. And so, half-consciously or subconsciously, she then provoked my anger in order to have a reason to take offense, cry, and, consequently, go to bed ahead of schedule...

A couple of words about her dragging her feet.

She didn't lift her feet while walking; she shuffled them along the floor. This delighted some of the children, who started to imitate her. This decrepit walk in a child struck me as unnatural, ridiculous, rude, and, I would add, contemptuous. A little later I discerned that it is not only natural, but peculiar to children at an age of intensified development. It's the walk of weariness.

In my private practice I have asked many times:

"Haven't you noticed that the child's walk has changed?"

"But yes, I have: she walks like an offended princess. It sometimes drives me to despair, to fury. She shuffles her feet as though she were a hundred years old or tired out by God knows what."

78. Doesn't this one example show how tightly integrated the world of the manifestations of the spirit is with its physiological foundation?

They are mistaken who believe that, having abandoned the hospital for the orphanage, I turned my back on medicine. After eight years working in a hospital I understood powerfully enough that everything that isn't as accidental as getting run over by an automobile or swallowing a nail can be recognized in a child only with a couple years' clinical observation, not rarely, in catastrophic illness, but daily, in her bright periods of wellness.

The Berlin hospital and German medical literature taught me to think about what we know and slowly, systematically, to move forward. Paris taught me to think about what we do not know but wish to, have to, will. Berlin is a workday, filled with minor cares and treatments; Paris is a bright tomorrow, with its dazzling sense of the future, tremendous hope, and unexpected triumph. Paris gave me the power of wanting, the pain of not knowing, the bliss of searching. The technique of simplifying, the inventiveness of trifles, the order of details – this I took from Berlin.

The great synthesis of the child – this is what I dreamt of when, in a Paris library, with a blush of emotion, I read the strange works of the classic French clinicians.

79. I owe my research technique and my discipline of scientific thought to medicine.

As a doctor, I note the symptoms: I see a rash on the skin, I hear a cough, I feel an elevated temperature, a whiff indicates an odor of acetone from the child's mouth. Some things I notice at once, the hidden things I seek out.

As a caregiver, I see symptoms as well: a smile, a laugh, a blush, crying, yawning, a shout, a sigh. Just as a cough can be dry, wet, or stifling, crying can be tearful, sobbing, or almost tearless.

I note the symptoms dispassionately. A child is feverish, a child is fussy. I reduce the fever, eliminating its cause to the extent possible; I weaken the intensity of the fussiness as much as I can without harming his spirit.

I don't know why my medical treatment doesn't achieve the desired result; I don't get mad, but keep looking. I observe that my directive is missing its mark, the order is not carried out by many children or by one; I don't get mad, but do research.

Sometimes an apparently minor and insignificant symptom speaks to a great law, an apparently unconnected detail is at its root bound up with an important problem. As a doctor and as a caregiver, I don't know trivialities, and I vigilantly pursue what seems incidental and worthless. A minor trauma sometimes devastates the powerful, corrective, yet fragile functions of the organism. A microscope reveals an infection in a drop of water that will ravage a city.

Medicine has shown me the miracle of therapy and the miracle of our efforts to peek into the mysteries of nature. Thanks to medicine I have many times seen a person die and the merciless force, tearing the mother's womb, with which the fetus, the ripe fruit, breaks forth into the world, into life, in order to become a person.

Thanks to medicine I learned to link – arduously – scattered details and contradictory symptoms into the logical picture of a diagnosis. And enriched by an experienced awareness of the might of nature's laws and the genius of scientific human thought I stand before the unknown – the child.

80. An angry look from the caregiver, his praise, admonition, joke, advice, a kiss, a story as a reward, words of encouragement – these are the therapeutic treatments that one must administer in smaller or greater doses, more or less often, depending on the case, depending on the individual qualities of the organism.

There are deviations, distortions of character, that one has to treat patiently with orthophreny.[35] There is an innate or fleeting anemia of spirit. There is innately poor resistance to moral infection. Everything can be diagnosed and treated. Too hasty or haphazard a diagnosis and an improper or overly vigorous treatment worsen the situation.

Hunger and satiety in the realm of spiritual life are just as material as they are in physical life. A child hungry for advice, some direction, will eat it up, digest it, and assimilate it; fed a moral, she will experience nausea.

A child's anger is one of the most important, most interesting fields.

You're telling her a story, she's listening inattentively. You don't understand why, but instead of being surprised like a naturalist, you grow impatient, get mad.

"You don't want to listen, that's fine. When you ask me, I won't tell you."

"Well then forget it," the child answers, "if it's such a big deal."

If she doesn't say it, she'll think it: you'll tell by her body language, by the expression on her face, that she doesn't care for the story...

Kissing, cuddling a little scamp, I was asking him to straighten out. He broke down crying and, with tears and despair, said:

"Sir, is it my fault that you just don't like rascals, you only like losers? So if you just tell one of them to be a rascal, then he won't listen to you, either."

His tears were not at all a sign of remorse. He wasn't protesting my caresses or my sweet words, because he thought them the harsh punishment he deserved for his many sins. He was merely thinking hopelessly about his future: this goodhearted, but stupid caregiver cannot understand that I cannot be different. Why does he punish me so cruelly with a kiss, which I hate; it would be better if he were to box my ear and order me to walk around all summer in torn pants.

81. Summing up the enormity of results that the clinical observation of the child in the hospital has provided, I ask what the orphanage has given us: nothing.

I ask the orphanage how many hours of sleep a child requires. Hygiene handbooks offer some table transcribed from book to book and established by nobody knows. The table announces that the older the child, the less sleep he needs: that's a lie. On the whole, children require less sleep than we think or, I would add, than we would wish. The number of hours of sleep shifts depending on the stage of development in which the child finds himself, and often the thirteen-year-olds go to sleep with the little ones, while ten-year-olds are sprightly and don't follow the prescriptions in books.

The very same child – today he cannot wait for the signal to hop out of bed, regardless of the weather or the temperature in the dormitory; when a year has passed, he suddenly becomes lumbering, with some effort he raises himself, stretches, and lingers, and the chill of the dormitory brings him to despair.

The child's appetite: he doesn't eat, doesn't want to, he gives it back, weasels out of it, uses trickery so as not to eat. A year passes: he eats, he devours, he – steals a roll from the pantry.

And favorite foods, and despised ones?

On being asked what his two greatest worries are, a boy answers: "The first, that my mother died, and second, that I have to eat pea soup." And there are children who will gobble down three portions of pea soup.

But can one speak of individual properties when the general laws remain unknown?

And that slouching comportment of children who, after a certain time, again straighten up, and again slouch? The pale ones blush and then go pale again. The mentally balanced suddenly become fussy, obstinate, incorrigible, only to find balance again sometime later – "straighten out."

How much arsenic debauchery and orthopedic swindling would vanish from medicine if we knew the springs and autumns of a child's development. Where would we research it, if not in the orphanage? The hospital is tasked with studying diseases, brutal changes, extreme symptoms; the whole jewelry case of hygiene, the micro-observation of its alterations – these should be worked out in the orphanage.

82. We do not know the child – worse, we know her through our prejudices. It's embarrassing how the same two, three works actually written beside the cradle are cited by everyone to the point of revulsion. It's embarrassing how the first conscientious worker to come along becomes an authority on almost every problem. The most minute detail in medicine boasts a richer literature than entire fields here. The doctor is merely the orphanage's honored guest, not its host. There's nothing strange in someone having stated sneeringly that the reform of the orphanage is the reform of walls, and not of the spirit. What always and ever reigns over the child of the orphanage is moralizing, not research.

Reading doctors' old clinical pieces, we see the meticulousness of studies that sometimes arouse laughter, and always amazement: they count the number of eruptions in diseases of the skin; the doctor hadn't stepped away from his patient day or night. Medicine today has a right to neglect the clinic a bit, placing its new hopes in laboratories.

And pedagogy, having skipped the clinic/orphanage, has immediately taken to laboratory work.

I have spent all of three years in the orphanage, enough to have a look around – and I am not surprised to have acquired a trove of observations, designs, conjectures; for no one has yet been to this golden country, they don't know of its existence.

83. We do not know the child.

The preschool-aged child – "school age" being a police designation in places where children are drafted into school. Teething, adult teeth, puberty.

It's no surprise that under the conditions for observing the child today we have discerned only his teeth and hair under the armpits.

We don't even know how to appreciate the striking contrasts in the child's organism: on the one hand, the vitality of the cells, on the other, their vulnerability to injury. On the one hand, excitability, stamina, strength; on the other, fragility, instability, fatigue. And neither the doctor, nor the caregiver knows whether the child is a "tireless" creature or a chronically exhausted one.

The child's heart? I know. A child has two hearts: the central, overworked one, and the peripheral one, with elastic vessels. That's why his pulse fades away so easily, but it balances out again just as easily.

But why do some children in a fit have a slowed, erratic pulse and others a fast, steady one? Why do some go pale, others go red? Who has listened to the heartbeats of children who've jumped rope a hundred times? Doesn't their apparent vigor stem from the fact that a child is inexperienced in economizing every last drop of his energy? Why is the pulse after a fit faster in girls than in boys, which means that a given boy has a "girlish heartrate response," but a girl has – a boyish one?

These are all questions not of the orphanage doctor, but of the caregiver-doctor in an orphanage.

84. The caregiver says:

"My way of doing things, my point of view." Even if he's had meager theoretical preparation and a modest number of years of practice behind him, he has a right to say this.

But let him prove that he has come to this way or perspective through work experience in such an area, under such conditions, with such child-material. Let him defend his position, cite examples, back it up with case law.

I even give him the right to the most difficult thing, what carries the greatest risk: prognosticating, predicting what the given child will grow up to be.

But let him always be aware that he can be wrong. May none of these views be an absolute conviction, nor a conviction for all time. May this day forever be merely a passage from the sum of yesterday's experiences to the greater one of tomorrow's.

Every problem should be examined independently of the general view – and each fact independently as well. For facts are contradictory, and it is only from their number on one side or the other that one can work out general laws.

Only under these conditions will this work be neither monotonous, nor hopeless. Each day will bring him something new, unexpected, unusual, every day will be a new monograph richer.

An unusual or rare complaint, lie, argument, request, offense, a manifestation of disobedience, insincerity, or heroism, will be valuable to him, as a rare coin, fossil, plant, or arrangement of the stars in the sky is to a collector.

85. It is only then that he will love each child with a judicious love, take interest in his spiritual content, his needs, his fate. The closer he is to the child, the more he will perceive in him qualities that are worthy of his attention. In research he will find both his reward and motivation toward further research, further efforts.

Example:

A mean, ugly, vexing little girl. If she takes part in a game, she disrupts it. She provokes insidiously, for she wants to be aggrieved so that she'll be able to complain. You show her good will, you encourage her. Weak intellect, aimless, no sense of honesty, no ambition, poor imagination.

I love her like a naturalist observing some paltry, nasty creature – look what's been born, such a poor, ugly little thing, nature's own Cinderella.

I had given a strict warning:

"Remember, don't you dare get out of bed."

And I returned to the evening's bandaging, which had been interrupted.

When, a moment later, a tremulous "Sir, come quick!" reverberated from the dormitory, I knew what it meant.

He hadn't obeyed, he got out of bed to finish getting even with a friend.

Silently, I meted out a couple slaps to the hand and, having tossed a blanket over his shoulders, took him to my room.

Earlier, half a year before, he would have resisted, broken loose, grasped at the bedrail, the doorframe. Today he already has the experience of a couple unsuccessful attempts, so he goes along. A strangely measured gait: a bit hurried would mean he submits, a bit slowed would already be resistance. I push him with my hand, very lightly, just enough that I know he's going because he's being compelled.

He goes, and a grim shadow has settled on his face, you would say a black cloud, which must condense into a storm; it is flowing from his soul.

He's standing, leaning against the wall, head lowered, not budging.

I finish up my minor efforts: I put iodine on a cut finger, smear Vaseline on a busted lip, a drop of glycerin on a hand, a spoonful of medicine for a cough.

"You can go back."

I follow him, for what if he hits someone on the way back? No, he was only looking, he slowed his step, maybe he was waiting – just let him provoke him, let him say, "Ha ha, you were standing in the corner!"

He reached his bed, got in, covered his head with the blanket, was maybe biding his time, maybe he wants me to return to my room.

I walk between the rows of beds.

He had already been on the straighter path, but today he had a bad day again. He slammed the door in anger, a glass door – a pane broke. He said it was the wind, a draft; I believed him.

While jumping rope, he didn't want to wait his turn, he took offense, didn't jump, he messed everything up. The other children complained. He didn't eat his supper: he didn't like the roll, the person on duty didn't want to exchange it.

It is difficult explaining to the children that they should be more forgiving of him.

The murmur of the drowsy room dies down. A peculiar moment: one then thinks with peculiar ease, and well.

My scientific work.

Weight curves, developmental profiles, growth index, the prognosis for somatic and mental evolution. So much hope: what will come of it? What if it's nothing?

But isn't it enough that I experience a feeling of joyful gratitude at their growing and getting stronger? Isn't that sufficient reward for my work? Don't I have a right to be a selfless devotee of nature? May the shrubs grow green.

Here's the brook that babbles, the grain-filled lea, the garden and its rustling leaves. Have I to pose my questions to the kernels on swaying stalks, ask the droplets what they're for?

Why rob nature? Let it keep its secrets.

Now they're sleeping, every one of them with a sin, if only the sin of a torn button they haven't sewn back on. How minor all this is in view of a menacing tomorrow, when a mistake sometimes takes its revenge with an entire devastated life.

All of you, so safe and quiet.

Where am I to lead you? Toward high ideals, noble deeds? Or merely to drill you in fulfilling the necessary obligations without which society will push you to the margins, but so that you could maintain your dignity? Do I have a right, for a bit of food and care over a couple years, to demand, to order, to want? Maybe for each of you your own way, even if it looks like the worst one, will be the only right one?...

Amidst the quiet of sleepy breathing and my own worried questions, there's an echo of sobbing.

I know that crying: it's him crying. There are as many different kinds as there are children, from quiet and concentrated cries, through capricious and insincere ones, all the way to those that are wailing and shamelessly naked.

It's sad when a child cries, but just this one's sobbing, stifled, hopeless, portentous, is foreboding.

A nervous child is one thing: how often we, not seeing the essence, satisfy ourselves with the name whose content we do not know. Nervous, because he talks in his sleep; nervous, because he's affectionate, because he's lively, because he's languid, because he tires easily, because he's developed beyond his years – *progéneré,* as the French say.

There are rare children whose years number more than the ten they have lived. They carry the baggage of many generations, the folds of their brains flow with the accumulated torments of many pained centuries and, with a slight stimulus, the latent, stored power of pain, grief, anger, rebellion is released, and one has the impression of a disproportion between the minor stimulus and the stormy response.

That's not the child crying, it's the centuries crying, it's the pain and longing moaning, not because he was standing in the corner, but because he has been oppressed, driven out, kicked around, accursed. Am I poeticizing? No, I'm just not finding the answer, so I ask.

It has to be a high-tension emotion if a trifle can knock it out of balance. It has to be a negative emotion, because you'll have a hard time bringing out a smile, a cheerful look, never the loud mark of childish joy.

I approached him and said in a firm yet gentle whisper:

"Don't cry; you'll wake the children."

He went quiet. I returned to my room. He didn't fall asleep.

This one sob amidst silence, stifled on command, is too painful, too lonely, an orphan's.

I kneeled down next to the bed; I didn't look up expressions and intonations in a textbook. I spoke in a monotonous half-whisper.

"You know that I love you. But I can't let you do whatever you please. The wind didn't break the pane, you did. You spoiled the other children's game. You didn't eat your supper. You wanted to fight in the dormitory. I'm not angry. You've already gotten better: you came on your own, you didn't run away. You're already better-behaved."

He is crying aloud again. Reassurance sometimes produces the exact opposite result: instead of calming, it agitates. But in gaining strength the explosion loses duration. He sobs loudly, only to go quiet a moment later.

"Perhaps you're still hungry? Would you like a roll?"

The last spasms in the throat. Now he's just crying, complaining bitterly with a soul strangely exhausted, aching, hurt.

"Do you want a kiss goodnight?"

He refuses with a shake of the head.

"Well, go to sleep, then, son. Sleep."

I touched his head lightly with my hand.

"Sleep."

He fell asleep.

Dear God, how will you protect this sensitive soul, that life not besmirch it with its mud?...

Summer Camp[36]

> *...Tell me instead what hopes you yourself carried, what illusions you succumbed to, what difficulties you encountered, how you suffered in your brush with reality, what mistakes you made, how you were forced to abandon hallowed notions in correcting them, what compromises you consented to...*[37]

1. I owe a great deal to the summer camp. Here it was that I first met with a flock of children and got to know the ABCs of practical childrearing in independent work.

With my wealth of illusions and poverty of experience, sentimental and young, I thought that I would be able to do much because there is so much I wish to do.

I believed that it's easy to win the love and trust of the child world, that one ought to give children free rein in the countryside, that it is my duty to treat them all identically, that good will quickly brings out remorse in every juvenile sinner.

For these children "of basements and attics," I wished to make the four-week stay at camp "a ribbon of happiness and joy" without a single tear.

Comrades – you poor things, who, like I then, cannot wait until the moment when it will finally get started. I'm sorry for you if, frozen at the gate, shaken to your foundations, ascribing the fault to yourselves, you do now know how to regain your balance quickly.

And you're enticed by the voice of someone else's experience:

"You see: it's not worth it. Do as I do: see to your own comfort. Otherwise the devils will take you, to the delight of the envious, with no benefit for the children you want to serve. Not worth it!"

You depend on the experienced: after all, they get by, while you, let's be honest, are standing there dumbstruck and helpless.

Poor things, how sorry I am for you.

2. Such an easy and rewarding task. You have thirty children out of a general population of one hundred and fifty, and no program. You can do as you please. Games, swimming, an excursion, a story – complete freedom of

initiative. The housekeeper will provide nourishment, your fellow caregivers will render assistance, the staff will maintain order, the countryside will give you beautiful grounds, sunshine, lovely smiles.

Impatiently awaiting the day of departure, I contemplated third-order and far-flung details, having no presentiment of the most immediate and important tasks. Thus I tried to get a gramophone, a magic lantern, I took out fireworks, I purchased checkers and dominoes just in case, for perhaps they won't have them among the games.

I knew that the children ought to be dressed in camp clothes, assigned places in the dormitory and at table, and before anything else I ought to learn the names and faces of my own thirty and maybe of all one hundred and fifty. This hadn't crossed my mind at all, it would take care of itself. In thinking about my children, I did not concern myself with who they are.

Naively trusting in how easy it would be, I clung to the charm of the task before me.

3. How do you learn thirty surnames, some of them difficult or similar, and thirty faces? None of the handbooks mentions this, yet without it the caregiver has no authority, nothing can be initiated.

This raises certain questions: what kinds of names, and what kinds of children, are first to be remembered? What are the individual properties of a caregiver's visual memory? How does this influence the children's fate and the general work in institutions with a significant number of them?

Experience teaches us that there are children whom you get to know easily, spontaneously, and those whom one must study. One may not leave this matter to time, for you will make a series of mistakes – you'll disgrace yourself repeatedly before you finally learn them all.

The first children you get to know are the disabled ones, those with a particular symptom, the unusual ones, i.e., those of small stature, or the tallest, or the oldest, the hunchbacked, redheaded, the exceptionally pretty or ugly. Sometimes a surname holds the caregiver's attention even earlier, before he has seen the child. If an auspicious name and packaging oftentimes determines the success of a cigarette brand or health remedy, the same happens, unfortunately, with people.

Out of a flood of impressions, we seize the easiest into our recollection; in assessing value, we seize onto what demands the least hardship to discern and evaluate fairly.

4. It is self-evident that, for the child who presents a certain positive value or knows how to enfold herself in it, it is important to be known. We turn primarily to the children we know, we give them instructions, we give them

the opportunity to get closer to us, to communicate with us, be distinguished by us. And they feel more self-confident, closer, and now privileged.

The child has an easier time turning to a caregiver who knows her, whether it's with a request or a question, and the caregiver hears her out more eagerly if he's heard, knows, remembers, recognizes. What the average child has to strive for, the child with an easily recalled appearance or name receives easily, quickly, without work.

Children who remain in shadow, with a sense of being wronged or a firm faith in their own meager worth, withdraw all the more, and wanting to get to know them you now have to seek them out. Otherwise you leave them to their own devices in their conflicts with the flock, and to their own experiences, without help or advice.

In every office, factory, and barracks, there are those who've been aggrieved merely by their superior not knowing about them, not knowing them, not remembering them. Valuable strengths are sometimes wasted in this way.

And the children, quick to gain experience, are waiting, they've strained their attention on their first encounter with you, and a little Mickiewicz[38] or Sobieski[39] is waiting for a joking question, a pretty child demands a sympathetic smile, while an ugly redhead or blockhead has a suspicious feeling that what awaits him in this new environment is new displeasures. And if you only take a longer, closer look at the pretty, kind, self-confident one, and read the unfortunate surname more quietly and quickly, you'll have affirmed the hope of the first, the fear of the second.

5. On account of their internal flaws and merits, you will be quickest in getting to know the violent and irritating children, the neglected, and those who are abnormally well-behaved. The pranks of the mischievous, the tearful whimpering of the bores alert you to their presence; the most impoverished cause trouble with their unruliness; the most affluent and insincere draw attention with their good manners. Finally, there will be those who are calculating and busy, who will rush to impose themselves on you with assistance, advice, information.

And all of them – the pretty ones, those with pleasant-sounding names, the most affluent, the insolent – demand that you quickly get to know them and put them first, at the expense of the regular crowd, which must remain in shadow, and they're surprised if you do not do this right away, and they seethe when you do not want to do it, and they employ every battle method that adults avail themselves of.

A young little prince in a school for the affluent, a village elder's son at a folk school, if he has not demanded it himself, then someone will whisper to him that he ought to, if he does not receive, that he ought to get his revenge: "Say that he beats you, that he didn't say his prayers, that he spoke coarsely about the authorities, that he's a bad teacher, that he doesn't care about us at all." Or else they smear your chair in chalk, they befoul the lavatory, they cause a ruckus during an official visit; dull and indifferent, they rebel, they embroil the most innocent children, those whom you most desire to shield from harm, in a nasty affair.

Joyfully anticipating the day of departure, I naively had no sense of how much careful tact I would need to rein in the menacing lot of them.

6. I was unconcerned when I saw that I had to remind a few of the children several times not to lean out the windows of the train car, not to run out to the stairs. Now one of them suggested to me that he stand at the door, he'd guard it, and another wanted to take down the names of those who were disobedient. I rejected both plans with a sharp remark:

"Just look after yourselves; how are you not ashamed, taking down the names of your friends?"

"They're not *my* friends," he retorted with contempt.

I seethed like a child.

There were likewise those who were dying from thirst; I explained to them, patiently and in vain, that they would have a drink of milk as soon as we get there.

With excessive care, I calmed a little boy who was crying at being separated from his mother; with too much vigilance, I saw to it that none of the children fell out the window; besides that, wishing to find common ground with my group, I lost precious time on trivial conversations: "Have you been to the countryside before? Are you worried that your little brother didn't leave with you?"

I quickly saw to the basic task of collecting money and postcards, I jokingly reprimanded those who handed in postcards that were already crumpled and soiled, I reluctantly assuaged those who, seeing me handling their property unceremoniously, advised me that their postcards are clean, and that the zloty coin handed over for safekeeping is shiny and new. What I was to do with the toothbrushes that they also wanted to give me, I did not know: "Those will remain with you for the time being."

7. I exited the train with a sense of relief, proudly noted that all the children were there, that it had gone smoothly. What remained was the carriage portion of the journey.

The least bit of experience would have allowed me to foresee that, unless they're warned against it, the children would throw themselves chaotically into the carriages, that the nimble and enterprising ones would occupy the seats up front, that the clumsy ones would lose their sacks of clothes and unfortunate toothbrushes, that they would have to be reseated, that there would be noise and confusion.

Maintaining order depends entirely on foreseeing. If I foresee it, I can prevent anything.

If I am taking them on a longer stroll around town, I ought to forewarn the children to take care of their business, for they will confide in me the secret of their need to go when we're on the tram or on the street...

On our stroll, we approach a yard with a well. I stop them:

"Form pairs. You'll approach the well four at a time."

If I don't forewarn them, the effort to keep order will be pointless. And if a fight breaks out, they smash the watering cup, they trample the garden, they break the guardrail – the fault lies not with the children, but with the inexperience of their caregiver.

These are trifles: with goodwill, this experience is quickly attained; but it is conditioned right away the first time they see you, which sometimes has an influence on the caregiver's entire future relationship with the children.

I found the journey to the camp to be anguish. When the first child got out of the carriage because he'd gotten bored with riding, he had to be ordered to get back in. I didn't do it. And so, with wild yelling, confusedly, some of them in the carriages, some on foot, losing their bags and prayer books along the way, jostling each other, excited, stunned, the children found themselves on the veranda.

8. None of the childrearing handbooks says anything about how wherever thirty children are getting dressed in institutional clothes there must be a few for whom all the shirts will be too long, too tight around the neck, or too restricting over the shoulders.

Piles of underwear and clothing – an active, temperamental lot – and a complete lack of experience on the part of the caretaker. Dressing a few of them convinced both myself and the children that good intentions are no substitute for skill.

With uncontained gratitude I accepted the help of the housekeeper, who effortlessly, unhurriedly, but quickly managed not only with the children, but with the underwear that I had already succeeded in making a total mess of. She assuaged the few of them who were dissatisfied with sleeves that were too long, a missing button, or pants that were too wide, saying it would be resolved tomorrow.

The secret to her triumph and my defeat lay in the fact that when I wanted to make everything please, fit, and on top of that to be aesthetic, she knew that it could not be that way, that while I was occupied with the first couple children, the others waiting impatiently, she immediately distributed half the shirts, giving the smallest to the little ones, the large shirts to the middle and biggest kids, leaving their more precise selection by exchange to their own initiative. It was the same with the pants and overshirts. And, consequently, there were children who were nimble and prudent, dressed to size, and impractical, clumsy ones dresses like little clowns at a carny circus. But the most important thing is that when the bell announced supper they were all dressed, their personal clothes packed in their sacks, numbered, folded, in the storeroom.

9. How should children sit at the table?

I didn't foresee this problem, either. I hastily decided at the last minute, in keeping with the prevailing principle of freedom: let them sit where they want. I had not thought, however, that there are actually only four distinct places – at the corners – that all the remaining places are identical; thus there would be quarrels over those four places, and the larger they are, the more enthusiasts they would have.

I did not foresee that the argument over those four spots would be repeated at every meal, that those who occupied them first would claim them on the basis of precedence, the others on the basis of equality.

I did not foresee that as far as getting to know one another and becoming friends was concerned, the children would change neighbors daily: thus, again, arguments just as we were distributing milk and soup, which by their nature spill and are wasted as the dishes lose their balance.

I did not foresee that in the constant change of places it would be harder for me to get to know the children.

I was even rather unwise in leaving the choice of a free bed in the dormitory to the children: one could sleep wherever he liked. Truly, if I had been given the choice, I wouldn't know which place to prioritize. The directive was so clearly nonsensical, however, that I quickly withdrew it, albeit it not quickly enough that there wasn't a lot of confusion and noise here as well. I accommodated the children according to a list, and I experienced enormous relief when relative peace reigned at last.

I had a vague appreciation of my own failures, yet I was too bewildered to seek out their sources.

10. The housekeeper called me to supper for the third time; the other caretakers had already left their rooms. I thought that one ought not to leave the children alone on the first evening: they might be afraid, they might cry; but the experienced housekeeper assured me that they were tired and would

fall asleep; how could I not believe her? The majority were in fact already sleeping.

I left, but not for long; I soon had to come back, and in a hurry, in order to bandage up a boy who had gashed his forehead on a buckle, while the second wrestler had a black eye that, over the course of several days, changed color from red to yellow, black, and dirty grey.

"The season's off to a great start," the housekeeper said.

I took this as a sardonic and insulting remark, not to mention an unfair one, since she was the one who had persuaded me to leave the room.

One ought to have foreseen that while some of the children will fall asleep, others, roused by the change in scenery, won't be able to; the annoyed can initiate quarrels and fights. I was instead prepared to hug the ones who missed home or were sad, not to reconcile those in conflict, while, wonder of wonders, the one who was crying on the way here was now fast asleep.

I didn't notice the most important thing: the fight, such a serious infraction, was a menacing sign – it proved that, on the very first day of my inauspicious activity, my authority had already been shaken.

I would add, parenthetically, that one of the fight's participants had a pockmarked face: that had surely played a certain role in the quarrel that ended so tragically for my pie-in-the-sky hopes: there hadn't been a single tear in the program, and there were already tears on the way to the camp – and now, blood.

11. I slept poorly that night. One of the children, unaccustomed to lying alone on a narrow bed, had slipped off the pallet freshly packed with straw and fallen to the floor with a bang. Someone moaned or blurted out something in his sleep, and again I was imagining that the one who'd been hit in the eye could lose his vision. I was all nerves.

I had ten years of tutoring under by belt; I was neither a youngling, nor a novice in the domain of pedagogy; I had read many books on child psychology. And despite that I stood there helpless against the mystery of the collective soul of the society of children. That it was making some new demands, that this painful surprise had caught me off guard, there was no doubt. My ambition was suffering, my weariness building – what, already?

Maybe I was still deluding myself that this first, admittedly exceptional day would be followed by those I had expected, rainbow-colored and smiling; but what to do to ensure a safe tomorrow, I did not know.

12. A fundamental error was my unenthusiastic rejection of help from the child on duty last year: he would have been an invaluable facilitator for the first days of our stay at the camp. Let him stand guard at the door to the train

car, let him even take names if that's how it's always been. Let him say how to keep the children from hiding the money they're carrying, how they usually sit at the table, how they sleep in the dormitory, which path to take to go swimming.

An analysis of all the mistakes made would be exceedingly instructive. Unfortunately, even if I did take notes, I skipped the failures: the wounds were too fresh, too painful. Today, fourteen years later, I don't remember the details. I know that the children complained that they were hungry, that their feet hurt from walking barefoot, that there was sand on the forks, that it was cold without cloaks, that an experienced caretaker looked indignantly on the disorder and anarchy in my group, that the housekeeper offered pointers that would be to my own benefit, which I jeopardized with my excessive zeal. I know that the custodian complained of littering in the woods, the veranda being ruined by the boys, who pulled bricks out of the pillars, that when washing it was my group that used up the most water, which had to be pumped into the tank.

Until the very worst thing happened on the fifth or sixth evening.

13. When the boys were lying in bed in the half-darkened dormitory, a racket broke out.

Someone had whistled sharply, someone crowed, another one barked, roared, and again someone whistled intermittently in various corners of the room.

I understood.

I no doubt already had allies among the children. I spoke to them, explained, asked, I saw both understanding and goodwill. But I did not know how to seek out my group's positive strengths, not to mention how to organize them. Thus the ambitious and the insincere, whose hopes I had disappointed, and whose desire to help I had rejected with disdain, came to a quick understanding; taking advantage of my inexperience, and having appraised my weakness, they had thrown down the gauntlet.

I walked among the beds with a slow step; the boys were lying exemplarily, their eyes closed, some of them covering their heads with a blanket, and they were harassing their caregiver, challenging him, taking a risk.

When I was in middle school we had a teacher whose one fault was that he was lenient and didn't know how to control his classroom. I recall with horror the orgies of malicious pranks we inflicted upon him.

Only slaves are capable of avenging themselves like this when they sense their power in the face of a hated authority. Every despotic school counts a similar victim among its staff, one who suffers and hides, is as much afraid of the authorities as of the children.

I lived through a lot in the course of those few minutes, which lasted an eternity.

14. So that's the response to my kindliness, enthusiasm, work? At first I felt like screaming bloody murder. The whole crystal edifice of my dreams had come crashing down, had fallen to rubble.

Anger and thwarted ambition: I'll be a laughing stock to those whom I surpass in feeling, those whom I wanted to convince, to attract with my example, maybe to impress.

I stopped in the middle of the room, I announced in a calm, if stifled voice that if I catch him, I'll thrash him. My heart was beating, my lips trembling! I was interrupted by whistling.

I caught him, pulled him out by the ear, when he protested I threatened to throw him out on the veranda, which the dog walked at night, let off his chain.

Do you know who it was that I beat? The one who'd whistled for the first time, just once. Why he had done it he could not explain.

What a superb lesson the children had given me.

To fetch pleasant impressions and charming memories, I was walking in white gloves, with a boutonniere in my lapel, to the hungry, the abused, the disinherited. I wanted to weasel my way out of my obligations with a couple of smiles and cheap fireworks; I hadn't even taken the trouble of learning their names, distributing the underwear, keeping the lavatory clean. I was waiting for them to like me; I didn't want to accept the flaws of those reared in the recesses of big-city life.

I was thinking not of work, but of fun; this children's revolt opened my eyes to a joyful vacation's negative aspects.

So then, instead of coming to terms with the mistakes I had made, I lost my temper and let the dogs loose.

The caretakers, my colleagues, had come here because they had to, for a wage, but I had come for an idea. Perhaps the children had sensed the insincerity and were punishing me?

15. Before evening on the following day, one of the boys warned me that the disorderly conduct was to be repeated, and if I were to strike someone they wouldn't relent, they'd defend themselves – they'd armed themselves with sticks.

I needed to act fast and energetically. I placed a bright lamp on the dormitory window; by the dormitory entrance I collected the sticks, which I removed to my own room: I'd give them back tomorrow.

Whether they understood that they'd been betrayed, or the bright light of the dormitory had made them timid, or the lack of defensive arms had thwarted their plans, it was enough that I was victorious.

A plot, revolt, betrayal, repression: that's how life had responded to my fantasizing.

"I'll discuss this with you tomorrow": that's how my threatening announcement sounded, instead of the sentimental "Goodnight, children" which I'd treated them to on the first evenings, and which was utterly useless.

I turned out to be a tactful victor. And life again taught me that sometimes good fortune flows from the place where we think that we've been touched by catastrophe, that a stormy crisis is often the start of recovery.

Not only did I not lose the children's goodwill, but on the contrary, our mutual trust grew. For the children the matter had been a minor episode, for me – a watershed event.

I had understood that children are a force that one can spur toward cooperation, that one can alienate with contempt, that must be reckoned with. It was the stick that, by a strange turn of events, had taught me these truths.

The following day, as we were talking in the woods, I spoke for the first time not to the children, but with them; I spoke not about what I want, but about what they want to and can become. Perhaps this is when, for the first time, I became convinced that one can learn a great deal from children, that they both assert their own demands, conditions, and stipulations, and have a right to do so.

16. Uniformity of dress burdens children not because the cut or color is identical, but because some of the children suffer physically for not having clothes that fit. The shoemaker will not consider the peculiarity of a child's foot if the caregiver's vigilance does not note it, understand it, and point it out. Give a bore comfortable shoes, and he might become active and cheerful. If the camp rules dictate that the children walk around barefoot in the summer, it will be to the delight of those who likewise went barefoot in the city, and torture for the certain number with exceptionally delicate skin. Anemic and less active children need warmer clothes.

How do you distinguish fickleness from actual need in an institution when it is no easy task in a family? How does one establish the boundary between what the child will easily get used to, what causes a passing hardship, and that which is a property of his organism, the individual difference of the one among the masses?

In the orphanage, sleep has to be uniform. And here the amount of sleep is calculated as the average need of a child, though the variations are significant. Thus you will have children who are chronically sleepy and those with whom you have to struggle, and fruitlessly, for a morning's peace in the dormitory. For it is agony for a child to lie in bed without sleeping, just as it's agony for him to stand when he's exhausted and drowsy.

Finally, there's uniformity of diet, which is not so willing to consider age differences, and which completely passes over differences of appetite in individual children of the same age.

This is why we have unhappy children in the orphanage, because they are dressed uncomfortably or not warmly enough, they're sleepy or incorrigible with regard to sleep, they're half-hungry or hungry.

These are challenges of the first order, decisive in the matter of childrearing.

17. There is no more painful vision than a hungry youngster's champing at the bit for a second helping or refill, arguing over a slightly larger hunk of bread; there is no more demoralizing factor than dealing with food.

It is against this background that we find the starkest conflicts between the conscientious caregiver and the conscientious housekeeper. Because the caregiver swiftly understands that one cannot rear a hungry child, because hunger makes a poor adviser.

Parents can say, "There is no bread": they lose neither the children's love, nor their respect; the caregiver has the right to say this exceptionally, but only exceptionally, and only when he is hungry himself. *The difference between children's average, normal diet and a larger appetite ought to be evened out with bread, as much as one wants and can eat.*

I know: the children will be carrying bread in their pockets, they'll keep it under their pillows, put it in the window frames and dump it in the toilet. That's how it will be for a week, with dimwitted caregivers for a month, but no longer. One may punish the child who does this, but one may not threaten:

"We're going to stop giving out bread."

Because then the more cautious of them, fearing the repressions that have been announced, will start hoarding.

I know: the children are going to stuff themselves on bread, and the regular meals will be added to the slop. Certainly, wherever sloppily prepared, poor-tasting food meets a youngster who is not utterly ravenous, the palate must give way to yesterday's unenticing, yet hardly repulsive bread.

I know: one moron or another will stuff himself – trouble, commotion – but believe me: he'll do it once or twice; only children who are excessively monitored have no experience.

18. There are conflicts even where there is complete harmony between the housekeeper and the supervisory staff. If the children are sated, it can

sometimes happen that a portion of the prepared food goes unused. A hot day, haste before an excursion, the milk slightly scalded, the housekeeper comes out with a reproach:

"Half of the porridge is untouched, but here's the bread we found under the veranda."

Let the caregiver drink down a full mug of scalded milk as an example, let him say that there will be no stroll if they don't finish their soup, let him distribute the bread in many small pieces, let him not discount the housekeeper's concern; but the bread must remain, there can be no capitulation, not for a single day.

Caregivers are inclined to disdain the housekeeper's worries; the housekeeper is inclined to detect disdain where there is none. Where there is goodwill on both sides, there are exactly the sorts of scuffles that there have to be between people who work in different areas of the same terrain. One must have tact, and I would remind the caregiver who is prone to forget himself in a moment of pique, who says, "How about you look after the pots and pans and not bother about the children," that the housekeeper has the complete right to respond, "And how about you wipe the children's behinds, because the laundress can't get their underwear clean."

Because if the housekeeper's duty is in fact to look after the cleanliness of the kitchen, then the duty of the caregiver is the cleanliness of the underwear. Goodwill will dictate the rules of tactful cooperation; it will provide the understanding that they serve the same good cause.

I say: where there is goodwill.

19. The children are now sated; you think that you've overcome the resistance – no, it's just biding its time. Perhaps the soup is over-salted today on purpose, the rice boiled down to paste. Perhaps the portions of meat are large on purpose, and besides that you can have as much potato as you like, and sour cherries for desert, "just let them get sick on him, he'll see how he likes it." All the rice in the wastebasket, after the salty soup the children will gorge themselves on water, gooseberries or cultured milk will finish it off.

Remember, young caregiver, that if a child knows how to be exquisitely cruel, he does this unconsciously, at someone else's instigation; when you get in an adult's way, their perversity knows no bounds.

The disinherited, those ill-treated by life, avenge themselves here for the injuries they've suffered. Disappointed in their ambitious strivings, here they relish their unappealable authority, they demand to be worshipped, they kindly allow you to serve them, they hand down orders despotically. The uninspired and awkward, the meek and hypocritical, here they'll find bread for the price of the filthiest labor and – silence. If you cross them, don't delude yourself that they're going to give in without a long, dogged, passionate fight; too fast and easy a victory contains the germ of defeat: they're waiting for you to grow tired, and in the meantime they want to put you off your guard or gather evidence against you.

If a young chambermaid has come to your room late in the evening to bring you something at the housekeeper's behest, or to ask you for something, it could be incidental, but it could also have a hidden purpose. The younger and less experienced you are, the more slowly you should act, the more careful you should be with your words, and the more suspicious you should be when something comes to you too easily.

20. If you do not want to go with the flow, submit to authority, indulge those who have a voice, rely on the clever and provident, kick the rank and file around, oppress the recalcitrant and incorrigible; if you want to scrutinize everything, meet every appropriate demand, resist abuse, give a complaint a full hearing – then you have to have enemies, whether you're a caregiver or a government minister. If you go into battle too presumptuously, incautiously, and confidently, you will get burned once or twice, and you may lose the desire for further experimentation at the cost of your peace, and sometimes of your livelihood and future. The more reckless the ascent, the more awful the fall…

And anyway, don't believe me: I lie, I'm an old grouch. Do as your feelings dictate, impulsively, full speed ahead, no compromise, straight for it… They'll chew you up, new ones will show up, they'll take your place, they'll take over. No negotiating with the dishonest; out of the way, you oaf!; the miscreant takes one in the kisser. You have no experience – all the better: if it shows you how you can creep along your whole life, you don't want it: you prefer to soar for, say, an hour… To the bald and grey, the vanquished will be unworthy of respect, but to the young he'll be a hero.

But don't take a half-step back…

Don't sulk – it's what you'd asked for…

Don't say that you hadn't been warned, that you've been deceived, lied to…

21. The speech about the noise was more or less as follows:

"I beat the boy, and it was wrong. I threatened that I would throw him out onto the veranda, where the dog would bite him; that was quite nasty of me. But who is guilty for my having done two nasty things? The guilt belongs to the children who deliberately made noise in order to anger me. It may be that I punished someone who was innocent. But who is guilty? The guilty are those children who used the darkness to hide. Why was it quiet yesterday? Because a lamp was burning. It's your fault that I was unfair. I'm quite ashamed, but you should be ashamed of yourselves, too. I have confessed, so now you confess. There are good children and bad ones; every bad child can set himself aright if he wants to; I'll gladly help him. But help me as well, so that I can be good, so that I don't go wrong by you. I find it quite unpleasant that one of the boys has a black eye, and another has a bandage on his head, that Mr. X is complaining about you, that the custodian is upset with you."

Then each of them said whether he is good, decent, or so-so, or isn't sure himself; then they said whether they really want to straighten out, or just a bit, or not at all. All of this was noted down. I learned which was the right wing of the group, which the center, which the left…

There are collections of political speeches, judicial oratory, church sermons. Why aren't there printed speeches by caregivers to children? Because to the masses speaking to the little souls of children seems so easy. I've worked on some of my speeches to children for a week or more.

22. We consulted with one another over what to do so that the children wouldn't litter the woods, make noise at the table, scatter bread everywhere, so that they would gather for a swim or a meal at the given signal.

I kept making all the mistakes I wish to protect you from, but I won the promise of aid from a part of my group.

The stupid things I did took their own revenge on me in efforts that came to naught, in a fruitless expenditure of energy. The children shrugged their shoulders, sometimes tried to convince me; I often relented.

I remember a conversation about grades for good conduct. I didn't want to give grades: they all deserve top marks, because each of them is trying to be good, and if he cannot, one shouldn't punish him for it.

"If I don't write to my father that I got top marks for conduct, he's going to think I'm misbehaving."

"But other caregivers, they have a rascal who gets at least a 'C,' but I'm polite and get nothing for it."

"If I do something bad and you give me a grade, then I know the matter's settled."

"If there's no grade, then I somehow don't feel like listening; I myself don't know why."

"I don't like it. If you give out grades, and I do something bad, then I think: let him give me a 'C.' But if there are no grades, it doesn't feel right."

Weigh each of these reasons, and you'll see how they raise important problems, how the children's individual differences clearly stand out in their light.

I gave in: each child determined for himself what grade he deserved, some of them regretfully: "I don't know."

23. For a pretty long time I gave in to the superstition that a number demeans a child. I was obstinate in not wanting to pair the children up, to seat them at the table according to their numbers. But children enjoy their numbers: he's nine and so is his number; he has the number twenty, and that's the same number of the house where his aunt lives. Is the guest at the theater demeaned because his ticket has a number on it?

A caregiver is supposed to know the children, to call them, in heartfelt conversation, by the diminutive form their mother uses for them.

One should know his ward's family, ask about the little sister who was frail, the uncle who lost his job. If the beds are arranged according to numbers, out of thirty there will be five who want to change places: because he wants to sleep next to his little brother, because his neighbor talks in his sleep, because he wants to be closer to the caregiver's room, because he gets afraid at night.

They go bathing in pairs according to their numbers; but if he feels like changing his so that he can go with a friend, if his partner walks too slowly, if he's hurt his foot, the number shouldn't hinder him: let him change his partner or his place.

Already in the first few days, the number can become the name the child's personality peeks out from, until his complete moral and intellectual character hatches. At that point the indispensable number brings no harm.

24. I had an affection for children who didn't want it, couldn't stand it, were afraid of it. I naively believed that over the course of four weeks I could ease every suffering, heal every wound. I wasted my time.

I devoted special care to the children who merited it least, instead of leaving them in peace.

I am moved by the recollection of how, yielding to my requests, they would open their game to those who would ruin it, how they would give in to the aggressive ones who were encouraged by the leniency I had commanded.

I give the wonder-ball to an idiot who, not knowing how to play, carries it in his pocket, because everyone has an equal right to the ball, which I would provide "fairly," taking turns.

I would extort promises to straighten out, exploiting the goodwill of the honest ones, who didn't want to take on commitments they couldn't meet.

I was pleased that it was going more and more efficiently, not counting the sleepless hours or the work spent in vain. I had contempt for the children, for their games, arguments, affairs, because I still found them "minor" back then.

25. Summer camp is an institution that is difficult and rewarding to lead. Right away you receive a significant number of children, whereas in any other place they arrive individually or in small groups to join those already there and well-behaved. The conditions for supervising large grounds are likewise not easy. The first week of organizing is difficult, the last demands increased vigilance: the children are already returning to the city in their thoughts and habits.

Here the conscientious yet inexperienced caregiver has the opportunity to test his strengths in practical labor, in the least painful manner, and he will quickly recognize the caregiving challenges of the orphanage; not responsible for the future to come, he can rate his shortcomings and vices more objectively. If he realizes his errors and mistakes, he has an opportunity in the following season, having no witnesses to the mistakes he's made and free of their consequences, to begin new work, on new foundations, with a new batch of children.

There's no need to conserve strength and calculate enthusiasm and energy for the long run. He'll get tired, the summer will pass – he'll relax.

The experiences gained in the first month will give him, in the second, the satisfaction of the progress he's made; he will quickly notice the difference, which will spur him toward further efforts.

It only seems that the work of the first season perishes irrevocably: in the second season there will be the acquaintances, relatives, and friends of the children from the first. Ask, and you'll learn that they already know you, they already know what you demand; before they've seen you, they already have a liking for you, and eagerness to acknowledge your authority.

26. The second season began under a lucky star. Having received the roster on the eve of our departure, I learned their names in turn. Some of the names aroused my confidence, others – my fear. That's not a joke: just think what a painter named Dustcloud looks like, a peasant named Snail, a cobbler named Wretch.

Armed with a gradebook and a pencil, I noted everything that struck me in a child during our first contact. A plus sign, a minus sign, a question mark placed next to the name was an assessment of the first impression. A brief "nice, a rascal, a nitwit, unkempt, cheeky" – these were the first characterizations, which could prove true or not, but which gave a general impression of the whole.

This is how a librarian flips through a substantial new shipment of books, casting a curious eye at the header, the dimensions, the cover. It's pleasant work: now that will be something to read!

I would note down those who had come specially recommended, were seen off by a large group, had been given many gifts for the road, had been late. The children already have questions, as well as requests, as well as advice; they're especially interesting for being the first. If someone drops his registration card, but his neighbor quickly picks it up and hands it over with a smile; if one of them answers "Here" quickly and loudly when his name is called from the roster, but another's mother answers for him; if one of them shoves another who had taken his seat, and the other protests; if one bows graciously, while another looks around him gloomily – all of this has tremendous meaning for the caregiver, it's noticed and preserved in memory or in a notebook; for him, it's valuable material for identification.

27. Collecting the postcards, I place them in slips of paper, numbered and folded in half, because some of them have been lined, others are grease-stained and crumpled. The children in the first season were quite rightly displeased that their own cards were not returned to them so that they could write home.

I wrapped the money in numbered pieces of paper and folded them in a handkerchief likewise prepared the day before.

This is a deposit, property that is all the more untouchable for the deposit having been compulsory. A child surrendering ten groszy is putting his entire estate into your hands: you are obliged to take it seriously.

Someone was standing on duty at the door to the train car, someone was on duty by every window. I had time to exchange a few words with each child; the details again made it into my notebook.

I noted those who pressed for water, who complained, who jostled by the window.

I collected the toothbrushes individually, tagged them with numbers on string.

The entire group marched past for a third time when I jotted numbers on their sacks with a ballpoint. And here, when I called out a name, some of them stepped forward quickly, others had to be called forward several times. There was also a group of the kind who, instead of looking out the windows, surrounded me, observing my work with curiosity. Someone was crying again: I sent a boy to comfort him, he'd do a better job of it, and anyway – let him cry.

28. I warned them that at the station we would be met by carriages, so now, on the train, was the time to take care of their business; that one was not allowed to crowd into the carriages, not allowed to get out on the way, that anyone whose clothes didn't fit would have them exchanged tomorrow. Two campers from the previous year would help distribute the milk; three others would help with dressing.

I struck up our friendship on a foundation of down-to-earth conversation, not empty flirtation.

I noted who had dirty ears, long fingernails, a dirty shirt; for if his mother does not tidy up her child before his departure, she is not only poor, but negligent, and sometimes the child is already self-sufficient, left to his own devices, or else doesn't have a mother. When I change his clothes and wash him, that detail will be lost.

I agreed to every proposal of help or assistance. For I knew that my task is to organize and keep careful watch, that I won't manage the lot of them myself, that I would pass the good caregiver examination if I have time for the most important matters and for taking care of the children who are exceptional for reasons of health, temperament, neglect, infirmity, or their great spiritual value.

And when the children had changed their clothes and were sitting at the table in numerical order, I started to learn their faces.

I already knew my group better than I had the last season's after several days.

29. I'll recognize one by his freckles, a second by his eyebrows, a third by the birthmark on the side of his nose, a fourth by the shape of his skull. There will always remain a few in whom one seeks a nonexistent likeness, who will not be recognized with more time. The classroom teacher does not know these difficulties, since he has the children every day, planted motionlessly on their benches. But the school janitor, the superintendent, the principal – they do know them. And for the child no one knows it is easy to have misbehavior go unnoticed while a couple of scapegoats answer for themselves and others.

"Oh, I know you. This isn't the first time – it's always you."

And the actual culprit is laughing into his fist.

This is why I place so much emphasis on the need to get to know all the children quickly, because all manner of damaging prejudice, as much to the children's advantage as to their disadvantage, has its source in their unfamiliarity.

It seems to me that I won't be far from the truth if I say that a pretty child with a kind, charming face has every reason to expect he will be taken for good, while an ugly or deformed one will be taken for bad. This is how we get the equally unfair prejudice of certain caregivers against pretty children. I'll say one more time that, absolutely and in every case, he who does not know at least one of his wards will be a bad caregiver.

30. In the evening, when they were settling down to bed, I had a chat about the boys from the season before.

"I'll tell you about the boys who slept on beds number five, eleven, twenty, and thirty-two.

One of them turned out to be very nice, the second was always dissatisfied with everything, the third really straightened out, the fourth had an unfortunate accident in the night – he'd gone in his bed, the boys initially made nasty fun of him, but then they came to see that he was poor, weak, and clumsy, so they looked after him. Where are they now? What are they thinking about?"

In these four true-life tales was hidden a moral, and a day plan, and the most difficult challenges of camp life.

I warned them about what they were to do if they were to be frightened at night, and what if they were to wake up early tomorrow.

And all but two of them fell asleep.

One had left an ailing grandfather and was thinking about him, the other always had his mother tuck him in before bed. The latter, one out of thirty-eight, needed a kiss in order to fall asleep that evening. I thought that it was precisely this one, among the most sensitive, who, in the first season, in its disorder and excitement, might have been berated or, through a simple mistake, taken by the ear.

On the first evening already I had time to jot down some notes, in a separate notebook, about the first day at camp, specifically, about each child. And already I had something, one minor detail to note about half of the children.

31. The following day, right at dawn, I was in the dormitory, and again, before they dispersed and got mixed up, I learned to recognize the children in my group.

The whole day long, I kept turning to another child to ask what his name was.

"What about me, sir? What's my name?"

The ones who were similar, or who seemed similar to me, I placed side-by-side and studied, and the boys turned their attention to the details by which one could recognize them and tell them apart.

The details that acquainted me with their personal life or with one or another domain of the child's spiritual life turned up by the hour.

Quickly and enchantingly, under the influence of the countryside and the beneficial formative influences, the crumpled souls, at first with astonishment and anxiety, then more and more confidently and joyfully, turn toward what is beautiful and harmonious.

But there is a range of caregiving possibilities that no miracle will change. A rich and alert soul will awaken, it had merely been exhausted by its conditions; but an impoverished and drowsy one will barely muster the painful grimace of a smile. Does that upset you? You only have four short weeks.

Integrity that is innate, inborn, will cling to the new forms of bright life; perversity will reluctantly subside.

There are shrubs that a single rain will revive, there are those that are sick and utterly wilted, there are weeds that stubbornly overcome culture.

32. I took a close look at how children's society is organized, and I understood the difficulties of the first season.

When children of positive value are just looking around their new terrain, they are apprehensive and restrained in getting to know each other and approaching each other; the negative force has already managed to organize itself, impose its tone, and be heeded.

The one who understands the necessity of rules, limits, and adaptations aids the caregiver's work passively, without hindering it, submitting to the programs that have the common good in mind. The one who wishes to take advantage of the caregiver's goodwill, scruples, hesitations, kindliness, or weakness assumes an active and aggressive role right away.

It is amazing how a twelve-year-old boy who's been separated from his family, in conditions that are foreign to him, under someone else's supervision, among new peers, can not feel self-conscious or embarrassed and, already on the first day, demands, resists, protests, conspires, selects his comrades, drags the passive and those without initiative over to his side, appoints himself dictator, and issues a demagogical slogan.

You don't have a moment to lose, you must spot him quickly and start negotiating with him. You are his enemy from the get-go, like any authority that demands and does not allow; convince him that you are a different authority than any he has encountered before.

33. An example:

On the train I bring it to a boy's attention that he is not allowed to go out onto the platform. He went out; he doesn't respond to my calling after him. To a sharp reproach, a contemptuous reply: "What difference does it make, I felt like having a drink." I ask him his name.

"I've taken it down."

"Big deal."

Now they're eyeing him curiously, he already has his allies, he's already impressing them. Sometimes just a "fine, fine" or a shrug of the shoulders is enough to recognize him. If that's how it is on the first day, just think how it will be tomorrow, or in a week.

I had a conversation with him that evening. The conversation was serious, to-the-point, as though among equals: we established the conditions for his stay at the camp.

In the city he sells dailies on the street, plays cards, drinks vodka, is no stranger to the police.

"Do you want to stay here?" "I guess." "You don't like it?" "I don't know yet." "Why did you come here?" "Some lady talked me into it."

He provided her first and last name and a false address, just in case.

"Listen, son: I want you to be able to remain here all month, I want you to like it. I only ask one thing: if you get bored, tell me; I'll give you a ticket, you'll return to Warsaw; don't run away, and don't deliberately make it so I'd send you away against your will. I'll let you do as you please, only don't spoil the order, don't ruin it for the other kids. Goodnight."

I offered him my hand.

Do not try to treat him as a child, because he'll laugh in your face or deceive you with feigned remorse, and once he's turned around he'll say something spiteful, something cleverly observed to humiliate you. Anything but insipid sentiment, because he will have contempt for you, exploit you, humiliate you.

34. There was another one:

In an intimate one-on-one talk, when the stupid, meek, cowardly little kids he disdained were not looking at him, he confided in me, was moved, promised to straighten out.

One is not allowed to invoke similar conversations, one ought not to demand that the pledges be fulfilled. When, a few days later, he smashed a bowl into the head of a boy who'd knocked into him at mealtime, I tactlessly reminded him, in a sharp manner, of the promise he had given me – he answered with a hateful look. A couple days later he stole some clothes, changed in the woods, and went to the station.

I would like to bring one thing to the attention of young practitioners who don't know children from impoverished spheres: among such children there are those who are raised most carefully and most neglectfully. These two categories of children not only avoid each other, don't like each other, have contempt for each other. But *the children of families* are afraid of the *children of the street* living right beside them. The imprudent social worker does not see the enormous difference between a moral boy and an immoral one, for they are both poor, live in an impoverished neighborhood on the edge of the city, belong to the same "sphere." It is precisely for this reason that the first fears the second, that he is a danger to him. No one has a right to force them to be friends.

"Just you wait, when we get back to Warsaw I'm going to pay you back": one often hears this threat from unfortunate compulsory friends during the final week of the camp season.

35. I was witness to the desperate efforts performed by a group of individuals to found children's clubs in Warsaw. I was reading a little book that reported on the attempts made in this regard in Moscow. The same mistake was producing the same difficulties. When the schoolchildren would demand that the miscreants be withdrawn, the director would say reproachfully:

"My son plays with them, but you don't want to: it's nasty."

Her son could play with them, because they don't beat him up when he's returning home from work in the evening; no one will yell at him, "Hey you, where are you taking that gal?" when he's on his way to church on Sunday with his little cousin; they won't accost him with "Hey you, lend me a dime for cigarettes."

If her son is taking a walk with his mommy and aunt and a little urchin comes up to her son, and his aunt asks in horror:

"Wherever did your Antoś make such acquaintances?"

Mommy will answer in a haughty tone:

"That's his friend from the settlement."

And she will be amused by her old aunt's god-fearing benightedness.

But a working-class mother will rightly fear and warn against similar friendship.

If an adult worker has the right not to want to be friends with a drunk and a cutthroat because it compromises him, even if he risks nothing by it, the worker's child has the right – has a duty – to avoid bad company.

And if the rascal is only feigning good conduct in order to use the chance encounter to get into the sphere of his peers, where he would not make his way otherwise? to exploit this acquaintance, take advantage of it?...

Manufacturing friendships between children who are completely different with respect to their moral value and life experience, which only their poverty binds into a single sphere, draws them harmfully into bad company – it is a reckless test of their moral fortitude.

36. I insisted:

"Go play with them."

I was working upon their ambition:

"There are thirty of you, one of him. So all of you can't straighten out one kid, but he's supposed to spoil all of you?"

"What do we have to do to make him straighten out? He doesn't want to play with us; if he agrees, it's going to spoil our fun."

It was the children, and not me, who had it right.

I understood significantly later that if a caregiver wants to have an immoral child among average ones, he carries complete responsibility for it, the whole obligation to keep watch. It's a hardship beyond children's power.

What looks like the most beautiful assumption has to be tested. The most obvious truth, difficult to execute in its practical application, should be examined diligently and critically. We are significantly more experienced than children, we know a great deal that children do not, but children know better than we do what they are thinking and feeling.

If a child wants something but doesn't know why, maybe he's hiding the actual reasons, maybe he's unsure of them. The art of caregiving will be finding out, sometimes piecing together, often doing the detective work to get at these half-conscious motives.

"There's something hidden here" – the more often the caregiver thinks this, the more quickly he will improve, the more assuredly he will avoid the persistent errors that flow from false assumptions.

37. I imposed the company of the sluggish, the clumsy, or the unkind upon the children.

It was absurd.

They're playing tag. The clumsy child knows neither how to run away, nor how to catch the others. The dishonest one will deliberately run away so that he's swiftly tagged, because he wants to be "it." If you force children to play with these two, they will avoid them deliberately, they won't tag them.

For the love of God, what adult would sit down to cards with a cardsharp or with someone who doesn't know how to play?

You let them have a ball, but under the condition that he will get to play too. Can you be surprised that they are reluctant to accept the heavy condition? Can you take them for bad because they feel an aversion? Won't they beat him up if they lose their round because of him – and whose fault would that be?

It takes great tact to look after children of this kind. One should take care not to let them be wronged, but also see to it that they cause no harm.

You always have to wait for him. The game is always spoiled by him. Because of him the caregiver was angry with us again, forbade something, took something away, threatened something.

During the first season I fought battles for the loser; in the second, I watched, moved, as one of the worst troublemakers took one of the quietest children under his care – on his own, out of his own goodwill.

38. Do not discount them!

Some boys were playing the game they call "jacks" or "knucklebones." It was already a familiar game to the poor children of ancient Rome. The player tosses five pebbles on the table or floor. Then he tosses one of the pebbles into the air, and before he catches the falling stone he has to quickly snatch one of the remaining four from the table. There are several levels of difficulty. For this game one needs to have dexterity and five smallish stones, the "jacks."

Complaints over who had taken one or all the stones were exceedingly common. I was at that time opposed to complaining.

"You don't have enough pebbles here? Go find yourself some more."

Three mistakes.

In the first place, everyone has a right to his or her own property, even if it's the most trivial and worthless object. That the loss is easily recovered – what does that prove? Let the one who took my jacks go look for others.

The one who did take them has committed an act that is clearly indecent, or at the least wrong. He has appropriated someone else's property.

When I started playing jacks myself, I learned that not all the little stones are uniformly advantageous. Thrown upon the table, those that are too round scatter too far, and those that are too flat settle down too close to each other.

Five pebbles selected for their shape and color are, for the player, like five horses with the same coat and size, five pearls in a necklace, five hunt-worthy dogs.

There are witnesses who saw, remember, affirm to whom the jacks belong. Right was on the children's side.

39. "He insulted my mother." After long hesitation: "He called me a son of a bitch." As a caregiver, I am obliged to allow for the fact that no small number of fathers give the same treatment to the foreman who's tormented them at the factory, the landlord when he doesn't want to fix the stove.

"You know what a grouch he is. He used to fight with everybody, now he only hurls abuse, he's already straightened out. It's true that they call people sons of bitches when they really want to insult them; they also call them jerks, bastards, rogues. Most often in anger, sometimes not thinking that at all. Because will someone truly think that a boy is a bastard because he didn't want to lend him a ball, or he inadvertently jostled him during a game of tip-cat? There are violent people and there are peaceful ones..."

I saw the boys' amazement at my pronouncing an accursed expression aloud and clearly. And I had said it aloud because what is whispered ferments, festers, and irritates, because there is no factor in childrearing more harmful than the deception of false modesty. If there are expressions that you're afraid to say, what will you do with an act that they might commit? A caregiver cannot be afraid of children's words, nor of their thoughts, nor of their actions.

Whoever wants to be a caregiver to the poor, let him remember that medicine distinguishes between *praxis pauperum* [practice among the poor] and *praxis aurea* [practice that brings income]; let him remember that there are lechers refined of speech and heroes of virtue who are vulgar in the maw. You have to know the sphere from which your wards are drawn...

40. It would be too risky to assert that impoverished children are more moral than affluent ones. There are alarming observations concerning one group and the other. One thing seems certain to me: the observations are made in the stairwells of urban apartment buildings, where the lack of room, the prohibition on loud yelling and running, and boredom and indolence compel the children toward powerful sensations and excitements that do not disturb the peace around them.

On the basis of my observations of children at summer camp I can state firmly that a normal child always prefers playing ball, racing, swimming, or climbing trees to withdrawing secretly into a corner for dreams known only to him.

One can calmly allow the boys and girls to run loose in the woods with minor supervision, since gathering wild strawberries and mushrooms will consume them so much that one can rather expect scuffles over a prize in the form of a mushroom, plunder on the part of the stronger kids, than displays of affection.

The cozy corner of an urban courtyard in an impoverished neighborhood and the space between the cupboards in a townie's well-appointed apartment – these hold secrets for which there is no room in the meadow or field. Just don't keep the children in their beds for more than eleven hours a day, for your own comfort, because they, especially in the summer, do not sleep more than eight or nine hours.

41. I was surprised to learn at the camp that the children are not averse to prescriptions and proscriptions aimed at maintaining the plan, order, harmony in the internal life, and they submit to them willingly. If someone breaks ranks, confesses his guilt honestly, and expresses remorse, at most he says:

"I know, but how can I help it?"

There are children who are carrying on a desperate battle with their innate liking, to the benefit of precisely this general harmony. One ought not to hinder this battle with excessive demands, for they will become discouraged or will run wild.

A caregiver should realize which prescriptions and proscriptions are absolute, and which allow for concessions. One is absolutely not allowed to swim in the river by himself, but one is sort of not allowed to climb trees. One is absolutely not allowed to be late for lunch, but one is sort of not allowed to be late when we are buddying up to take a walk: let those who are late catch up to us when we've already gone half a mile; for a lively child does not want to stand in place and wait for everyone else to assemble.

For exceptional children, with the others' consent, there are exceptional rules: this is the most difficult and rewarding of the caregiver's tasks.

If one boy out of a hundred and fifty swims so well that nothing threatens him, he lives on the Vistula, spends half his day in the water swimming across the river without difficulty, if the children allow it, you can even allow him to swim on his own. You have to have the courage to assume the relative fear for his life upon yourself.

42. Social instinct is characteristic of children. They might accept a certain engagement mistrustfully, because they don't trust adults, because that have not understood, but they soon accept it when they take part in it themselves.

What to do so that the children don't scatter bread around the woods, so that they aren't late to lunch, so that there isn't fighting or cursing? Even if similar discussions won't remedy a given malady, they will always raise the moral level of the children in general, consolidate the sense of group responsibility and social obligation.

Note down how many children were late before the discussion, how many fights were recorded over a day. Record how many after the discussion, graph it, and you'll see that they're less frequent. They're more frequent again – a second discussion.

The loveliest speech is tasked with sparking enthusiasm, engagement, but never consolidation.

Some people ascribe too much weight to the word, they expect too much; others are too dismissive of it, because they've been let down. Both groups are mistaken. You won't do anything with words, but you won't get any work done without them. The word is your ally, never your substitute.

This is the only effect you can expect.

43. A meeting on untidiness in the loo.

"When there's a fire or a flood, the best run for help, risking their own lives. When one must do something difficult or unpleasant, it's always the best people who go. We have difficult and unpleasant work to do, and we are turning to the best among us… So, who will take on voluntary duties, each for half a day?"

Understandably, lots of them sign up. But that's just the beginning. For the first two days you choose the energetic, the easily enthused, the less rigid, for the watch will be hardest during the first couple days, and it's a new thing, so they will see to it with all the more enthusiasm. Tell them why they're going to go first.

You don't accept the quarrelsome child's offer, because you're afraid of arguments, because they don't like him, because they'll let him have it out of spite.

You reject the overly impulsive: "Because you'll get in a fight, better not to get involved in this."

You assign the serious children to the days following: you trust that their enthusiasm won't wane.

The quiet one is for later: "You'll have an easier time of it then, you won't manage tomorrow."

You warn him that there will be those who call him "shithead" or "potty-watcher." Don't be offended: they're morons!

You will warn him as to what the person on duty is to do if a little blockhead soils his toilet unintentionally; what to do if he does it intentionally, out of spite; what will happen if he doesn't manage to spot the guilty party.

You have to arm him with a broom and a washcloth. You have to drop in yourself during the day, when there's the most frequent use, in the morning or after lunch, take a quarter-hour shift yourself, in case of doubt take the broom and washcloth into your own hands.

There's no point in getting angry, caregiver: "How many times have you been told?" It doesn't help, and it won't help. So why talk? Because a certain number of children will understand the commitment of a pledge freely given, and to the unconscientious child I will say, "What did you promise for?" That's a real asset.

For a child does not have the cynicism of adults, who reply:

"And must one fulfil one's commitments?"

44. The children's assistance is indispensable to the caregiver, under the condition of constant, vigilant inspection and shift change. For only in this way can one avoid your young coworkers' taking over. Power corrupts! One must explain gently and carefully that being on duty provides no privileges, that it's an act of honor.

Every day I changed those on duty as meals were being served on account of the accepted custom that whoever was on duty received a larger portion of food. This was a bother for the housekeeper, but I considered it necessary.

There were those on duty for making beds, one for each row; for handing out bowls for washing hands; for picking up toys; one who made sure that the towels were hung evenly on the bedrails.

Those whose duty had been to pick up broken glass so that children running wouldn't cut their feet.

It is easier to get to know children in minor activities than in the classroom: there, one has to consider the pupil's abilities, his preparation, the case. Here, we immediately discern children who are volatile and mutable in their likings, ambitious, aggressive, conscientious, or dishonest.

45. If, over the first couple of days, one pays careful heed to how the children get to know each other, one is easily convinced that the forces of good need help, support, and above all else careful and vigilant protection from the two or three for whom your system is inconvenient.

If the government's duty is to safeguard society from violence and abuse on the part of harmful elements, then the caregiver's duty is to safeguard the children from a fist, a threat, an insult, their property (whether a pebble or a stick) from being appropriated, to protect their organization (whether it's a game of ball or building sandcastles).

When this great task is performed once, light maintenance suffices to keep it from slipping or sliding.

All the time saved thanks to the children's help, and a large part of best practices in childrearing, we can devote to the exceptional persons whom we wish to occupy ourselves with separately and individually, because we want to or we must, because they are meritorious, dangerous, or just simply don't fit the average norm.

We have not only exceptional children, but also exceptional situations that occupy a lot of our time. A child has suddenly gotten sick; it's dusk, and four children haven't come back from the woods; there's a complaint about throwing stones or pinecones at a beggar; theft.

The greater their number, the more of these exceptional children and situations there are. Anger won't help anything here: it's how it has to be. The whole rationale of organization depends on everything going its own way in spite of this, on the little things taking care of themselves, so that you'd always be able to say:

"See to it on your own, because I'm busy…"

46. Self-confidence and prudent foresight are cheery and understanding; inexperience is sulky and unstable.

Out of thirty or forty children, there has to be one who's abnormal or immoral, one who is quite neglected, one who's spiteful and asocial, at odds and disliked, one who's violent, with an unbridled, uncommon individualism, one who's clumsy or frail. It has to be this way!

You're organizing an excursion: there has to be one who's weak, one who's offended, one who's reluctant to go because everyone else is eager to set off:

"Oh great, an excursion!"

One will be looking for his hat, one will get into a fight in his excitement, at the last minute a third will run to the loo, a fourth will have disappeared no one knows where.

On the way, one's head or feet will start to hurt, one will cut himself, one will get offended, one will feel thirsty.

You're telling a story; inevitably, one of them will interrupt you:

"Excuse me, sir, what kind of bug it that?"

Another:

"He's poking me in the ear with some straw."

A third:

"Oh, they're herding the rams!"

Youthful sulkiness threatens:

"If someone interrupts me one more time..."

Experienced forbearance waits it out with a smile.

In getting angry at exceptional situations, doesn't the caregiver realize that the work would be deadening, monotonous, boring without them, that the exceptional children provide us with the most abundant material for contemplation and inquiry, they teach us to improve and dig deeper? If not for them, how easy it would be to submit to the illusion that we have achieved the ideal. And who is so unwise as not to know that beyond a relative good it is always possible to attain something better?

47. A minor point, though not without value. If you're diligent, conscientious, and more talented as a caregiver – judge your comrades kindly. Don't let them feel their inferiority. If you wish the children well, it is for their good that you must steer clear of all clashes with your colleagues.

I was the most ardent of the caregivers at the camp; it could be no other way. I longed to work among children, while they'd had enough of it. I nestled into the simple conditions of country life with satisfaction, while they found charm in neither the straw-stuffed pallets, nor in the cultured milk.

Once, when a boy had an unfortunate accident and, for this reason, an argument broke out with the washer-woman, I washed the soiled shirt and bedsheet at the well. But I saw the washer-woman's confusion, the housekeeper's embarrassment, the amazement of my colleagues, which I had counted on in advance. Had someone else done it, he might have heard a contemptuous:

"Good for him. Let him see how he likes it. It's his kid anyway."

One ought to steer clear of lovely gestures calculated for effect. If your insincerity is buried in actions, ostensibly quite positive ones, they will irritate more than words.

And one ought never ever to consider eagerness, nor minor improvements introduced over the first days or weeks of work in a new area, as a service. On the contrary, if it were otherwise, it would say the worst of any new worker: he's supposed to be the most enthusiastic and to see the lacks that are already imperceptible to the exhausted and accustomed eye.

48. I said it in my introduction, I've repeated it, and I'll say it one more time, with emphasis: the caregiver is also a nurse, he's not allowed to disdain, nor to talk his way out of this obligation: the child who's wet himself at night, the child who's throwing up, the one with discharge from his ear, the child who's soiled himself, with a rash on his body or on his head – the caregiver has to help him with the potty, wash him, tend to him. And he has to do so without a trace of disgust.

Let him do what he wants, let him practice it in a hospital, on a cancer ward, at an infant daycare, but he must inoculate himself.

Besides this, the caregiver to poor children must acclimate himself to physical filth. Pediculosis is an endemic disease among impoverished children all over the world; from time to time the caregiver must find a louse on his own clothes. One cannot speak to the child about this disease with indignation, nor with disgust, because children's parents and siblings deal with this phenomenon calmly and objectively, and thus one ought likewise to see to the children's cleanliness calmly and objectively.

The caregiver who is nauseated by children's dirty feet, who cannot stand an unpleasant odor, who loses a whole day's peace of mind when, the horror!, he has found a louse on his coat – may he go all the more quickly to the store, the office, wherever he likes, but may he quit the folk school, the orphanage, because there is no more humiliating role than earning one's bread with revulsion.

"I despise filth, but I'm a good caregiver," you say with a shrug of the shoulders.

You're lying: in your mouth, in your lungs, in your blood you have the air that the children have befouled.

Fortunately, my activities as a doctor liberated me once and for all from the fatal sin that a caregiver might commit. "Yuck" does not exist for me. Perhaps that's precisely why my wards love cleanliness.

49. Fabre[40], the ingenious French entomologist, vaunts the fact that he made epoch-making observations of insects without killing any. He studied their flight, their habits, their worries and joys. He observed them attentively as they were rejoicing in the rays of the sun, fighting and dying in battle, searching for nourishment, building their shelters, stocking up. He was not indignant; with an intelligent gaze, he followed the mighty laws of nature in their barely discernible flickers. He was a folk teacher. He did his research with the naked eye.

Caregiver: be the Fabre of the world of children.

The Orphans' Home[41]

1. The technique for directing an orphanage depends, in its minute yet decisive details, on the building in which it is housed and the land where it is built.

How many bitter accusations fall upon the heads of children and staff for the mistakes of the builder, how many unnecessary impediments, how much work and anguish is brought by negligence in the construction plan. If an alteration is possible, how much hardship will it take to discern it and to convince others of its necessity? There are mistakes that cannot be corrected.

The Orphans' Home was constructed under the sign of mistrust of children and staff. To see, know, and prevent everything. The enormous recreation room – it's an open square, a marketplace. A single watchful person takes everything in. The same goes for the great barrack-like dormitories. Such a building has real virtues: it allows you to get to know the children quickly; appropriate to summer camps and for the main bureau from which children would arrive to other, differently constructed orphanages, it is wearying that it lacks a "quiet corner." Noise, commotion, jostling each other – the children complain, and they're right to.

If, in the future, it were possible to add an extra floor, I'd speak in favor of a hotel system: a hallway, with small rooms along both sides...

Besides an isolation room, quarters for sick children, it is necessary to designate a space for children who are just not feeling well. A bumped leg, a headache, having slept poorly, in a fit of anger – let him have a snug corner where he can spend a certain time alone or with a comrade. One such child, getting in the way, knocked around between everyone else having fun, resentful, isolated, arouses sympathy, sometimes angers those around him...

The toilet and urinal have to form a whole with the large dormitory, or else even be located within the dormitory. Placing entrance halls and corridors between them is nonsense. The more we hide the toilet, the filthier it will be…

Placing the snug apartment of the institution's director far from the children removes him from essential pedagogical influences. He can monitor the office, the accounting, can represent the institution, correspond with the authorities, but he will be a stranger, a guest, and not the host of the orphanage. For the orphanage is "the minor details" – one mustn't forget that. The builder is obliged to situate the person who runs the institution so that he must be a caregiver, so that he sees and hears the child not only when he is answering a summons to the office.

2. I once came across the opinion that philanthropy, without healing any of society's wounds, without satisfying any of its needs, fulfills two important tasks.

It seeks out ills that the state has not yet noticed, not yet appreciated. It researches, it initiates, yet seeing its powerlessness, it demands benefits; in the end it passes the obligation over to the local community or to the state, which can render aid fully.

Its second task is innovation, seeking out new ways in what the state does schematically, routinely, and cheaply.

Besides state care for orphans, everywhere there is also private care, which is sometimes better: grander edifices, a richer diet, a more liberal budget, more elastic governance. Here, however, the tyranny of bureaucratic regulations can be replaced by the unpredictable and menacing caprice of a powerful benefactor.

If we consider that at times the entire initiative, all the effort of those in charge, amounts to indulging the tastes of inexperienced caregivers who know neither the difficulties, nor the mysteries of raising children communally, we will understand why it is so hard to incline more worthy types toward work in child welfare institutions, which is why they bring in the dregs and the wasters.

If the powerful patrons saw what kind of poison an irresponsible worker is for the institution, they might renounce once and for all the imposition, or at least just the recommendation, of persons who are admittedly unsuitable, yet "worthy of our support." The patronage system is an offense – a criminal one.

The child-protégés also demand discussion as well:

"The child must be accepted. An exceptional circumstance."

The child who doesn't quite meet the criteria[42], who brings everyone else harm, will be of no benefit to himself. No pressure, let alone violence, is acceptable in making the caregiver keep a child in his institution against his own better judgment.

The caregiver must have the right to say, "This child is harmful." We must trust him. The caregiver must have many rights, because orphanage work is hard. In matters of caregiving, his voice is decisive.

The caregiver ought to have a certain monthly budget to use exclusively at his discretion, for there are objects that can seem unnecessary, there are costly expenses that one can put off, but to the caregiver they are necessary, and immediately so.

An important point.

If the orphanage has several trustees, there should be *a book in which the trustees record their remarks, demands, and questions.* There will be fewer of them, they will be more moderate, there will be no contradictory directives.

A couple words on volunteer staff. They are a significant benefit; they give the institution an extravagance of care for which the regular staff, buried in the drudgery of daily work, has neither the time, nor the imagination. Someone shows up to tell a story, someone else takes a group of children on an excursion, offers supplementary lessons to a few. But do not let them be their own burden on the staff, let them abide most strictly by the regulations, let them manage on their own, asking nothing and requiring nothing.

3. The year the Orphans' Home was constructed was an unremarkable one. Never have I better understood the prayer of work and the beauty of genuine action. Today's square on a map, a piece of paper, has tomorrow transformed into halls, a room, a corridor. Accustomed to arguments over viewpoints, principles, convictions, here I was witness to construction. Every volatile decision was a directive to the artisan, who made it manifest for all time. Every idea has to be assessed, evaluated on the basis of cost, feasibility, and functionality. And it seems to me that the caregiver who doesn't know that out of wood, sheet metal, cardboard, straw, and wires one can create dozens of objects that facilitate and simplify his work, that save valuable time – and thought – hasn't been sufficiently educated. A little shelf, a notice board, a nail, when stuck in the appropriate place, solves pressing challenges…

The building was to be ready in July; in October, it was still not finished. And so on a gloomy, drizzly afternoon the children, freezing, excited, cocksure, armed with sticks and twigs, arrived noisily from the countryside to an institution filled with craftsmen. They were given dinner and sent to bed. The former shelter had been located in an unsuitable rented location with haphazard furnishings, tattered clothes, and the incompetent care of a stupid housekeeper and a clever cook.

I calculated that, with new quarters, new conditions, and prudent care, the children would immediately accept the new rules for their cohabitation. But they had declared war before I had managed to appreciate the situation. I believed that my camp experience would shield me from surprises. I was wrong. For the second time, I had encountered the children as a threatening pack before which I stood powerless; for the second time, clear and mighty truths had started to take shape in painful experiences.

Against the demands placed on them, the children assumed a position of absolute resistance that the word was incapable of breaking, and compulsion aroused aversion. The new building they'd dreamt of all year was becoming repugnant. It was only significantly later that I understood the children's fondness for their former life. In its disorder, in the Gypsy poverty of its conditions and the total lack of means there was ground for free initiative, an extravagance of individual, powerful, and short-lived efforts, a fantasia of lush willfulness, the verve of a powerful act, the need for self-restraint, no care for tomorrow. Thanks to the authority of a few, order suddenly appeared for a short time. Here there was supposed to be permanent structure bolstered by impersonal necessity. That's why the children on whose help I had counted the most wilted and disappointed. And it seems to me that the caregiver forced to work in chaos and a scarcity of means should not sigh for structure and comfort overmuch – there are great difficulties and significant dangers there.

4. How did the children manifest their resistance? In trifles that only the caregiver can understand. Minor, elusive, and all the more unbearable for being numerous. You tell them they're not allowed to leave the table with bread; one inquires as to why that has to be, several hide bread, one stands up ostentatiously: "I didn't even get to eat yet." They're not allowed to hide anything under their pillows and bunks: "They're going to take things from my lockbox." You'll find a book under a pillow – he'd though that a book was allowed. The washroom is closing: "Hurry up." The response: "One second." Why doesn't he hang up his towel? "But I have to hurry." One has taken offense, three imitate him. During lunch, a rumor that there was a bug in the soup – a plot: they don't want to eat the soup. You see a couple of blatant ringleaders in this stubbornness and resistance; you sense there are several in hiding. You see the insidious ruination of something you'd thought was established, you encounter unforeseen difficulties in every initiative. In the end you are no longer conscious of what manifests accident, what is incomprehension, and what is conscious ill will.

A key is lost, a moment later it's found; and you hear an ironic remark: "I'm sure you were thinking I hid it, right, sir?"

Yes, indeed: you had been…

To the question of "Who did it?" you receive the constant response: "We don't know." Who spilled this, smashed this, broke this? You explain that it's not a big deal, you ask them to own up to it. The silence – it's not fear, it's a conspiracy.

It has happened that while addressing them my voice has broken and my eyes have welled with helpless tears.

Every *young* caregiver, every *new* caregiver, has to endure these hard hours. Don't let him be discouraged, don't let him say prematurely, "I don't know, it's impossible." It is only apparent that words don't work, a collective conscience is slowly awakening, the number of adherents to the caregiver's good will and of more judicious direction will increase from one day to the next, the camp of partisans for the "new direction" is growing stronger.

A Recollection

One of our worst rascals broke a rather expensive faience urinal while cleaning it. I didn't get angry. A couple of days later the same boy shattered a five-liter bottle of cod liver oil. And this time as well I gave him only a mild talking-to.

It helped: an ally…

How easy management is when the caregiver rules over the flock; what hell the work is when the caregiver thrashes around powerlessly, and the flock knows it, feels it, and is a vengeful antagonist. He is in such danger of acceding to a system of the most brutal violence for the sake of his own security.

5. Fifty out of a hundred children who are taken to the Orphans' Home from their former shelter were, in the final tally, the familiar kind who bound their mutual experiences and hopes to ours; who took a great liking to Miss Stefania[43], the Orphans' Home's main caregiver; who resisted being organized but were capable of it. In a short time, a new fifty, and thus new difficulties, had been taken in. In our home, a day school had been established, which allowed me to confirm the gulf that divides the teacher-aristocrat from the Cinderella-caregiver.

The administrative year ended in our triumph. One housekeeper, one caregiver, a guard, and a cook – for a hundred children. We became independent of any kind of staff and the tyranny of the shelter personnel. The host, worker, and director of the home became – the child himself. Everything that follows here is the children's work, not our own.

The Notice Board

In a visible spot on the wall, not too high up, hangs a board upon which you use thumbtacks to post all the directives, notices, and announcements.

Without a board, life is anguish; you say, loudly and clearly:

"Children: A, B, C, D" – they go, they take, they do – "such and such."

Suddenly E, F, and G come up to you…

"Me too?" "And me?" "What about him?"

You repeat yourself; it doesn't help:

"What about me, sir?"

You say:

"Go ahead, go get…"

Again, questions, noise, confusion.

"When? where? what for?"

Questions, demands, pushing – they pester and frustrate. But it couldn't be any other way. For not all the children have heard, not all of them have understood, not all of them are sufficiently sure that they know precisely, and ultimately even the caregiver could overlook something in the tumult.

In the chaos of current affairs the caregiver must issue directives that are immediate, not well-thought-out, not carefully studied, and are therefore imperfect; he must decide quickly, and thus based on his temperament and presence of mind; something unexpected always surfaces at the last moment. The notice board initially forces him, and later accustoms him, to work out the plan for every undertaking in advance. Caregivers do not know how to communicate with children through the written word – that's a big mistake.

Even where the majority of children don't know how to read, I would hang an announcement board: not knowing the letters, they'll learn to recognize their names, they'll feel the need, they'll sense their dependence upon those children who do read.

An announcement:

"New clothes will be issued tomorrow at ten o'clock. Since not all the clothes are ready, the following will not receive them: A, B, C, D… The old clothes will be collected by: F and G…"

An announcement:

"Has anyone found or seen a small key with a black ribbon?"

"Whoever broke the windowpane in the lavatory, please come forward."

A notice:

"Yesterday the boys' dormitory was filthy again."

"The children are destroying the books, scattering the pens."

"It isn't 'eye-adine,' it's 'iodine.'"

"It will be Easter in one month. We request that the children offer ideas and suggestions for how to spend the holidays pleasantly."

"Whoever wants to change his place in the dormitory (or at table) should report to his classroom at eleven o'clock."

Notices, warnings, and requests are now posted no only by the caregivers, but by the children as well. All kinds of things. The board is alive. You'll wonder how you could have ever gotten along without it.

"Excuse me, sir, but me too?"

"Check the board."

"I don't know how to read."

"Ask someone who does."

The board gives the caregiver and the children the opportunity for initiative. A calendar, a thermometer, important news from the daily paper, a picture, a riddle, a graph of fights, a list of damages, the children's savings, weight, height. As before a shop window display, a child will stand before it when he has time and desire – he'll stare. One can even post major cities, the population of each, the cost of grocery items. You won't anticipate everything...

The Mailbox

The caregiver who has acknowledged the utility of written communication with the children will be quickly persuaded of the need for a mailbox.

The notice board provides the caregiver a habitual answer, and one that therefore requires no effort: "Read it." The mailbox provides the opportunity to defer every decision by responding: "Write it down."

It is often easier to write than it is to say. There is no caregiver who wouldn't accept letters with a question, request, complaint, apology, confidence. It has always been this way: the box codifies a prudent custom.

In the evening you remove a fistful of papers unskillfully scrawled over, and just as you're reading them attentively in peace and quiet you'll think about what you would have discounted for lack of time and thought during the day.

"Can I leave tomorrow because my mommy's brother has arrived?"

"The other kids tease me."

"You're not being fair, sir: you sharpen everyone else's pencil, but you didn't want to sharpen mine."

"I don't want to sleep by the door, because at night it seems like someone's coming in."

"I'm angry with you, sir."

"The teacher from school was saying I'm better behaved now."

"I would like to speak to you about a certain very important matter."

At times you'll find a little unsigned poem: it came to mind, he wrote it down, didn't have anything to do with it, tossed it in the box.

You'll find an anonymous note with uncensored invective or a threat.

There are everyday letters, ordinary ones, rare and exceptional ones. Something gets repeated constantly – you'll think up how to sort it out, remedy it, but tomorrow, not today. You'll muse longer over the content of an exceptional letter.

The mailbox teaches the children:

1. To wait for an answer: not right away, not on demand.

2. To distinguish between the minor and fleeting grudges, worries, wishes, and doubts and the major ones. Writing it down requires a decision (and nevertheless the children will often want to take back a letter they've tossed into the box).

3. It teaches them to think, to state their case.

4. It teaches them to want, to know how.

"Write it down and put it in the box."

"I don't know how to write."

"Then ask someone who does."

At first I made a mistake I'd wish others to avoid: I dispatched the chronic bores to the box, not without some irony. Having understood the insult, they quite rightly got offended at me and at the box.

"One cannot talk to you at all now, sir."

I heard a similar accusation from the caregivers, too: isn't written communication with the children too official?

I maintain that the box does not hinder oral communication with the children, but facilitates it. I choose the children with whom a longer, confidential, sincere, or serious conversation is necessary; I choose a moment that suits myself and the child. The box saves me time; because of it, the day becomes longer.

There are unquestionably children who do not enjoy writing, but they are perhaps exclusively the ones who rely on their personal influence, a smile, a kiss, coquetry, special treatment, and a moment luckily seized. They don't want to ask, they want to extort. Whoever's sure of himself counts only on being right, submits his application, and calmly awaits a decision.

The Shelf

A shelf can complement the board. We don't have one yet in the Orphans' Home, but we feel the need. On the shelf: a dictionary, a collection of sayings, an encyclopedia, a description and map of the city, anthologies, a calendar, a collection of games and toys (a tennis handbook, footballs, etc.). A couple of checkers sets for general use. A library is necessary; handing out games at certain hours and on certain days, monitored by the person on duty, keeps them from being destroyed; but it should be the college and research station for the children's unmonitored social instinct. They will destroy and lose things – too bad.

There is room on the shelf for notebooks written by the children. One records the songs he likes best, another jokes, a third riddles, a forth dreams; a notebook of fights or arguments, of tardiness, damages, of lost objects. Dailies and monthlies edited by the children on nature, travel, literature, and society.

Duty reports and journals can be placed here. The caregiver's journal can rest here. Not every journal has to be kept mandatorily under lock and key. It seems to me that a journal in which the caregiver confides the disappointments he has felt, the difficulties he has encountered, his mistakes, pleasant and joyful experiences, as well as painful ones – this can play a large role.

Here's the place for the log of who goes into town, what for, when they go and come back, and for a "notary book." Children eagerly exchange, desert, and sell items from their own minor property. We shouldn't be averse to this, much less forbid it. If a pen knife or strap is a child's property, why can't he exchange it for a pencil case, magnet, or magnifying glass? If we're concerned about fraudulent transactions, arguments, and feuds, we introduce the notary book, which will prevent abuses. If the children are reckless and inexperienced, let's give them the opportunity to acquire the necessary experience!

(Since I ascribe significant value to the caregiver's journal, I will quote a couple of excerpts from my own:

"Today I got angry at one of the boys unfairly. Unfairly, because he could not have done otherwise. But what am I to do if my duty is to stand guard over the equal rights of everyone? What would they say if I were to allow one of them to do what I reprimand others for?..."

"The older children gathered this evening in my room. We discussed the future. What are they in such a hurry for, why do they want to be grownups so badly? Naive, they think that being older means doing what you want. They don't see the chains that weigh upon our adult will."

"Another theft. I know that where there are a hundred children one must find one – or more? – who's dishonest. And yet I cannot resign myself to it. I might as well resent the lot of them."

"He's really straightened out. I was afraid to believe it prematurely, but I've been observing closely for two weeks already – maybe he's made himself a good friend. I sure hope he has."

"I have once again learned of a certain distasteful affair. I'm pretending I don't know. It's so unpleasant to just keep grumbling, griping, getting mad, investigating."

"Strange boy. Everyone respects him. He could have great influence, but he keeps his distance from all of our undertakings. Strangely separate and reserved. It's not egoism, not ill will on his part; he can't go about it any other way, and it's a shame."

"What a lovely day. Everyone healthy, active, cheerful. Everything somehow went well, smoothly, quickly. Oh, to have many days like this!")

Lost and Found

The caregiver casts a reluctant eye on the contents of the children's pockets and drawers. They lack for nothing: pictures, postcards, shoelaces, little nails, pebbles, rags, beads, boxes, small bottles, stained glass, stamps, bird feathers, pinecones, chestnuts, ribbons, dried leaves and flowers, paper figures, tram tickets, fragments of what had been, the germs of what is soon to be. Every trifle has its own often rather intricate story and distinct origin and different worth, sometimes a very great sentimental value. Here there are remembrances of the past and longing for the future. A small seashell is a dream of traveling to the sea, a screw and a few wires – an airplane, proud fantasizing about aviation; the eye of a long-broken doll – the sole memento of a beloved who no longer is and will not be again. You'll even find the photograph of a mother and, wrapped in pink crepe, two pennies from a dead grandfather.

New objects show up; some of the older ones lose their value. Thus one exchanges, gives away, then regrets and takes back.

I'm afraid that the caregiver-brute, not understanding, and thus discounting, in his anger over pockets wearing out and drawers getting jammed, mad about arguments and unrest, because what gets lost gets found – scattered, disorderly, with impunity – that in a fit of ill humor he gathers these treasures into a pile and tosses the garbage into the furnace. He's committing an astounding abuse, a barbaric crime. How dare you dispose of someone else's property, you pig! How dare you then require that the children respect anything or love anyone! You're not burning scraps of paper, but beloved traditions and fantasies about the sweet life.

The caregiver's task is to demand that every child has something that constitutes not the anonymous property of the institution, but his own, that there be a secure hiding place for this property. If the child puts something in his little drawer, he has to be certain that no one will touch it, because two beads are his expensive earrings, a chocolate wrapper is a rentier's promissory note, a journal is a secret document deposited in an archive. Beyond that, duty commands that we facilitate the child's finding what he has lost.

Thus, a glass cabinet for found objects. The most minor object has its owner. Whether something is lying under the table or has been left on the window or is half-buried in sand in the yard – it must find its way to the cabinet.

The fewer ownerless objects there are in a given orphanage, and the more minor property there is, the more acutely you feel the plague of constantly giving back and seizing found trifles and of the complaints that something's missing. How do you store what they give you as found? You put it in your pocket: an example of dishonesty.

In the Orphans' Home there is a lost-and-found box. The one in charge of the box carries it to the glass cabinet and returns it at the appointed hour.

During a period of intense struggle for order I have surrendered every errant hat, apron that hasn't been hung up in its place, every book left on the table – to the lost and found.

The Shop

A plague of rightful, appropriate demands from the children: a notebook, a pencil, a nib, a shoelace, a needle, a thimble, a button, soap – from morning till night. Something is forever running out, breaking, tearing, something's always needed – never a moment's peace.

Thus, the shop: a small room or perhaps a wardrobe, even just a cabinet. But you issue items once a day, at an appointed hour. Whoever's late or has forgotten has to wait until the following day. Anyway, do you need convincing?

In issuing items, one records who received what and when. If you accuse a child of breaking nibs, you have the opportunity to confirm it with facts, figures, to compare them with others. The shop issues certain items for free, others at low cost.

The Broom Stand

I ought to have provided the heading, "Duties." I preferred to write "the broom stand" in order to emphasize that duties are worthless if we do not at the same time win respect for the broom, washcloth, bucket, garbage pail.

The tools of manual labor have already acquired a certain respect. And no matter how a book continues to occupy a privileged position, it is now the hammer, the plane, the pliers that have come out of hiding in their dark corner, from a box under a bed, and the sewing machine has been allowed into our stately rooms.

At the Orphans' Home we dragged the broom and washcloth from their hiding place under the stairs, we put them not only in view, but in a place of honor next to the dormitory's front entrance. And a strange thing: in the light of day this common folk was ennobled, they grew in spirit, they rather pleased the eye with their aesthetic appearance.

The two dormitories have six brooms. If there were fewer, how many arguments, quarrels, and fights we'd be witness to. If we take the position that a well-scrubbed table is tantamount to a carefully written page, if we take care that the children's work not replace the paid work of the staff, but that it elevate and educate them, then we must examine it not any old way, but thoroughly, put it to the test, divide it among everyone, and monitor it, and adjust it, devote a great deal of thought to it.

A hundred children – a hundred workers for maintaining order and running the house, a hundred levels, a hundred degrees of strength, know-how, a hundred temperaments, character traits, good will or indifference.

Settling upon duties is not the beginning of the organizational work, but its conclusion – not a one-time "sit-down" with the children, but several months of labor, both the manual kind and that of an alert and creative mind.

One must first of all know the work and know the children. I have seen such incredible sloppiness in the division of labor in orphanages that the duties corrupted the children, bedeviled them, taught them to hate any kind of work.

There are easy duties that demand neither physical strength, nor skill, nor moral attributes – they're easily managed, passively performed, without tools. For example, setting up chairs or picking up scraps of paper.

Whoever dusts already has a dust towel for which he's responsible.

Classrooms that have up to four children on duty demand a harmonious coordination of activities.

There are morning duties and evening duties, daily ones and weekly ones (distributing underwear, bathing, cutting hair), one-time duties (beating the mattresses), summer ones (outhouses), winter ones (shoveling snow, etc.).

Every month one draws up and posts a new roster of children on duty. This activity is preceded by written applications submitted by the children. Thus:

"I want to have dormitory duty." "I want to mop the classroom and look after the bath towels." "I want lavatory duty, and if not that, then cloakroom duty." "I want toilet duty and to give out the food at Table 8."

Every duty has candidates who reserve the positions to be vacated in advance, set it up, win consent; there are numerous negotiations. Someone who's bad at his duty must run around a lot, make a big fuss, make many promises before he secures himself a place.

"I don't want to be with you, because you argue, because you're late, because you're lazy."

Not a tenth of this great pedagogical work reaches our attention. Every office has its good and bad sides, every job demands harmonious coexistence. A child receives a raft of new and pleasant emotions and encounters unexpected difficulties in his new duty. The fact that he is doing something new spurs his efforts; barely has he managed to get bored when he sees the need to redouble his energy if he is to gain the right to his sought-after place or retain the one he occupies.

Here one achieves total equality of age and sex: a younger but diligent child advances quickly; a boy obeys a girl.

Where there are several children on duty on the same terrain, one is older. Every floor has its responsible child on duty. There is nothing artificial in this division. Administering others' work is a burdensome obligation; responsibility is no fun. Those uninitiated into our organization would make accusations on account of this gradation. Each should monitor himself; as in life, however, everything doesn't always happen as it should. Among children, too, one comes across a certain percentage of careless, unconscientious, and frivolous workers; anyway, someone must not only monitor, but teach and assist. And here the caregiver, wanting to have time for longer conversations with individual children in particular cases, should communicate with the mass of children in writing. Those on floor duty and the older ones in charge of more important branches of household management provide an account of their duty every evening in little diaries to be handed in.

Albeit that only a portion of the duties at the Orphans' Home are paid, I am of the opinion that they should all be paid. Wanting to produce good citizens, we don't need to create idealists. The Orphans' Home is not deigning to look after children who have no parents, and in substituting for the dead parents in their material care it has no right to demand anything from the children. Why don't we have to teach the child as early as possible what money and compensation for work are, so that he feels the value of the independence that a wage provides, so that he learns the good and bad sides of possessing. No caregiver will raise a hundred idealists out of a hundred children; a few of them will emerge of their own accord, and woe to them if they don't know how to count. For money provides everything except happiness; it even does provide happiness, and reason, and health, and morality. Teach the child that it also offers unhappiness and illness, that it takes away reason. Let him eat his fill of ice cream from the money he's earned, and let his stomach ache; let him argue with his friend over ten groszy; let him gamble it away, lose it, have it stolen from him; and let him regret his purchase, let him be tempted by a lucrative duty and learn that it wasn't worth it, let him pay for the damage he's caused.

The Tutorial Board

Instead of explanations, I am providing the journal of one of our pests, which he wrote for a young female tutor, alongside her notes.

April 16
I would like to be a carpenter. Because when I'm gearing up to travel I'll be able to make a case, and I'll be able to put different things in that case— clothes, and food, and I'll buy a sabre, and a shotgun. If wild animals attack, I'll defend myself. I'm deeply in love with Hela, but I'm not going to marry a girl from the Orphans' Home.

The tutor's note: Hela likes you, too, but not so deeply, because you're a troublemaker. Why don't you want to marry a girl from our institution?

I don't want to marry anyone from our institution because I'll be embarrassed. When I'm already gearing up to travel in order to discover a part of the world I'm going to learn to be a good swimmer, even on the ocean. I'm going to America, I'm going to work hard, I'll make money, I'll buy a car and drive all across America in my car. But first I'm going to the savages and I'll be there three weeks. Goodnight.

The tutor's note: Goodnight. And are you going to write to me?

R. and I were discussing what it was like for us at home. I said that my father was a tailor, and R.'s father was a shoemaker. But now it's like we're in prison here, because we're not home. And if someone doesn't have a father and mother his life is worthless. I told about how my father would send me for buttons, and R.'s father would send him for nails. And there was more. Because I forgot.

The tutor's note: Write more clearly.

This is how it has to be. When I return from my travels, I'll get married. Please advise me about whether I should marry Dora, Hela, or Mania. Because I don't know who I should take for my wife. Goodnight.

The tutor's note: Dora said that you're a brat, Mania doesn't give her consent, and Hela laughed.

But I wasn't asking you to ask them, I only wrote which one I love. Now I'm worried and am embarrassed; all I did was write who I love. Now what? Now I'm embarrassed to go up to them. Please tell me what table I'm supposed to sit at so that I behave well, and write me a long story. And please don't show this to anybody, because I'm afraid of writing a lot. And I really want to know what an Australian looks like, what they look like there.

The tutor's note: If they're not embarrassed, you shouldn't be, either. One cannot write stories in a small notebook. If they'll let you, sit at Table 3. I'll try to show you an Australian. I won't show them your journal.

I think that being twelve will be a great joy for me. When I leave, I'm going to say goodbye to everybody. I don't know what to write.

The tutor's note: You said that you have so much to write that you don't know if you have enough room, and now you don't know what to write.

Please give me advice, because I'm terribly troubled and I don't have a clean conscience. I'm so worried because in class I'm the one, and I don't know why, who always has one fault on his mind, but I'm afraid of making this fault real. It's that I'd steal. But I don't want to trouble everyone, and I'm trying as much as I can to straighten out. So I don't think about this fault, I think about traveling. Goodnight.

The tutor's note: You've done a very good thing in writing to me. We'll have a talk, and I'll give you some advice. But don't get offended when I tell you something.

I've already straightened out. I'm becoming friends with G. – he's already straightened me out. And I'm really trying. But why can I go out only every two weeks? I'm the same as everybody else, after all, so why do they have to be better than me? And they go out every week, and I only every other. I want to be the same as all the other children. My grandmother asked me to come see her every week, and I'm ashamed to say I can't.

The tutor's note: You know why you're not allowed to go out like everyone else. I'll ask, but I doubt it will work.

I was already in trouble, too, because I was thrown out of the school, I was supposed to be thrown out of the Orphans' Home if they don't let me into the school. And now I'm already going to school again. I already know thirty-five nations. I have a book about travel. A real book. I really want to have some kind of box. Please respond.

The tutor's note: I'll look for or try to get a box to give you. But can you write to tell me what you'll use this box for?

I really need the box, because I have a lot of things, and letters, and little books, and a whole lot of necessary things. Now I'm not friends with anybody anymore, because I don't have anyone to be friends with. When this notebook is used up, will I get a new one? I wrote it sloppily because I write on two lines. I'll write everything, I'll record my troubles, the bad things I've done, what I'm thinking about, and different stuff. I have a whole lot of interesting things to write…

The boy was nine years old, his tutor – twelve.

The Sit-Down Discussions

A child thinks not less, not worse, not more poorly than adults; he thinks differently. In our thinking, the images are faded and ragged, the emotions dull, dusty. A child thinks with his emotion, not his intellect. That's why it is so difficult to communicate with them, it's why there is no more difficult art than speaking to children. For a long time it seemed to me that one must speak to children easily, intelligibly, absorbingly, vividly, convincingly. Today I think differently: that we ought to speak briefly and with feeling, picking over neither our expressions, nor our phrases – openly. I'd rather say, "My demand is illegitimate, harmful, unfeasible, but I must demand it from you," than justify it and demand that they admit its legitimacy.

Gathering the children, griping in front of them or scolding them – and forcing praise upon them – this is no discussion.

Gathering the children, lecturing them, stirring them up and choosing a few to take on an obligation and responsibility – this is no discussion.

Gathering the children, lecturing them about how you cannot manage, so let them come up with something so things will be better – this is no discussion.

Noise, havoc – slapdash voting – is a parody of a discussion.

Frequent lectures and frequent discussions trivialize this kind of appeal for a group suggestion for initiating something or explaining some matter, the malady of the day.

A discussion should be practical, the children's remarks listened to carefully and honestly – no insincerity or pressure – the decision postponed to a time when the caregiver is working out a plan of action. If the caregiver does not know, doesn't have the skill or the ability, the children also have a right not to know, not to have the skill or ability.

And no unfeasible promises! The stupid and the mindless children make promises, the reasonable and honest ones get angry and sneer.

One has to work hard for the possibility of communicating with the children. It doesn't come on its own! The child has to know that he is free to speak up and that it's worthwhile doing so openly, that it won't provoke anger or aversion, that he will be understood. What's more, he has to be sure that he won't be laughed at or suspected of wanting to kiss up – by his friends. A discussion demands a pure and dignified moral atmosphere. There is no more pointless farce than setting up elections and voting that are supposed to come out in a favorable spirit for the caregiver.

Beyond that, the children must learn the technique of leading discussions. It is not easy to debate as a pack.

One more condition. Compelling people to participate in deliberations and voting is unjust. There are children who do not want to take part in deliberations – are you going to force them?

"It's just blah blah blah, and there's no order."

"What should we come together for, sir, when you'll just do what you want?"

"What kind of discussion is it when no one can say anything because they laugh or get angry?"

One shouldn't discount this criticism, nor explain it away as dictated by ill will. The more critical children are right to complain…

If I judge sit-down discussions harshly today, it's because when I first started working at the Orphans' Home I overestimated their value – my mistake was the abuse of the word.

One way or another, discussions stir the collective conscience of the flock, they elevate the sense of mutual responsibility, they leave a mark. But beware. There is no unconditional camaraderie and solidarity in a flock, nor can there be. I'm bound to one by nothing more than a common roof over our heads and the morning bell to get up, to another by a shared school, to a third by what we like, to a fourth by friendship, to a fifth – by love. Children have a right to live in groups and individually, by their own effort and their own thinking.

The Newspaper

A pedagogical institution without a newspaper seems to me to be the haphazard and hopeless pacing and grumbling of the staff, going around in a circle without direction or monitoring for the children, something ad hoc and random, without tradition, without memories, without an evolutionary line into the future.

The newspaper is a powerful link: it joins one week to the next and binds the children, the staff, and their support into one indivisible whole.

The newspaper is read aloud in front of all the children.

Every change, improvement, reform, every ailment and complaint finds its expression in the newspaper.

One can treat it in the couple lines of a news brief, in a short column, or in the lead article.

One can merely note:

"A got into a fight with B." Or: "There's more and more fighting. Once again we must record a fight between A and B. We don't know what they fought over, but does every argument necessarily have to end in fighting?" Or: "Enough with the Fist," or "This Has to End" – the matter is discussed under a sensational headline.

For the caregiver, who has to understand the child and himself, the newspaper is a perfect regulator of words and deeds. The newspaper is a living chronicle of his work, efforts, and mistakes, of the difficulties he has struggled against. The newspaper legitimates his competence, bears witness to his activities, defends him against potential accusations. The newspaper is an invaluable scientific document.

Perhaps it won't be long before colleges offer lectures on pedagogical journalism.

The Collegial Court

If I devote disproportionately numerous passages to the court, it is because I am convinced that a court can become the seed of a child's equal rights, it leads toward a constitution, it compels one toward an announcement – a declaration – of the rights of the child. The child has a right to have his affairs taken seriously, to have them weighed fairly. Until now, everything has depended on the goodwill and the good or ill humor of the caregiver. The child has not had any right to protest. One must put an end to despotism.

The Collegial Court Codex

If someone does something bad, it's best to forgive him. If someone has done something bad because he didn't know, then now he knows. If he has done something bad unintentionally, he'll be more careful in the future. If he does something bad because he's having a hard time adjusting, he will try. If he has done something bad because he was talked into it, next time he won't listen.

If someone does something bad, it's best to forgive him, to wait for him to straighten out.

But the court must defend the quiet children so that they're not harmed by the aggressive and the impudent ones; the court must defend the weak so that they're not tormented by the strong; the court must protect the conscientious and the diligent so that they're not held back by the careless and the lazy; the court must see that there's order, for disarray is most harmful to good, quiet, and conscientious people.

The court is not justice, but it should strive for justice; the court is not truth, but it desires the truth.

Judges can make mistakes. Judges might punish for acts that they themselves commit, they can say something is bad when they do it themselves.

But it is shameful when a judge consciously hands down a perfidious verdict.

How Does One Bring a Suit?

The notice board hangs in a visible place. Everyone has the right to register his case on the board: his own name and that of the person he's taking to court. He can sue himself, any child, any caregiver, or any adult.

The clerk records the cases in a book every evening and collects statements the following day. Testimony can be made orally or in writing.

The Judges

The court meets once a week. Judges are chosen by lot from among those who have not been brought to court in the last week. Five judges are drawn for every fifty cases to be judged.

It can happen that there are a hundred and twenty cases. That needs fifteen judges. And there aren't that many who haven't had a single case in the course of a week. In this instance lots are drawn from everyone, and groups are established in such a way as to not have anyone judging their own case.

Verdicts are handed down according to the codex; additionally, the clerk has the right, with the judges' consent, to refer certain cases for examination by the Judicial Council or for a court session, to be examined in everyone's presence, so that everyone hears and knows precisely. The court clerk is the caregiver. Verdicts are recorded in a book and read out to everyone. Those not satisfied with the verdict may submit their cases for reexamination, but no sooner than after a month has passed.

The Judicial Council

The Judicial Council consists of the caregiver and two judges chose by secret ballot for a three-month term.

Besides verdicts, the Judicial Council works out the rules incumbent on everyone.

Since the judges on the Council might also have cases, five judges are chosen for the Judicial Council, of whom only three judges hear cases.

The Clerk

The clerk does not hear cases; he only collects statements and reads them out during sessions. The clerk keeps the court's notice board, the book of statements and verdicts, and the table of damages, he administers the compensation fund, he maintains a graph of the verdicts, and he edits the newspaper.

How the Court Maintains Order

If someone is late, makes noise, causes a disturbance, doesn't put his things away, cuts into line, litters, makes the home untidy, goes where he's not allowed to, teases, argues, and fights – then he is disorderly. One must consider what to do.

The court can forgive him, say that he's misbehaving, or ask the Council to permit him to shirk the rules a couple times or a few times a month.

The Council can give him time to think over what he's done.

The Council can allow one person to do something that no one else is allowed to do: let him be an exception.

Taking Care that an Obligation Is Met

Whoever doesn't want to study or work, who does everything carelessly, harms himself and is no use to anyone else.

If the court does not help, one must turn to the Council. Perhaps he's sick, perhaps give him time to adjust, perhaps release him from work altogether?

Taking Care of People

Different people are all together. This one's little, that one's big; one is strong, another weak; this one's smart, that one less so; one is cheerful, another sad; one is healthy, another has an ache. The court sees to it that the big one doesn't hurt the little one, and that the little one doesn't get in the older one's way. That the smart one doesn't exploit or make fun of the stupid one. That the quarrelsome one doesn't annoy, but that the others not bother him, either. That the cheerful one doesn't make stupid jokes at the expense of the sad one.

The court must see to it that each has what he needs, that no one is miserable or embittered.

The court can forgive, but it can also say that someone has acted inappropriately, badly, very badly.

Taking Care of Property

The garden, the yard, the building, the walls, the doors, the windows, the stairs, the stoves, the windowpanes, the tables, the benches, the cabinets, the chairs, the beds – if they're not looked after, they'll be broken, destroyed, filthy and ugly. The same goes for the coats, clothes, hats, handkerchiefs; the plates, mugs, spoons, knives – if they're lost, scratched, smashed, shattered – that's just a shame. The same goes for the books, notebooks, pens, toys – one ought to respect them and not destroy them.

The loss is sometimes small, sometimes big; the concern is sometimes minor, sometimes great.

The person who has inflicted the damage is registered with the court, which weighs whether he is to make up for the loss himself or whether the court will cover the cost with its own funds.

The same thing applies to the children's private property.

Taking Care of Health

Illness, disability, and death—these are a great misfortune. A windowpane can be replaced, a ball purchased for the one that was lost; but what do you do when someone knocks out an eye?

Even if there has been no misfortune, everyone has to remember that they must be careful.

The Judicial Council determines how long an announcement about an unfortunate accident or an illness caused by neglect has to remain on the court's notice board.

No One Knows Who...

No one knows who did it. The culprit doesn't want to own up to it. If one really tries, one can always find out. But how unpleasant it is to search, investigate, suspect. If something happens, and no one knows who did it, the unknown person is sued in court, there's a trial, the judges judge, and the verdict is posted on the court's notice board. If it's an act that brings shame on the entire institution, the Council rules that a black mourning banning will be stitched onto the institution's flag.

Everyone Does It

If something is repeated often and judgement cannot fall on everyone, one must think through what to do.

"Everyone's late. No one hangs up his hat."

Untrue – not everyone, but many. One child does it a couple times a week, another once a month. But it's true that there's disorder.

The Council decides to post a graph or undertakes something else so that there isn't chaos.

Exceptions

A certain child cannot conform, a certain child breaks the rules. You've tried – nothing helps. What do you do? If we allow one to do what is forbidden to the others or release him from what is prescribed to everyone, will something bad come of it?

The Judicial Council can make an exception for someone until such a time as he has asked that it be removed. The Council determines whether to place these exceptions on the court notice board.

§§ 1-99

There are ninety-nine articles of acquittal, or those that say that the court has not weighed in on the case. And after the case it's as though there is no case, or else a trace of guilt obliges the accused to try not to do it again.

§ 100

The court says that he is not at fault, offers no reprimand, doesn't get angry, but, regarding § 100 as the minimum punishment, includes it in the table of court verdicts.

§ 200

Two hundred says:

"He has behaved inappropriately."

Tough, it happened. It can happen with anyone. We ask him not to do it again.

§ 300

Three hundred says: he's done a bad thing.

The court condemns him. If in Article 100 and Article 200 the court asks him not to do it again, here it demands that it not be repeated.

§ 400

Four hundred: serious guilt.

Four hundred says: you've done a very bad thing, or: you're behaving very poorly.

Article 400: this is the final attempt, the final willingness to spare the guilty party shame, the final warning.

§ 500

Article 500 says:

"Whoever has committed such an act, whoever is so indifferent to our requests and demands, does not respect himself or does not care about us. Thus we, too, have no opportunity to spare him."

The verdict is announced with his first and last name on the newspaper's front page.

§ 600

The court posts the verdict for a week on the court notice board and announces it in the newspaper.

If Article 600 has been handed down because someone repeatedly does the same thing, his behavioral chart can be posted for a longer period, but instead of his full name only his initials are provided.

§ 700

In addition to the consequences provided in Article 600, the content of the verdict will be sent to the family.

For it may be that he will have to be expelled. Thus one ought to warn the family. If you were to tell them right away, "Get him out of here," the family might complain that they hadn't been given warning, that it had been concealed from them.

§ 800

Article 800 announces: "The court is no help." Maybe punishments that were once used in pedagogical institutions would help, but we don't use them anymore.

We offer one week for reflection. During that week, he can neither bring a case to the court, nor will we bring him to court. We'll see whether he straightens out and for how long.

The verdict is announced in the newspaper, posted on the notice board, and the family notified.

§ 900

Article 900 announces:

"We have lost hope that he will straighten out."

This verdict says:

"We do not believe him."

Or:

"We are afraid of him."

And finally:

"We don't want anything to do with him."

In other words, Article 900 expels him from the institution. He might remain, however, if someone assumes responsibility for him. Expelled, he might return if he finds a tutor.

The tutor answers for all his faults before the court.

The tutor can be a caregiver or one of the children.

§ 1000

Article 1000 announces:

"He is expelled."

Every expellee is entitled to request re-admittance after three months have passed.

The Chart of Verdicts

Just as every patient in a hospital has a fever graph, a chart of illness and health, the court notice board features a chart of the institution's moral health – and one can know whether things are going well or poorly.

If the court has issued four verdicts according to Article 100 (100 x 4 = 400), six verdicts according to Article 200 (200 x 6 = 1200), and one of Article

400, all together that would be 400 + 1200 + 400 = 2000, and on the chart we register that this week the sentences amounted to two thousand.

The Codex

The court does not judge the case.

§ 1. The court declares that A has withdrawn his complaint.

§ 2. The court regards the accusation as meaningless.

§ 3. The court does not know what really happened and therefore recuses itself from judging the case.

§ 4. The court expresses its belief that nothing of the kind will be repeated and is therefore not judging the case.

Note: the accused must express his consent to judgment under this article.

§ 5. The court recuses itself from judging the case in anticipation that these offenses will soon disappear on their own.

§ 6. The court is postponing the case for a week.

§ 7. The court has been duly informed of guilt.

§ 8. ...

§ 9. ...

The court offers praise, thanks, or expresses regret.

§10. The court sees no fault in A's act, but rather an example of civil courage (bravery, integrity, noble impulse, honesty, goodness of heart).

§ 11. The court thanks A for informing it of his guilt.

§ 12. The court apologies for the inconvenience of the court summons.

§ 13. In expressing its regret for this having happened, the court nevertheless does not find A guilty.

§ 14. ...

§ 15. ...

§ 16. ...

§ 17. ...

§ 18. ...

§ 19. ...

The court sees no fault.

§ 20. The court acknowledges that A has met his obligation (has behaved as required).

§ 21. The court finds that A had a right to act (to speak) as he did.

§ 22. The court finds that A was in the right.

§ 23. The court finds that A has committed no offense against B.

§ 24. The court finds that A has told the truth.

§ 25. The court finds that A has done nothing wrong.

§ 26. ...
§ 27. ...
§ 28. ...
§ 29. ...

The court assigns fault to the circumstances / the instance / to several people / to someone else.

§ 30. The court acknowledges that A could not have done otherwise.

§ 31. The court assigns fault to the circumstances / the instance without faulting A for what happened.

§ 32. Since several people did the same thing, it would be unfair to condemn one.

§ 33. The court assigns responsibility to B for the act committed by A.

§ 34. ...
§ 35. ...
§ 36. ...
§ 37. ...
§ 38. ...
§ 39. ...

The court calls for forgiveness.

§ 40. The court finds that B should not be angry with A.

§ 41. The court asks that he be forgiven.

§ 42. ...
§ 43. ...
§ 44. ...
§ 45. ...
§ 46. ...
§ 47. ...
§ 48. ...
§ 49. ...

The court forgives because it sees no evil intent.

§ 50. The court forgives A, who might not have known or understood, and expresses its hope that it will not be repeated.

§ 51. The court forgives A, who did not quite understand, and expresses its hope that this will not be repeated.

§ 52. The court forgives A, who did not know this would happen (he did it inadvertently, through carelessness, by mistake, out of forgetfulness).

§ 53. The court forgives A, because he had no intention of causing an offense against B.

§ 54. The court forgives A, because it was a joke (a stupid joke).

§ 55. ...

§ 56. ...

§ 57. ...

§ 58. ...

§ 59. ...

The court forgives in consideration of extenuating circumstances.

§ 60. The court forgives A, because he did (said) it in anger and is impulsive, but he will straighten out.

§ 61. The court forgives A, because he did it out of obstinacy, but he will straighten out.

§ 62. The court forgives A, because he did it out of false ambition, but he will straighten out.

§ 63. The court forgives A, because he is quarrelsome, but he will straighten out.

§ 64. The court forgives A, because he behaved this way out of fear, but he wants to be more manly.

§ 65. The court forgives A, because he's weak.

§ 66. The court forgives A, because he behaved this way after being teased.

§ 67. The court forgives A, because he behaved this way out of a lack of consideration.

§ 68. ...

§ 69. ...

The court forgives because there has already been a punishment, since it sees his regret.

§ 70. The court forgives because A has already been punished for his deed.

§ 71. The court forgives, because A regrets having acted in this way.

§ 72. ...

§ 73. ...

§ 74. ...

§ 75. ...

§ 76. ...

§ 77. ...

§ 78. ...

§ 79. ...

The court is trying to forgive.

§ 80. The court forgives A, because it is of the opinion that only kindness can straighten him out.

§ 81. The court is attempting to issue an acquittal.

§ 82. The court forgives without losing hope that A will straighten out.

§ 83. ...

§ 84. ...

§ 85. ...

§ 86. ...

§ 87. ...

§ 88. ...

§ 89. ...

Exceptional acquittals.

§ 90. The court forgives in consideration that A wanted it so badly that he didn't have the strength to restrain himself.

§ 91. The court forgives, because A has not been with us long and cannot understand order without punishments.

§ 92. The court forgives, because A will be leaving us soon, so the court does not want him to depart from us with resentment.

§ 93. The court forgives A, because it finds that he was spoiled by excessive good cheer on everyone else's part; the court warns A that everyone is equal before the law.

§ 94. The court takes under advisement a friend's (brother's, sister's) fervent appeal and forgives A.

§ 95. The court forgives A, because one voice among the judges insisted steadfastly upon it.

§ 96. The court forgives A, because A did not want to say what might have justified his actions.

§ 97. ...

§ 98. ...

§ 99. ...

§ 100. Without offering forgiveness, the court states that A did that of which he stands accused.

§ 200. The court finds that A acted inappropriately.

§ 300. The court finds that A behaved badly.

§ 400. The court finds that A behaved very badly.

§ 500. The court finds that A behaved very badly. The verdict is to be announced in the newspaper.

§ 600. The court finds that A behaved very badly. The verdict is to be announced in the newspaper and posted to the notice board.

§ 700.The court finds that A behaved very badly. The verdict is to be announced in the newspaper, posted to the notice board, and conveyed to A's family.

§ 800. The court strips A of his rights for one week and is summoning his family for a discussion. The verdict shall be announced in the newspaper and on the notice board.

§ 900. The court seeks a tutor for A. If a tutor is not found for him after two days, he will be expelled. The verdict shall be announced in the newspaper.

§ 1000. The court expels A from the institution. The verdict shall be announced in the newspaper.

Supplements to the Verdict

a) The court is grateful for the truthful testimony.
b) The court is surprised that A did not report this himself.
c) The court asks that this not be repeated.
d) The court appeals to the Council and asks that it prevent this in the future.
e) The court asks the Council that it allow the verdict not to be carried out.
f) The court expresses its fear that A might grow into a harmful person.
g) The court expresses its hope that A will grow into a courageous person.

The Court Gazette 1
On the Collegial Court

Grownups have courts. These grownup courts are not good. So every few years they change them a little. Courts for grownups lay out different punishments: monetary fines, arrest, prison, hard labor, even the death penalty. These courts are not always fair – sometimes they're too lenient, sometimes too strict, sometimes they're wrong: someone says he's not guilty, but they don't believe him; sometimes he is guilty, but he gets away with it. And people are still thinking about what can be done to make the court fair. And there are also people who think about what to do so that courts wouldn't be necessary, so that people didn't do bad things.

In schools, it's the teacher who judges; in schools, the teacher lays out the punishment: he stands you in the corner, throws you out the door, puts you in detention, often he shouts, sometimes he hits. There are punishments like missing lunch or not being allowed to visit your family.

And here anger is not always appropriate, punishment is not always appropriate.

So here, too, people are thinking about what to do, what to change. There have been various attempts, there will be various attempts. One such attempt is our collegial court.

The collegial court says that someone is not guilty or is guilty, but the court forgives him; or else the court does not forgive – it *gets angry*, it invokes Article 100, which means that the court is a little angry, or Article 200, 300, 400.

The court doesn't get mad, doesn't yell, doesn't hurl insults, doesn't offend; it calmly says:

"You acted inappropriately, badly, very badly."

Sometimes the court tries to shame someone: if they're ashamed, maybe they'll control themselves more.

Our court has already held five sessions. It gathers together every week – it has weighed 261 cases. And though it's hard to say whether the effort has succeeded, one can already say something about it.

The first week provided us with thirty-four cases. All of the accused submitted to the court themselves.

We had posted a slip of paper three times.

On the first paper was written:

"Whoever was late yesterday, please register with the court."

Thirteen registered.

On the second paper – a couple days later – was written:

"Whoever went out without notice, please submit to the court."

Six registered.

On the third paper – a couple days later – was written:

"Whoever made noise in the dormitory yesterday, please submit to the court."

Fifteen registered.

In this way, we gathered the thirty-four cases that the court examined at our first session.

The court forgave everyone.

In the introduction to the collegial court, the following was written:

"If someone does something bad, it is best to forgive him."

And the court forgave.

Only nineteen times did the court say:

"Guilty."

Only ten times did the court say:

"Article 100."

Only six times:

"Article 200."
Only twice:
"Article 300."
Only once:
"Article 400."
We know: there are those who do not like that the court forgives so many things.

Our codex has an Article 1.
Article 1 announces:
"The complaint has been withdrawn."
This means that the person who brought the case to court forgives it himself.
Of all the articles, this first article is repeated most often.
There were 120 cases in which one person brought another to court. And here, the one who brought the case himself later forgave in sixty-two instances.

There are those who say:
"What punishment is that – Article 100 or 200?"
For some, it's a punishment, for others, not:
"So what? They yelled at me, they're angry with me – but I don't care."
There are those who say such things.
It also happens that if someone is thrown out the door, locked in the classroom, or even beaten, he'll also say:
"So what? I just stood there behind the door – I just sat in detention for an hour – it didn't hurt at all."
Whoever says that Article 100 is not a punishment, let him answer, but honestly: does he want to have a trial and get Article 100 or 200, or doesn't he?
If § 100 causes no great distress, we actually do want everyone to conduct themselves well, not wanting to receive even a small punishment, a minor distress.
We even want everyone to conduct themselves well without fear, without anger, without a court. And maybe that's how it will be in the future.
§ 100 is a punishment – everyone understands that. And whoever says otherwise either hasn't thought it over or doesn't want to tell the truth.
The longer we have the court, the more we'll lose the habit of anger, reprimands, and punishments, the greater the significance will be not only of Article 100, but also of those articles that forgive.

There are those who say:

"Take every foolishness to court right away."

And that's not appropriate at all.

We don't always know whether someone is submitting himself or someone else to court as a joke.

We have Article 2, which says:

"The court finds that it is not bothering to weigh cases like this."

Out of 261 cases, the court has found that it is not worth judging a case only four times. Only four times! But here, too, we cannot say whether it was a joke, a dimwitted joke.

Sometimes a minor matter hurts a lot. People are different. One person cries over what makes another one laugh.

The matter of calling names – is it nonsense, or not? Sure, it's nonsense, but how many tears have been shed over it?

We had forty-three cases of name-calling. And there were those who really suffered, because it is hard to say what's an innocent nickname, what's an insult or, worse – persecution.

Is it a minor matter if they pour water on someone as a joke, or take something and tease and don't want to give it back? If I am in a good humor, I'll be laughing about it myself; but if I am upset, the joke makes me feel angry or hurt; I have the right not to want jokes today, or else not to joke with everyone.

The court has been around for a month now. Not everyone understands yet. We are sure that there will be fewer and fewer insignificant cases as the court wins respect.

There are those who say:

"How's that shrimp going to judge me?"

First of all, there are five judges, and there is always one older child among them. Secondly, not every little kid is stupid. Thirdly, one needs to be honest to judge, and a little kid can be honest, too.

It might be unpleasant to an older child that a little kid is judging him. But a court isn't there to be pleasant.

"It's unpleasant being a judge," the voices rang out.

We believe that it is. And that's precisely why judges are chosen by drawing lots. And this way is better than voting.

If someone judges often, judges for a long time, he can go bad quickly – he learns to look on other people's guilt as though he were himself without sin. But when someone is a judge once, he can learn a great deal, too: he'll see how hard it is to be just, and how important justice is.

We have now had the court for five weeks. There is not much we can say, but it seems to us that the court has already been beneficial to many.

If someone were to say, "Stop, or else I'll take you to court," and he stops, then although the court knows nothing about it, it has still brought a benefit: defense.

We know that they often say with a laugh, "I'm going to take you to court." Who is so stupid that he can't tell a joke from the truth? It also happens that someone says with a laugh, "So sue me."

This is sometimes an innocent joke, and sometimes it is spite directed at the court, which looks into every case seriously, calmly, and honestly, and which never refuses anyone help when they turn to it – it always has the time to make inquiries, hear out complaints or defenses, it does not hurry and does not jokingly brush off even the most minor case, which always contains someone's sorrow or anger.

Yes, the court is unpleasant for those who are called "bootlickers," of whom one says that "still waters run deep" – and for the wily ones who do a lot of bad things, but carefully. The bootlicker knows that they like him, so there's a lot he can get away with so long as it's nothing awful. The quiet one sometimes teases more than the one who yells and hits. But a clever one will manage to weasel out of the disagreeable matter, too. And that's why they find it more convenient without the court, so they want to ridicule and destroy it. But the court takes no offense, it will just go on carefully seeking improvements and changes, at the same time performing its duty to the best of its knowledge and skill.

It is now, and it will always be, that one person will have ten cases in a month, while another – one in a year. There is nothing to be done about this, and there is no need to do anything about it. Let each person figure out for himself what he wants to do with the court.

There had been great concern over whether the court would manage if there were too many cases. Now the concern is gone. The court can, over an hour or at most two, take care of a whole week's cases, even if there were a hundred or more. And anyway, we know that the beginning is always difficult.

If the court could bring about such order that there was no longer any need, neither for getting angry nor for keeping watch, just to spend an hour each week taking care of sweeping out all the week's wrongdoing, the way a room gets swept in the evening or morning, that would be quite nice and convenient indeed.

Let us now consider a few cases from past weeks: they will perhaps convince us that the court is of benefit precisely in that it is calm, that it is never in ill humor, nor in good, that it neither likes nor dislikes anyone, that it calmly gives their explanations a full hearing.

Case 21. One is not allowed to make noise in the dormitory. But they messed up his bed, therefore he scolded them angrily, and thus loudly. § 5.

Case 42. They poured water on him as a joke. What is he to do? Pour water on them, too? hit them? quarrel with them? This can be forgiven. He himself will no doubt forgive, but not now, not right away. He will forgive, but they shouldn't do this again.

Case 52. A girl is walking on stilts. A boy walks up to her: "Give me your stilts." She doesn't want to give him her stilts. The boy starts to beat her up, tears the stilts away, pushes her, hits her in the face. The girl cries – instead of a happy game, she has sorrow. What for? Why? She takes the boy to court, but then she forgives him. § 1.

Case 63. Everyone calls him names. It really worried him initially, but then he got used to it. Tough – one cannot fight and argue with the entire world. Suddenly a court appears, heralding a new, better order. And so he chooses the one person who calls him names most often, most hurtfully, and takes him to court. We summon him a month later: "Do they call you names less now?" "Yes, they do." With a smile of gratitude for the court, which has defended him.

Case 67. She was late coming home from her family. Why? She has only one aunt, no one else. She wouldn't go see her aunt, because she didn't like her. Why is not our concern. She finally did go, made up with her family, took a stroll with her cousin – they sat down on the grass, they talked. She forgot that she had to return home. The court forgave her.

Case 82. The person on duty wants the child to trim his nails; he claims that he needs them to dig holes in the earth (he works in the garden). The work is done in four days – then he allows his nails to be trimmed. Is he in the right? § 61.

Case 96. They have run through the old list of sheets to be aired out; a new one has not been written yet. The person on duty asks, "Who wants to air out their sheets?" No one does. So he turns to two boys: "Do yours." They do not want to – they had done it recently. § 1.

Case 107. She had removed a book from the reading room and taken it to the yard, where she had been peeling potatoes. She forgot it, left the book on a bench. A two-year-old child came and tore the book up. § 70.

Case 120. A rolling hoop flew into the neighboring yard. They went to find it. A little boy found the hoop and did not want to give it back. An argument ensued. We received a complaint that the boys behaved impolitely. § 3.

Case 127. He put on someone else's jacket by mistake. Scabies can be spread by similar mistakes. § 31.

Case 144. He took a belt and did not want to give it back. He took it for fun and is having fun not giving it back. He runs away, laughs. "Give it back this instant!" "Here," he teases, and he runs away. Certainly, it is not an especially important case. But cases like these teach us that not everyone likes jokes, and those who do like them do not want to joke all the time and with anyone. § 54.

Case 153. He slammed the door – he registered his own case. So what if not everyone who slams the door registers on the board? So what that someone else will do a truly bad thing and hide it. These minor cases are particularly interesting because they are the expression of an alert conscience. There are quite a lot of these cases; we imagine that there will be more. There are people who are sorry for having done something bad that they're not punished for. § 31.

Case 160. One is allowed to go out to the front yard only at certain hours. One of the older girls goes out to the front yard; the child on duty, a younger boy, forbids it. She does not like this; she doesn't want to listen to a younger child. What is he to do? He takes her to court. The court will not take your head off. It forgives, but it expresses the hope that this will not be repeated. And the court's hope is binding.

Case 165. A case of false suspicion. We had several of these cases. False suspicion often hurts worse than being hit. A girl is counting pennies. Up walks a boy: "Show me." She says, "I don't want to." "You don't want to show me because you stole it." Yesterday he lost a penny and was looking for it. She does not know about that, and even if she did, how would she recognize his, and what right does he have to insult her? § 1.

Case 167. They have broken a girl's bead necklace; she is picking up the beads and threading them; she is upset. She is leaning over, and just then they put cherry pits on her neck. "Stop it," she says angrily. "And what will you do if I don't stop?" "I'll take you to court." "Go ahead." The court date arrives: the complaint is withdrawn. § 1. We mentioned that there were upwards of fifty such cases. We may be mistaken, but it seems to us that they teach some people respect for their neighbors, and others forbearance.

Case 172. He climbed a tree to show a friend he knows how, but he registered with the court because he knows it is not allowed. § 90.

Case 206. He washed a bowl in the cloakroom; he did not know it was not allowed. He learned it was not, and he registered with the court. § 51.

Case 218. He was talked into going to court. He did, and now he sees that he has done a stupid thing: better to go to court when you have a complaint. § 1.

Case 223. Four boys were having a lesson at a table. After the lesson the table was covered in ink. The court had a hearing, and it turned out that only one had written on Table 36:3, and one had his ink splattered. If not for the court, the anger would have fallen on them all. § 4.

Case 237. They were joking around, chasing each other, until one of them hit another hard with a stick. His arm hurt badly, so he registered with the court; it stopped hurting, he invoked Article 1.

Case 238. Some people will find this case funny as well. Both were relieving themselves in the toilet; one accidentally, unintentionally sprinkled the other, who then deliberately did the same to him. § 200.

Case 252. The floor monitor has a lot of trouble with him. He forgets, he has to be sought out, he does a sloppy job tidying up. She has threatened to take him to court many times. It has not helped. She has finally lost her patience and taken him to court. But she has forgiven him: maybe he will straighten out.

Case 254. Those on duty are sweeping the courtyard in the evening. One of them still has to clean the toilet, and both have to wash their feet before bed. And that's when they lock them out in the yard and don't want to open the door. § 100.

Case 258. She is always late. The child on duty tells her to finish up in the lavatory, and she gets angry, does not listen, calls names. "When I feel like it," she says. "You're just angry at me."

And it is all forgiven after a couple days, but in the meantime taking her to court substitutes for an argument. § 1.

Case 260. He was making noise in the morning before the wake-up call. He registered himself with the court. The court forgives and asks that it not happen again. § 32.

The Court Gazette 9

They are not afraid.

The court does not help. They are not afraid of the court – one often hears such opinions.

So some people do not want to take others to court, and so they keep things from the court. Others invoke Article 1, because the court won't do anything anyway. Still others finally say, "Go ahead and take me to court. I'm really scared."

And increasingly the cases did not come to the court's attention. Until finally H., who had been dismissed from his duty, neither thought it necessary to register with the court, nor did any of those who knew about his having been dismissed take him to court. Not only did H. stop using the court, but so did the older girls, and then the boys as well.

It is all the more interesting that some nevertheless submitted to the court up to the last moment. This shows that there are honest people everywhere who do not do what "everybody" is doing, but who conduct themselves according to their conscience and their own judgment.

The court does not help.

It is always easier to say that something is not worth it than to think. One can always find tongues for wagging, but it is difficult to find a head for thinking. Somebody has said, "It doesn't help," and the rest, like sheep, repeat in a chorus, "It doesn't help."

And those who have shouted the loudest are the ones for whom the court was inconvenient, a hindrance, dangerous. For the court has given people the right to make a complaint and to have it weighed on its merits.

"He will receive Article 4 or Article 54."

For one, § 1 would be enough, or §4, or § 54; for another, even § 800 will be without consequence.

The court's task is to introduce order among people, but it cannot make miracles, nor does it want to.

It would be a miracle if, after getting § 100, a slacker were suddenly to become hardworking, or if someone who is aggressive, noisy, and quarrelsome were to become peaceful and kind. In the same way, no one in school changes from a dunce into a model pupil after receiving an "F" or "D."

But the court gives everyone the right to say:

"Starting tomorrow, I'm going to be careful. I am determined not to do this again. I want to be careful."

And should someone want to get in his way, he can take them to court. Example:

Someone who starts fights resolves to stop. Certainly, they will anger him on purpose, because there are those who do not like when someone wants to straighten out: he sues those who are provoking him. So what if they sue him back for taking them to court frivolously? The court will know what to think about this.

The court does not make miracles, but neither does a request, or a threat, or anger, or the rod make such miracles. And where there are punishments, there are those who say:

"So what? It didn't hurt at all."

And they do not straighten out, but fall to ruin, they vulgarize.

"It doesn't help. So what should I do – do I have to keep turning to the court?"

What, then? Is it so much work?

At first, C. was provoked constantly and by everyone; he took them to court, they laughed at him, they teased him, but he kept doing it. Finally they stopped getting on his case, so he stopped suing them.

I am sure that if someone who has abused his power on duty were sued three times a day over the course of two weeks, he would have to finally straighten out. Only those on floor duty were too lazy to register; it was more convenient to get mad, argue, wring their hands over how they cannot manage. Because, in taking it to court, they are exposed to the fact that *the court might not rule in their favor,* because they think themselves infallible, because often, instead of speaking softly, they start arguing – because they do not have the patience to wait a couple days.

There is too much anger; that is why the court has served as a tool for revenge. This anger demanded that the accused at least have his name posted immediately, and that is why § 4 or § 100 has not been enough for anyone.

When we were talking about anger over the summer, one of the boys wrote:

"When I am angry, I could kill."

The court did not kill anyone, so they have born a grudge against it.

There have been other grievances as well:

"The court hears out one side, and it doesn't listen to the other."

If a small child would sue an older one, the older one wouldn't show up, though he had been summoned. There was no way around it.

In general, the older children did not come to the classroom, though they had been asked to attend.

Contempt of court was the proof that it had been completely misunderstood. And worse still: not understanding it, it was subject to contempt and ridicule.

Judging was a game for some, for others – an unpleasant obligation they felt like weaseling out of.

"I'm taking something to court on purpose so I don't have to judge."

This was either a falsehood or an ugly deceit.

Instead of teaching the truth, the court taught lying; instead of teaching honesty, the court taught shiftiness; instead of producing courage, it built up cowardice; instead of inspiring thought, it made people lazy.

There were more and more unknowns; no one wanted to own up to anything. Why? If they were not afraid of the court, why hide? He fishes around other people's lockboxes, but he does not have the courage to say, "I did it." He's taken a pen: he isn't afraid of the court, but he won't say, "I took it."

And worse still: they got mad at those who were saying that something of theirs was missing. It got to the point that if someone had something taken, he was afraid to mention it, because he also knew that he wouldn't find it, he would just have unnecessary heartache.

So some, instead of looking for it, accuse the unknown party, and others – the decent ones – accuse no one, because they are afraid.

And Article 1?

He sued someone, forgot about why. A person who knows how to think says to himself:

"If I don't even remember what I was suing for, I should invoke Article 1. Why take the time, why trouble them unnecessarily?"

They don't show up. They don't invoke Article 1. Why not? Because they don't understand that no one has ordered them to, no one is checking up on it, no one is threatening them – it's just what they're supposed to.

And the court statements?

It was often embarrassing to listen to them, embarrassing to record them. And yet it was so easy to say:

"I did a wrong thing."

Three times, only three times out of 1,950 cases.

It seemed that, thanks to the court, the adults could gain greater respect for the children; no, on the contrary, even those who had had that respect have lost it.

And it was still worse: the judges plotted either not to sentence people at all, or to do so lightly. Because that's more convenient. It finally reached the point that one judge hit another for judging according to his conscience.

It was difficult to wait any longer: the court is of no benefit; on the contrary, the court brings harm; the court does not introduce order; on the contrary, the court is bringing about disarray: the court is not straightening anyone out; on the contrary, it is spoiling those who had been more worthy. Such a court could not exist one day more.

Half a year's work wasted. Whoever does serious work in the future will see how this hurts, how it makes one sad.

Unfortunately, they are not afraid of the court, and precisely because they are not afraid, they have no respect, and because they have no respect, it is no longer to the court that they lie, but to themselves. For they do not want to think about and evaluate themselves, nor to muster the effort to right themselves.

I know that the court is needed, that in about fifty years there will not be a single school, a single institution of learning without a court. But for the Orphans' Home the court is harmful because they do not want to be free people, because they want to be slaves.

H. I am selecting only certain of his cases.

Twenty cases of name-calling. Nine times he received § 1, nine times they forgave him – it did not help. Twice § 60. Twice § 4, plus § 63 and § 82. Three times § 100, once § 200, once § 300.

Eleven cases of provoking, teasing, and ridiculing. Twice § 1, four times § 54, twice § 82, once each § 41, § 100, and § 200.

One case of disrupting work: § 300.

Twelve cases of fighting. Three times § 1, twice § 54, §§ 32, 60, 80, 81; twice § 100, once § 200.

Ten cases about duties. Twice § 1, once § 4, §§ 32, 82, twice each of §§ 100-400, 500, 700.

Three times, poor conduct in class. §§ 80, 82, and 200.

Three times, getting his head dirty. §§ 1, 54, 200.

He did not wash his hands: § 100.

He broke an inkpot: § 81.

He broke a mug: § 31.

He gave his food away: § 4.

He cheated at a game: § 100.

He backbit: §§ 60 and 200.

He was tardy: §§ 70, 82.

He butt in: § 100.

Incorrigible, and yet there was no brave person with the courage to sentence him under § 800, thereby revoking his right to use the court.

The Court Gazette 19
"The Judicial Council"

For half a year we have had a court without a Council. It was necessary to try out the court up front, then to expand and improve it.

The court alone has not been enough. Having a hundred cases a week, it has had to dispose of more important cases perfunctorily for lack of time.

The Judicial Council has been at work for ten weeks already; it has examined seventy cases, or seven cases a week.

Cases such as these are referred to the Judicial Council:

1. All cases of tardiness in returning from a visit to one's family.
2. Cases where, besides a sentence, some rule incumbent on everyone has to be issued.
3. Cases with monetary damages (a broken window, something destroyed).
4. Cases where the sentence may come under an article higher than 500.
5. If someone brings enough suits in a single week that they all have to be considered summarily.
6. More difficult cases where it is necessary to question both sides long and carefully in order to find out who is right.

The court clerk says:
"We are referring this case to the Council."

Most often the judges agree to this. In a couple cases, the judges have ruled that they can judge for themselves.

It happens that those who have a case themselves ask that the case be judged by the Council. The clerk approves, but not always.

For the time being, this is not sufficiently regulated, but thought is going into it.

The First Case

H., a small boy, has already had many cases. No sentences have helped. He has laughed openly at the court, he has become impossibly spoiled, and he has clearly demonstrated that the court on its own, the court alone, does not help at all. There were two roads: either to rule that the court is utterly worthless and shut it down, or to exclude this one person from the court.

Brought to court once again, he insulted the court in a vulgar manner, and for insulting the court he was referred to the Council.

H. testified that the court makes him angry, that they tease him by constantly taking him to court, that they are constantly threatening him – wherever he goes, whatever he says, right away he will hear:

"I'm going to take you to court."

Finally, all out of patience, he told A. and the court most coarsely:

"I don't want a court, I'd rather they box my ears and rap my knuckles."

Entirely understandable: he prefers to wage war without punishment and to have his knuckles rapped one time out of a hundred than to straighten out and obey the regulations that apply to everyone else.

The judges on the Council split into two camps. Some wanted to forgive him this time, too. Others demanded § 900. H. was finally sentenced to § 800. H. was excluded from the court for a week, and for that week he had what he had wished for:

1. On Saturday he did not receive fresh stockings because he was late when they were being distributed.
2. On Sunday his knuckles were rapped because he did not want to clean up.
3. On Tuesday his ears were boxed for a brawl while peeling potatoes.

Given that he had been locked out of the court, he did not have a single case.

Besides his initial case H. had one other: that he had called an older girl a vulgar name long and loudly, with guests present. Since he had already received § 800, the court forgave him and assigned § 60.

The Second Case

An irredeemable, quarrelsome slacker. He is convinced that he is always right; he takes offense whenever something is brought to his notice. Poor at his duties, an unconscientious worker.

Because of him, the soup was thin: it lacked twenty pounds of potatoes. § 90.

He now has a job.

There has already been a complaint for his laziness.

The Third Case

An older girl.

Without asking for permission, she took scissors that are the private property of her caregiver, misplaced them, and in four weeks not once did she come to explain herself; she does not even look for them. § 400.

The Council considered three more cases at its first session.

1. I., on duty, did not want to pick up garbage. § 55.
2. They were roasting potatoes in the boiler room. § 41.
3. He is late to his duty assignment. § 30.

The Second Week

The Council had only one case on the second week.

A boy reads books during lunch and dinner; he does not respond when this is called to his attention.

Asked by the Judicial Council whether he wants to be an exception so that the Council would allow him to read during meals, he answers that he categorically does not want it. § 4.

The Third Week

Because of cases of untidiness around the lockboxes, the clerk is proposing a plan.

I. To completely get rid of keys, which are unnecessary in light of the fact that they do not protect the mysteries of the objects contained in the lockboxes, or
II. to designate responsible persons on duty who would sit at a separate table next to the safe from morning to night, or
III. to keep the cabinet locked and open it for an hour twice a day, or
IV. to track down the insolent pest.

The Council rejected the plan. It sentenced the unknown party to § 3 (no one knows how it happened), since:

1. many children allow others to go into their lockboxes while they are absent;
2. children share books among themselves and often exchange them without their owner's knowledge;
3. sometimes they accidentally go into someone else's lockbox.

If not for the Judicial Council, the cabinet might really have been locked up, and that would have been an inconvenience.

A certain B. has eight cases.

    Eight cases in one week.

1. A girl is standing there quietly, and he starts pushing and hitting her. "I'm going to take you to court." "Go ahead." And he keeps pushing and hitting. § 63.
2. A girl is holding a letter. B. tears her letter away, runs around the room with it, threatens to tear it up. § 63.
3. A boy is sitting by himself. B. starts pulling him, pushing him, yanking him. § 63.
4. A girl is standing next to the wastebasket. B. puts the wastebasket over her head. § 63.
5. One of the boys plays with him in the morning, but in the evening he does not want to. B. hounds him, accosts him, will not leave him alone. "I couldn't deal with him." § 63.
6. He goes up to a girl:
"You want me to beat you up?"
"Go away."
He does not want to leave her alone, he hits her and tosses her out of her chair. § 63.
7. He goes up to a girl:
"Have you had scabies?"
He hounds her and says that she had scabies. § 63.

    Furthermore, he has been reported for conducting himself poorly in his job. "He haggles over work, has a hundred answers for every remark, he butts in on everyone, he's disobedient." § 93.

    B. got out of these cases in one piece because the complainants stood up for him.

    "B. is not a bad boy, but he's annoying, irritating, unambitious. When anyone says, 'Go away, leave me alone,' it doesn't even occur to him to go away – he laughs and keeps provoking them. He is not stupid; it's sometimes pleasant talking with him. B. says that he is sad because there isn't anyone truly kind who would want to help him be different. In the store they forgive him for many things, so he's become spoiled, but he's already straightening out."

Other Cases

A case of two small children poorly behaved at table. § 81.

A case of two middle children leaving the school of their own accord. § 41-50.

A case of a girl on floor duty bearing false witness against someone else on duty. The Council ruled that he is to be rehabilitated.

The Fourth Week

There were only three cases on the fourth week, of which one was about a handkerchief being tossed into the laundry or sewing room.

The Burned Shoes

In the boiler room, two boys burned up two pairs of clogs and one pair of shoes. The housekeeper had ordered them to do it.

"It's not right. You could have repaired them."

"They were useless."

"Even the worst shoes can be repaired."

§ 33: the boys had fulfilled an order that was given to them – it is not their fault.

The Sewing Room

On Sunday, the boys enter the sewing room to sew some buttons, etc. One took the cotton, which they are not allowed to take; another wanted to sew a pocket, though he had one undamaged pocket that was completely adequate.

They tell him, "Get out." And he says, "You see her there? She'll tell me I can't, she's going to order me, yeah, to sew it, so what are you going to do about it?"

"She wanted to kick me out like a dog. Some people have two pockets – one of mine had a little hole."

At the end of the case, the first received § 40, the second § 200; it was decided that the repairs should be done in the recreation room, not in the sewing room; the older girl from the sewing room should keep a small book like those on floor duty do; and one must find out whether it is not in fact better to sew with cotton than with cheap thread.

The Fifth Week

Five cases.

Another person has been found who hates the court.

G. has five cases.

He makes noise in the dormitory. He does not feel like getting undressed, he approaches various beds, converses loudly; if you call this to his attention, he does nothing about it. In the lavatory he sings and whistles; if they say to him, "Stop it," he says:

"So sue me."

When he is on duty, he does what he wants to, he gets offended and does not clean up or does so carelessly. He behaves just as he pleases. He lies: he says that he has swept the dust out from under the stove, but it is not true.

Taken to court, he does not show up to give testimony: "I'll go if I feel like it."

A sick boy is lying down:

"What are you lying down for, what's wrong with you?"

He received no answer, so he beat him.

But this is how G. explains it:

"I can't stand the court, I hate it, I don't want to have anything to do with the court. I don't want to explain myself, not orally, not in writing, because I know that I'm often in the wrong. Everybody holds the court over my head, that's what makes me maddest. Let them take me to court, but don't let them hold it over me." § 700.

The court is not pleasant – that much is true. But it also hasn't been introduced for fun. Its task is to stand guard over law and order – the court's goal is for the caregiver not to be forced, like a cowherd or farmhand, to force others into obedience crudely, with the cane and yelling, but to consider, advise, and evaluate calmly and judiciously, with the children, who often have a better sense of who is right or else to what degree they are wrong. The court's task is to replace the brawl with the work of thinking, to exchange outbursts with pedagogical impact.

The Case of B.

He is once again before the Judicial Council.

Lazy, disobedient, and careless when he is on kitchen duty, all the same he is now being transferred to a new duty. He does not peel the potatoes there, and here he does not sweep the stairs. No matter that all the children are going to have thin soup, no matter that they are waiting for him before they can wash the stairs, because one cannot do so before they are swept.

"I'm just not going. I don't feel like it."

They approach him three times – nothing.

"If I had to take him to court, I'd have to take him to court every day. He doesn't bring the dustpan, he throws the garbage out the window or sweeps it under the stove. If he does happen to bring the dustpan, he doesn't put it back. He doesn't put away the broom, doesn't put away the washcloth. But if you mention it to him, he's always in the right."

"He's good, but impulsive. He gets offended and talks back in anger. He thinks it over later, you just have to put it right in his face. Not punctual!" § 82.

These are the workers who ruin the reputation of the Orphans' Home.

It is increasingly difficult to find good positions for our boys.

As we know, they complain about B. at his job: he has not been working long.

A Brawl

The kitchen. M. walks in and says:

"Hey, I ran into your sister, and she asked me to give you her regards."

"Big deal!"

"Some sister you are, you don't even want to know that your sister sends her regards."

"I already heard you."

Those present begin to laugh.

M. turns to another girl:

"Would you say the same thing if I ran into your sister?"

Laughter.

D. grabs a weight and throws it at one of the girls. When she is mad, D. often causes a brawl. § 200.

While Playing Dominoes

It used to be that when someone was called a "cheater," we did not know why. Now that one is allowed to play for candy or money, there is an ever greater influx of cases of dishonest play. For what had been done in secret now takes place openly and is monitored by the court. Why forbid everyone from doing something when there are only three or four cheaters? And what good is a prohibition if it cannot enforce whether they play dominoes or checkers just so, or for candy? And if someone loses toffees, which one must purchase, or money – what difference does it make? Some spend their money productively because they are sensible – they rarely play, they learn caution; and the frivolous and the stupid spend their money stupidly, and they gamble it away stupidly. If someone loses a stamp while playing against a cheater, maybe he will be careful, and when he grows up he will not gamble away his entire estate or someone else's money, because that happens, too.

The first case of dishonest play ended with one of the small children being barred from playing for a month, but that was too long: at his request, the ban was reduced to two weeks.

§ 3. No one knows how it was. These cases are always very difficult to judge.

The Sixth Week

Two important cases were settled: taking linen up into the attic, and giving away toys. We have taken the first step toward sorting out prayer time.

Unhelpfulness

"I always have so much trouble when we have to take the linen up. The boys don't want to carry it or carry it unwillingly. One is tired, another doesn't have time, and a third will come later. Unfortunately, it just happened that I sued the one who carries the linen more often than the others. But it happened that way because I don't approach the ones who refuse at all anymore. It made me angry that he said he was tired, and I knew that he wasn't tired, because it was already a half hour since he'd gotten back from school."

"What do I have to explain myself for? They'll say I'm guilty anyway, because they only ever believe the girls. I don't like going up to the attic, because they're interrupting me reading or playing, plus she makes this face that makes me mad. And anyway, I'm the one who always takes it on himself to get the boys together to carry the linen, we'll do it ourselves from now on. Just don't let her think I'm doing it because she took me to court." § 5.

"They were playing dominoes. I say, 'Come shake out the vests.' They answer that they already did some, though he hadn't, but he's tired. He showed up ten minutes later. But it was already too late."

"I had taken a letter to 99 Marszałkowska Street. I was playing dominoes – I wanted to finish the round. I'll shake out the vests from now on so I'm not called a lazybones." § 4.

Games

"I took them to court because I can't deal with it anymore. They take the games and don't give them back, they leave them on the table, they lose the cards for Old Maid and the checkers pieces. This makes a lot of trouble for me."

"The second I take something, someone else reserves it. I went to clean the classroom, so I lent it out for that time. I didn't know it would be lost."

"I took the picture Old Maid deck and was suddenly called out for my bath. So I had to put it away in my lockbox because I didn't have anyone to give it to." §§ 40 and 50.

At the Judicial Council's request, the Committee for Positive Recreation has established the following Regulations:

I.   One can play Old Maid or dominoes for candy, postcards, or money only on Fridays and Saturdays beginning at 4:30.

II.   One can quit the game after having lost thirty cents.

III.   One may lose at most fifty cents.

IV.   Those who owe money ought to pay it back within one week.

V.   Marked dominoes must be thrown out.

VI.   Whoever takes an Old Maid deck should see to it:

    a.   that there are no scraps of paper under the table,

    b.   that the deck is returned in a timely manner,

    c.   that they have agreed whether there are four or five players,

    d.   that they assume responsibility for lost cards.

Note: checkers are issued after 6.

One may not take games fifteen minutes before the time to return them. Games should be returned five minutes before meals.

Prayer Time

"He's always goofing off at the table, and during prayer he makes these faces that make everyone laugh. He's nice and cheerful, but during prayer he should behave properly."

The clerk has suggested that the Council issue rules on removing those who behave improperly during prayer from the room – for a week.

The Council resolved to set this case aside until such a time as a new boy starts reciting the prayers.

The accused received § 4.

A Judge before the Court

His lot had been drawn: he had to judge. He did not show up – he did not feel like it.

Why?

1.   Because then they resent you because they hand down punishments that are too harsh or unfair.

2.   Because he does not like the court, he does not want to have anything to do with the court.

The clerk proposes § 50 and exclusion from the court lottery for one to three months…

He does not understand!

He does not understand that judging is not a pleasure, but a social obligation, perhaps an unpleasant one.

He does not understand that the court can exist only insofar as there are judges.

He does not understand that "I don't like it, I don't want to" does not mean "I'm not going to." For every person often has to do what he does not want or like to do.

If the court were worthless, no one would turn to it; if they do turn to it, that means it has some benefit, and thus everyone is obliged to facilitate its work and not hinder it.

They say that it is strict, that it is unfair – they can turn to the court a second time, they can appeal. Of the 3000 cases judged since the beginning there have now been four appeals. Whoever does not just blather on about whatever pops into his head but sees to the fairness of the sentence can again submit his own case to the court after four weeks. The careless and dimwitted do not do this – they prefer to get mad.

The Experiment's First Year

I rated the value of the court and the benefit of the codex during its yearlong trial. There were 3500 cases. The smallest number of cases in a week was fifty, the largest – 130.

Twenty-five issues of *The Court Gazette* came out over the course of the year. The first, printed here in its entirety, was published after the first trial month.

The ninth issue was published a half-year later when the court was suspended for four weeks. After the break, the Judicial Council was introduced, and its activities are featured in issue 19 of *The Court Gazette.*

It seems to me that it would be most fitting to tell how things were:

I learned immediately in the initial weeks that many minor cases that vex the children, that incense them and upset the order, do not come to the caregiver's attention, and cannot. The caregiver who maintains that he knows everything is consciously lying. I have become convinced that the caregiver is not an expert in matters that concern the children; I have become convinced that the caregiver's authority elevates his competencies, that there is an entire hierarchy wherein every older child has a right to kick around or just simply to disregard anyone two years younger, that willfulness is apportioned precisely according to the ward's age. And the guard over this den of injustice is the caregiver himself. *Sic volo, sic jubeo*[I want this, I order this].

No matter that the caregiver does not give a beating or prod in that most rare instance when *someone, encouraged by his impunity, hits a younger or weaker girl in the face and takes her stilts.*

There had been a custom, a tradition, that the thirteen-year-olds would borrow pens or blotting paper from the little ones, but when a little one demanded it back he would hear this polite reply:

"Buzz off. Don't bother me about this."

There were several dozen of these "minor" cases. One had to learn – to study them laboriously – to understand them.

Many cases were still settled out of court. The conviction that "it's better to talk it over" than to conduct trials for any old thing was so ingrained that there was no way to combat it. This diminished the court's authority. If the older children don't acknowledge the court, if a raft of the most important cases don't make it to court, the court is something between a game and a dismissive brushing off of those cases about which one knows not what to do. Instead of "Leave me alone," the new formula sounded like "So sue me."

The accusation that the court doesn't help because they're not afraid of the court, because they get nothing out of the court, would resound unbearably and disruptively. One should emphasize that this is how it worked in an orphanage where there were officially no punishments.

When we speak of punishments, we always have our mind on switches, detention, deprivation of food, etc., skipping over the fact that a punishment like yelling, anger, a "dressing down," a threat, changing your attitude toward the child from friendly to hostile is a severe punishment.

The "litigiousness" of the little ones was fatal for the court. They would sue for "anything at all." Half of the cases were the minor feuds of a small group of the youngest children. Laughing over how little Mr. X or little Miss Y is a loyal customer of the court, the mood of mockery became fixed. "Sue me" was a constant formulaic response to a proper grievance. "Find some way to limit the number of cases" – the apparent necessity of this was building.

But how?

By saying that they weren't allowed to bring "foolishness" to court? I categorically maintain that this cannot be done. And it's an odd thing: if the judges have been inclined from the beginning to discount all the little ones' cases, even all the cases of hitting, name-calling, interfering – they nevertheless quickly acknowledged the correctness of the view that the gauge of a case's importance is the hurt it has called, the sense of injury that the complainant has.

Why is a broken window a serious matter, but destroying a child's private property has to be "foolishness"? Is cheating at a game of conkers not punishable dishonesty only because they're playing for chestnuts and not for money?

Playing conkers has provided a large number of cases; it has been the source of innumerable arguments. What does the caregiver do in these instances? He forbids them to play! Forbidding, he inflicts violence; forbidding, he makes it harder for himself to know the children gambling, when those character traits that have enormous import in life reveal themselves most easily, traits like frivolousness, greed, impetuousness, dishonesty, etc. A prohibition on play would be, in my opinion, as much harm to the caregiver as to the children. Playing conkers has been the little ones' first schooling in the rule of law. At first, unheard-of things took place: he has lost a hundred chestnuts and cynically declares that he won't hand them over. Why not? Because he doesn't want to. They band together: they'll pool their chestnuts, but then they've fought over them, and "I'm not going to give you my chestnuts." Some testimonies dumbfounded me. In broad daylight, among many witnesses, a boy loots a girl's chestnuts and blatantly mocks her: "I do what I want – what are you going to do about it?" Her only recourse is to turn to an older comrade who will assist her, but in what form? She'll bash him on the back of the neck, tug, push, throw him to the ground. Sinhalese customs in a properly run orphanage in the capital of a civilized country. And yet it wasn't long ago that not only did I, too, agree to a similar state of affairs, but it even had a certain grace: I was inclined to make light of the case because a cheery little rascal was closer to me than a slightly awkward "girly" was. However, the fact that this nice rascal tyrannizes a certain group of children, buttering me up at the same time, the fact that the little predator conducts himself with a sense of entitlement to disentitle others, was something that had gone unnoticed – it was beneath the threshold of my pedagogical awareness.

Often a single case typified a child for me better than working with him for a couple months. Sometimes a single case typified the milieu better than broad observation over the course of several months.

As the court clerk I got to know its ABCs, I developed, finally I was becoming an expert in their affairs.

A pile of irritating garbage – shriveled, flaking chestnuts – is revived. There were unremarkable chestnuts, those exceptionally suitable for game play, chestnuts as mementos and those that were especially lucky. "I always win with this chestnut – I said up front that I wouldn't play for this chestnut."

I ask: what caregiver has the time to weigh cases like these; who has the desire to weigh them against righteousness, the law, and not – give them a forgiving smile?

Thanks to these "minor" cases I was forced to rethink all the convoluted guesswork of communal life. An asocial, antisocial type, an individual who doesn't want to seize control over his habits and preferences, was emerging and, exceptionally forcefully, demanding an answer to the eternal question: what is to be done?

"I hate the court; I'd rather have them rap my knuckles and box my ears, I'd rather anything but the court." "I hate the court, I can't stand it. I don't want to take anyone there, and I don't want them to take me."

There were several like this. The court had surprised them as an unexpected and most threatening enemy-registrar, enemy-openness, enemy-light.

He doesn't want to explain himself, doesn't give a hoot about being right, doesn't think to push himself. He might succeed or not – and it is in this gamble that he finds pleasure: chance excites him, he lives from one adventure to another, he steers by the mood of the moment, outbursts suit him.

If there is that lucky one who has the opportunity for scientific study of the courts' pedagogical significance, I heartily recommend that he observe these children in particular.

And it is typical that this small handful has overthrown the court. In suspending the court, I did not doubt that it was a merely a weeks-long break for us to introduce certain changes and additions. Despite this, I experienced the break as a painful failure. For I understood how much hardship it would take for the court to clear a road for itself at other pedagogical institutions led by other people.

I know that all better caregivers wish to jettison the pesky necessity of grumbling, griping, mouthing off, and floundering, insofar as they do not want, after the fashion of German schools, to bash their preferred instrument dispassionately and proudly into wherever the rules dictate. But I know that the court must defer their hope for an easy, fundamental, and, most importantly, quick resolution of the hundreds of minor offenses, faults, infringements, dodges, and conflicts that occur in the life of a flock that has to be remade into a society of the rule of law. The court will not replace the caregiver, won't even assist him, but it will extend the range of his intercession, hinder and complicate his work, deepen and consolidate it into a system.

One can provide the children with notebooks, pencils, and pen nibs at different times, registering it only mentally – then there will be disarray; one can give them out at a certain hour on certain days, noting the date of distribution – there will be order and even a certain fairness. Sure, there may have been the sorts of orphanages where there are no fixed hours for meals, and the children eat when they want, the cleverer ones more, and more often, than the quiet and meek. One can apportion and mete out punishments, chastisements, reprimands, and reproaches without a court. There is disarray without diverging from what is generally accepted. The caregiver gets by somehow, and so do the children.

It is amazing how every unresolved problem, every shoddily cobbled-together prescription or proscription, every oversight comes to light and is avenged in court. Evening unrest in the dormitory, noise in the dormitory – a long line of irritating cases in various forms – announced persistently over the course of the entire year, raised the alarm with mathematical vigilance and precision, that the matter of the children's sleeping hours had not been resolved, that it still needed regulation. The court was actually powerless here, because what is needed here is either completely open violence – the cane – or a solution to a difficult problem that is in keeping with the physio-psychological needs of children.

Every impractical, and therefore pedagogically lousy demand, tirelessly "knocking to be let in," begs for deviations and concessions. Every child who doesn't allow himself to be brought under the general law has to be an exception to the law.

And what is needed here is the conscious, creative, and devoted thought of the caregiver.

An incompetent teacher doesn't know how to deal with his classroom. The court shows up, and now the pupils work diligently, are polite – what a miracle this would be, and in addition to being a welcome one to the caregiver it would be lethal to the children.

Before deciding to suspend the court, I sat through many hard hours. The children, admittedly a certain small but exasperating group of them, were exploiting the court for their own benefit. They respected the court when it was convenient for them to do so; they sneered at it when it got in their way. Disarray crept in, at first in minor details; but what will happen if the sense of impunity becomes hardened? One cannot wait a week with everything. "I'm not going to peel potatoes, I'm not going to clean." Taken to court, he still doesn't peel potatoes. What is to be done? It's been worse: "If I'm taken to court, I don't need to clean; I'm not going to clean, since I'm already being taken to court."

And the sentences were light. No group of judges dared reach beyond § 400. The opposition attentively maintained this resistance to applying the higher articles. Between a court of jurors and the collegial court there is the fundamental difference that here the judges and the accused know each other, they are bound by the thousandfold threads of mutual relations, that handing down a big sentence is to expose oneself to trouble. We know how unpleasant and troublesome courts of honor sometimes are. And the main thing, what's the point of inflicting violence on oneself and exposing oneself to unwelcome remarks when a heavy sentence won't help anyway?

Opinion on the court was divided. Besides the few of the court's enemies and allies, a considerable majority held the position that the court is beneficial but requires changes.

"The court is needed, but it brings no benefit."

"For some children, the court is good, but it's no help to others."

"Our court will be very useful in time."

"If it were a different court, it would be quite necessary."

These few opinions from a questionnaire are a good illustration of the children's attitude toward the new institution.

Treating the court as an experiment that might come to naught, I tried first of all to make the most precise use possible of the enormous factual material it had provided. With no time at my disposal, I at least sketched the outlines of each case. The statistics were interesting as well, the case law, the common and exceptional cases, the attitude of the accusers, the accused, and the judges toward one another – in me, it augmented an awareness that, in the future, the director-caregiver (and not one person serving as caregiver and administrator) must be the court clerk.

The court is needed, necessary, irreplaceable.

The court must have enormous pedagogical significance. Unfortunately, we have not yet grown into a court. Not yet, or – not yet us.

The court hasn't come to us ceremoniously as a major legislative act; it slipped in timidly and apprehensively. And yet in suspending the court I had a distinct feeling that I was committing a coup d'état, and I might be deluding myself, but the children sensed it, too. Now what was going to happen?

Some children "heaved a sigh of relief," rid themselves of a watchful supervisor. Some, wanting to prove that the court was unnecessary, conducted themselves better. A certain group enquired as to whether and when the court would be restarted. Beyond that, a hefty handful of children had as little interest in the court as they did generally in all matters of cohabitation.

In the accusations leveled against the court from outside, theoretically, one is repeated most often:

"The court habituates children to litigiousness."

For me, and no doubt for any caregiver, there are no "children" – there are individuals, so various, so extremely disparate, each reacting so differently and in their own way to what surrounds them that a general accusation must summon a forgiving smile. Over the entire year, there wasn't a single piece of evidence that would justify accusing the court of fostering litigiousness, whereas many facts seem to speak in favor of the court's having taught the children how inconvenient, harmful, and nonsensical litigiousness is. Enormous work took place, in my opinion, under the court's influence and auspices – that of realizing the conditions and rules of cohabitation. Whoever does not discount the society of children, whoever understands that it is a world and not a "little world," the figure – 3,500 cases – will convince him that I cannot go into details, since the work would have to encompass several thick volumes. There is just one thing I wish to stress: among one hundred children, only one boy could not be cured of his litigiousness, but a great many children were, and no doubt for the long term.

After its hiatus, three important modifications were introduced to the court.
1. Those dissatisfied with the verdict have the right to appeal after a month.
2. Some cases are excluded from the court and referred to the Judicial Council.
3. The children have the right to take adults and the staff to court.
    I cannot get into the details.

Over the course of half a year, I submitted myself to the court five times. Once for boxing a boy's ears, once for kicking a boy out of the dormitory, once for putting someone in a corner, once for insulting a judge, once for suspecting a girl of theft. In the first three cases I received § 21, in the fourth case § 71, in the last case § 7. Each time I submitted an extensive written statement.

I maintain with complete conviction that these few cases were the cornerstone of my upbringing as a new, "constitutional" caregiver who doesn't wrong the children not because he likes or loves them, but because there is an institution that protects them from the caregiver's injustice, willfulness, and despotism.

The Parliament of the Orphans' Home

The duty posts already have a seven-year history at the Orphans' Home; they've undergone trial by fire at many orphanages. Kitchen, laundry, inventory, building maintenance, monitoring the younger children – these are assigned to the wards who have transformed from ten-year-old children on duty into fourteen- or fifteen-year-old members of staff. The institutional newspaper continues; the court has been at work for two years without pause. We have matured into attempts at self-governance. It is by this path that we got a Parliament, of which we cannot yet say anything for certain. The Parliament numbers twenty delegates. Each has a constituency of five children; whoever gets four votes becomes a delegate. Everyone votes; only one who has not had a single court case for dishonesty can be a delegate; those who have been dishonest (theft, cheating) are granted the right to rehabilitation. The Parliament ratifies the laws issued by the Judicial Council, or else it rejects them. The Parliament approves the days of the calendar and acknowledges the right to commemorative postcards. If the court is empowered to decide on a ward's forced expulsion, the Parliament should strive to have the matter of admitting new children and dismissing older ones, or even the staff, depend upon its decision. Caution is advisable; the limits of the Parliament's authority ought to be expanded slowly; let its limitations and reservations be many, but let them be clear and open. Otherwise, let's not hold elections, let's not stage games of self-governance, let's not lead ourselves or the children unto error. Because the game would be tasteless and harmful.

The Calendar

I am providing a few articles from the proposal:

§ 6. The Parliament designates special occasion days besides religious holidays, whether as a result of a delegate's suggestion or in connection with the approval of a commemorative postcard.

§ 9. December 22. Slogan: "Not Worth Getting Up" (because it's a short day). Whoever wants may sleep in without getting out of bed. Whoever wants may not make his or her bed. The details will be worked out by the Parliament's legislative commission.

§ 10. July 22. Slogan: "Not Worth Going to Bed." Whoever wants may stay up all night. Weather permitting, a night march through the city.

§ 12. The first snow day. Slogan: "Sledding Day." The first snow day will be designated by snow falling with a temperature below one degree Celsius. Playing in the snow, an excursion, sledding for those selected by a vote.

§ 18. Day of the Dead. During morning prayer, we commemorate the names of deceased wards.

§ 19. Lunch Number 365. The housekeeper receives candy for all her hard work. Same for those on kitchen duty. Slogan: "The Kitchen's Name Day."

Note: proposals for honoring the laundry are requested.

§ 22. Pigpen Day. Slogan: "No Washing." Whoever wants to wash on this day must pay a fee to be determined by the Parliament.

§ 2…. Watch Day. After making a promise, an unpunctual shoemaker straightened out and all year brought the shoes at an appointed day and hour. The Parliament has awarded him a postcard for punctuality. In commemoration of this, the children are allowed, on the day of the Parliament's resolution, to remain in town for an extra hour.

§ 27. Day of the Careless. Whoever is voted most careless about his clothes receives an article of clothing so that he will not look like a slob on special occasions.

§ 28. Cauldron Day. Since one of the older boys unaccommodatingly refused to help move a cauldron when the elevator from the kitchen to the dining room was broken, on this day two older boys chosen by lot will carry breakfast up, even if the elevator is working.

§ 32. Encouragement Day. Whoever has had the most convictions over the course of the year receives acquittals for an entire week's offenses. If he or she wants, he or she can be a judge. Encouragement Day is being introduced to commemorate an instance when one of the biggest rascals went an entire week without a single case brought against him.

§ 40. The Parliament legislates the number of years a given day is to figure into the calendar.

Commemorative Postcards

Not yet passed by the Parliament, the "Temporary Statute on Commemorative Postcards" includes the following articles, among others:

§ 3. The caption on the reverse side of the image says: "By act of Parliament on (date), (name) has been awarded a commemorative postcard for…" The date when the postcard was awarded can be designated as a special occasion day and included in the calendar.

§ 4. The person applying for a postcard should submit his or her application on an unfolded sheet of paper upon which he or she has, in his or her own hand, writing carefully and legibly, enumerated the actions and facts that he or she wishes to remember. The actions can be good and bad, beneficial as well as harmful, praiseworthy as well as reprehensible; the postcard can be a pleasant keepsake or an unpleasant one, an encouragement or a warning.

§ 5. If the Parliament wants to underscore the memorialized fact more powerfully, it includes it in the calendar of victories and defeats, of commendable effort or negligence, of evidence of strong or weak will.

§ 7. The content of the image on the postcard should be appropriate to that for which it has been issued; therefore:

1. For getting up immediately after the morning bell, a winter landscape is issued during the winter season; for getting up during the months of spring, a spring scene, etc.
2. For peeling 2,500 pounds of potatoes – "the flower postcard."
3. For fighting, arguing, not abiding by the rules and resolutions, "the tiger postcard."

4. For looking after the little and new children – "the caring postcard," etc.

§ 10. Whoever has conscientiously performed the same duty for more than a year has the right to receive a postcard with a view of Warsaw.

The Parliament recognizes the Orphans' Home as a small piece of Warsaw and wishes to offer a keepsake all the more precious to those who might leave their native city in the future.

§ 12. Besides commemorative postcards, the Parliament will devise a way to issue anniversary ones. For example, someone who consistently gets up early and therefore possesses postcards of the four seasons might receive "the strong will postcard," etc.

§ 14. We should also slowly introduce "the health postcard" (whoever has not once gotten sick, is growing quickly, does sports), commemorative postcards for participation in plays, games, working for the newspaper and the court.

§ 17. The farewell "forget-me-not" postcard is the final postcard – with the signature of the children and the caregivers.

A postcard is not an award, but a keepsake, a memento. Some children will lose it on the road of life, others will keep it for a long time.

Notes

1 *How to Love a Child*, a work in four parts, appeared in print for the first time in 1920. Korczak had written most of the text during the First World War, during his military service as a junior resident doctor in a division field hospital. *The Child in the Family*, the first part of the tetralogy, most likely arose in its entirety while Korczak was serving in the First World War. The text first appeared in print in 1918 as a separate work entitled *How to Love a Child*. *The Child in the Family* grew primarily out of the experiences and observations Korczak had acquired in his pediatric hospital and private practice. *The Orphanage*, the tetralogy's second part, addresses the question of children's community. Here, Korczak drew first of all on the observational and factographic material that had emerged from his work at the Orphans' Home (1912-1914) [see note 39] in the two years before the First World War broke out. *Summer Camp*, the third part of the tetralogy, refers to Korczak's experiences in connection with his work as a caregiver at summer camps [see note 14] in 1904, 1907 and 1908. *The Orphans' Home*, the fourth part of the tetralogy, contains the principles and models for organizing the social life of children that Korczak had developed together with his closest collaborators over four years of work (1912-1914 and 1918-1920) as director-caregiver in the Orphans' Home. It is thus a peculiar chronicle of the beginnings of Korczak's "pedagogical project." To the fourth part of the text he appended authentic documents from the institution's operation (*The Court Gazette*, the codex of the collegial court, a ward's journal with a tutor's notes). The present publication is a translation of the second edition of *How to Love a Child* (1929).

2 Juliusz Słowacki (1809-1849) - a poet and playwright, one of the most outstanding Polish artists of the Romantic period. Author of, among other works, the symbolic epic *Anhelli*, quoted here by Korczak.

3 Stefan Żeromski (1864-1925) - an author of many novels and stories, one of the most outstanding Polish writers of the turn of the twentieth century. Korczak is quoting here from a story entitled "Oblivion" [Zapomnienie]. The quotation is imprecise.

4 A reference to the Russian Partition. Poland was partitioned by its neighbors three times until, in 1795, it vanished from the map of Europe, its territories divided among Russia, Prussia, and Austria. Poland regained its independence after the First World War in 1918. Warsaw, the city where Korczak lived and worked, belonged to the Russian Partition.

5 The source from which Korczak draws the quotation has not been confirmed.

6 Korczak abandoned direct hospital and outpatient medical practice when he assumed the directorship of the Orphans' Home in 1912. He had worked before this at Bersohn and Bauman Children's Hospital. Korczak's "divorce" from medicine, however, was never quite realized: he treated children at the Orphans' Home and at Our Home [see note 29], as well as his friends' children, and he remained interested in new medical advances.

7 Stanisław Kamieński (1860-1913) - a Warsaw pediatrician. Józef Polikarp Brudziński (1874-1917) - a pediatrician and neurologist.

8 In Poland, inoculation against smallpox became a general mandate beginning in 1919, effectively preventing the spread of the smallpox epidemic.

9 Groszy and zlotys - the currency of Poland. One zloty is subdivided into 100 groszy.

10 *Magna Carta Libertatum* (Magna Carta) - an English bill of principles issued by King John in 1215 and granting particular rights to the barons, it is regarded as the basis for civil liberties. Korczak's brochure *A Child's Right to Respect*, included in the present volume, can be regarded as a "Child's Magna Carta."

11 Colette, *The Complete Claudine*, trans. Antonia White (New York: Farrar, Straus and Giroux, 2001), p. 239.

12 Stanisław Witkiewicz (1851-1915) - a Polish painter, architect, and theorist of art working at the turn of the twentieth century. Here Korczak is quoting Witkiewicz's story "Jędrek Czajka."

13 See note 21.

14 Summer camps for children were conceived in 1876 by Walter Bion, a parish priest in Zurich. The first camp in Poland was organized in 1882 in Warsaw through the efforts of, among others, Dr. Stanisław Markiewicz (1839-1911), a physician and community activist. Dr. Markiewicz co-founded the Summer Camp Society, of which Korczak had been a member since 1900.

15 Octave Mirbeau, *Abbé Jules*, trans. Nicoletta Simborowski (Sawtry, UK: Dedalus, 1996), p. 115.

16 Stanisław Brzozowski (1878-1911) - a Polish philosopher, writer, publicist, and literary and theatrical critic. He worked at the turn of the twentieth century. Korczak is quoting here from Brzozowski's most famous text, "The Legend of Young Poland: Studies in the Structure of the Cultural Spirit" [Legenda Młodej Polski. Studia o strukturze duszy kulturalnej]. Brzozowski devoted a sketch in his book *The Contemporary Polish Novel* [Współczesna powieść polska] to Korczak's literary output.

17 Jean Martin Charcot (1825-1893) - a world-famous French scientist, clinical neurologist, and professor at a Paris university.

18 Leo Tolstoy (1828-1910) - a renowned Russian author writing in the second half of the nineteenth century and into the twentieth, he is read throughout the world. Interested in education and childrearing, in 1859 he founded a free school for peasant children at his Yasnaya Polyana estate. He published his pedagogical reflections in his own journal, *Yasnaya Polyana* (1861-1862).

19 Pedology - the experimental science of the physical and psychological development of children and youth, developed in the first quarter of the twentieth century. It drew attention to biological and environmental conditions, in accord with its fundamental principle, the so-called Two-Factor Theory. Today pedological interests fall within the range of developmental and child psychology. Korczak described himself as a pedologue on more than one occasion.

20 King Krakus - the legendary ruler of the Poles and founder of the city of Kraków.

21 The terminology and phrasing used by Korczak in this and the following fragments, racist by contemporary standards, are translated in accord with the spirit of the original.

22 Adam Mickiewicz (1798-1855) - a poet and playwright, one of the most outstanding Polish artists of the Romantic period.

23 Orthophreny - a therapeutic pedagogy concerned with physical and mental deviations from the norm.

24 Alexandr Kuprin, *Yama: The Pit*, trans. Bernard Guilbert Guerney (Library of Alexandria, 2014), p. 69.

25 Cezary Jellenta (1861-1935) - a Polish writer and critic of literature and art at the turn of the twentieth century. The source from which Korczak draws the quotation has not been confirmed.

26 See note 19.

27 See the "Collegial Court Codex" included in *The Orphans' Home,* the fourth part of *How to Love a Child.*

28 Korczak's *A Child's Right to Respect* is included in the present volume.

29 Maria Falska (1877-1944) – an educator, well-known social and political activist, Korczak's long-time friend and coworker. From 1919, she was the director of Our Home,well-known social and political activist, an orphanage for Polish children, where Korczak spent many years as a doctor and educator.

30 Joseph Gabriel Prévost (1793-1875) - a French philanthropist, founder of the orphanage in Cempuis (1853), to which Korczak refers here. The institution developed rapidly beginning in 1880, when its directorship was assumed by Paul Robin (1837-1912), a French labor activist, educator, and supporter of integral education – a secular education rooted in the child's harmonious mental and physical development. He rejected the model of religious and authoritarian education.

31 See note 41.

32 Johann Heinrich Pestalozzi (1746-1827) - an outstanding Swiss pedagogue and thinker, the father of modern social pedagogy. Korczak had been particularly interested in Pestalozzi's thought since his youth. The two shared an ideological kinship.

33 This quotation was probably translated by Korczak.

34 "Fame" [Sława] - a short story by Korczak published in 1913. The action takes place among pupils in a primary school.

35 See note 23.

36 See note 14.

37 The source of the epigraph remains unclear. It is most likely a self-quotation.

38 See note 22.

39   Jan III Sobieski (1629-1696) - king of Poland (1674-1696).

40   Jean Henri Fabre (1823-1915) - an outstanding French entomologist. He researched and masterfully described the habits and instinctive behaviors of insects. He introduced the experimental method into entomology.

41   The Orphans' Home arose through the initiative of the "Orphans' Aid" Society, of which Korczak had been a member since 1909, and whose goal was to assume total care over orphaned Jewish children in Warsaw. In 1910 the Society purchased a plot at 92 Krochmalna Street, and in autumn 1912 it brought the children to the newly constructed building. Korczak became the Orphans' Home's director, and Stefania Wilczyńska became his assistant and the head caregiver (both performed their duties without payment). In 1940 the Orphans' Home was forced to relocate to the area of the Warsaw Ghetto, first to 33 Chłodna Street, and subsequently to 16 Sienna Street. In August 1942, as part of the liquidation of the Warsaw Ghetto, the wards and caregivers of the Orphans' Home were transported (together with other orphanages) to the Treblinka German extermination camp, where they were murdered.

42   Children were admitted to the Orphans' Home based on their qualifications. In the institution's early days, the process was as follows: one had to submit an application, which would then be followed up by visits to the applicants' place of residence. Children who had sufficient care were not admitted, nor were children who were gravely disabled, ill, or developmentally delayed. Children came to the Orphans' Home following one of two regimes: permanent residents, and those in the day program (from 8:30 in the morning to 8:30 in the evening).

43   Stefania Wilczyńska (1886-1942) - an educator and Korczak's closest colleague, she co-directed the Orphans' Home where together with Korczak she realized the pedagogical concepts and principles of their system of caregiving and education. She perished alongside Korczak, the remaining caregivers, and the children in the Treblinka German extermination camp. The children called her "Mrs. Stefa."

The Events of Childrearing[1]

Translated by Danuta Borchardt

Introductory Reflections

I.

In medicine, the science of diagnosing disease is of primary importance. A student examines a series of individuals, learns to observe, explain and connect symptoms, and then arrives at a conclusion.

If pedagogy is to follow medicine's beaten path, it must devise diagnostic strategy for raising children, based on an understanding of the symptoms.

Just as fever, cough, and vomiting are symptoms to a physician, so must a smile, a tear, a blush be to a caregiver. Every symptom has meaning. One must make a note of it, consider all possibilities, reject what is fortuitous, seek similarities and search the governing laws. Not how to demand and what to demand of a child, not how to impose or forbid, but instead to find out what the child lacks, what it has in excess, what it demands, what it can give.

A childcare institution, as well as a regular school, is both a research territory and a child-raising clinic.

Why does one pupil, as he arrives in class, check all nooks and crannies, chat with everyone, and why a school bell can hardly get him into his bench? Why does another pupil take his place immediately, then reluctantly leave it for a break? Who are these youngsters, what qualities, what kind of things can a school provide, what can it demand in return?

Why one pupil, when called to a blackboard, goes willingly, her head raised, with an impish smile, and with an energetic move wipe the blackboard and, pressing hard on the chalk, write in big letters? While another child, dragging her feet, hems and haws, adjusts her clothes, her looks downcast, approaches the blackboard, wipes it on command, and proceeds to write in faint and small letters – why?

Which child is the first, which is the last to run out of class for a break? Which one raises his hand frequently because he knows the answer and wants to say it, which one does this seldom, and which one never does it?

During silence in class, which pupil is the first to cause a rumpus, and which one, in the general rumpus, remains silent?

Which child (and why) chooses one place over another, on the front or the backbench, or chooses one over another of his classmates as his neighbor?

Which children walk home alone, which ones go in pairs or in a group? Which child switches friends, which remains faithful?

Why, when we expect laughter, there is none? Why hilarity when we expect tender emotion? How many times has the class yawned during its first and last hour? For lack of interest? If so, why?

Instead of sulking that things turned up differently from what we had the right to expect, a scrutinizing and searching "why" emerges, otherwise no experience is gained, no creative action, no move forward, nor any new knowledge.

This material does not provide a pattern for conducting such studies. It is a document, which shows the difficulty of photographing with words what is right before one's eyes, and it shows how fruitful, though sometimes erroneous, can be commenting on what one has observed – an "event" recorded on the fly; it is an individual pupil's or a group's particular symptom.

II.

The more skilled caregivers begin writing a diary but soon abandon it because they don't know the technique of making notes, they haven't acquired, in their seminary, a *habit* of recording their work. Expecting too much of themselves, they loose confidence in their ability; demanding too much of their notes, they loose faith in their value.

Some things gladden me, others sadden, surprise, worry, anger and discourage me. So what to record and how?

A caregiver has not been taught this. Having grown past the level of writing a school boy's diary, which he had hidden from his dad under a mattress, he has not matured to the level of writing a chronicle to be shared with a colleague, or discussed at meetings and conferences. He may have been taught to take notes of other people's lectures and ideas, but not of his own.

What kind of difficulties and surprises have you encountered, what mistakes have you made and how have you corrected them, what defeats have you experienced, or what triumphs have you celebrated? Let your every failure teach you consciously, and serve to help others.

III.

How do you spend the hours of your life, how do you use the store of your young energy? What's happened to your enthusiasm, if any, which has waned over the years – has it not enlightened you or hewn out anything? And your experience? What were its component parts? No longer for the sake of science in general, no longer for others, but just for you.

You can't work for the good of your country, or for society, or for the future, unless you first work for the enrichment of your soul. Unless you take you cannot give. Only by the growth of your own spirit you can take part in the growth of others. The notes contain seeds from which a forest and a field of grain have grown, they are the drops that create a wellspring, these are the things with which I feed others, quench thirst, gladden, and protect from travail.

Your notes are a reckoning of your life. They document that you have not wasted your life. Life has a way of letting you achieve only part of what you wanted to do. When I was young, I didn't know, but now, grey-haired, I know, however, I no longer have the strength. Your notes will be the defense against your conscience, which says that this was not enough, not as it should have been.

I. Public School – First Grade

A note: A student doesn't have a pen…

Commentary: What to do? Should a teacher have a few spare pens to loan? Which pupil often forgets to have a pen? Make a note – how many times, but don't exaggerate, like "you *always* forget." Perhaps in the morning before the first class: who has forgotten what?

A note: [a five-minute observation during the last quarter of an arithmetic class.]

Bolek rubs his chin, pulls at his ear, shakes his head, looks out the window, jumps up and down in his bench, crosses his arms, sways his hips, measures the width of his table with his exercise book and with his hand, then turns the exercise book pages, hangs down from the edge of his bench, bends forward and lurks, swings his arm, pats the bench, shakes his head, looks out the window (it's snowing), bites his nails, puts his hands under his bum, pulls up his shoe, fans himself with his exercise book, puts his hands in his pockets, stretches himself, wiggles his hips impatiently, rubs his hands, then says: "Ma'am, I'd like to go to the blackboard."

Command: "Write!" He grabs his pen, waves it in the air, blows at it and dips it into an inkwell. A few more robust wriggles with his hips. "Ma'am, I… oh, my!" He bangs his forehead with his hand, jumps up and down.

Command: "Add 332+332." In no time, he makes the addition, turns about. Teacher:"You did it?" he whispers: "I work fast, like the *wiiiiwind…*" he then clucks his tongue and sighs.

Commentary: This is how a child protects himself, dissipates his mounting energy that has no outlet, this is how he struggles to not interfere with the flow of assignments, pleads for action, expresses regret, wields the tool of his work, and, finally, expresses his hidden longing, with a poetic analogy to the "*wiiiwind.*"

Observe the torture of a lively, excitable child, how wisely he deals with it, gives vent to a half or even a quarter of his energy so as not to incur the teacher's displeasure, how hard he tries before he finally can't help exploding with something that provokes the teacher's remark: "Sit still!" How "fortunate" is an apathetic, sleepy child!

A note: "Be quiet!" How many times per hour?

Commentary: variations: a) teacher's exclamation "be quiet!" is superfluous because disciplining (read: a fist bang) brings on quietude; b) repeating "be quiet!" frequently and without conviction gives no results; c) one can allow the rumpus, and thus give up teaching; d) one can try to reach an understanding with the children. Thus: total silence or relative silence. What interrupts silence during class: a question, a request, a remark, an unsolicited response, laughter, conversation with a neighbor? When and to what degree do you allow this? Depending on your mood, or have you thought it through? If you have, you must facilitate the children's understanding.

A note: Uncertain replies to the simplest questions, cautious responses.

Commentary: A teacher will rarely refrain from adding something even to a pupil's correct reply, "faster, slower, louder, once more, good, go on."
"There is three boys."
"Not is, there are three boys."
A pupil doesn't always know if he has counted correctly or expressed something badly. This results in a feeling of having made a mistake, having given a wrong answer.
Any work is hard enough, and mental work is downright impossible when someone stands over your shoulder and badgers you or interferes.
This is what sometimes happens:

Teacher: "So how many pounds did he have left?"
Pupil: "Five."
Teacher: "Give me a full sentence."
Pupil (guessing): "Six."
So perhaps – let him finish, or correct later? An important matter.

A note: The teacher says "there are no witches." Zbyszek, a quiet boy, after thinking a while, whispers to himself "but there are witches in the world."

Commentary: How often the home's authority is in conflict with the school's authority! Sometimes the authority of adults must give way to that of an older classmate.

A note: How does the noise at a class break rise after the first, the second or the third hour: the number of fights, quarrels, or complaints? How does the anxiety of the class rise as indicated by the number of reprimands directed to the class as a whole, or to individual children?

Attention: To order a child to sit for four hours on an uncomfortable, ill-fitting bench is the same torture as ordering her to walk, for the same number of hours, in shoes that are ill-fitting, too tight.

A note: "Wait, don't write yet." Or: "Write faster, hurry up, because they're waiting."

Commentary: With his "faster," or "not so fast," the teacher tries to bring the entire class to one and the same level. Too bad! Both his "faster" and "slower" miss the mark, demoralize the children, and just hang in the air.

A note: "Well, how many is it?" The pupil doesn't know. The others prompt him "forty eight." Teacher: "Well, how many?" The pupil keeps silent.

Commentary: This is a most interesting phenomenon. Why does the teacher keep demanding a useless reply, why does the pupil, quite logically, refuse to give it? Which pupils are reluctant to take advantage of prompts?

A note: "What kind of book is this?" (She calls for adjectives). The pupil: "with pictures."
What does the teacher do in this case?

A note: All pupils are already drawing. Adaś is only just about ready to begin. The bell rings. Everyone has finished, while he is reluctant to stop his work.

A note: "Show me your drawings." An embarrassed smile, he drags his feet, he wavers.

Commentary: Has anyone noticed how serious a child becomes when he's drawing, how he strives, how painfully his spirits flag?
"Why did you draw it like this?"
"Because it's pretty, that's how I fancied it."
Janinka drew something like a branching cactus, a small bird sitting on each spike.
"What is this?"
"That's how a girl drew it at our orphanage."

A note: A child who sits by a balcony is cold (it's windy there).

Commentary: This leads to lapse of attention. If the classroom is cold and the children are lightly dressed, one will sit still, stiff in the cold, another will be wiggling about to counteract it.

A note: Something is bothering a pupil in the mouth, he keeps moving it, perhaps it's a loose tooth.

Commentary: A factor that disrupts attention.

A note: The treasury of a pupil's pocket – a pen case.

Commentary: The teacher has prevailed not to bring to school balls, dolls, magnets or magnifying glasses. However, she allows a pen case, yet its contents are a source of distraction. But doesn't the child pay attention because he's playing with it, or, is he playing with the pen case because he's not paying attention? And, having relaxed by playing and satiated his need for being absent from the issues of the lesson, will his attention return faster or will his lack of attention persist? Or, on the contrary, in the absence of the pen case, will he sink into thoughtless apathy that much longer?

II. Preschool and First grade in a Private School[2]

A note: A girl on duty wipes off the blackboard. Małgosia purposefully, (and with malice), smears it with a piece of chalk. That's strange.

Commentary: Sometimes a child's behavior surprises us. If child A has done this, it would be understandable, but this one? It makes us question our previously established diagnosis. Our reprimand for her will sound like this: "Well, well, so that's how it is? But I thought… I was wrong… from now on… etc." We feel hurt and offended that we've been misled. Yet it sometimes happens in an exceptional case, that a child B is imitating someone, says or does "like others do." Małgosia saw yesterday or a week earlier that someone else was teasing a girl on duty, someone she admired and wanted to be like her.

A note: "Girls, please stop talking."

Commentary: Why does such a reprimand work in a school for "well-behaved children"? Punishment in the form of a gentle reprimand, of an impatient gesture, of a look of surprise, or of a shoulder shrug. Punishment: an ironic remark – instead of a birch twig that lashes the bum, a word that flogs a child's self-respect. "That's not nice, it's not seemly." A sharp remark inflicts a wound. Perhaps I'm at the root of an important issue; namely, whence grows man's appalling dependence on the opinion of others, his immobility at the threat of ridicule all the way to a dog-like alertness to what will a waiter, a hotel porter think of us?

A note: A child doesn't know something – should we keep asking?

Commentary: A child has not learned his lesson of German words. If it were only possible to photograph his behavior! A numb gaze, a meek posture, a wan smile or an expression of anger, a rebellious frown, or a deceitful hemming and hawing, lip movements without words (he knows but can't remember, oh, he knows, will say it in a minute, oh, he has no idea why he doesn't know). The teacher keeps asking her questions. This reminds one of torture, creates a bad impression.

A note: Besides the children who arrive late, an equally uncomfortable issue for the school is of arriving early, should also be discussed.

A note: Who likes to sit in the first row of benches, and who in the last row?

A note: "Olek, give me back my eraser." Olek returns the eraser, but instead of placing it on the bench, he puts it on his classmate's head. It's boring to put the eraser on the table.

A note: "You still don't know? I repeated it so many times. You should be ashamed."

Commentary: Ah, well, too bad – he doesn't know it. Instead of a reprimand, ask "why"? What if a doctor said to his patient, "You should be ashamed, you've gone through a whole bottle of the medicine, and you're still coughing, your pulse is weak, and you haven't had a bowel movement."

A note: Władzia enters the classroom, puts down her books, she then wanders – to the blackboard, to the pictures on the wall, to the teacher's table, back to the blackboard, to her own bench, to the last row, she then swings between the rows, sits down, then vigorously swings her legs. Enter: Janka. She goes to the window, stands still as she looks through it. Commotion – the children are moving the benches around. Janka turns around, she frowns, takes no part in it; then, with a sudden move goes to her own bench. (By the way, some pupils become as attached to their places as prisoners do to their cells).

A note: Stasia, observed for eight minutes. 1. She runs to a different bench from her own. 2. She kneels at her bench. 3. Back to another bench, whispering something. 4. Back to her own bench. 5. She talks to her neighbor who then leaves her bench and Stasia takes her place. 6. She's then at the teacher's table. 7. She returns, and in the passage between benches she lifts herself on her arms, then she bends down. 8. As she leans against her bench she talks under her breath with two other girls. 9. Laughter and conversation with a group of five. 10. She goes quickly to the fourth row with some news. 11. She returns to her seat. 12. She returns, peaks into a neighbor's book.

A note: "You, children, just don't want to think, you're not paying attention" (this in a tone of helpless and hopeless despair).

Commentary: In this cage the teacher is locked up with the children; not only must she restrain them but also be restrained, and while she's torturing them she's torturing herself. Perhaps at one time she tried, she searched how to do it. But if not, it was because she didn't know, she didn't know how, conditions made it impossible. Perhaps she made a mistake in choosing her profession. Who's to blame?

A note: Władzia raises her hand (I have a fleeting thought not to make a note, because it spoils my previously made diagnosis).

Commentary: I reluctantly make a note that Władzia, this frivolous, fidgety girl, wants to say something. Why? Since this is contrary to my negative view of her as a student, I should gladly greet it and scrupulously note this fact. Władzia, as I *want* her to be, should not be raising her hand, she should be happy to be left in peace, and that no one is forcing her to respond. This is my crime that I *want* her to be what I have decided her to be. Instead, I should really see her as she is, most fully, in her various aspects.

But I'm lazy, I want Władzia to be easy to know, I've pinned a label on her, it's done. Her raised hand is a new manifestation, needs re-consideration, an effort to think anew and to deepen my perception of her.

I'm impatient, I'm in a hurry. Having become "acquainted" with her as an easy child, I rush on to other, more difficult ones. I deal quickly with one sick person, and make a hasty diagnosis because others are waiting. My ambitious self is concerned about my discovery, perhaps exactly because it's so slipshod and was easily reached. I'm not sure and I'm concerned that this new event will somehow destroy the label – alms given in passing. I'm sorry I have to admit that I can hardly spell this out, that I must take time and care to decipher the alphabet of symptoms, to somehow roughly stammer out their meaning. There is within me a puffed-up authority that will, with precise insight, immediately identify "the little squirt." There lives within me a demoralized bungler, trained by his school, to shirk the duties of acquiring real knowledge. Little Władzia's raised hand is a protest by a live human being who is not to be disposed of easily, who objects to a label, to a tag, someone who says: "you do not know me." What do I know about Władzia? That she fidgets? Her teacher's casual remark: "she's a lazybones" was to my taste, so I assimilated it. But perhaps Władzia is not a lazybones. Perhaps I should discard a facile diagnosis, admit my error and let a few self-critical remarks be my reward.

Perhaps Władzia the teaser is capable of a lively interest in things, perhaps she is fighting against her teacher's prejudice. Her raised hand may signify a) "actually, I do know the answer, I'm not what you think I am," or b) "if something interests me, I know it and want to respond in class." Or perhaps, this lazybones has today decided to improve herself and, perhaps having had a talk with her mother or with her girlfriend has decided to begin a new life? Shouldn't I help her in this effort or, having noticed this, just wait what will happen later, perhaps tomorrow, or next week?

No, this is not the grimy hand of a preschool kid, but a question to which I can't find an answer.

A note: A chat, about a mouse, etc. (then about a rat, a bee, etc.).

Commentary: There's no book that will discuss the technique of having a conversation with children, or a chat (not a lecture). It seems easy, perhaps that's why we don't know how to do it. I remember those lovely talks at summer camps and those in the evenings at my orphanage, who hasn't experienced them, surely there are caregivers who remember them? Can't all this be transferred into schools?

A mouse – someone borrowed a cat to catch the mouse, then there is a story about a dog's fight with the cat – a rat was on auntie's pillow – one time they found a mouse inside a fish – rats can swim – there were small fish in a bath – there are gold fish – when we go on a boat ride we see fish – some flowers are poisonous – a bee stung my daddy – my grandma has beehives.

A topic for conversation – a few children want to talk all at once. One tells me something, another one starts telling his neighbor something, groups are formed. Someone starts a rumpus – the call for relaxation – the moment is gone. But there are ten minutes left to the bell, so what to do?

If I were to establish turns, let them sign up, but the children would be shy because they are not used to it and have little to say. How is one to protect from destruction a child's interesting and totally un-researched language of storytelling?

An example, not from school but from the kindergarten, a story told by the five-year-old Wiktor:

"Where did you see the apples?" I ask. "Apples – I saw apples – so tiny – the trees so big – you can lie down and swing – there was this dog – and when one apple falls – he's lying there and sleeping – mommy's coming – I want to go by myself – and there's a chair – there's the dog – some dog – he bit – he had *shhharp* teeth – so when he was asleep, that one bit him – he should be smacked for biting – there's a lady – and teeth like this – I forgot what he's called – Foks, he's called – he bit and bloood – he was chewing a bone – scram, Foks, scram! – and his eyes popped out and he bit – he dropped the bone and bit – I threw the dog an apple – and when I took an apple from the tree and threw it far – this hard apple – as sweet as could be – he just sniffed it – and then a soldier came – bang at the dog – bang – so pretty – pretty – pretty.

I took notes, as much as possible, not in shorthand. Compare Wiktor's "*shhharp, bloood*" with Bolek's "*wiiiwind.*"

III. Helcia

Territory of observation – a kindergarten. A large room, in a corner a piano. By the walls small cane armchairs and small tables for individual children. In the center six small tables and four small armchairs next to each one. By the door a closet with toys and Montessori equipment[3]. The heroes of our observation: Helcia, a three-and-a-half-year-old, Jurek and Krysia, both three years old, Haneczka, five years old, Nini, six years old. Time of observation: two to three hours over the course of two school days.

Helcia is self-assured, used to being admired, she beguiles people with her intellect and charm; she and her older brother are a couple of charming, healthy, lively children who captivate one's mind and heart.

I happen to know Jurek from his home situation. When he's not being a confirmed tyrant, against my will I look at him – it's a slipshod observation; his "ruined reputation" follows a fracas when he, the "turk," made an attempt to hit his mother with a whip.

Krysia – here my medical knowledge stands in the way. I don't like when a certain kind of child catches measles or whooping cough. She's one of those diminutive, almost filigree, serious, focused children, there's something in them that evokes dreaminess, wistfulness, sad forebodings – hence a tender concern and respect. I'm apt to prescribe them cod liver oil and kiss their little hands.

Haneczka, how to describe her? She has a good head on her shoulders, she's "been around," you can't push her into a corner or lead her astray, she's "a piece of work," yet she's a "pick of the crop," and she knows her limits. I'd like to say she lacks charm but that's not a kosher thing to say; one can surely predict that she'll be a brave human being.

It's impossible to characterize Nini. I've noticed something of a child conspirator in her, which evokes mistrust. She prefers to be with her one-year-old brother and with children younger than herself.

I began my observations without any program or plan, just casually: "What are the little ones doing?"

My first note in pencil:

Helcia, (drawings).

"It has a red tongue (a dog). Why?"

Nini: "Because it's a small dog."

"Do small dogs have red tongues – *sometimes*?"

(Helcia' story about a small dog that was barking even though "we weren't doing anything to it.")

Krysia is playing with a ball.

Nini: "Oh, Krysia is *also* using just one hand to play."

I understand that a child, looking at a picture, will notice separately a tail, ears, a tongue, and teeth – details that adults don't notice. We minimize this because they are pictures for children, however, we behave similarly in a painting gallery. We're surprised by children's perceptiveness because we make light of them, we're surprised that they're human beings and not dolls.

I explain to myself that Helcia's question why small dogs have red tongues is her wish to chat with Nini just about anything: it's because Nini is above Helcia in the social hierarchy, as her hobnobbing with a seven-year-old girl indicates. My impression is confirmed by her word "sometimes" inserted for no good reason. This is how a simpleton who encounters an aristocrat will interject a fanciful word or expression into a meaningless conversation, just to show that he too knows, and can do, a thing or two.

Nini's remark that Krysia is playing, her "also" shows surprise – she sees for the first time that Krysia is indeed playing.

Nini about a ball:

"I can play with one hand – can you?"

"No." (Hel., quickly).

"I can even toss it up."

Krysia exchanges a good ball for a defective one.

Nini's response:

"Eeee – let's not swap them – OK?" (Nini).

Krysia squishes the defective ball that has lost its air.

I've here recorded two events. On many occasions I've established Helcia's noble veracity. If she lies, it's because of pride, in defense of her dignity. It's painful for her to admit that she can't do something, so by her quick response about not being able to play with one hand she obviously wants to change the subject of conversation.

The other event concerns Nini. Krysia exchanges a good ball for a bad one. Nini eagerly catches the ball and laughs; in a moment, she'll say: "You, silly, this ball is losing air, it's worthless, it doesn't bounce." But she has a sudden thought – it's better to conceal that she's made a good bargain, so she quickly responds with "let's not swap them." A needless ploy: Krysia is pleased with the swap, she's trying out the punctured ball and no longer wants to play. Just as Helcia did not tell a lie by quickly and softly saying that she doesn't know how to catch the ball with one hand, so did Nini not cheat Krysia. Thus the boundaries of numerous human flaws and transgressions become erased, as well as virtues and good deeds.

> Playing-cubes are on the floor.
> Nini: "I'll build *you* a ship – a furnace – yes, a furnace on a ship."
> Helcia: "And you know how to build a ship like this?"
> Nini, not looking at Helcia: "Yes, I do."
> Krysia – Helcia – a train.

The six-year-old Nini, while playing with the younger ones, looks down on them. She'll build not for herself but for them. Helcia doesn't want to agree with this or to accept Nini's authority. So she asks a tactless question and receives a demeaning reply, namely, does Nini know how to build something that she, Helcia, knows how to build? Nini isn't looking – of course she can.

> Nini tells a story about vipers.
> "Wasn't the ending funny?" she asks.
> "No," Helcia replies.

I'm completing my notes from memory. Nini is fighting for her authority by telling a story about vipers. Helcia doesn't know what a viper is and is not interested in the story. Nini, anticipating a defeat, has posed a risky question and received an unpleasant reply. Now, quite unnecessarily, I ask Nini a few questions about vipers. "A viper is like a thread and can eat up two hundred people." Helcia scowls at Nini, tension between them rises, the atmosphere thickens. Two people of different ilk have run into each other by accident; after a phony conversation and unwelcome encounter they part in mutual disdain.

> Cubes and lettered blocks – a long while – a castle.
> "You know how to build?" (Helcia) "Nice one like this?"
> Nini – 22.
> Krysia – 0.
> Helcia – 14.

They return to the building blocks. Soon Nini spews out twenty-two words, Helcia – fourteen, Krysia – not a word. I note that in less than twenty minutes of unforced play there were 1. pictures. 2. a ball. 3. cubes. 4. a story. 5. cubes.

> Envy – emulation.
> Helcia is more and more insistent:
> "It's pretty, you know how to build like this?"
> She topples Nini's house.
> "I'm going to build all by myself."
> Nini:
> "I'll build a house for Krysia."
> (She whispers something into Krysia's ear).
> Krysia turns around and topples Helcia's house.
> (A blank in my notes).

I forgot to mention that they're all sitting on the floor. A fight going on for Krysia, this small, calm, silent and serious person who, when she picks up a ball, evokes surprise. I watch the course of this drama with bated breath: Helcia's suffering, the rancor rankles her, she's angry at Nini, she's fighting for Krysia but senses it's for nothing, Krysia is looking at Nini's building. Revenge follows – Helcia topples Nini's house. Nini ignores this with disdain, it's not proper to pick up a fight with a weak adversary; she merely underscores that Krysia belongs to her. There's so much missing in my notes! I fill them in from memory: after Helcia's coarse deed, Krysia gently moves toward Nini, meets Helcia's rebellious stare with a calm gaze, then turns toward Nini. All this lasted one tenth, one hundredth of a second, Nini's order and Krysia's swift toppling of Helcia's building. Helcia keeps quiet, she feels guilty and helpless vis á vis Krysia.

A blank in my notes, the evidence of my emotions and of a whirr of feelings that all this had stirred up in me. Isn't there something of a human being? I don't remember any such strong moment since my research on infants.[4]

Helcia has established a relationship with Nini – but how?

I don't know. I don't remember. I lost a series of interesting events. Actually, I wouldn't have trusted any notes if there were no "blank spaces," and honest confessions that an observer hadn't remembered, hadn't noticed or forgot something.

Haneczka arrives and goes to Nini.

Jurek goes to sit in Helcia's chair. Helcia is watching for a long while. (I wait) – nothing happens!

Haneczka removes a cube from Helcia's house. Helcia watches this for quite a while.

"Haneczka, please don't take my blocks."

Haneczka takes Helcia's blocks. Helcia bangs her on the head with a block.

Helcia grabs her last block and gives it to Jurek:

"Here – here – here!"

Jurek turns to me:

"This girl has nothing to build with, has nothing to build."

"What?" I ask (in my deep, harsh voice).

"She took everything."

Helcia looks at Jurek (Jurek at Helcia).

"She – that good girl."

Haneczka divvies out eight cubes, Jurek adds his ninth.

Haneczka, to play hazard, adds another one.

"Jurek, I gave her back all of them, I gave her back everything."

(I have tears in my eyes).

I begin with my "what"? the one harsh word, and alien in spirit and sound to everything that was happening here. The children understood each other, while mine was a pretense not to understand. My brain cells, my vocal cords, my entire being, including my past when so much happened, all this was a personification of sordidness and falsehood as compared to wonderful mysteriousness of sounds, and to ephemeral and silvery tones. There was no room here for scientific reasoning, this was a state of mind, a saintly conversation between feelings that science has no right to touch. I'll keep pondering on this, even though I'm being injurious toward myself.

Jurek goes to sit on Helcia's chair, next to her table. Helcia looks at him, it's impossible for her to be thinking she's all emotion. She's missing those long moments when she sat by her table, far from the other children and watched them from aside. But this has passed and will not return. She has left her quiet little nest, having suffered so much, and there's no return. Now it's Jurek who sits there, the same one who pushed her a few days ago. But Helcia has forgiven him and has surrendered her quiet haven, her secluded, little abode. She now longs for something that will not return.

The children keep grabbing her blocks, she's meekly asking them not to do it, she knows that life is unfair, but she's unable to defend herself and doesn't want to run away. It's not words but a soft, sad voice, as are her posture and facial expression. No actress will ever be capable of thus pleading for help, for tolerance and mercy. What a genius nature is that it allows a three-year-old child to be a personification of such a plea. And what about words? They are so simple: "Haneczka, please don't take my blocks."

Haneczka who personifies life does not know mercy: she snatches the blocks. Helcia hits Haneczka over the head with the remaining block; she's scared of retaliation, in her three-fold "here," while she's squeezing the last block into Jurek's hand, there's so much dramatic power here! Thus it is with a soldier, who while dying in battle, renders his flag to the next one at hand, as long as it's not the enemy.

It's not until now, when she's been repelled and mistreated, that Helcia notices me and turns toward me. Poor thing!

Haneczka is somewhat impressed by Nini though her talkativeness bores her.

Helcia fixes the damaged ball.

"See how it's done?"

Helcia to Jurek:

"Give me the box."

Jurek – a defensive move.[5]

She strokes his face. He doesn't give it to her – walks away. Now Helcia grabs it from him, runs off and sits by me.

(A blank space).

Helcia: "Do you know how to build like this?"

Jurek: "No, bzz – bzz – bzz."

Finally, but how grotesquely, I won't be surprised if she were to sigh.

These notes are indicative of my weariness. I don't stop making them because they're valuable, yet I'm tired, totally tired, and I make a mess of them. Here's a note on the last event because I don't want to trust it to my memory. Helcia, who so badly wants to hear from the others that they don't know what she knows how to make something, finally reaches her goal – Jurek doesn't know. He's embarrassed to admit it, so he retorts with his "*bzz – bzz – bzz,*" which makes light of it and changes subject of conversation. As Helcia did a while ago.

Teacher: "*À sa place.*"[In its place]

Helcia to Nini: "What does 'place' mean?"

Helcia turns to Nini, not to me.

Prayer time. Haneczka and Krysia take part in it. After the prayer, Helcia, having been crushed earlier, says firmly to Jurek:

"This is my place, it's mine."

Jurek gives it up and moves to his own place.

After marching exercises, Haneczka pushes Jurek from his armchair, so he meekly moves to another place.

Helcia, at her seat, bangs her table with her legs, rattles the table, bangs the table with her hand.

(A blank space).

Helcia has a few blocks, takes one out, gently strikes the table with it; her movements are sluggish, she rests her head on her hand. Then she begins to build a gate on to Haneczka's palace, doesn't succeed; the triangle top keeps falling off its base three, four times. Helcia returns the blocks to the box.

A blank space – it's my defeat. I briefly turn my head away, leaving Helcia troubled and alone. I find her to be disappointed and unhappy, but here lies the box with the blocks – when has Helcia taken it from the closet, how? I don't know. Wearied, I spaced out.

I read what I've written. It's written badly. I understand it, but a reader will only understand by carefully reading it several times. There will be few such readers. I must write simply, more accessibly. On my next day of observation, I choose another, a new method. First, all notes set together, then the course of events is juxtaposed with the story's action, and finally – a commentary.

The following is my plan for a student of a seminary[6]:

1. Distinctive traits of the child he's observing.
2. Conditions for observation.
   a) plan of place.
   b) notes about oneself: how many previous works, how has he met the child, what did he know, has heard and remembered about the child before he undertook his observation.
   c) his own state of mind – has he undertaken the observation willingly, with a goal in mind, or fortuitously? Is he in good physical health, of a cheerful disposition, etc.?
3. Notes *in crudo* [in the rough], including "blank spaces," (which are breaks in observation). There should be a question mark in brackets where he is unable to read his notes. Important: preserve abbreviations.
4. A concise story of the course of events.
5. A commentary to the notes.
6. His personal material, i.e. his own experiences and reflections.

I think I made this plan in its main outline subconsciously. Something like a theater reportage, an essay on a well-known theater stage drama. The lack of clarity in my work comes from the fact that when I read an essay about a drama by Shakespeare or Sophocles I'm familiar with Hamlet or Antigone, while here the reader isn't familiar with the heroine, Helcia, or the drama. My reason for leaving my first day's observations in their present form is to show its shortcoming, what it should not be like. I'm not sure if the second day will be any better.

(NB what disturbs me is the fact that I don't write on the day of my observations but four days later: I make comments on my Tuesday observations on Saturday.)

Day two of observations

My notes:
Helcia doesn't even look at her table.
Krysia is playing with Mania.
Helcia starts talking to Stasia – no response.
Helcia starts talking to Janek – a prolonged silence.
Helcia yawns.
Helcia with Wika:
"I'm eight years old."
"Władek is also eight."
Wika goes to check this, Helcia isn't sure.
Hel.: "Wł., how old are you?"
Wł.: "seven and a half."
Krysia by the table of the older children. Helcia is watching her.
Prayer time, marching exercises. Helcia loudly, as a provocation, "Oh, an apron, mommy told me to wear an apron." Runs. Topples a table.
Loudly to the teacher:
"It fell over."
To me:
"My sleeves turned."
She looks ugly.
The next moment she turns pretty, having forgotten about herself, she now struggles to button up her apron at the back.
"Please, sir…"
When I'm about to…
"I'll do it myself."
Turns her apron around, tries to widen the hole with her finger.
"Please fasten it."
I reach with my hand, she backs off, tries again, (her last try, just as adults do, just in case at the last moment she'll succeed, this is her last chance).

(A blank space).

I button it, "try to unbutton it, that's easier." She doesn't want to, walks over to the table with letters, walks to Krysia.

She's learning to respect real merit.

Helcia, the letters – she's dreaming about power. I'm at the table, she turns to Mrs. N.

Fiddles with the letters, "Is this correct?"

"No."

(How entirely elders' admiration demoralizes children!).

To me: "This is how it's set, right?"

"No."

"Please have a look."

"No."

She moves over one letter.

"Please have a look."

"It's not right."

She doesn't let me show her.

I insult her: "You're too little (because she's annoying me).

She walks away, shows Mrs. N. that the table is broken – shows a doll: "Is it badly dressed?" Recounts items of the doll's dress.

"I have something like this in my pocket. Guess what it is."

"I don't know, how could I? Do you know what I have in my pocket?"

"I do." (She peeks in).

To the letters:

"Please look if this is right," she asks Mrs. N.

"No."

(She works at it – can't reconcile herself.)

Mrs. N. shows her how to arrange the letters, Helcia isn't watching, she's bent on charming, reigning, not working.

Then she asks me: "What about now?"

"No!"

She's back to the broken table, shows it to Janek.

Conversation with Mrs. N. Helcia looks at a picture book, while looking, she hums one of the songs from the kindergarten, "Polishinelle".

"Ma'am, do you know how to draw a cat? Because I do."

(At home, she knows how to do something that adults don't).

A conversation with Tadzio, she's forbidding him something.

She's bored.

"Take some blocks, houses, just like Haneczka does."

"Like Krysiaaaaa?"

"No, like Haneczka."

"I don't want to. That's easy. And you, sir, do you know how to sew an apron?"

"No."

"But I know how."

"Yet you don't even know how to button it."

"Yes, I do."

"No, you don't."

"But I do." (We're teasing each other).

"And do you know, sir, how to draw a cart?"

"No."

"I do. And a cat?"

"Yes, I do."

I give her a pencil and a piece of paper: "Draw it."

"And I know how to draw a pencil."

She draws a duck (like a three-year-old). I admit, though coldly, without enthusiasm, that it's good.

"And can you do it?"

"Yes."

She looks surprised, then draws.

"What is this?"

"I don't know."

"Come on, something legs," she says.

I draw a duck.

"Please gimme paper I draw a bowl."

"Draw it on the same piece of paper."

"Eeeee." But goes on with her drawing.

Instead of a bowl, a girl with a basket.

"You were supposed to draw a bowl."

"Isn't it a pretty bowl?"

"Ask Krysia."

Helcia talks briefly with Krysia.

"What did Krysia say?"

"Isn't this a nice little basket?"

"No, bad."

I draw one. "Which is better yours or mine?"

"This one." She points with her finger at mine.

I feel sorry for her.

1. Admiration.

2. Antipathy, anger.

3. Commiseration.

I align myself with Helcia against Krysia. Everyone admires Helcia, but they actually adore Krysia. Krysia tries to be the first in the marching exercises. Helcia wants to force her way in. Krysia waits for things to evolve naturally.

Girls like Krysia are:

1. Passive, they don't waste energy.

2. Quiet – they'll sneak into anything, they'll watch who does anything best, and they take their time to watch.

3. They win without much struggle – just with a sudden burst, with a single attack.

I want to help Helcia, to teach her.

"Give me a piece of chalk."

She can't find it. Krysia finds it and brings it to me. I draw a house on the blackboard. She tries, badly. She adds windows to my house.

Lala passes by.

Hel.: "Look, isn't it pretty?"

Lala: "You draw well."

Hel.: "Oh, look at the windows."

Hel. realizes there's a misunderstanding she's embarrassed.

She draws trees, doesn't want to use a mop to wipe them off, just a piece of paper. She uses her hand, looks at me with a contrary smile.

Hel.: "Please draw something."

I draw a man. She adds fingers, makes some improvements.

She demands a new drawing. I draw a bird.

Hel.: "This is a bird or a *lark*." (She awaits admiration for having spoken a new word).

For a brief moment I walk over to Krysia who is pasting something.

Soon Helcia arrives, pulls me away (envy). Loses the chalk, looks for it a long time, finds it.

The chalk falls to the ground, breaks. She looks surprised, writes something with a piece of it on the blackboard, throws it down and watches it (experiment.).

She demands a new drawing. I draw a flower. She improves on it.

"What's this?"

"Glasses."

"What are they for?"

"To see better."

"And what's this for?"

"To hold them in place."

"Couldn't they just use nails?"

"Nails would hurt."

I take off my glasses, show them. She smears me with the chalk.

"Helcia, you're making me dirty."

"Is this a new suit?"

"No, it's old."

"I have a new dress. Zosia made it."

"And who is Zosia?"

"Here is a man with a head, hands, and a brow."

"Why the mustaches?"

Her dad shaves. I can't because I have no money to buy. She suggests I make it out of gold or paper. I cut it according to her instructions out of paper. As a result there are two holes in the piece of paper. She places it on her face and tries to scare me. (She's waiting for "oh, dear, I'm scared, oh, I'm going to hide."). I say nothing.

"Isn't it scary?"

"No."

I give her a mirror so she can see if it's scary. I ask Krysia if it's scary.

"No."

Helcia draws something on the mask to make it scary.

"How about now?"

"No."

She screws up her face.

"And now?"

"No."

I ask her: "Did anybody get scared?" She doesn't reply. She tries the mask on me, then on Krysia.

Breakfast.

Hel., loudly:

"I know where is my bottle (of milk)."

(NB., Krysia says "t" instead of "k". Perhaps this speech defect makes her close-tongued, unsociable; caregivers ought to be aware of this and prevent her isolation).

(It wasn't Helcia I've been observing for two days but rights of nature, of a human being).

There're only two little girls in the kindergarten: Helcia and Krysia. According to our precepts of "you two play together," they'd be forced to do so; if not thus forced, they're inclined to socialize with the older children, this promises them something more than play. Mania prefers to talk with and to take care of the little ones. Krysia has noticed this and, as the close-tongued, quiet and serious one, has attracted Mania to herself. Helcia is only just beginning her search. She approaches Stasia – a wrong choice. Then –

Janek – a good choice: he's been in the kindergarten only a week and hasn't yet felt his way around; he's ill at ease, hardly knows anyone, this blurs their age difference, they chat. However, Helcia lacks patience, so she nabs Wika, awkwardly, by mentioning the brother's age, but she's not sure if she's right about his age (eight), so she is embarrassed. Fear of ridicule thwarts Helcia's expression of feelings, her every move. This is why she doesn't take part in prayer, in marching, in gym. She's suffering but she's scared, she can't. When the children march in rhythm to the piano music, she wants to attract attention, and needlessly raises her voice about her apron and topples the bench – all to her discredit. She announces these things with surprise in her voice and a forced smile, she then quickly changes the subject of conversation by telling me that the sleeves of her apron have been turned (inside out). She reverses them, puts on the apron, but can't button it. I want to help her, she declines. She finds the button hole too small (the apron's closure is at her back). She turns to me for help, but at the last minute she suddenly steps back and tries again. Turning for help a second time, doesn't let go of the button and keeps trying.

This is a very frequent phenomenon not only among small children but also among older ones and among adults. When, as a student, I worked in a hospital, I once witnessed the following scene: my colleague H. wanted to extract a patient's tooth but was unable to do it. He turned to the doctor in charge who approached him, but the student didn't give up his forceps and tried again. The tooth broke.

Letters on a moveable abacus are set in compartments of a box, like types in a printer's case. In the morning, the letters having been scattered, the children who are not familiar with them are supposed to reset them according to their similarity. Krysia knows how to do it but Helcia wants to fake it instead. I suspect: at her home she scribbles something on a piece of paper and says she's written something; since the adults agree with this, she believes them. No wonder – if a three-year-old thinks that it's easy to read (murmurs to herself) to draw, or to write, then a six-year-old is unwilling to make any effort to struggle. Helcia angrily insists that she's placing the letters correctly, doesn't want any explanations or to be shown and helped. She wants to do it herself! Her unceasing questioning "do you know how?" can be easily read as something the adults in her home do by pretending not to know what she knows. So many times it has been observed, in so many variations. A three-year-old jumps down a step: "see, I can do it." Enter a cheery uncle: he pretends he can't, he's scared, he falls, acts like a clown. The child laughs, pushes him, eggs him on with her contrariness, malicious pranking, disdain and faking. The three-year-old makes a smudge on a piece of paper: "it's a horse." The uncle feigns surprise: "what a beautiful horse," and says he can't do it, he tries by using a pencil with the blunt end, the pencil falls out of his hand, the paper falls to the floor. The child tries to explain, gets annoyed, at times hits the uncle. Had the cheery uncle realized that the child is only laughing excitedly because she knows that the fun will end with being rocked, hugged, and kissed, while another child may react with fury and irritation. If the uncle had realized that one child's sparkling gayety and reveling laughter, and another child's half-surprised, half-angry gaze remind him of unruliness in his private rooms and defiance in his boudoir, perhaps he would be more circumspect in the future. If nannies behave likewise, who knows, perhaps they picked it up from the cheery uncles, they have not brought it from the countryside, from the humble cottage, where, as far as my observations go, relation to a child is serious and dignified.

My anger, as expressed in my disdain toward Helcia: "You're too little," was most likely addressed to those cheery uncles (and aunties), who can't look at a pretty two-year-old without subconsciously or unconsciously thinking what a piquant person will the child eventually be. Thus this contagion travels to children's rooms, thus the youngest are crippled, and later, in the kindergartens, they rectify their warped souls but lose confidence in adults and their attachment to home.

The "no's," "absolutely not," "I definitely know," "definitely can," are also from the cheery uncles' repertory. The uncle says: "I'll buy you from your mommy," or "your eyes are ugly." Their inventiveness is great indeed! So the child says: "Not true, you won't; mommy, not true, he won't?" "Oh, yes," "oh, no." This passes for teasing. Some children hate it, others like the jokes where anger, dislike and fear provide much excitement.

Helcia promises to draw a small bowl, but she then realizes her drawing has no resemblance to a bowl, so, let it be "a girl with a basket." The adults are such idiots anyway, they'll believe anything. She twice changes the subject of conversation which is so unpleasant to her. She honestly admits that my drawing of the basket is better, but when Lala takes my drawing of a house on the blackboard to be Helcia's, Helcia doesn't have the gumption to clear up the misunderstanding.

The incident with the chalk is interesting. Helcia does not expect it to break when it fell. If a glass falls it becomes useless, a pencil breaks. When the chalk breaks, she carefully tries to use it, and it works. She throws it down – what will happen? Now she knows this – for the rest of her life.

A few days ago, Uglie tried to dip the chalk in water and write. All of us had a moment in our life when we asked what happened to sugar dropped into tea; when told that it dissolved, an unfamiliar word was added to an unfamiliar phenomenon. We didn't understand this until we experimented with sugar, with salt. I remember placing salt water in the sun to see if dry salt would be left in the flask; I waited long and in vain, and the solution of the issue was left hanging. A child likes to stir sugar with a spoon but mommy doesn't like this because, more often than not, the glass falls over.

Conversation about glasses. These are not only pieces of glass to improve vision, but also bits of metal – what for? If the glass pieces don't stay in place, why not use nails? I reply that it can't be done, but I don't laugh. There have been many solutions for fixing pieces of glass: an eyeglass, a pince-nez, a spyglass. It's not so simple to recognize ears as something that small wires can be hooked over. The fact that the three-year-old Helcia doesn't know, what took centuries of a joint effort of specialists to discover, is not funny. However, it's indeed to my discredit that I, not until my fortieth year, and only in response to Helcia's question, thought about it for the first time. If you sneer at a child when she doesn't know something, you kill her wish to find out.

Who'll admit that he hasn't read *Faust*, not seen Rubens paintings, doesn't know who Pestalozzi was? Our reading is slapdash, our way of observing is slapdash, our acquiring knowledge is careless; there are only certain individuals who create civilization, only cliques make politics, while the dumb populace, led by the nose, would rather die than admit the embarrassment of not actually realizing that it is led by the nose, as long as no one's laughing. Whoever laughs at a three-year-old who wants to nail pieces of glass to the eyes is a traitor, a corrupt person.

Helcia doesn't know how the glasses are attached, but she has a new dress. There, that's how we finally understand each other.

The conversation about money, paper and gold, is just a scrap of actual, overheard conversations. I cut out two circles out of a sheet of paper (coins) according to Helcia's instructions. She notices the likeness of the sheet of paper to a mask with which the good uncle likes to scare children. While entangled in a talk about money, Helcia wants to disentangle herself so as not to betray her ignorance. She puts the "mask" on her face and tries to scare me and Krysia. She doesn't succeed. There must be something wrong with the mask, so she contorts her face. This doesn't work either.

It seems to me that Helcia is beginning to understand that her home is just kidding her, having fun, pretending and lying; that things are different there from what she thought. She's scared, yet she's also attracted to this new, real life, which calls for effort and struggle, where contribution, not charm has value, there are more indifferent gazes than smiles, more snares than helpful hands. Her home impedes rather than helps her.

The above note did not turn out as I had wished. I wanted to provide the seminary student a model for recording observations and supplement them with commentaries. Instead, I wrote a model for myself how to move from a minute observed event such as a child's question, to manifold and general matters. This proves how various frameworks, plans and road signs are a hindrance to independent thinking.

IV.

I always thought that a great obstacle to rational raising of an individual child is something one is not always aware of yet it is a constantly present idea, namely "it's not worth it." As a caregiver of dozens and dozens of children, I have a sense of much greater responsibility. My every word echoes in a hundred minds, my every move is followed by a hundred watchful pairs of eyes. If I manage to arouse feelings, to convince, and move to action, then my fondness, my faith and action will mount to the power of one hundred. Even if almost all children disappoint me, there will always be one or two, if not today, then tomorrow, who will convince me that they had understood and were "with me." While raising one hundred, I know no loneliness, I'm not afraid of defeat. While devoting hours, days, months of my life to one child – what do I do? At the price of my own, single life I build only a single life. My every act of self-sacrifice feeds only one child. It's much easier to overcome my irritability, my weariness and bad mood, and to begin afresh to tell stories when I have one hundred listeners.

If I came across a caregiver who for the sake of one or two children left a group, in other words, she preferred a private situation to the day care center or an orphanage, I thought she had no passion for her profession, that she was merely interested in profit, better conditions and less hard work.

After I spent only two weeks with Stefan, an eleven-year-old boy, I became convinced that observing one child provides material just as rich, bringing as much satisfaction and as many concerns as observing a large number of children. In this one child one notices more issues, one's feelings are more subtle, and one thinks through every fact more deeply.

In my opinion, a weary caregiver of a group has the right, perhaps even a duty to use work rotation, namely to move away for a while from a crowd to tranquility, and then to later return and work with a crowd. As far as I know, this has not been happening so far; instead, caregivers separately specialize in individual and group education and raising of children.

My notes were in the form of a diary, and I thus presented them here. As a document and in spite of unusual conditions of time and place, they may have a certain value.

NB. I was at that time, the head of a ward in a field hospital. During a lull in war hostilities I took a boy from an orphanage; he wanted to study craft, and there was a carpentry workshop at the hospital. I spent only two weeks with him; when I fell ill and went away the boy remained there a while longer. When the army was on the march again, the orderly returned him to the orphanage.

Thursday, March 8, 1917

This is his fourth day. I wanted to make notes from the first day. Unfortunately, as is often the case with notes, there's always more to write than time allows. This discourages many people. I regret that many strange emotions are lost to the record.

I'm now used to the boy's presence.

His name is Stefan. His mother died when he was seven years old, he doesn't remember her name. His father is still fighting in the war, or imprisoned, or dead. Stefan has a seventeen-year-old brother living in Tarnopol. He first lived with him, then with some soldiers, and for the past six months at the orphanage. Orphanages have been formed by a conglomeration of cities, and they are run by anyone available, of any merit. The government alternates between allowing and disallowing to teach there.[7] These are not educational institutions but garbage dumps, where children are thrown in like refuse from the war, a sad debris from dysentery, typhus, and cholera; parents are swept away, actually only mothers, because fathers are fighting for a novel division of the world. The war is not a crime, it is a triumphant procession, a feast of crazed, drunken, merry-making demons.

No sooner had I asked him if he wanted me to take him in, than I regretted it.

"Not now, I'll come for you on Monday. Ask your brother tomorrow if he'll let you. Ask his advice, think about it."

We're on the road – the moon – the snow. What's he thinking? He looks around with curiosity – a church, a railroad station, train carriages, a bridge. His face is just ordinary. Allegedly, he's a keen worker; there's a carpentry workshop at the hospital, I'll give him to Mr. Duduk to study.

Result of an examination: He hasn't forgotten how to read.

A test in arithmetic: How old is he at present?

I sense he doesn't understand what "at present" means.

"At present? Present what?"

I don't correct him.

His brother gave him fifty kopeks, he bought cakes filled with jam, and candy, and, at my place, he ate some cold headcheese – Mr. Płaska's masterpiece. In the evening he had belly ache, in the appendix area. That's bad. I would rather he ate his soldier's fare until it's decided if he's to stay with me. I wanted him to have a definite daily plan of activities.

Walenty[8] sighs:

"What on earth do you need this for?"

Stefan has an innate sense of orderliness. When his class is over he places his books on the side of the table and his pen next to the inkwell. When one edge of his towel hung lower, he adjusted it.

Why did he spend all his fifty kopeks on sweets?

"Why should I scrimp? On money?"

This is not likely his opinion but some authority's, Nazarka's or Klimowicz's (Klim. is good at drawing).

"Your father will be back," I tell him.

"Great if he is, same if he isn't."

This too he must have heard. I could have said a lot of nonsense such as "Pshaw, how can you talk like that… about your father…, etc." But right now he's interested in other things.

"What are those holders by the mirror for?"

"One is for soap, one for a comb, and one for a toothbrush."

"When this cigarette case was new, was the leather rumpled?"

"Yes, it's sort of like crocodile leather."

A notice to caregivers. When you arrive in a child's home as a tutor, let the child be in your room when you're unpacking, let him help you open your bag or suitcase and take out and place the various items around. There will be conversations about your watch, your penknife, your vanity case. It will quickly and naturally bond you with him. This is how the child bonds with his peers. It's worth to consider how often adults make acquaintances through their children and by talking about them (in a park or a summer home). Boys bond with each other by playing ball, girls by playing with dolls. If you tell the child that it's not nice to touch your belongings, to question everything, you'll embarrass him, you'll generate animosity. You can tell him this a month later, or in three months' time, and when it pertains to a stranger. Because you are now "colleagues."

"How much did this cigarette case cost?"

"About two or three rubles. I don't know, I don't remember, I've had it quite a while. Look, the lock is damaged, won't snap to."

"Can't it be fixed?"

"Probably, but it's no problem because the cigarettes can't fall out anyway."

I'm not his tutor just yet, I'm just observing, trying not to make any comments so as not to alarm him. However, during the past four days I had to instruct him twice.

The first time. During my lesson with Stefan, a hospital assistant arrives. I'm on call: sick people are being brought in.

"They bother you all day," Stefan says, annoyed, his voice raised.

Both his tone and facial expression indicate that this isn't his opinion. This is how Miss Lonia or a cook presumably talk at the orphanage.

"Don't talk like that," I say gently and after the assistant leaves.

"But he buts in while I'm reading."

He's surprised that there are two hundred and seventeen sick and wounded people in the hospital.

"So you, as the one on call, have to check them all."

"No, only the new ones, so they don't place someone infectious next to non-infectious patients."

"Is it true that measles is an infectious disease? When I had it, I kept choking and couldn't talk. Dad gave me mineral oil to drink and I felt better. Dad had never gone to a doctor, and he knew how to treat everything himself."

"Your dad was a wise man," I say with conviction.

"Sure he was wise," he affirms, nodding his head.

I'm dying to ask him why he said that if his dad didn't return that it would be great too. No, it's too soon for that…

The second time.

"Listen, Stefek, don't address Mr. Walenty by just Walenty but Mr. Walenty."

"But I do say Mr. Walenty." This is an echo from the orphanage: to wriggle out.

It's my fault, now, when I'm talking with Stefan I make sure to always say Mr. Walenty.

An important matter, especially in an orphanage. A caretaker, a dishwasher woman, a laundry woman resent the children when they call them by their first names. While talking with the children one should always say Mr. Walenty, Miss Rózia, Mrs. Skorupska.

It's been validated what I've said with reference to illness in an orphanage: illness in a family brings a child closer to it. As a rule, parents and their children mention fondly or at least remember well those moments. At an orphanage an illness means unnecessary trouble, which often leads to distancing.

I had a lot of trouble to make it possible for Stefan to write in bed. I had to empty a big box and I placed an inkwell in a tin can, which Walenty had earlier turned into an ashtray for me. On one side I had to prop up the box with a pillow and the other side with books. He thanked me with a smile. The orphanage can't afford such luxury.

"Are you comfortable?"

"Yes," with a smile.

He settles himself at this table by placing books at his side and a pencil between the slats of the box, all according to his innate sense of orderliness. A new situation, he isn't following established pattern and is acting on his own initiative.

He's now sitting and copying a poem from a primer, whispering.

"A white – white – white..."

And finishes it, with a mental effort:

"A little white shir – white shi – a little shirt."

He sighs.

"A little white shirt... I'll give her a little white shirt for the road."

Even so he makes a mistake and writes "wite."

"Look, instead of 'white' you wrote 'wite.'"

He smiles, embarrassed.

"I'll write it again."

"Better leave it for now, you'll change it after tea."

"No, now."

Again silence, interrupted by concentrated whispering. He looks gloomily because there are mistakes in his rewrite. In the first copy, I let go of a few mistakes so as not to discourage him, but not this time. The other evening he made mistakes in his reading but didn't know why.

"Because you're hungry," I said. I wanted to know if he remembered my remark.

"What do you think: why didn't it work out as well now?"

"Because if it turns out badly at first, it gets worse later."

Then, in desperation:

"I'll copy it once more."

He blushed, tightened his fists. I kissed the top of his head – an idiotic kiss; he moved slightly aside:

"Poor, poor little orphan..."

At this precarious moment (while copying, Stefan misses an entire stanza) Walenty brings tea.

"For the road – for the road I'll give her – I'll give her for the road."

Walenty drops a sugar cube into the tea. Stefan casts a fleeting glance, continues writing.

"The knife was found," Walenty says.

Stefan looks up attentively: a knife, what knife? He rests his head on his arm, any moment he'll ask a question, no, he resists the temptation, concentrates again. Walenty smiles, I make a quick note, and outline an interesting event, Stefan doesn't notice anything. Then triumphantly, after a brief period full of expectation, he says:

"There, sir," a smile.

"Well done, but you 'swallowed' one letter; do you want to look for it?"

Stefan drinks his tea, furrows his brow, searches for the "swallowed" letter.

Too bad I haven't looked at my watch to check how long he's been writing.

"My watch, my watch!" No matter how many times I remind myself, I always forget.

Two thoughts:

During my long months with the group of children I failed to notice if any of them smile. It was something too subtle, too slight, below the threshold of my awareness. Only now do I realize that this is an important symptom, worth studying.

When Stefan casually asked me:

"Will I be able to ride a horse?" with a winning smile (?). My reply was evasive: "It's slippery now, and the horses aren't shod well; perhaps in the summer." Children know that their smiles bind you to a response.

My second thought: for a child, copying is not a thoughtless activity. On the contrary, it requires a lot of effort not to miss a letter, a word, or an entire line; not to copy the same word or line twice, not to make any mistakes; to fit a word into a line without parsing it into the next line; the letters must be the same size and equally separated. Who knows, perhaps it's by copying that the child finally comes to understand the text that he is reading. It's obvious that creative minds are soon bored by passive transcribing. While transcribing, Stefan was like an apprentice copying a master's artwork. Pity the teacher who must correct the scribbling in forty notebooks, unless he perceives and senses the effort of the work as for a group.

For a child, not only reading presents him with the difficulty of setting letters, it's a series of incomprehensible words and surprises in grammar. So he reads:

"Ap-p-l-es, app-l-es." (a pause during which he figures out the meaning of the word) then quickly and fluently reads, "apples."

More in a ditty:

"Cause the lill Polish song, songie, (with disbelief), song, song (murmurs to himself), what a songie (ends loudly), the Polish songie the birdies have taught me."

We, acrobats in fluent reading, who from two letters catch an entire word and from two words an entire sentence, are unable to realize neither the difficulties with which the child struggles nor the means by which to make his work easier.

In a story, just a while back, Stefan read "Franek" instead of "Felek." I didn't correct him at the time. Now, when he finished it, I asked him:

"What was the boy's name?"

"Franek."

"Try again."

"Well, Franek."

"I bet you it's not Franek."

He then read:

"Fra-Fre-Fe-Felek."

"See, good thing you didn't take up the bet."

"Good thing."

"You probably know a Franek?"

"I do."

"And what about Felek?"

"I don't know any Felek."

The same thing happened in an arithmetic lesson. Instead of "blueberries," he read "blackberries" twice.

"Five blackberries." He announces.

"That's not how it begins."

No response, then definitely with a trace of irritation:

"Five it is."

"Five it is, but not blackberries."

"What then?"

"Look, and you'll see."

"… bla …blue …blueberries."

"See: listen Stefan, perhaps as a magician or something, you're making Franek into Felek, and blueberries into blackberries."

He's so charming in his surprise, when caught off guard, his how did this happen? so I kiss him. (Totally unnecessary. When will I unlearn this?).

Stefan is annoyed at an unfamiliar construction.

He reads:

"A saleswoman has nine apples. How many apples will be left if four boys take two apples each."

He mumbles under his breath:

"What's this 'each'?" (Then aloud.) "One apple."

"Two coins… coins, ah, I know it but I forgot."

This seemingly illogical sentence has a rational base – if he doesn't know because he's forgotten, perhaps it will come to him later.

At about the twentieth sentence he suggests:

"I'll read softly then I'll write down what I found."

"Good, and I'll nod if it's correct."

He's not the first to make such a suggestion. I don't know if a child wants to introduce more diversity into his work this way, or if there's a deeper wish here, a need for silence while he's concentrating on his work.

Evening

He said his prayers, kissed my hand (an echo of his family home, a nest broken by war, one of many hundreds and thousands). I'm writing. He lays quietly, his eyes open.

"Sir, is it true that after shaving one's hair, it doesn't grow any more?"

He's concerned that an overt mention of my baldness may offend me.

"It's not true. If one shaves one's beard it grows back."

"Some soldiers have beards all the way to their waists, like Jews. Why?"

"This is their custom. The English even shave their moustaches."

"Is it true that there are many Jews among Germans?"

"Yes, among Germans, there are Russian Jews, there are Polish Jews."

"You're saying Polish Jews. Are the Poles Jews?"

"No, Poles are Catholics. But if somebody speaks Polish, wishes Poles well, and wants their good, then he is also a Pole."

"My mom was a Ruthenian, my dad a Pole. Boys follow their father. Do you know where is Podgajce? My dad is from there."

"How old is your dad?"

"He was forty two, now he's forty five."

"Your dad might not recognize you because you've grown."

"I don't know if I'd recognize dad."

"Don't you have his photo?"

"Of course not! Some soldiers look like my dad."

Silence. Evening – a very important time for a child. Most often it's time for reminiscences, for quiet reflections and softly spoken conversations. It's like that at the Orphans' Home, it's like that at a summer camp.

"Are you writing a book?"

"Yes."

"Did you write my primer?"

"No."

"So did you buy it?"

"Yes."

"You probably paid half-a-ruble for it."

"No, only twenty-five kopeks."

Again silence. I light my cigarette.

"Is it true that sulfur can poison you?"

"Yes. Why?"

I don't understand the reason for this question.

"Because they'd matches like they went on maneuvers…"

An echo of his father's blurred account about the superior quality of some brand of matches, something his father told him about the time when he was a bachelor and served in the army; there happened to be some sulfur in the soup and soldiers were poisoned.

I don't understand, Stefan is talking in a sleepy voice, he's muddled, falls asleep.

In my childhood, I wanted very much to see my guardian angel. I'd pretend I was asleep, then suddenly I'd open my eyes. Not surprisingly, he'd be hiding. In the Saxon Garden[9], you'd think a guard was nowhere close, but as soon as you'd run on a lawn for your ball, he'd be there, threatening you from a distance. I was upset that this angel of mine was actually a "guard."

Day five

Duduk was praising Stefan for being industrious. When I went to the workshop Stefan was sawing wood. I wasn't at ease watching him: the board was moving to all sides, the blunt saw was jumping all over the board, and it would be so easy to sever your fingers. But I said nothing. It would be nonsense to tell him to be careful. I had already cautioned him enough.

"Don't go outside barefoot. Don't drink un-boiled water. Aren't you cold, do you have a belly ache?"

This is actually what makes "our" children self-conscious, it corrupts and dulls them.

He comes home from the workshop at six.

He doesn't want to go to Tarnopol on Sunday.

"What for? It's been hardly a week so why go there again? Will Mr. Walenty go with us? How long we'll be there?"

He doesn't want to write to his brother.

"I'll see him there soon enough."

"But what if he's not at home?"

"Well, all right then."

"So how will you begin your letter?"

"Blessed be Jesus Christ."

"And then?"

"How am I supposed to know?"

"Do you want to write that you've been sick?"

"No!"

I've a hard time restraining myself from a caustic question "How about the cake with jam and the headcheese?"

His short letter: I'm working in a carpentry shop, I like doing it, my tutor shows me how to read and do arithmetic, you needn't worry about me.

"How will you sign it?"

"Stefan Zagrodnik."

"Perhaps you can say 'lots of kisses.'"

"Naah, no need."

"Why?"

"Because I'm embarrassed," he whispers.

I then suggest:

"Do you want to make a clean copy of what you wrote first, or shall I write it on a piece of paper and then you'll copy it?"

I give him a letter sheet and an envelope. He tries twice, but no luck. Wastes a lot of paper. All right, tomorrow he'll copy from my piece of paper.

We spend an hour and a half on arithmetic without a break.

"Isn't this enough?"

"No, till the end of the page."

Who knows, perhaps a set of exercises is the best primer for practicing reading. Exercises, puzzles, charades, playful questions – a child not only must but also wants to understand them. Although, I don't know, perhaps distracting the child's attention is not advisable. Suffice it to say, that in our today's lesson, exercises have eliminated and substituted reading.

"How many cigarettes, sir, do you smoke a day, probably fifty?"

"No, twenty."

"It's bad for your health to smoke; when a boy once blew on a piece of paper it turned yellow. When there's cotton wool in the cigarette, it stops the smoke."

"Did you ever smoke?"

"And why not?"

"In the orphanage?"

"No. When I lived with my brother."

"Where did you get them?"

"When they lay on a table or on top of a wardrobe. Do you, sir, get dizzy?"

"Perhaps a little bit."

"I got dizzy... I don't want to get hooked on them."

A pause.

"When it gets warm we'll ride horses, right?" (This is important to him, he remembers my promise).

"We better not ride but stay put."

"Yes, but I'm thinking – to Tarnopol."

"Horses are scared of cars."

"So what, if one carries us off a bit..."

"And what if it jumps sideways?"

I tell him that once, near Łomża, a horse almost toppled off a mountain. Stefan goes to bed. I wind up my watch.

"Watches can be wound up both ways, right?"

I show him that my watch can also be wound up "both ways".

I move on to my writing, to tidying my notes.

"Sir, I put in a new pen nib because the other one was cutting into the paper."

"It got bad so soon because you were writing on the table, wood blunts a nib." Only now, I casually remark upon his usual bad habit. Such remarks, as I observed many times before, carry more weight.

Silence...

"Why do you tear up so many sheets of paper?"

I explain what it's like to make hasty notes, and what it's like to work on them thoroughly.

"For example, I note something about a patient: cough, fever. And then, when I have time, I write it up properly."

"My mom used to cough, spit up blood, a medic assistant came and said it's hopeless. She kept going to the hospital till she died."

(A sigh, then a yawn. The sigh is mimicry – that's what one does when talking about the departed).

Day six

No sooner had he drank his tea than he ran to the workshop. He whisked by at lunchtime, and returned at six in the evening.

I began an interesting test: I looked at my watch to check how much time he spent reading a particular story and how many mistakes he made. I didn't correct them while he was reading, not until he finished. So he read twice, the first time it took him four minutes and thirty-five seconds, and he made eight mistakes. The second time – three minutes and fifty seconds, and only six mistakes.

A major quarrel about the horse. We're playing checkers. In the orphanage, some boys played well and didn't want to play with Stefan. "Who's going to play with me when I'm no good at it?" However, he learned from them the mannerisms of a good player, to wit, twiddling his fingers in the air before making a move and then descend on his adversary's piece like a hawk; or to smack his lips, or to hit a piece nonchalantly with his nail with a disdainful expression and a supercilious puffing up of his lips. These are unpleasant mannerisms even in a good player, and more so in a bumbler like Stefan; to encourage him, I sometimes declare a no-win.

So, we're playing. Suddenly:

"Please, sir, you go by train tomorrow, while I and Mr. Walenty ride the horse."

"You silly. Do you think horses are for transport? Ask the colonel."

"Will he give me permission?"

"Fiddlesticks."

"Well, sir, it's your move."

He sounds irritated and, having decided to win at all cost as revenge, he begins to cheat.

"Eee, what's this move... hurry up... you're so clever."

I pretend not to notice but play more carefully, in order to win as punishment.

"You're sure to lose, sir."

"You'll lose because you're cheating," I say calmly but firmly.

If I give in to a child's wish, disdain is bound to creep in. It is necessary to counteract with facts, not by griping, to maintain one's authority.

Few big pieces are left, I strike a painful blow, and he loses his queen.

"I don't know how to play with queens," he says with resignation.

"Nor do you play well with small pieces, but you'll learn."

While I was washing my hands, he poured some water for me from a mug, handed me a towel, and told me to drink my tea before it got cold. I did not say a word that he had offended me and, just as subtly, he asked forgiveness for what he had felt toward me.

In the quarrel about the horse, he showed not only anger but also disdain. Where did it come from, what was its source? Perhaps from my asking him: "do you want to do arithmetic, or to read, or to write?" Perhaps this had annoyed him. Children like some coercion: it eases their struggle with their inner recalcitrance and saves them from mental effort to make a choice. Decision is the result of voluntarily relinquishing certain things and amplifying one's responsibility for results. A demand is external while free choice is internal. "If you leave a decision to me you are either stupid and therefore ignorant, or lazy and loathe to make it."

Whence this minor shadow of disdain on Stefan's part? I give him pretzels while I eat plain bread. He offers me the pretzels twice, takes the better ones, more thoroughly baked, no one has taught him the insincerity of minor social sacrifices that are supposed to indicate readiness to make greater and more genuine sacrifices.

This trifle, this nothing that I view as the quarrel about the horse proves that the time to keep encouraging him has passed, and that I can slowly begin his upbringing. I am collecting materials for that conversation.

In the evening I check his dirty shirt – of course there is a louse there.

"What is it?" he asks with concern.

"A louse."

"That's because they didn't change sheets in the orphanage. The comforters were dirty."

"Never mind, there won't be any lice here. Why didn't they change sheets?"

"I don't know, perhaps they didn't feel like washing them."

The first conversation about the orphanage.

"They're not afraid of an orderly but they're scared of a military guy. Actually, the military won't hit you, that's forbidden, the teacher will scold him for it. Sometimes, when he yells he'll use his belt, but doesn't hit you."

"Did you ever get the belt?"

"Well, why not?"

It seems that they hit but don't hit. Yet Stefan is right: they don't hit, it's forbidden, but sometimes when a military guy screams and threatens he will, in secrecy, use the belt.

I used to laugh at this seemingly illogical talk. However, about three years ago I ceased to laugh after Lejbuś said:

"I love to go on boat rides."

"Have you ever gone on a boat?"

"No, never in my life."

This is an error in expression, not lack of logic: he's sure it would be a pleasant thing to do.

Day seven

Mr. Checkov had guests for a card game. Supper was late. Walenty was on duty in the dining hall. I finally left at midnight in a bad mood. When I returned to my quarters I lit a lamp, Stefan was nowhere around. What the deuce? Going out the door, I ran into Stefan.

"Where were you?"

"In the kitchen. I kept going in and out, looking through the window, and you were sitting there. Then I looked and all of a sudden you were gone. So I ran to catch up with you."

"Were you scared?"

"Why should I be scared?"

No, he wasn't scared. He had waited, looked around, ran to be with me.

I hadn't seen my people for two years. Then six months ago – a brief letter, all crumpled up, it may have gotten through a cordon of bayonets, controllers, and spies. And now, I'm not alone anymore.

I experienced boundless gratitude toward this child. There is nothing notable about him, nothing that would attract me to him, or to rivet me. A simple face, a countenance without charm, his mind average, little imagination, total lack of soft-heartedness – nothing that makes children attractive. And yet, through this unremarkable child, like through any ordinary bush, it's nature and her primeval laws that talk, like God. Thank you, child, that you are just – so simple.

"My little son," I thought with tenderness.

How am I to thank him?

"Listen, Stefek, if you have any questions, any worries, or want something, please tell me."

"I don't like to bother you."

I tell him – no bother at all.

"If it's a bother, I'll tell you, and explain it to you. For example with that horse; horses are for lugging wood, for carrying bread and to transport the sick..."

"I'd like you to bring me some pretzels."

"Good, you'll get you some pretzels."

As it happened, our proscribed supply ran out today.

We went to Tarnopol on sleighs. Stefan looked sad. He didn't make any of those child-like comments, which direct us to something we no longer notice or reminisce on something we used to see very, very clearly.

Stefan was to go to church with Walenty, then to visit his brother, while Walenty went shopping. I was to look for an eye doctor who might be working at a military hospital. We would re-join back at the orphanage. On our way, Stefan changed his decision several times: he would first go to the orphanage, no, to his brother first, no, he wanted to go with Walenty.

At the orphanage, a teacher called to him, but he stood there strangely dumb, colorless, replied to her questions in a soft, apathetic tone. Not until we left the teacher's room at the orphanage did I realize why he didn't want to go to Tarnopol, why he was so sad on our way there, why he was so quick to say "Well, let's go."

Stefan was afraid that I would leave him behind.

We had to buy a teakettle.

"So I'll go with Mr. Walenty, I know where we can buy one."

I took out my wallet.

"Oh, so you'll give Walek (not Mr. Walenty) ten rubles and we'll buy some cakes."

His cheeky tone now signified: "I was not scared at all, I knew you wouldn't leave me there…"

He's been strangely reluctant to talk about his brother. I never knew why. He didn't want me to meet his brother: what had been the meaning of this?

He was reading, then finished.

"So, how many mistakes did I make?"

"Guess."

"Five."

"No, only four."

"So it's two less than the first time."

He'd read it incorrectly, but right away he corrected it himself.

"Are you counting this, sir?

He read the same ditty for twenty seconds the first time, for fifteen seconds the next time, and the third time also for fifteen seconds.

"Can't I go on reading it faster?"

He tried to read faster.

"Scrach – scra – scra – scarecrow…"

Not to lose time he quickly turned the page.

Yesterday he read the poem *Vistula* three times, today – four times; the result – very interesting:

Yesterday: twenty seconds, fifteen, eleven.

Today: eleven seconds, ten seconds, seven seconds, six seconds.

The same with the poem *An Orphan*:

Yesterday: twenty seconds, fifteen seconds, fifteen seconds.

Today: fifteen seconds, twelve seconds, ten seconds.

He carried through the gain he had made from yesterday's third reading in its entirety.

I made a note in the form of an equation: the numerator was the number of seconds, denominator was the number of errors. Thus 24/3=24 seconds and 3 errors. Since I graded the time and quality of his work, I could forego to grade his reading skill.

While reading, he became confused with the word "ditty," lost a lot of time, gave up:

"Eee, this will take a lot of time."

Walenty remarked:

"Just like a horse, when it gets snagged it can't pull."
I let Stefan to begin again.

Day eight

Yesterday I wrote: those child-like comments, which direct us to something we no longer notice. Here are a couple of examples.

"Oh, look, sir, at the label on the tea." (When he dropped in a sugar cube, bubbles of air came to the surface).

"How many cubes did you put in, sir?"

"One."

"Look, sir, there are two cubes." (as seen through the glass cup).

Concerning a pretzel:

"What is poppy made of?" "It grows," I reply. "So why is it black?" "Because it's ripe." "Is it true there are little partitions inside, and inside those there are a few more, right?"

"Hmm."

"Can a garden produce a full plate of poppy?"

His concept of a garden consists of four or five images, mine of a hundred or a thousand. This was so obvious, but it was only thanks to his question that I began to ponder on it for quite a while. A child's numerous, seemingly illogical questions, are at the root of this. This is why it's so difficult for us to communicate with children, because they use the same words but they attribute to them other meanings than we do. My garden, my father, my death are not his garden, his father, his death.

A father-physician shows a bullet he has removed during surgery from a wounded man.

"Will they kill you, daddy, with the same bullet?" his eight-year-old daughter asks.

Equally, countryside and city don't understand each other, nor do a lord and his slave, or a satiated and a hungry man, or a young one and an old one, perhaps only a man and a woman do understand each other. We only pretend that we understand each other.

For a whole week, Stefan watched, without any interest, all his peers sledding down hills and hillocks. Such a strong temptation, yet there he was, working at the carpenter's. He worked until lunchtime with Duduk, constructing beds for the sick, and in the evening he came home with a sled.

"I'll only go downhill twice."

"Only twice, not three times?" I asked, incredulously.

He smiled and took off. He was gone for a long while. There was silence in my room, it was empty; it was a mystery to me, why Walenty, who kept complaining about the boy's bother and uselessness wanted to call him twice into the house. Perhaps he too needed my evening lessons with Stefan.

He returned, sat down and waited.

"Was the sled all right?"

"Not yet properly adjusted."

This was a dispassionate question so as not to betray that I was totally on his side and forgave him his tardiness thanks to his blush, breathlessness and his cheerful, healthful emotions. He understood and wanted to take advantage: he reached for the checkers with a questioning look.

"No, sonny."

Without any shadow of protest, he seemed pleased to pick up a book. I sensed that had I complied with his request, he might have been hurt.

"But without a watch," he quickly added.

"Why?"

"Because with a watch, it's like someone standing over my head and hurrying me up."

Then he read. Like never before. This was inspiring. I was surprised and couldn't believe my ears. This was not a reading but like sledding over the book, conquering obstacles with hundredfold will power. He transferred his entire sport hazard on to learning. I was now sure that correcting his reading mistakes would be nonsensical: I became invisible to him, nor should he see me – all to himself, his own will rushing him on.

I picked up my pen and made notes.

Here are some mistakes, as he tried to master the text and understand its meaning:

He read "the children 'walked' instead of 'talked', "one 'needs' bread instead of one 'kneads' bread." He read "he gave a signal," instead of "he gave a 'sign." "Hanusia" instead of "Anusia" (cf. Felek and Franek).

He read: "the doctor signaled granny to take 'they' (the children) out instead of 'them."

A struggle for meaning:

"In a dig book, no – in a big book. When the teacher has learned the verses – oh, no – the ditties."

These were mistakes because thoughts muddle vision.

The text:

"The children kneeled with granny… they cried and called: 'oh, God, oh God, spare our dear mommy from death. Intercede for us, the Holiest oh, Mary! Let our mommy recover."

Then: the granny "kneeled" instead of "led" the children to bed.

The text:

"At this hour, mother busied herself with dinner. The whole family gathered to dinner. At the chief seats sat the old folk bent by age: granddaddy and granny Jasia.

Granddaddy was eastwhile (instead of 'erstwhile')..."

The grotesqueness of written language: one pronounces wen and spells when? Even if a child doesn't say it, one can infer from his tone, facial expression, pauses in reading and his accent that it surprises and sometimes annoys him.

If we don't badger a child's reading with constant corrections and explanations, we may arrive at some excellent observations.

To wit:

Stefan read "to br, br brake." I corrected him "to bake," he repeated "brake," and went on reading, he didn't hear what I had said, busy working, immersed in his reading...

Children don't like to be interrupted because it interferes with their reading. Stefan read "cornice." He noticed that I wanted to explain what it meant, so, preempting me, he said quickly: "I know what cornice means," and went on reading...

Other difficulties: construction of phrases, incomprehensible words, quirks of written language, unfamiliar grammatical forms, for example:

Stefan read, "he gave 'to' the boy," and softly to himself: "he gave the boy the cherries."

When he finished reading, I wanted to check his understanding of the text, so I asked:

"What's this about?"

"About a slovenly boy."

An echo of a fleeting thought about an unfamiliar grammatical form: about a boy, he vaguely remembered that it was somehow different in the book, different that he thought it should have been.

How interesting that just today, after his sledding escapade the necessity for a watch became a burden to him. At first, I paid no attention to it.

I'm standing by a heating stove and pondering on today's lesson. Stefan, already in bed, suddenly:

"You promised me."

"Promised what?"

"A fairy tale."

This is the first time that he reminds me about a fairy tale.

"Do you want to hear a new one?"

"No, the one about Aladdin... but please sit down."

"Where."

"Here, closer, on the chair."

"Why?"

"All right, so just tell me, stay by the stove."

Seemingly nothing, yet full of meaning.

Of the three fairy tales: *Cinderella, Puss in Boots* and *Aladdin* he chooses the one closest to him, where a magician comes to a poor boy and with his magical lamp influences the boy's fate. While here, a stranger-physician (an officer) suddenly appears and takes the boy from an orphanage; in the fairy tale, Negroes bring him delicacies on gold platters, here Walenty offers him pretzels.

"But, please, sir, sit down," Stefan whispers. This tells me why children in general, while listening to a fairytale – they want closeness to the one telling it: I should sit next to him. My questions: "where?" "why?" annoy him. He feels too embarrassed to admit why. This is the result of depravity on our part, which makes a child to be brazen and say: "I like you so much, I want to be close to you, I'm sad, you're so good." Stefan was embarrassed to sign his letter to his brother with "I kiss you," and "your loving..."

During breakfast, Stefan says:

"Instead of eating the pretzels, you give them to me."

I reply "hmm," to which he's nothing to add.

After the fairy tale, I try to explain that the presence of a watch while he's reading should not rush him.

"If the first time you read, it took you three minutes, the next time it was less by five seconds, this was good." Then: "If today it took you longer to read than yesterday, you might wonder why – perhaps you were sleepy today, or more tired from working at the workshop, or the sledding was a problem."

"So I read badly today?"

"What do you think?"

"I don't know," after a moment's hesitation: "I think I read well."

"Yes, you read well today..."

Now my right eye is hurting me as well, it's watering. I've trouble writing – I must take a rest. Too bad to skip making notes. They are such an immeasurable treasure.

Day nine

Stefan has scabies. In the orphanage, he had it twice. The first time the treatment lasted three weeks, next time it took six weeks. No wonder he was afraid to mention it, and in child-like fashion he delayed the catastrophe. I only now understood why he had asked a couple of times, if and when the baths would be available. I ignored his questions – obviously a mistake. An unusual zeal for cleanliness, of this child of war, should have struck me. By not paying attention, I probably attributed it to his wish to visit and try the unfamiliar to him public baths (he had heard that sick people take such baths).

This discovery made great impression on Walenty – what will happen to our laundry, our food?

"I never had such a thing," Walenty is full of reproach, thinking, and I don't know why, that he's sure to catch it.

A brief lecture on scabies, its etiology, the degree of its infectiousness, and treatment that would take three days.

"Go, sonny, to your workshop, and I'll put some salve on you after dinner."

Yes, both tender words and a kiss were needed here.

"I never had pimples like that when I lived at home," he whispers.

Before he went to the workshop, he spent a lot of time sledding. When I arrived at the workshop, Stefan looked at me with concern that I might tell Duduk about it.

All this was most unfortunate and disturbed my equanimity. Just today, having collected the necessary materials, I wanted to have a talk with him: about his having torn out a page from his notebook, and taken a grenade to the workshop without asking if I'd allow him to show it; about making a sled not knowing if I would permit it; about not telling me the truth: he didn't want me to meet his brother, so he was hiding something; he told me that they hadn't been hitting kids at the orphanage, then admitted that he had been hit with a belt.

I wanted him to know that I was pleased with him, but that there were certain small details I wanted to mention to him, to let him know that even though I keep quiet, I'm noticing things. Now there is the scabies that he was hiding from me to be added. I plan a talk about all this for a few days hence, when his skin and my eyes are healed. It's of the utmost importance that we let reprimands pile up and address them rarely in the form of a friendly conversation. We're usually concerned that a child will forget, but he remembers very well, we are the ones who are likely to forget and therefore prefer to deal with issues in the heat of the moment, in other words, at the wrong time and brutally.

This evening Stefan was reading badly. Yesterday: twenty seven lines in six and a half minutes, today: sixteen lines in seven minutes.

I made him recount what he had read. During the past few days, he was telling the story briefly, in his own words, beginning in a child-like way: "So this is how it went..." Today, and I didn't know why, having recounted the first story, he asked:

"I told it badly, right?"

He decided to tell the next story in the words of the book, just like at class. Right away, he fell into an awful, monotonous, thoughtless, fawning tone of the telling a school-like story, furtively peeking into the book, selecting sentences haphazardly and without making sense.

He plays checkers much better, his bluffing moves have ceased – he plays with attention and in earnest. I get it: he's been wont to imitate, to copycat other contestants, the experts, and now he begins to play by himself.

I keep helping him, drawing his attention to errors.

"But just don't tell me what to do. If you tell me, I'll accept it too easily."

Correcting every reading or writing mistake has the same result, namely the child makes light of his own work.

The table is wobbling. Stefan spills some tea on it and makes a trail of his finger to the edge, so the tea trickles down.

"Look, sir, how I make the tea trickle down."

"Hmm."

"It just trickles down."

Clearly, a child has certain sensitivity – I'd call it a grammatical and spelling consciousness. I've noticed many times that a child, having heard an ungrammatically constructed sentence tries to change it, but doesn't know how to correct it. Doesn't methodical education annihilate this consciousness? Don't we make the child's work more difficult with our unintelligible, inaccessible explanations?

A child's mind is a forest, where tops of trees move slightly, where branches intertwine, leaves tremulously touch each other. There are moments when a tree touches its neighbor and thus conveys a vibration to hundreds, even thousands of other trees, to an entire forest. Our every "good, bad, be careful, do it again" is like a gale launching chaos. I once followed a dandelion seed, the seed suspended from a white plume. I followed it for quite a while: it gently flit from one stalk to another, from one blade of grass to another, stopping here, flitting off there, until it latched on and began sprouting. Oh, human thought, we don't know the laws that govern you, we wish we knew but we don't, and mankind's evil genius takes advantage of it.

Instead of "tears" Stefan reads "teens."

In the arithmetic exercise, the word "it came to" annoys him.

"The 'it came to' surely means 'he got.'" (mumbles to himself). "So surely, three... he got six plums."

He reads:

"Distrustfully," (then once more, carefully): "distrustfully," and a third time, with resignation, "distrustfully."

He continues…

He reads:

"Fluent… fluent… or 'affluent'?… It says here 'fluent'."

He puzzles over the grammatical phrase "you, child, are sitting." After re-reading it and making sure he's read it correctly, he ponders on it.

"Please, sir, is the hand in your watch made of gold?"

"No, it's just ordinary."

"Because there are gold ones."

"Have you seen any?"

"I have, Miss Lonia has one."

Another time:

"Why don't you buy yourself a nail file for your nails?"

"Why?"

"Just like the one that Miss Lonia has."

It seems to make him uncomfortable that I, a man, an officer and his present guardian, seem to be below par to Miss Lonia, handicapped by my lack of a gold watch hand and of a nail file.

Before turning in for the night I rub him with the salve.

"So it'll all be gone in three days?" he asks in disbelief.

"Why didn't you tell me about it?"

"I was embarrassed," he whispers.

"Why so? That you were sick?"

"At home I never had any pimples," he dodges a reply, he doesn't want to say that at the orphanage they would laugh at him, that they were disgusted with scabies.

"You have the salve all over you, sir."

"I'll just wash it off."

While in bed, he asks:

"I didn't go sledding for too long, did I?"

Considering my kindness toward him, he's worried about the sin he's committed. This is how I explain to myself his question, so out of the blue: "he's not mad at me for anything. Why isn't he, perhaps he doesn't know what I've done? I did go sledding, while he wanted me to study. I went sledding for a long time, but perhaps it wasn't so long after all?"

A brawl and reconciliation.

Walenty is on duty. I pour Stefan some tea.

"Why did you pour me just half-a-glass?"

"So you wouldn't spill it on the table."

"Eee, I'll pour myself some more."

I don't respond. He keeps pouring, puts the glass back and, while he's squeezing between the table and the bench, the table wobbles and a lot of tea spills. Stefan gets embarrassed. He goes to fetch a dishrag.

I speak calmly but firmly:

"Please, Stefan, don't take any of Mr. Walenty's things because he doesn't like it."

"I wanted to wipe the table."

"What do you know, perhaps this dishrag is for wiping glasses."

All befuddled, he takes back the dishrag. I tilt the table and wipe the rest with a paper towel. Stefan keeps quiet, but finally with an uncertain voice, he tries this:

"Why are there letters H.S. on the glass (of the lampshade)?"

"Probably these are the initials of the manufacturer."

He follows it up with more questions. This means "we're just talking; the other thing is now forgotten. Who would bother remembering such trivia?"

And yet he did remember. In the evening:

"I'll pour the tea, all right?"

"Good."

He pours me a full glass, not much more than half for himself.

"Please, sir, hold on to the table," he says, squeezing past it. "Now it didn't get spilled."

If it were not for my eyes, I would have described this more fully, I omitted several details. In the morning, he said "thank you," and handed me a towel. He apologized not with words but with deeds.

A child watches himself, analyzes his actions. We just don't notice this work because we don't know how to read between the lines, between words tossed casually. We want the child to confide in us all his thoughts and feelings. While we're not particularly disposed to confidences, we don't want to or don't realize that a child is more bashful, more touchy, and more sensitive about our brutal vigilance of his own spiritual tremblings.

"I didn't say my prayers today," Stefan says.

"Why not?"

"I forgot." (A pause). "When I wash myself in the morning, then right away I say my prayers, but if I don't wash, I forget to pray."

He doesn't wash himself because of the scabies.

Stefan has difficulty saying "sir."

"Guess what, 'sir,' wait, 'sir,'don't talk, 'sir,'vis á vis 'you, sir, have a guess."

Or again:

"You, sir, would rather be writing, while I'm prattling and I'm disturbing you."

I'll bring up with Stefan the issue of the sleds in our general conversation. Soon, there'll be no snow. How fortunate that I didn't reprimand him right away. Here's the secret of his having missed work:

"I was so scared at the workshop, about the master smelling the salve. When he was in one place, I would immediately go somewhere else. In the morning I would go sledding to air out the smell."

There are two customs hung over from the orphanage.

Stefan laughs softly, covering his mouth.

"Why don't you want to laugh loudly?"

"Because it's not nice, the teacher says."

"Perhaps because there are lots of kids there and it would make a lot of noise..."

Second: every morning he leaves a piece of pretzel on his plate and some tea at the bottom of his glass. Obviously, there's something behind this.

"Tell me, Stefek, why do you always leave something?"

"I don't, I eat it all."

"Listen, sonny, if you don't want to tell me why, just say so. There are times when one doesn't want to tell something. (A right to have secrets!). But you do leave things."

"Eee, because they say that eating everything looks like one hasn't eaten all year."

Realizing that this presents some difficulty, I don't press him for more. I've inadvertently hurt his feelings. I too would feel hurt if I had done something to show off my knowledge of social manners and then suddenly realized that doing so isn't at all in good taste.

Imitation.

"Please, sir, I want to write capital *K* like you do."

In the Orphans' Home, many children adopt some of my letters, assuming that letters, which adults use, are better, more valued. I remember the time when I would struggle learning to write capital *V*, like my father did addressing his envelopes "Venerable." I thought this would impress my teacher, but instead, I was met with a harsh rebuff:

"When you're a dad, you can write as you wish."

Why? What's her problem? What's bad about it? I was both surprised and hurt.

Today during dictation, a hospital attendant arrived with some paperwork. I didn't notice that Stefan watched attentively how I was writing. After the attendant left, he began to write so fast that there was no way of deciphering what he had written.

As a teacher, I have only three lines of absolutely slapdash writing, while as a caregiver, I have a more perceptive sense of rebelling against his own imperfection.

"I want to write as fast as you, I want to be like you."

Well, let's try:

"Look, young fellow, how you have scribbled here. Blam... dram... bram... Why do you think the three lines came out so badly?"

"I don't know," (a bashful smile).

"Perhaps you were tired?"

"I wasn't tired."

He doesn't want to lie, yet he can't tell the truth.

We were checking his progress in the proficiency of his reading. Since we were now reading a book with small lettering, we had to count the letters.

"There were thirty seven lines with seventeen letters each, which means six hundred and twenty nine letters. You read this for two hundred and ten seconds, so three letters per second. Since there were sixty five lines, with twenty seven letters per line, you read them in six and a half minutes. So almost five letters per second."

He wasn't much impressed even though he watched my calculations with interest.

Before going to sleep.

"Shall I kiss you goodnight?"

"Am I a saint or something?"

"Is it just..."

"Or a priest, or something?"

I like to encounter easy words to pronounce in reading such as "she called, she's pleased, she lit," but difficult words such as "bare" or "bear" annoy me.

An easy assignment; he has already done a hard one, but now he gets confused, makes mistakes. Why on earth?

"Oh, look, sir, here's a pimple."

"Where?"

"Here," and he shows me his neck. "Isn't this scabies?"

"No, you'll have a bath tomorrow and will be well again."

Now the arithmetic goes without a hitch.

Day eleven

When I put on my dark glasses, Stefan asked softly:

"Do your eyes hurt a lot?"

Smile and whisper – it's thanks to Stefan that I notice them; I wouldn't have at the orphanage.

"I'm well and you're sick," he said that evening.

This was an honest way of showing compassion. We adults talk nicely but feel less deeply. I was grateful to Stefan for what he said.

I didn't know why he said:

"These days, I don't think about my brother at all."

"That's too bad. You should think both about your father and your brother."

Infamous war.

He cried when I went to the hospital. I thought it was probably a reminder of the family nest: one must cry when someone goes to a hospital, or dies.

He and Walenty paid me a visit at the hospital.

"Sir, are the officers here also sick?"

"Yes."

"Because of their eyes?"

"No, from various illnesses."

"And do they play cards for money?"

Notes

1   *The Events of Childrearing* first appeared in print in 1919 and contained three of the final four chapters: *Public School – first grade, Preschool and first grade in a private school* and *Helcia*. Korczak collected the materials to the second and third part during his observations at the Polish private educational establishments in Kiev: in the kindergarten run according to the Montessori system (*Helcia*) and, most likely, in the grammar school (*Preschool and first grade in a private school*). It was not possible to ascertain from which school came the observations used in the first part. The materials for the last part, titled *IV*, included in the second book edition of 1924, Korczak collected during his military service as a junior resident doctor in a division field hospital near

Tarnopol in 1917. The present publication is a translation of the second edition of *The Events of Childrearing* (1924).

2   Private schools functioning in Poland (on the territory of the Russian Partition [see *How to Love a Child*, note 4]) at the turn of the nineteenth and twentieth centuries had the status of secondary schools of liberal education (grammar schools). They often provided introductory classes (where education began with a primer). Usually, children in middle and higher classes did not begin their schooling at public grade schools but went directly to introductory classes of private grammar schools.

3   Maria Montessori (1870-1952) – Italian community activist, a physician, a pedagogue, and a reformer of children's preschool education. In 1907 she began to organize so-called "Children's Houses." The Montessori method of education consisted of an all-inclusive development of children's senses: eyesight, hearing, touch movement, etc. This goal was achieved with the aid of a rich collection of didactic tools: rollers of various height and thickness, small stairs, colorful boards, bells and whistles, a moveable abacus, a collection of numerals, and other such items.

4   Korczak presented the conclusions of his observations of infants in *The Child in the Family* (among other publications), the first part of the tetralogy titled *How to Love a Child*, included in this volume.

5   I call the move "defensive" when a child, unwilling to give up an object, raises it with his hand and hides it behind his head that has twisted toward the raised hand (author).

6   A reference to teachers' seminary. *The Events of Childrearing* came out as a separate small volume of the "Library of the Polish Public School Teachers' Union."

7   This was happening during the Revolution (in 1917) in the present Ukraine – then Tsarist Russia transforming itself into the Soviet Union. It was a chaotic time of changing regime, varying decisions, and of military lawlessness.

8   Korczak's orderly.

9   The Saxon Garden – one of the most popular city parks in Warsaw, located in the city center. Established in the seventeenth century, it was the first public city park in Poland.

A Child's Right to Respect[1]

Translated by Sean Gasper Bye

Disdain – Mistrust

From the very beginning, we grow up believing something large is more important than something small.

"I'm big," a child joyfully declares when placed on a table.

"I'm taller than you," she says proudly when measuring up against a peer.

It is unpleasant to stand on tiptoe and not reach; keeping up with adults is hard if you have short legs; small hands can lose their grip on a glass. Climbing onto chairs, into vehicles, or up a flight of stairs is awkward and laborious; a child cannot grasp door handles, look through windows, take things down or hang them up, because everything is too high. In crowds, she is blocked, unnoticed, jostled. It is uncomfortable, disagreeable to be small.

What is large, takes up more space, inspires respect and admiration. Small is ordinary, uninteresting. Small people have small needs, small joys, and small sorrows.

Great cities, high mountains, tall trees: these are impressive.

We say:

"A grand deed, a great man."

A child is small, insubstantial, there is less of her. We must bend over, lower ourselves to her level.

What is worse, a child is weak.

We can pick her up, toss him in the air, sit her down against her will, forcibly stop him from running, and frustrate her efforts.

If ever he does not obey, I can resort to strength. I say: "Do not wander off, do not move, get out of my way, give it back." He knows he has no choice, making so many attempts before he understands, surrenders, and gives in.

Who would dare to shove, pull, or strike an adult? And when, under what extraordinary circumstances? Yet how commonplace and innocent to slap a child, jerk him hard by the hand, or squeeze him painfully in affection.

The feeling of powerlessness engenders a veneration for strength; anyone – not merely an adult, but anyone older and stronger – may forcibly express his unhappiness, using strength to bolster a demand or enforce obedience, he may do harm with impunity.

By our own example, we teach disdain for the weak. This is a poor education, a dark omen.

The countenance of the world has changed. Now it is not muscle power that labors and defends us from enemies, not muscle power that reclaims the earth, the forests, and the sea, that grants control, gratification, and security. The machine is our subjugated slave. Muscle has lost its unique privilege and no longer wields the upper hand, giving way to increased reverence for intellect and knowledge.

The questionable cabinet of curiosities and the contemplative's modest cell have developed into the lecture halls and edifices of the researcher. Libraries add additional floors, shelves sag under the weight of books. Proud reason's temples teem with people. Persons of knowledge build and command. Time after time, hieroglyphs made of numbers and pen-strokes fling new achievements to the crowds, testifying to the power of humankind. Our memory and understanding must come to grips with all this.

The arduous years of learning continually lengthen; schools, examinations, and printed words multiply. But a small, weak child, his life yet so short, has not read, is not able...

It is a daunting question how to share out the regions we have conquered: upon whom shall we bestow what tasks and what payment, how can we cultivate the globe we have mastered? Where and how do we distribute workshops to sustain hands and minds hungry for work; how do we maintain obedience and order among the human ants; how do we safeguard against the individual's ill-will and madness; how do we fill the hours of life with labor, rest, and recreation; and how do we fend off apathy, satiety, and boredom? How do we confine people in penal institutions, how do we facilitate understanding, when do we distribute and divide up? Speed and encouragement here, restraint there; ignite here, extinguish there.

Politicians and lawmakers make tentative efforts, but time and time again they fail.

When it comes to children, they advise and reflect, but who would naively ask a child for her opinion or approval? What could she have to say?

Apart from good judgement and knowledge, in the struggle for survival and power, it is important to have quick wits. With foresight, a person may catch wind of something and earn more than honest accounting would consider their worth. Such people swiftly and effortlessly climb to the top, charming others and earning their envy. A shrewd understanding of human nature is called for – not the altar of life, but the pigsty.

Yet a child awkwardly toddles around with schoolbooks, balls, and dolls; he can tell important, powerful things are taking place without his participation, over his head, which will determine fortune and misfortune, which will punish and reward. And shatter.

A flower is a harbinger of fruit to come, a chick will become a chicken that lays eggs, a calf will one day give milk. In the meantime, however, there comes effort, expense, and worry: will they survive, will they not fail?

We fuss over a young one; though the wait to adulthood is long, perhaps when we are old they will support us and pay us back. But life knows droughts, frosts, and hail that blasts and destroys crops.

We search for signs, longing for foresight and certainty, in restless anticipation of that which is to come, while ever more neglecting that which is.

The young have little market value. Only in the eyes of the Law and of God is the apple blossom worth as much as the apple, or are green shoots equal to mature grain.

We nurse, protect, feed, and educate. A child accepts our offerings, unconcerned; what would she be without us, to whom she owes everything?

Only, solely, nothing but – us.

We know the paths to success, we offer directions and counsel. We encourage virtue, stamp out vice. We guide, correct, and train. She is nothing – we are everything.

We give orders and demand obedience.

Morally and legally responsible, with knowledge and foresight, we are the sole judges of children's actions, movements, thoughts, and intentions.

We give instructions and see to it they are fulfilled according to our will and understanding. Our children are our property – hands off!

(In truth, things have changed somewhat. Today there is more than just the will and exclusive authority of the family – there is also a present, if still cautious, social control. Only a little, barely perceptible.)

A beggar may dispose of his alms as he pleases, but a child has nothing of his own and must account for each object he has acquired at no cost and for his own use.

He may not tear, break, or soil; he may not give gifts, may not reluctantly throw away. He is to accept and be glad. Everything in its proper place and time, rationally, and according to its purpose.

(Perhaps this is why he values small, worthless objects that earn astounded sympathy: after all, castoffs – a string, a box, some beads – are his only true property and treasure.)

In exchange a child is to give in, merit good conduct – he should ask, wheedle, so long as he does not demand. Nothing belongs to him, we give it out of good will. (A painful analogy comes to mind: a rich man's girl-friend.)

Because a child is poor and trapped in material dependency, the relationship of adults to children is rotten.

We disrespect a child because she does not know, cannot reason out, and lacks intuition.

She does not know the trials or complexities of adult life, she does not know the causes of our periods of excitement, discouragement, and weariness that drive away our calm and sour our mood: she has no knowledge of grownups' failures and bankruptcies. It is easy to put her mind at rest, deceive the naive little one, and put on a masquerade.

A child believes life is simple and easy. There is papa and there is mama, father earns and mama purchases. She knows nothing of betraying one's duties or fighting for one's share and more.

She herself is free of material woes, powerful temptations, or disruptions – once again, she does not know and cannot evaluate. We analyze a child on the fly; seeing through her with a casual, piercing glance; exposing her feeble ruses without investigation.

But perhaps we delude ourselves, thinking a child is only what we wish her to be. What if she hides from us, what if she suffers in secret?

We plunder mountains, cut down trees, exterminate animals. Communities proliferate where once there were forests and swamps. We continually settle people in new territories.

We have subdued the world, put iron and animals to our use, subjugated the colored races, coarsened relations among nations, and placated the masses. A righteous order is still a long way off, while injury and misery grow.

The doubts and uncertainties of a child seem frivolous.

A child's clear democracy knows no hierarchy. For the moment, the sweat of laborers and the hunger of his peers, the suffering of a tormented horse or a slaughtered hen pains him. Dogs and birds, butterflies and flowers are his friends; in pebbles and seashells he finds his brothers. With the haughty pride of an arriviste, he lacks solidarity for his fellow man, unaware only humans have a soul.

We disrespect a child because she has many hours of life ahead of her.

We feel the labor of our own steps, the burden of actions undertaken in our own interest, the repression of our perceptions and feelings. But a child runs and jumps, she gazes without purpose, she is surprised and inquiring, she cries at the drop of a hat and is generous in her joy.

In autumn, the sunlight is rarer and so there is value in a beautiful day; springtime will be green no matter what. Nothing particular is needed, it takes little to make a child happy – why make an effort? We hurriedly and carelessly brush her aside, neglecting the abundance of her life and the joy we can so easily bestow.

For us, important quarter-hours and years are slipping away. A child has time yet, she will get there, she will live to see the day.

A child is not a soldier, he does not defend the homeland, though he suffers along with it.

There is no need to court a child's opinion, for she cannot vote: she does not threaten, demand, or speak.

A child is weak, small, poor, and dependent until he becomes a citizen.

Lenient, coarse, or brutal treatment – but always disrespect.

A tiny tot, just a kid – a future person, not one right now. Not real until later.

Keep an eye on her, do not let him out of your sight for a moment. Keep an eye on him, do not leave her alone. Keep an eye on her, do not step away.

She falls down, hits, cuts and soils herself, spills, tears, breaks, ruins, flings, loses things, starts fires, and lets burglars into the house. He hurts himself and us; injures himself, us, and his playmates.

Keep an eye out – no independent action – we have the unlimited right to control and criticize.

A child does not know what to eat or how much, when and how much to drink, does not know the limits of fatigue. So be ready to watch over his diet, sleep, and rest.

For how long, until when? Forever. With age, mistrust changes, but does not lessen, and even increases.

A child cannot distinguish the important from the trivial. Order and systematic labor are foreign to her. Absent-minded, she forgets, ignores, and neglects. She does not know what responsibilities she will have one day.

We need to caution, guide, drill, contain, rein in, correct, warn, prevent, impose, and combat.

Combat frowns, caprices, and stubbornness.

Impose a program of vigilance, caution, fear, and concern, of foreboding and of dark predictions.

From our experience, we know danger lies all around, ambushes, traps, misadventures, catastrophes.

We know the greatest caution offers no absolute guarantee, and are the more suspicious for it: so that our consciences remain clear, so that in times of sorrow we find no fault in ourselves.

A child enjoys pushing the boundaries of insubordination, he is strangely drawn straight to wickedness. He gladly surrenders to negative urges, following the worst examples.

He easily goes wrong and is difficult to set right.

We long for goodness, wish to ease the way, and we offer all our experience wholeheartedly: it is ready, he needs only reach out his hands. We know what harms a child, remembering what harmed us – let him steer clear, be spared, avoid danger.

"Remember, know, understand."

"You will learn, you will see."

He does not listen – seemingly on purpose, seemingly to spite us.

We must ensure he obeys, ensure he accomplishes his task. On his own, he will openly tend toward evil and choose the worse, more dangerous path.

How can we tolerate a child's thoughtless pranks, silly antics, and baffling outbursts?

A suspicious, primitive creature. She seems submissive and innocent, but is in fact cunning and treacherous.

She knows how to slip through our fingers, dull our vigilance, and deceive us. She always has an excuse prepared, a defense; she will dissemble and outright lie.

She is untrustworthy and suspect.

Disrespect and mistrust and suspicion and blame. The analogy is painful: a troublemaker, a drunk, a rebel, a madman. How can we live under the same roof?

Reluctance

Never mind. We adore children. In spite of everything, they are a consolation, encouragement, and hope; a joy and repose, the shining light of life. We do not frighten, burden, or harry them, they feel free and happy…

Why then do they seem to be a weight, a hindrance, an inconvenient addition? Why look on a beloved child so unfavorably?

Confusion and limitations creep into a family's life even before their child has greeted the unwelcoming world. The short months of long-anticipated, deserving joy collapse irreversibly.

A long period of heavy incapacity is followed by sickness and pain, restless nights and unplanned expenses. Troubled peace, spoiled order, an unbalanced budget.

Alongside the sour stench of diapers and the piercing cry of a newborn, the chains of marital slavery rattle.

Communication is onerous when the other is incomprehensible. Inventions and guesswork become necessary. We wait, perhaps even patiently.

When he can finally speak and walk, he gets underfoot, he moves everything around, he peeks into every corner, the little ragamuffin – the despot is just as good at getting in the way and sowing disorder.

He causes damage, resists our rational will, makes demands, and understands only what he cares to.

We must not ignore small things: we resent children for too-early mornings and for crumpled-up newspapers, for stains on dresses and wallpaper, for wet carpets, broken binoculars and souvenir vases, spilled milk and perfume, and doctors' fees.

A child does not sleep when we wish, he does not eat what we want; when we think he is about to burst into giggles instead, frightened, he cries. And he is frail: any error risks illness, presages new difficulty.

If one adult forgives, another accuses and antagonizes all the more; not only mother, but father, the nanny, the maid, and the neighbor shape a child's reputation – dealing out punishments in secret or contrary to the mother's wishes.

A little schemer can cause friction and hard feelings among adults; someone is always hostile or offended. Where one is lenient, another is vindictive. Often, ostensible goodness is mindless negligence, and the child is held responsible for others' faults.

(Older boys and girls do not like it when we call them children. This word they share with the very youngest forces them to answer for the past and share the bad reputation of babies – while they themselves are targets of just as many accusations).

How rare a child who is just as we desired, how often is her growing up accompanied by feelings of disappointment?

"After all, by now she should be..."

In exchange for what we have given in good will, she is meant to do her best and reward us; she is to understand, accept, and abandon, but above all – feel grateful.

The demands and requirements increase with age, most often in a different way and less than we had hoped.

We hand over a portion of time, responsibilities, and authority to school. Vigilance is redoubled, responsibility is deepened, divergent competencies collide. Gaps are revealed.

Parents will kindly forgive, their leniency flowing from a clear sense of guilt at their responsibility for bringing their child into being, of the harm done to an imperfect child. How often does a mother seek to use a child's alleged illness as a weapon against others' accusations and her own doubts?

By and large, a mother's voice is not appreciated. She is partial, unauthoritative. Instead, we turn to the views of educators, experts, experienced people: does a child deserve kindness?

In private homes, a tutor rarely finds conditions conducive to living with children.

Constricted by mistrustful supervision, he is forced to maneuver between others' instructions and his own views, between external requirements and his own peace and comfort.

In taking responsibility for a child entrusted to him, a tutor suffers the consequences of questionable decisions made by his breadwinners – the child's legal guardians.

When forced to mislead and avoid difficulty, he may easily become corrupted – by hypocrisy – or embittered and indolent.

Over years of work, the gap widens between what an adult demands and what a child desires, and the tutor grows more proficient in impure methods of bringing a child to heel.

A complaint for this thankless labor emerges: whom God would to punish, He makes a children's educator.

An active, noisy child, curious about life and its mysteries, exhausts us; her questions and astonishments, his discoveries and undertakings with often-unfortunate outcomes tire us.

Advisors and comforters are rare, while strict judges are common. A summary verdict and punishment has only one result: *the antics of boredom and rebelliousness grow rarer, but stronger and more perverse. So we strengthen supervision, overcome resistance, guard against surprises.*

Thus is the decline of a tutor:

> *disrespect, mistrust, suspicion, investigation, discovery, reprimand, accusation, and punishment; ever more frequent prohibitions and more absolute coercion in search of suitable means of prevention, ignoring a child's efforts to carefully fill up a piece of paper or an hour of life, saying coldly: "Wrong."*

The sky-blue of forgiveness is rare, the scarlet of anger and indignation – common.

The more understanding is required in raising a group of children, the easier it is to fall into the error of accusation and resentment.

A single small, weak child is wearying and an individual transgression is infuriating, but how maddening, beleaguering, demanding, and unpredictably impulsive is a group!

Understand once and for all: not children but a group. A bunch, a gang, a pack – not children.

One is accustomed to thinking one is strong; suddenly, one feels small and weak. A group is a giant, with tremendous combined power and huge combined experience; in a moment, it rises up in unified resistance, then only to collapse into dozens of pairs of arms and legs – or heads, each concealing different thoughts and secret demands.

How difficult it is for the new teacher in a classroom or the new caregiver in an orphanage, where children are governed by strict discipline and where the unruly and alienated have organized themselves on the principles of thuggish violence. How powerful and threatening when they attack one's will in united effort, aiming to burst the dam – not children, but an elemental force.

How many hidden revolutions, whereof a caregiver does not speak out of shame at accepting he is weaker than a child?

Lesson learned, he resorts to any means to tamp down and control. Familiarity or innocent jokes are not tolerated: no curt responses, shrugs, stubborn silences, angry glances. Uproot and vengefully destroy insolence and stubborn recalcitrance. Buy the ringleaders off with privileges, select confidants, have no regard for fair punishment – the stricter the better, to make an example, to stifle the first sparks of rebellion, so even in their thoughts the horde-colossus makes no attempt to demand or go on the prowl.

A child's weakness may elicit affection, but the strength of a group is enraging and terrifying.

There is a false allegation that kindness emboldens children, that gentleness will be answered with impunity and disorder.

But let us not mistake carelessness, incompetence, or feeble stupidity for goodness. Among caregivers, apart from cunning brutes and misanthropes, we also encounter incompetents, spurned by all workplaces and unfit to take on any responsible post.

Sometimes a teacher wishes to get on children's good side and quickly, cheaply win their trust with no effort. They wish to romp around when in good humor, not laboriously organize the life of the group. Often paternalistic leniency is interspersed with sudden outbursts of bad temper. They make fools of themselves before the children's very eyes.

Sometimes ambitious people believe it easy to reshape a child through persuasion and friendly moralizing; that it suffices to touch the emotions and extract a promise of improvement. Such people are wearisome and tedious.

Sometimes the apparently kind, showing support in insincere platitudes, are the more insidious enemies and wrongdoers. They provoke disgust.

Ill-treatment will be answered with disdain, kindness with reluctance and rebelliousness, and mistrust – with conspiracy.

Years of work have made it ever more clear that children deserve respect, trust, and kindness; that they enjoy a sunny atmosphere of gentle feelings, cheerful laughter, lively first efforts and surprises; of pure, bright, loving joy; where work is dynamic, fruitful, and beautiful.

One thing has caused doubt and concern.

Why, at times, does the most certain child disappoint? Why are there rare, though occasional, sudden explosions of insubordinate group action? Perhaps adults are no better, but they are more reliably level-headed, confident, and calm.

I have stubbornly kept seeking and, little by little, have found an answer.

1. If caregivers seek out qualities of character and values they consider especially worthwhile, if they desire to shape children to fit a single model, to pull everyone in one direction – then they will be led astray. Some children will imitate these dogmas, others will honestly give in to suggestion – for the time being. But when the child's true face is revealed, not only will the caregiver sense failure, but the child as well. The more effort is made to maintain a facade or submit to an adult's influence, the stronger the backlash will be; once a child's underlying tendencies are unveiled, he no longer has anything to lose. How important the lesson that comes from this.

2. Caregivers have one measure of morals, while groups of children have another. They both see a richness of spirit: the caregiver waits for them to develop, while the children wait to see which of these richnesses will be of use today, whether he will share what he has or – haughty, jealous, selfish, and miserly – consider his privileges his and his alone, refusing to tell stories, play games, make drawings, assist, lend a hand: "he's only doing it as a favor," "you'll have to ask him." Isolated, he aims for a grand gesture to ingratiate himself into the community, which gladly accepts

his conversion. He is not ruined immediately, on the contrary, he has understood and made a correction.

3. When they have disappointed collectively, when the group has done harm.

    I found an explanation for this in a book about training animals and I will not conceal the source. It says a lion is not dangerous when angry but when playful, wanting to have fun, and a group of children is as strong as a lion…

    We must seek solutions not merely in psychology, but rather in books of medicine, sociology, ethnology, history, poetry, criminology, and prayer as well as training manuals. *Ars longa* [Art is long][2].

4. Now comes the sunniest, and let us hope not the final, explanation. A child can become drunk upon the oxygen in the air just as an adult can on vodka. Excitement, impairment of the centers of control, risk, mental cloudiness; and the reaction – embarrassment, heartburn, a feeling of distaste, and guilt. My observation is specific – clinical. Even the most honorable person may have a weak mind.

Do not reproach: children's cheerful drunkenness is thrilling and virtuous; it does not distance or set apart, but brings closer and unites.

We conceal our own faults and reprehensible deeds. Children are not permitted to criticize or point out our vices, addictions, or amusing qualities. We masquerade as perfection. On pain of deepest resentment, we defend the secrets of the ruling clan, the caste of initiates – we are dedicated to a higher cause. Children are the only ones who may be shamelessly undressed or spanked.

When it comes to children, we play with marked cards, trumping the weaknesses of young childhood with the aces of adult virtue. Cheats, we stack the deck so as to oppose their worst with that which is good and precious in us.

Where are our slobby and reckless, our covetous gluttons, idiots, idlers, ne'er-do-wells, troublemakers, cheats, swindlers, drunks, and thieves? Where are our violence and crimes both notorious and concealed? How much discord, deceit, jealousy, spitefulness, blackmail, cutting words, shameful actions? How many quiet family tragedies in which the children suffer, first victims of martyrdom?

How dare we blame and accuse?

After all, the community of adults is assiduously sifted and filtered. How many have sunk into the grave, the jail, or the madhouse, been swept into the sewers of residue and scum?

We tell children not to reason, to obey the older and more experienced; but their nearest more experienced elders are adolescents, with their meddlesome provocations and pressure.

Delinquent and unbalanced, they run wild, knocking into children, pushing them over, doing injury and infecting others. And all children are assigned joint responsibility (since at times they are a slight nuisance to us as well). These few outrage sober-minded public opinion, standing out like clear blemishes on the face of childhood life, dictating the norms of treatment: brief, though oppressive; harsh, though wounding; and stern, meaning brutal.

We do not allow children to organize. Disdainful, untrusting, and reluctant, we do not provide the necessary care: we cannot manage without the assistance of experts, and the experts are the children.

Are we so gullible as to consider the caresses with which we torment children to be kind? Do we not understand that in cuddling a child it is we who cuddle up to them; helpless, we hide in their embrace; we seek protection and escape in hours of homeless pain and derelict abandonment; we burden them with our sufferings and yearnings.

Every other caress, if not fleeing to our child and begging for hope, is shamefully searching within them and arousing sensual feeling.

I hug because I am sad. You can have it if you give me a kiss.

Selfishness, not kindness.

The Right to Respect

It is as though there are two kinds of life: one serious and respected, another forbearingly tolerated and less valued. We say that they are future people, future workers, future citizens. That they will be, that their life will truly begin later, that it is not serious until the future. We condescend to let them dally alongside, but we are more comfortable without them.

But this is wrong, for children have been and will be. They have not dropped out of the blue and only for a short time. Children are not friends we come across fleetingly, whom we can hurry past, whom we brush aside with a smile and our best regards.

Children make up a large percentage of the human race, the population, the nation, its inhabitants, our fellow-citizens – they are permanent comrades. They have been, will be, and are.

Does life exist to be treated jokingly? No, the years of childhood are long and important ones for life, for a person.

The cruel but candid law of Greece and Rome[3] permitted killing children. In the Middle Ages, fishermen pulled drowned corpses of infants from rivers in their nets. In seventeenth century Paris, older children were sold to beggars and babies were given away free in front of Notre Dame. Not so long ago. To this day, children are cast aside if they get in the way.

The quantity of illegitimate, abandoned, neglected, exploited, depraved, and abused children is growing. The law defends them, but is its protection sufficient? Much has changed and old laws require revision.

We have become wealthier. We no longer benefit from the fruits of our own labor. We are heirs, executors, co-owners of an enormous fortune. How many cities, buildings, factories, mines, hotels, and theaters do we own, how many goods are on the market, how many ships transport them – sellers surge forward, asking to use their goods.

Let us strike a balance, let us estimate how much of the general budget belongs to children, what share falls to them, but not as a favor, not as charity. Let us thoroughly examine how much we set aside for the use of the race of children, the nation of the little-grown, the class of serfs. How much is their inheritance, how should it be divided, have we dishonest caregivers not deprived them of it, expropriated it?

Life is cramped for children, stifling, impoverished, dreary, and harsh.

We have introduced universal education, forced intellectual labor, we have enlistment and conscription for school. We have burdened children with the hardship of reconciling the contradictory interests of two equal authorities.

School makes demands and parents are reluctant to oblige. Conflicts between family and school weigh on a child. Parents accept the school's sometimes unfair accusations against their child while defending themselves against taking care as the school demands.

The strenuousness of soldiers' service is also preparation for the day when they will be called to action, and yet the government ensures all their needs are met. The state provides a roof over their head and food, uniforms and rifles; their pay is earned, not charity.

Yet children must beg from their parents or community while still being subject to the constraints of universal education.

The lawmakers of Geneva confused obligations and rights. The tone of the Declaration[4] is one of persuasion, not of insistence: it is an appeal to goodwill, a request for kindness.

School creates a rhythm of hours, days, and years. School officials are meant to fulfill young citizens' present needs. A child is a rational being, intimately familiar with the requirements, difficulties, and obstacles in her life. What is called for is neither despotic command, nor imposed discipline, nor untrusting control, but tactful understanding, trust in experience, cooperation, and coexistence.

A child is not a fool, there are no more idiots among them than among adults. Bedecked in the crimson robes of age, how often we impose thoughtless, uncritical, impossible demands. Often a reasoning child stands amazed at our malicious, geriatric, sneering stupidity.

A child has a future, but she also has a past: unforgettable events, memories, many hours of essential solitary reflection. No differently than we, she remembers and forgets, cherishes and disdains, logically reasons – her errors are also out of ignorance. She weighs carefully whether to trust or doubt.

A child is a foreigner, ignorant of the language, of where the roads lead, and of laws and customs. Often, she prefers to explore for herself, asking for directions and advice when she finds herself in difficulty. She requires a guide to courteously answer her questions.

Respect for her lack of knowledge.

A villain, a swindler, and a rascal exploits foreigners' ignorance, gives incomprehensible responses, and deliberately misleads. Simple folk mutter reluctantly. We snap and quarrel with children, chastising, reprimanding, punishing, not kindly informing.

How lamentably meager would a child's knowledge be if she did not draw it from her peers, from eavesdropping, from snatches of adults' words and conversations.

Respect for the work of acquiring knowledge.

Respect for failures and tears.

Not only the torn stocking, but the skinned knee; not only the broken glass, but the gashed finger and the bruise, and the lump, and so the pain.

A blot in a notebook is an accident, a vexation, and a failure.

"When papa spills his tea, mama says: 'no harm done,' but when I do it she always gets angry."

Children, unaccustomed to pain, hurt, and unfairness, suffer acutely and are quicker to cry; even a child's tears prompt teasing remarks, seem less important, cause anger.

Whining, blubbering, sniveling, squealing.

(A selection of words the adult lexicon has invented for use with children.)

Tears of stubbornness and caprice are really tears of powerlessness and revolt, a desperate attempt to protest, a call for help, a complaint of negligent care, testimony that adults foolishly restrict and compel, a symptom of discomfort, and always a sign of suffering.

Respect for children's possessions and their budgets. A child agonizingly shares in his family's material woes; he is aware of shortages, he compares his poverty to a friend's prosperity and frets over the bitter pennies by which he worsens his parents' destitution. He does not wish to be a burden.

What can a child do when he needs a hat, and a book, and a movie ticket, a notebook when the old one is full, a pencil when one is lost or stolen, when he wishes to give a keepsake to a kind person, and buy a pastry, or make a loan to a friend. So many essential needs, wishes, and temptations, but no money.

Does the fact that theft makes up the majority of cases in juvenile court not call out to us, not rouse us to action? Disregarding children's budgets takes its toll and punishing them does no good.

Children's possessions are not rubbish, they are a beggar's materials and work tools, hopes and keepsakes.

The worries and cares of today, the bitterness of young years and of disappointment – these are not make-believe, but essential.

A child grows. She lives more strongly, her breath hastens, her pulse quickens, she builds up – becomes larger, reaches deeper into life. She grows by day and by night, when sleeping and waking, when happy and sad, when she misbehaves and when she stands repentant before you.

There are springtimes of redoubled development and autumns of retreat. Sometimes the skeleton grows and the heart cannot keep up; too little here, too much there, a new chemical system of glands vanishing and awakening, new worries and surprises.

Sometimes the urge to run matches the urge to breathe, she wants to wrestle, to move, to conquer, and then hide, dream, and bind together wistful memories. Resilience alternates with a need for calm, warmth, and comfort. She wavers between intense, passionate desire and discouragement.

Fatigue, suffering from pain or congestion; too hot, too chilly; drowsiness, hunger, thirst, surfeit, shortage, discomfort – these are not caprices, not ploys to get out of school.

Respect for the secrets and vacillations of the hard work of growing.

Respect for the current hour, for today. How can he know how to face tomorrow if we do not allow him to live an aware, responsible life today? Don't trample, don't mistreat, don't enslave him to tomorrow, don't turn out the lights, don't hurry, don't rush.

Respect for each individual moment, for these will die and never come again. Always treat these seriously, for a wounded moment will bleed and the ghost of a murdered one will haunt a person with bad memories.

Let a child eagerly drink in the joy of young life, let him trust. This is precisely what he wishes. He does not regret time spent telling a fairytale, talking to a dog, playing catch, carefully examining a picture, or practicing his letters – he does all this warm-heartedly. He is the one who has got it right.

We naively fear death, not realizing life is a succession of moments dying and being reborn. A year is merely an attempt to grasp eternity for everyday purposes. One moment lasts as long as a smile or a sigh. A mother wishes to raise her child. But she will not see the day: over and over, a new woman will greet a person and then bid him farewell.

We clumsily divide our years into the more and less mature, yet there is no unripe today, no hierarchy of age, no higher and lower ranks of pain and joy, hope and disappointment.

When I play with or talk to a child, two moments from my life and his intertwine, equally mature; when I am with a group of children, I always take time to say hello and goodbye to one of them with a look and a smile. When I am angry, we are once again joined together – but my anger, a single vengeful moment, violates and poisons this mature, important time of his life.

Do we go without for tomorrow's sake? What attractions does the future hold? Too often we paint it in dark colors. This is a self-fulfilling prophecy: the roof collapses because the building's foundations have been neglected.

A Child's Right to Be What He Is

"What will become of him," we ask nervously. "What will she be when she grows up?"

We long for children to be better than us. We dream of the perfect man of the future.

We must vigilantly catch out this lie, deride the hidden selfishness of this platitude. It seems self-sacrificing but in truth is a downright swindle.

We have come to an understanding with ourselves and are reconciled, we have forgiven ourselves and no longer demand betterment. We were raised badly. It is too late for us: our faults and vices are now deeply ingrained. We forbid children to criticize us, though we do not control ourselves.

Absolved, we have renounced the struggle with the self, and pass the burden of it onto our children.

Caregivers readily grow accustomed to adult privilege, watching over children but not themselves, noting the children's faults but not their own.

Whatever is detrimental to our peace, ambition, and comfort we consider to be the fault of children; whatever jeopardizes and angers, disrupts our routines or requires time and thought. We do not believe in wrongdoing without ill-will.

A child does not know, has not heard, has not understood, has misheard, mistaken, failed, is unable – everything is blameworthy. Every difficult moment a child has – whether failure or discomfort – is willful and blameworthy.

Too quick or not quick enough, or not performing a task well enough – to us, this is carelessness, laziness, forgetfulness, foot-dragging.

Not carrying out a dangerous or impossible task – blame. Having angry, misplaced suspicions – blame again. Our anxieties and suspicions are the child's fault, even if he is attempting to better himself.

"You see: you can do it if you want to."

We always find an accusation to make, greedily increasing our demands.

Do we tactfully give in, avoid needless friction, do we ease our lives together? In truth, is it not we who are stubborn, fussy, aggressive, and capricious?

A child compels us to pay attention to her; the only moments we notice and remember are when she bothers and disturbs us. We do not see when she is calm, serious, focused. We disregard the sacred moments when she talks to herself, to the world, to God. She is forced to hide her longings and urges in the face of mockery and harsh comments, to conceal her desire to understand, not to disclose her resolution to better herself.

She obediently hides her penetrating gazes, surprise, worries, regrets – and her anger and rebelliousness, too. We wish to see her jumping up and down and clapping, so she puts on the smiling face of a jester.

Bad actions and bad children speak louder, drowning out the whispers of the good, though there are a thousand times more good ones than bad. Good is strong and it stubbornly endures. It is untrue that it is easier to break than to repair.

We keep our attention and imagination sharp by uncovering bad behavior, spotting it, ferreting it out and tracking it down, catching it red-handed; by making unfavorable predictions and holding harmful suspicions.

(Do we keep watch over the elderly to stop them from playing soccer? Yet how vilely relentless we are in sniffing out masturbation in children.)

One door slammed, one bed unmade, one coat flung on the floor, one blot in a notebook. When we are not scolding, we are at least grumbling, rather than being glad it was only one.

We do hear complaints and arguments, but so much more forgiveness, acquiescence, aid, care, favors, good deeds, profound and beautiful influences. Even truculent and angry children do more than shed tears, they also sow smiles.

We lazily wish for perfection – that out of ten thousand seconds of school time (count them!) not one should be difficult.

How can the same child be good in one teacher's eyes and bad in another's? We demand a uniformity of virtues and moments – and more than that, we demand they fit our predilections and standards.

Has history ever known such tyranny? A generation of Neros has proliferated.

Good health comes with bad; virtue and morals exist alongside deficiencies and flaws.

Beside the few children of joyfulness and celebration – for whom life is a fairytale and a splendid legend, who are trusting and kind – there is the mass of children, to whom since their earliest days the world has proclaimed grim truths in austere, unyielding declarations.

Broken by the contemptuous ill-treatment of coarseness and want, or broken by the tender, sensual neglect of satiety and refinedness.

They may be filthy, untrusting, alienated from others – but they are not bad.

It is not only the home that provides a model for a child, but the entryway, the corridor, the yard, and the street as well. A child speaks in the words of his surroundings, states his views, rehearses gestures, follows examples. There is no such thing as a pure child – each one is tarnished to one extent or another.

Oh, how quickly a child emancipates and cleanses himself; he does not need healing, only to be wiped clean, and he will gladly lend a hand, pleased to have found a role. He has waited, yearning for his bath, beaming at you and at himself.

Every caregiver celebrates such naive triumphs from storybook tales of orphans, and cases like these lure gullible moralists into believing it is easy. The incompetent relish them, the ambitious claim credit for them, the brutish are furious it does not always work out this way; some wish to repeat these results everywhere by increasing the dose of persuasion, others – the dose of pressure.

Alongside the merely soiled we find the mutilated and wounded. There are slashes that leave no scars, knitting themselves back together under clean dressings. Lacerations take longer to heal and painful scars remain, which must not be aggravated. Pustules and ulcers demand more effort and patience.

We commonly say: the body is healing, but we ought to add: so is the soul.

There are so many scrapes and ailments in schools and orphanages, so many temptations and meddlesome whisperings, and so many fleeting and innocent influences. No need to fear dangerous contagions if the aura of the institution is healthy, if the air is fresh and full of light.

How intelligently, slowly, and marvelously the healing process occurs. How many noble secrets hide themselves in human blood, fluids, and tissues. How hard each disrupted function and wounded organ works to regain balance and be equal to the task. How many miracles there are in the growth of a plant and a human being; in the heart, the brain, the breath. At the smallest excitement or effort, the heart already beats stronger, the pulse quickens.

A child's spirit possesses the same power and persistence. It possesses moral balance and sensitivity of conscience. It is not true that children are easily tainted.

Correctly, though sadly belatedly, pedology[5] has found its way into school curriculums. Without understanding the harmony of the body, one cannot fathom respect for the sacred mystery of children's betterment.

Incompetent diagnoses lump active, ambitious, thoughtful children, each of whom are flawed, but healthy and clean – in with the miserable, moody, and mistrustful or the polluted, tempted, and reckless, who are meekly obedient to adverse examples. Immature, careless, and superficial examination confounds and mistakes them for those rare immoral children who are freighted with malice.

(We adults have known not only how to render the stepchildren of fate harmless, but also how to deftly exploit the labor of these dispossessed.)

Healthy children forced to coexist with the bad suffer in dual measure: they are marred and drawn into immorality. But do we not recklessly accuse them all, do we not impose collective responsibility?

"You see what they're like, what good are they?"

This is perhaps the worst possible injury.

The progeny of drunkenness, violence, and madness. Their transgressions are the echoes not of voices from without, but of commands from within. Dark moments when he sees he is different, that life is hard, that he is maimed, that others will curse him and egg him on. He makes his first decision to combat the urge to do wrong. What others have obtained for free and with such ease, what in others is commonplace and trivial – clear days of internal equilibrium – for him is a reward for bloody struggle. He seeks help, holds fast to those he trusts, asks, demands: "save me." He has confided a secret, he wishes to set himself right once and for all, instantly, in a burst of effort.

Rather than prudently restraining this reckless impulse, deferring a child's resolution to better himself, we clumsily encourage and accelerate it. He wishes to break free, but we do our best to ensnare him; he wishes to escape, but we hypocritically lay traps. While his desire is clear and honest, we teach only to dissemble. He gives us a whole, long, unblemished day, and we reject him on account of a single bad moment. Is this worthwhile?

A boy used to wet himself every day, though now it's less common, it had been better, but it has gotten worse again – there is no harm in that. An epileptic has longer gaps between attacks. A child with consumption coughs less often and his fever has gone down. Not even improvement, simply not getting worse: a doctor would record that as a successful treatment. Here, tricks and coercion will do no good.

Desperate, rebellious, contemptuous of the submissiveness and fawning of common virtue – these children stand before their caregivers retaining a single, and perhaps the ultimate, saintly quality: aversion to double-dealing. And this is what we wish to strike down, to execute. What a bloody crime we commit! We overpower them with hunger and torture, yet our brutality does not break the rebellion, but instead drives it underground. We are recklessly fanning the flames of the hatred of deceit and hypocrisy.

The children do not forsake their plans for revenge but postpone them until the time is right. If they believe in good, they bury this urge in absolute secret.

"Why did you let me be born? Who asked you to give me this miserable life?"

I am reaching for the highest level of initiation, the most challenging revelation. The only thing transgressions and offenses call for is patient, kind understanding; wrongdoers require love. Their angry rebelliousness is justified. We must bid farewell to easy virtue and take the side of the lonely, maligned offense. When will they receive the flower of a smile, if not now?

Yet correctional centers still contain the Inquisition, the torture of medieval punishments, uniform obstinacy, and vindictive ill-treatment. Can you not see the best children feel sorry for the worst: of what are they guilty?

***

It is not long since humble doctors dutifully gave their patients sickly sweet drinks and bitter concoctions, strapped down the feverish, practiced bloodletting, and starved their patients in gloomy antechambers of the grave. They indulged the powerful and were cold to poverty.

Until they began to demand – and they received.

For children, doctors[6] have obtained space and sunlight, just as – to our shame – generals[7] have given our children exercise, thrilling adventure, the joy of selfless service, the resolution to lead an upstanding life as heard in a tale told by the fire under the camp's starry sky.

As caregivers, what is our role, what is our share of labor?

A guardian of the walls and furniture, the calm of the yard, the cleanliness of ears and floors; a shepherd for the youngsters so they do not stray into strange pastures, do not bother adults at work or happily on their days off; a steward of ragged knickerbockers and shoes; and a miserly dispenser of porridge. A defender of adult privilege and an idle perpetrator of unprofessional caprices.

A little jumble-store selling anxieties and admonitions, a market stall offering moral odds and ends, a seedy dive selling denatured knowledge which intimidates, confuses, and lulls to sleep instead of awakening, enlivening and cheering. Agents of cheap virtue, we are meant to force honor and humility onto children while warming adults' hearts and touching their positive emotions. Build a solid future on a shoestring budget, mislead and conceal that children are a multitude, a will, a power and a law.

Doctors have snatched children from the jaws of death; now the task of caregivers is to give them a reason to live, give them the right to be children.

Researchers have declared that a fully-grown person is driven by reason and a child by impulse; an adult is logical, a child excitable in misleading flights of fancy; an adult has character, an established moral countenance, a child is tangled in the chaos of instinct and craving. They investigate a child as a baser, weaker, and poorer psychological being, rather than a distinct one. As though all adults were learned professors.

Yet an adult is a muddle, a backwater of opinions and convictions, herd mentality, superstitions and customs, the reckless activities of fathers and mothers, and the whole of irresponsible adult life from top to bottom. Carelessness, sloth, obtuse stubbornness, thoughtlessness, adult preposterousness, madness, and drunken mischief.

Yet children possess seriousness, sagacity, and stability, unwavering commitment, expertise in their area, a wealth of fair judgements and assessments, tactful restraint in their demands, sensitive intuition, and an unfailing sense of right and wrong.

Does everyone who plays chess with a child win?

Let us demand respect for bright eyes, bare cheeks, youthful efforts and confidences. Why should dim gazes, knitted brows, rough grey hair, and stooped resignation deserve the greater honor?

The sun rises and sets. We pray in the morning as well as the evening. Both inhaling and exhaling, the heart both contracting and relaxing.

A soldier when he goes off to battle – and when he returns, covered in dust.

New generations grow, new waves arise. They come with vices and virtues, so provide them the conditions to grow up better. We cannot defeat the coffin of hereditary illness; we will not command cornflowers to turn into grain.

We are not miracle-workers – and we do not wish to be charlatans. We renounce hypocritical longing for the perfect child.

We demand: the eradication of hunger, cold, damp, airlessness, cramped spaces, and overcrowding.

It is you who sire the sick and infirm, you create the conditions for rebellion and plague: your recklessness, thoughtlessness, and irrationality.

Beware: it is the strong brute who molds modern life, *homo rapax* [rapacious man]: he dictates the way forward. His concessions to the weak are lies, his respect for the elderly, the equal treatment of women, and his kindness to children is dishonest. Emotion roams homeless – like Cinderella. And it is precisely children who are the princes of emotion, poets, and thinkers.

Respect, if not reverence, for pure, bright, immaculate, holy childhood.

Notes

1   *A Child's Right to Respect* was probably first published in late 1928 or early 1929. The booklet contains a synthesis of Korczak's views as they had appeared since his earliest works. It is an expression of the consistent struggle for children's rights Korczak had conducted since the start of his career. This struggle and his views harmonized with the development of an entire social movement for rights and care for children in the years following the First World War.
2   The full saying, *Ars longa, vita brevis*, means "Art is long, life is short."
3   In the Greek states (e.g. in Sparta), physically disabled infants and mentally disabled children were killed. In Ancient Greece and Rome, neither the law, nor religion, nor philosophy, nor morality condemned the abandonment of children (which often condemned them to death) – it was one of the methods of population management.
4   A reference to the Geneva Declaration of the Rights of the Child, adopted by the International Save the Children Union (*Union Internationale de Secours aux Enfants*) on February 23, 1923. On September 26, 1923 the Declaration was endorsed by the 5th

Session of the League of Nations in Geneva. In response to a renewed appeal from the International Save the Children Union in 1948, an expanded Geneva Declaration was proclaimed, and on November 20, 1959 the United Nations General Assembly adopted the Universal Declaration of the Rights of the Child, alluding to the Universal Declaration of Human Rights. Currently the Declaration has been superseded by the Convention on the Rights of the Child, in force since September 2, 1990.

5 See *How to Love a Child*, note 19.

6 A reference to Dr. Stanisław Markiewicz (1839–1911) – a medical doctor and community worker in Warsaw and the co-founder of summer camps for impoverished children. See also *How to Love a Child*, note 14.

7 A reference to Scouting – the system of social and moral education for girls and boys as well as the youth movement started in the United Kingdom by Lt. Gen. Robert Stephenson Baden-Powell (1857–1941), which subsequently spread to many countries. Here, Korczak is referring to the Scouts' classes: field exercises and games, camping, exercises in observation, physical labor, and acquiring "badges" for various practical skills.

Index

Lightning Source UK Ltd.
Milton Keynes UK
UKHW010659210221
378983UK00009B/255